T0190036

Second Edition

Threat Assessment and Management Strategies

Identifying the Howlers and Hunters

Second Edition

Threat Assessment and Management Strategies

Identifying the Howlers and Hunters

Frederick S. Calhoun
Stephen W. Weston

CRC Press
Taylor & Francis Group
Boca Raton London New York

CRC Press is an imprint of the
Taylor & Francis Group, an **informa** business

CRC Press
Taylor & Francis Group
6000 Broken Sound Parkway NW, Suite 300
Boca Raton, FL 33487-2742

© 2016 by Taylor & Francis Group, LLC
CRC Press is an imprint of Taylor & Francis Group, an Informa business

No claim to original U.S. Government works

Printed on acid-free paper
Version Date: 20150916

International Standard Book Number-13: 978-1-4987-2184-4 (Paperback)

Library of Congress Cataloging-in-Publication Data

Calhoun, Frederick S., author.
   Threat assessment and management strategies : identifying the howlers and hunters / Frederick S. Calhoun and Stephen W. Weston, J.D. -- Second edition.
      pages cm
   Includes bibliographical references and index.
   ISBN 978-1-4987-2184-4
   1. Violence--Prevention. 2. Violence--Psychological aspects. 3. Aggressiveness. 4. Police training. 5. Criminal behavior, Prediction of. 6. Threats. I. Weston, Stephen W., author. II. Title.

HM1116.C353 2016
303.6--dc23   2015033145

Visit the Taylor & Francis Web site at
http://www.taylorandfrancis.com

and the CRC Press Web site at
http://www.crcpress.com

To Austin James Calhoun (1918–2006)
and John Wayne Weston (1926–1992)

Contents

Section I
THREAT ASSESSMENT
AND MANAGEMENT STRATEGIES

Contents   xi

Appendix: When Should Threats Be Seen as Indicative of Future Violence? Threats, Intended Violence, and the Intimacy Effect   **211**

DEBRA M. JENKINS

Index   **251**

Preface to the First Edition

Robert L. Burke settled his disputes with bombs. At work, Burke frequently threatened his fellow employees in the air traffic control tower at Walker Field Airport in Grand Junction, Colorado. Several of his colleagues complained that talking with Burke often left them in fear for their lives. During one conversation with Gary Mueller, his supervisor, Burke bragged about owning two guns, including a .357 Magnum. When Mueller asked why Burke needed two pistols, Burke replied that two guns increased his killing power. "Why a .357?" Mueller asked. "You'll find out," Burke told him. During this same conversation, Burke demanded that Mueller do things Burke's way because Burke was the only person who knew how to do things right. If Mueller did not follow Burke's instructions, "something big was going to happen" and "Mueller would be sorry" because Burke "had nothing to lose." After nearly a year of such conversations, threats, and references to violence, in March 2004, Serco Management Services terminated Burke's employment.[*]

Burke took up a nomadic existence, moving frequently with his belongings packed into a maroon van. In July 2005, he bought a used ambulance from a couple in Derby, Kansas, but then failed to take possession of it. When the owners sold it to another buyer, Burke rejected the check they sent him for reimbursement. He e-mailed them on July 19 saying, "If/when it comes time to get 'the information' I will…and then My Farewell Tour will begin." The tour began on February 1, 2006.[†]

Burke left his first bomb on the roof of Serco Management Services headquarters in Murfreesboro, Tennessee. It exploded around 4 p.m. but did little damage and resulted in no injuries. Twenty-seven days later, on February 28, Burke arrived in Derby, Kansas, and left a bomb on the porch of a house belonging to a neighbor of the ambulance sellers. Its explosion also did little damage. A month later, Burke returned to Grand Junction and, early in the morning of March 25, planted five bombs at the homes of his former coworkers, all of whom had testified against him during his dismissal proceedings from Serco Management. Three of the bombs went off; the other two were disarmed by police. The three that exploded caused minor damage, primarily from the fire resulting from the incendiary accelerant Burke had added to the explosives. When police searched a storage shed used by Burke, they found a piece of paper containing the addresses and phone numbers of several of his targets.[*]

On April 3, a man claiming to know Burke called a *Grand Junction Daily Sentinel* reporter to arrange a meeting. The man claimed that Burke had stored information on a computer that "would affect every contract [air traffic control] tower in the country." The reporter, however, suspected the caller was actually Burke, so he alerted police. When the "informant" called back April 5, the reporter agreed to meet him at a motel in Orem, Utah.

---

[*] Morris, E., Saccone, M., & Harmon, G. (2006, March 25). Feds take over serial bomber case. *Grand Junction (CO) Daily Sentinel*, Morris, E. (2006, March 27). GJ bombs similar to one in Tennessee. *The Daily Sentinel*, and Harmon, G., & Morris, E. (2006, March 27). Burke still at large. *The Daily Sentinel*.
[†] Harmon, G. (2006, April 6). Burke linked to 7th bomb. *The Daily Sentinel*.

A police surveillance team caught Burke hiding behind the Orem Walmart, his van parked in such a way as to hide the rear Colorado license plate.* At trial, Burke pled guilty to the Colorado bombings and received a prison sentence of 10 years. "This was personal," the judge noted in handing down the sentence.†

Burke qualifies as what we call a *hunter*. Simply defined, hunters intentionally use lethal violence. Their behaviors in carrying out the violent act follow a defined trail which we call the *path to intended violence*. Burke developed a grievance against his employer and coworkers, decided to act violently against them, then researched their locations, built his bombs, delivered them, and set the timers for detonating them. That the bombs did not do as much damage as intended does not detract from the hunting process in which Burke engaged. Like all hunters, Burke intended to act violently, then engaged in all the requisite behaviors necessary to consummate that lethal violence, including, ultimately, exploding the bombs.

Around the time Burke planned his hunt, again according to press reports, Suffolk County, New York policeman Michael Valentine met a woman on Match.com, an Internet dating service. Beginning in November 2005, they dated about 6 weeks before she broke up with him. Unwilling to let her go, Valentine hacked into her e-mail account and essentially stole her online identity. He began sending himself and some 70 other men e-mails in which he pretended to be her. These e-mails expressed romantic interest toward each recipient. On at least two occasions, men showed up at her house believing they had arranged a date with her. Suffolk County computer-crime detectives believed Valentine used several computers, one belonging to the police department. In April 2006, the district attorney obtained a 197-count indictment against Valentine, charging him with stalking, computer trespassing, official misconduct, and tampering with evidence. Valentine's lawyer promised a vigorous defense.‡

On June 30, 2006, Valentine copped a plea. He resigned from the police department and pled guilty to two counts of Unauthorized Use of a Computer. The district attorney dropped all of the other charges. The judge sentenced Valentine to 1 year of "conditional discharge." The judge also issued a 3-year order of protection for the victim.§

Valentine is what we call a *howler*. Simply defined, howlers engage in problematic behavior toward their targets, but that behavior does not result in lethal violence. Valentine developed a brief relationship with a woman, then targeted her after she rejected him. However, at no time did he appear to entertain thoughts of committing violence against her, nor did he take any of the steps along the path to intended violence. Instead, he embarked on a high-tech harassment campaign to embarrass, inconvenience, and perhaps even frighten her. By stealing her online identity, Valentine wreaked havoc on her social life and seriously embarrassed her by attributing messages and emotions to her through forged e-mails. As despicable as these actions were, at no time did he put her in physical danger.

Herein lies the distinction between hunters and howlers. Burke wanted to kill his targets by blowing up their residences or burning down their houses. He measured his success

---

* Suspected bomber arrested in Utah after tip. (2006, April 7). *Salt Lake City Tribune*.
† Harmon, G. (2007, February 3). 'This was personal' judge blasts GJ bomber with 10 years in prison. *The Daily Sentinel*.
‡ L.I. officer charged with cyberstalking. (2006, April 4). Associated Press.
§ Brian Creter, Senior Investigator, Gavin de Becker and Associates, to Frederick S. Calhoun, e-mail dated October 3, 2014, in author's personal possession.

in terms of death or destruction. Valentine wanted to harass and embarrass his target. He sought emotional and mental injuries, not physical. He measured his success in terms of inconveniencing, embarrassing, or frightening his former dating partner. Hunters deal in lethal violence; howlers cause stress.

This book explores in detail the differences between those who hunt and those who howl. Its intended audience goes beyond law enforcement or security specialists. Rather, anyone involved in managing potentially violent situations or problem individuals, such as human resource staff, mental health professionals, staff attorneys, employee assistance professionals, school administrators, teachers, guidance counselors—even potential targets— might gain from reading it. Our approach avoids theory in favor of practical concepts that can be readily applied by anyone involved in managing threatening situations or individuals. We are pragmatists who recognize that at workplaces, schools, homes, courts, and all the other venues of intended violence, threat management requires a multidisciplined team approach. We write for every member of that team and use the generic term *threat manager* to address them all.

Taken together, hunters and howlers represent problem individuals. More precisely, they are individuals who purposefully intend to cause problems. At one end of the spectrum, the problems involve lethal violence. At the other end, the problems entail establishing harassing or binding attachments. In between are threats, intimidations, stalking, vandalism, physical abuse, and other forms of disruption. Threat managers must manage both ends of the spectrum and everything in between, although clearly, the killing end takes precedence. But that precedence in no way means that howlers can be ignored. By their very nature, problem individuals of every stripe insist on having their problems addressed. That insistence requires responses from threat managers.

This book, we believe, offers threat managers several benefits. First, it arms them with ways to identify problem behaviors and associate those behaviors with either hunters or howlers. Knowing with whom one is dealing is a crucial first step in any threat management process. Second, unlike any other study on threat management, we focus as much on problem individuals who intend to harass or intimidate (the howlers) as we do on individuals who intend lethality (the hunters). No other study gives as detailed a definition of howlers, yet howlers comprise the vast majority of problem individuals in any social setting. Third, through actual case studies and case analyses, we offer the best practices for assessing problem individuals and recommending the best protective response and management strategy.

Implementing an Effective Threat Management Process

A successful threat management process does not necessarily depend on large staffs or huge resource commitments, but instead on attention to detail and a thoughtful approach. It consists of 10 elements, each integral to the others, and they constitute the golden rules of contemporary threat management. Following them will allow the threat manager to implement an effective threat management program. We present them in Chapter 1 by way of introducing the approach to understanding hunters and howlers.

Threat management cases are not about investigating or solving crimes; they are about managing the behavior of an individual. Threat managers do not have a caseload of crimes assigned to them. Rather, threat managers manage problem individuals. Consequently, a threat manager's caseload is a hybrid between a criminal caseload and a parole or proba-tion officer's caseload.

Hence, we shy away from such traditional terminology as opening or closing a threat management case. Rather, we find the following designations best suited for managing threat management cases: active, inactive, chronic or habitual, or long-term.

Contemporary threat management seeks to avert violence altogether. Organizations must expand their security from simply fortifying physical security countermeasures and reacting to violent attacks. They need to incorporate an effective threat management pro-cess for defusing the risks of violence before the violence erupts. We are not talking about *predicting* violence. Predictions are the provinces of angels and fools. We advocate estab-lishing procedures to enable the threat manager to identify potential problem individuals, assess the seriousness of the risk, investigate the circumstances, and then devise the appro-priate strategies for managing the subject. Implementing an effective threat management process requires organizations to follow the 10 golden rules. Doing so will further enhance their security.

Because hunters and howlers have entirely different purposes, they behave in very dif-ferent ways. This book explores those behaviors in order to make each more recognizable. In between those explorations, we offer detailed case analyses to show how being able to distinguish hunters as hunters and howlers as howlers can offer profound benefits to iden-tifying, assessing, and managing both situations. Because hunters and howlers behave dif-ferently, threat managers need to deal with them in different ways. That requires being able to separate those who hunt from those who howl. This book discusses how to do exactly that.

Preface to the Second Edition

We take the opportunity of this second edition to expand our scope. The content of the first edition remains intact, although we updated many of the examples and illustrations. In this edition, we added a new section. "Section I: Threat Assessment and Management Strategies" offers our current thinking on how to conduct thorough threat management processes. We draw on the latest research as well as ideas and concepts from our previous books. Overall, the second edition allows us to integrate the sum of our careers in threat management—both our individual experiences managing problem situations and our research and writing on the topic—into a single volume. Our purpose with this second edition is to create a stand-alone volume on how to develop a threat management program and how to run it effectively.

In Chapter 1, we discuss the necessity for establishing threat management processes, then offer guidance on how to do so. Chapter 2 covers how to identify potential problems by conducting protective fact finding. As facts are gathered, we then describe the best methods for assessing those facts to determine the level of risk in Chapter 3. On the basis of those ongoing assessments, in Chapter 4, we discuss how to select the most appropriate threat management strategies to defuse the risk. Section I, then, provides the necessary skeleton for setting up threat management processes.

"Section II: Identifying the Howlers and Hunters" reprises the subjects presented in the first edition, effectively adding flesh and tissue to the bones of Section I. It defines two types of problem individuals. *Howlers* make disturbing and inappropriate communications but never go beyond those disturbances. *Hunters* do go beyond to launch attacks and inflict harm. Both pose problems; both have to be managed; neither can be ignored. Yet, understanding their differences informs both the threat assessment and the selection of the most appropriate threat management strategies. Howlers and hunters differ considerably. Threat managers need to understand and exploit those differences. Chapter 5 introduces the twin concepts of hunter and howler. Chapter 6 presents precise definitions for each concept. Chapter 7 offers insights into understanding hunters, while Chapter 8 does the same for howlers. Throughout, each concept is illustrated with numerous examples drawn from real-life events.

Chapter 9, "Working with the Intimacy Effect and the Law," discusses how the degree of intimacy between subject and target affects the credibility of threatening communications and reviews the case law on domestic violence, the most intimate venue for violence. Chapter 10, "Working with the Hunter, Howler, and Other Concepts," summarizes the importance of recognizing hunters and howlers and also reviews a number of important concepts.

The appendix reprints a summary of research on the intimacy effect written by Debra M. Jenkins. Nothing has emerged from subsequent research in the field of threat management to disabuse her 2009 conclusion that the intimacy effect factors into the credibility of threatening communications. The more intimate the relationship between subject and target, the higher the likelihood of carrying out the threatened action. The more distant or impersonal the relationship, the less likely the threatened action will occur. The intimacy effect affects both hunters and howlers. Understanding it and applying its principles in threat assessments give the threat manager better insights into the degree of risk and how best to manage the situation.

We view working on the second edition of *Threat Assessment and Management Strategies: Identifying the Howlers and Hunters* as a great opportunity to consolidate our thinking on threat management into one volume. For a quarter of a century, we—individually and as partners—have pondered the perplexities of managing problem individuals. Over that time, we developed practical ideas and approaches that we applied to our own work, to our writings, and to our teaching. In this edition, we draw on the latest research and on our previous works and ideas to present to the reader a comprehensive approach to setting up a threat management process. Our purpose is to provide guidelines, not prescriptions. Dealing with hunters and howlers is a volatile, slippery challenge that belies rules, order, and predictions. It requires approaching the problem intelligently, flexibly, and, with each new problem, with originality. In this edition, we set up the parameters for implementing a successful threat management process. The threat manager must provide the intelligence, flexibility, and originality.

About the Authors

Frederick S. Calhoun, PhD, was the lead researcher and principal architect in developing the threat assessment process used by the U.S. Marshals Service for analyzing risks to federal judicial officials. He also developed the service's policies and procedures for conducting protective investigations. At the request of the National Sheriffs' Association, Dr. Calhoun coordinated the curriculum and led a nationwide training program on contemporary threat management for local law enforcement. He also wrote the curriculum and led the training of deputy U.S. Marshals Service threat investigators and their supervisors. Dr. Calhoun earned his PhD from the University of Chicago and is the author of 13 books, including *Hunters and Howlers: Threats and Violence Against Judicial Officials, 1789–1993* and *Defusing the Risk to Judicial Officials: The Contemporary Threat Management Process* (with Stephen Weston). In 2013, he and Mr. Weston released their newest book, *Concepts and Case Studies in Threat Management: A Practical Guide for Identifying, Assessing and Managing Individuals of Violent Intent.*

Dr. Calhoun also teaches a periodic 2-day seminar entitled "Managing Threats: Reducing the Risk of Violence." This seminar is designed to train law enforcement officers, mental health professionals, and private security officials to identify, assess, and manage individuals of violent intent. Instruction includes defining inappropriate communications and contacts, assessing problem individuals, and employing effective threat management strategies.

Stephen W. Weston, JD, is a 32-year veteran of the California Highway Patrol. From 1991 to 2006, he managed the unit responsible for the investigation of threats against California state officials.

Mr. Weston has been on the staff of the Los Rios College District since 1978 as an instructor in dignitary protection, threat assessment, and major event planning. He was an instructor in the nationwide contemporary threat management training sponsored by the National Sheriffs' Association. Mr. Weston has served on the faculty of California State University, Sacramento, in the Criminal Justice Division, teaching the course "Violence and Terrorism." In 1996, he graduated from Lincoln Law School in Sacramento and was admitted to the California State Bar.

Stephen Weston is the coauthor, with Frederick S. Calhoun, of *Defusing the Risk to Judicial Officials: The Contemporary Threat Management Process* and *Concepts and Case Studies in Threat Management. A Practical Guide for Identifying, Assessing and Managing Individuals of Violent Intent.* Mr. Weston consults with government and private organizations in the management of threatening situations and lectures throughout the country on public official threat management. He has served as president of the Northern California Chapter of the Association of Threat Assessment Professionals.

Threat Assessment and Management Strategies

I

Establishing Threat Management Processes

1

We designed the second edition of *Threat Assessment and Management Strategies: Identifying the Howlers and Hunters* as a kind of user's manual describing the threat management process. The basic process enlivening threat management consists of three basic steps: *identifying*, *assessing*, and *managing* problem situations or problem individuals. Establishing an effective threat management process requires mastering those three steps. As simple as this may sound, in practice, each step presents its own unique challenges, its own unique obstacles. Overcoming them opens the way for establishing a successful threat management process.

We intend for these processes to apply to threat management activities in a variety of venues. We recognize that the threat manager's role varies depending on the context in which that role operates. Threat managers, and the teams with whom they partner, differ depending on the size of the organization or institution, whether it is public or private, whether it is law enforcement or not, and who or what is being protected. The threat manager's authority and the scope of the threat manager's functions also vary from venue to venue. Threat managers specializing in celebrities face different challenges from threat managers working in schools or universities. Protecting judicial officials raises different demands from protecting corporate chief executive officers (CEOs). Gathering places such as sports stadiums and shopping malls also have special issues that threat managers face. The threat manager's role likewise depends on whether the threat manager's functions are in-house or outsourced and whether the threat management process is an ongoing function within the organization or institution or a one-time response to a specific event. Yet, regardless of the venue, the threat management process remains the same.

Therefore, we will walk through each step. In this chapter, we provide a general overview of the component parts of the process—the specific steps an organization or individual has to take to establish effective threat management processes in any environment. In the following three chapters, we detail in depth the processes for identifying, assessing, and managing problem individuals. As always, we strive to present practical, operational tactics that we have found effective in running our own or observing other threat management programs. This is not an ABC or a by-the-numbers instruction manual. Situations requiring threat management are far too volatile and much too convoluted for that. Each situation has to be treated on its own. No two problem situations are alike. Subjects have different motives, targets have different attractions, and every situation has its own unique context. Rather, we present in the second edition guidelines for thinking through the threat management process from taking steps to recognize the initial inappropriate approach to applying the most effective strategies for managing the problem individual. Threat management, culled down to its most elemental facet, is—above all else—the progression of recognizing and thinking through a problem situation to its successful outcome.

Fortunately for those just entering the profession, the current state of the field presents an opportune time and climate. A diverse number of different, but complimentary, professionals now populate the field. These include law enforcement, psychologists, behaviorists, private security companies, social science researchers, and analysts. Their different perspectives enrich the profession by offering different ways to understand problem situations and problem individuals. The field, too, has begun producing scholarly studies, dissertations, and research reports. It boasts of its own quarterly *Journal of Threat Assessment and Management*. Threat managers should be encouraged to make good use of these expanding resources.

Recognize the Need for Threat Management Processes

Why do law enforcement, public entities, and private organizations need threat management programs? Because the angry and the outraged necessitate it. Problem individuals may turn to violence or harassment for exoneration, vengeance, even salvation. They direct their anger, their revenge, and their fears at the individuals or organizations who they perceive wronged them. Without competent threat management processes to identify, assess, and manage those who intend to cause problems, organizations risk missing any opportunity to intervene and defuse the risk.

Tragically, no one individual, organization, or institution enjoys immunity from violence. That lack of immunity constitutes the most compelling reason for establishing threat management processes. In September 2014, the Federal Bureau of Investigation (FBI) released a study of "active shooter" incidents. The Bureau defined an active shooter using the agreed-upon definition employed by agencies within the federal government. An active shooter is "an individual actively engaged in killing or attempting to kill people in a confined and populated area." In its study, the FBI broadened the definition to include more than one individual and dropped the word "confined," thus enabling it to include incidents that occurred outdoors.*

Using that definition, FBI researchers identified 160 shooting incidents between 2000 and 2013 that matched. The shootings occurred across the entire spectrum of venues for violence, including private companies; public gathering places, such as movie theaters and political events; schools and universities; and military installations. Analyzing those incidents produced a number of disturbing findings that directly support the need for organizations and individuals to develop threat management processes. FBI researchers found the following:

- An average of 11.4 incidents occurred each year of the study.
- An average of 6.4 incidents occurred in the first 7 years but increased to an average of 16.4 in the last 7 years of the study.
- 70.0% of the incidents took place in either a commercial or business venue or at an educational venue.
- Active shooters acted in 40 states and the District of Columbia.
- 60.0% of the incidents ended before law enforcement officers arrived on the scene.†

---

* *A study of active shooter incidents in the United States between 2000 and 2013.* (2014). Washington, DC: Federal Bureau of Investigation.
† *A study of active shooter incidents*, p. 6.

Not only have these incidents been increasing in recent years, but also the lethality of recent incidents has increased. The last 6 years of the study, from 2007 to 2013, experienced the incidents with the highest number of casualties:

- 32 killed, 7 wounded at Virginia Tech on April 16, 2007
- 13 killed, 32 wounded at Fort Hood, Texas, on November 5, 2009
- 12 killed, 58 wounded in Aurora, Colorado, on July 12, 2012
- 27 killed, 2 wounded at Sandy Hook Elementary School in Newtown, Connecticut, on December 14, 2012.*

Of course, these 160 incidents represent the most horrific and publicity-grabbing events over the last 14 years. But they had no monopoly on violence. Between the December 2012 massacre of 26 elementary school children and school staff in Newtown, Connecticut, and October 2014, 87 more shootings occurred at schools across the United States, an average of one school shooting a week.[†]

Other venues also suffered terrible tragedies. Domestic violence, workplace violence, violence against judicial officials, and violence against public figures also occurred, thus exposing individuals and organizations to the need for threat management processes. Why the need for threat management processes? Because those processes offer the only way to prevent a potential shooter from becoming active.

Assign Responsibility to Manage Inappropriate Situations to Trained Threat Managers

Calling threat management a *process* rather than a *program* avoids any implication that threat management necessitates full-time personnel and the dedication of significant resources. Establishing threat management processes depends on the size of the organization or institution; the nature of its interaction with insiders, clients, and the general public; and the projected workload requiring managing. As a result, the staffing of the threat management processes can range from a fully staffed, full-time group to someone working part-time as a collateral duty when the need arises. The process can also be outsourced to a qualified threat management consultant. The Secret Service obviously dedicates significant full-time resources to carry out its threat management responsibilities. The Transportation Security Administration's (TSA's) national Workplace Violence Prevention Program employs one full-time national program manager and part-time, as needed, local coordinators at the larger airports. The coordinators all have other responsibilities. In some organizations, a qualified threat manager is contracted on an as-needed basis. Vulnerability and workload are the determinants.

We strongly recommend using teams composed of subject matter experts as an integral part of the threat management processes. The composition of those teams depends on the resources available to the organization or institution and on the nature of the threat itself. Not every expert will be needed for every situation, but they should at least be on call. In

---

* *A study of active shooter incidents*, p. 7.
† Valinsky, J. (2014, October 24). There have been 87 school shootings since Newtown. So why does no one seem to care? News.Mic.

addition to qualified and trained internal or external threat managers, these experts include human resource specialists, attorneys, supervisors, security managers, ombudsman staff, internal affairs, and other specialists appropriate to each organization or institution. For simplicity, throughout the second edition, we refer to the team as the threat manager.

Whatever the size or composition of the unit, whoever is assigned threat management responsibilities should be trained and qualified, as well as willing and able to take on the responsibility.

Provide Training and Liaison with Potential Targets and Administrative Staff

Regardless of the size of the processes, the threat manager needs to train the workforce or others associated with the organization to educate them on what behaviors to avoid, what behaviors to report if witnessed in others, and where and how to report that information. In setting up new threat management processes within an organization or institution, the threat manager's first challenge is to educate everyone within the organization on the spectrum of behaviors considered inappropriate. The lesson is that members of the organization should control their own behaviors and report inappropriate behaviors they may witness others engaging in. For example, TSA created a 1-hour course every employee is required to take online. The course explained the threat management processes while emphasizing the types of behaviors to avoid and to report. Officers in the California Highway Patrol's specialized unit responsible for investigating threats to California elected officials spend considerable time educating those officials *and their staffs* on what should be reported and how to report it.

The point is to use people as an early warning radar system. The threat manager cannot begin to make threat assessments if he, she, or the team does not get reports on inappropriate or suspicious behaviors or events. Posting signs listing inappropriate behaviors that should be reported can be an effective educational tool. The Kaiser Permanente facility in Reston, Virginia, hanged posters in its restrooms addressing domestic violence, with information on where victims can get help. The TSA used the following chart to educate its employees on inappropriate behaviors they should avoid engaging in and—at the same time—those same inappropriate behaviors they should report if they witness another employee engaging in them (Figure 1.1).

Training the staff helps the threat manager get the initial facts, one hopes unembellished by exaggeration or worry, as quickly as possible. The key staff members who should be trained may not correspond to the usual organizational hierarchy. Although CEOs, principals, victims of domestic violence, and public officials should be well briefed, the majority of reports the threat manager will receive will come from potential targets, receptionists, mail handlers, website managers, social media coordinators, perimeter security officers, parking lot attendants, telephone operators, cafeteria staff, gardeners, and other individuals who are in a position to observe what is going on in or near a particular venue. These are the people who deal most with the public and the outside world. They are more likely to see or hear or receive any inappropriate contact, no matter who is targeted.

Once the threat manager trains the staff on what and how to report information, the threat manager will begin receiving reports of alleged inappropriate situations. We say "alleged" because not all of the situations reported actually cross the threshold of being

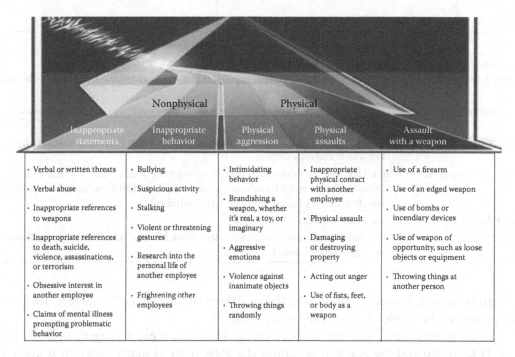

| Nonphysical | | Physical | | |
Inappropriate statements	Inappropriate behavior	Physical aggression	Physical assaults	Assault with a weapon
• Verbal or written threats • Verbal abuse • Inappropriate references to weapons • Inappropriate references to death, suicide, violence, assassinations, or terrorism • Obsessive interest in another employee • Claims of mental illness prompting problematic behavior	• Bullying • Suspicious activity • Stalking • Violent or threatening gestures • Research into the personal life of another employee • Frightening other employees	• Intimidating behavior • Brandishing a weapon, whether it's real, a toy, or imaginary • Aggressive emotions • Violence against inanimate objects • Throwing things randomly	• Inappropriate physical contact with another employee • Physical assault • Damaging or destroying property • Acting out anger • Use of fists, feet, or body as a weapon	• Use of a firearm • Use of an edged weapon • Use of bombs or incendiary devices • Use of weapon of opportunity, such as loose objects or equipment • Throwing things at another person

Figure 1.1 Spectrum of inappropriate behaviors. (From Authors' personal possession.)

inappropriate and thus warranting the implementation of the threat management process. The national program manager of TSA received reports with some regularity that an employee felt "threatened." When asked for details, the employee would say that his or her supervisor threatened the employee with some disciplinary action. The program manager then had to explain that disciplinary actions fell well within the authority of any supervisor. Threats of discipline did not warrant engaging in the threat management processes. Similarly, the U.S. Marshals Service, the agency responsible for protecting federal judicial officials, occasionally received reports from a federal judge claiming that a citizen threatened the judge with impeachment. The judge felt threatened by the citizen exerting his or her constitutional right to seek the judge's removal, but responding to that stretched far outside the Marshals Service's scope of authority.

We recommend that the reporting processes be made simple and user-friendly to those who report information. The threat manager should foster an atmosphere where all information is received with gratitude and in a timely manner to encourage future reports. None of the threat management processes can work without first setting up viable reporting procedures.

Create an Incident Tracking System with Well-Documented Files

Controlling the flow of information requires information management. Depending, again, on workload, managing the information can be as simple as an index card system or as sophisticated as a computer database. The system needs to be designed to retrieve information quickly and efficiently. It should include not only demographics on the subjects of

Table 1.1   Variables for a Threat Management Database

Variable	Explanation
Situation synopsis	A brief description of the circumstances of the situation
Situation specifics	Situation specifics as to what happened and who was involved, especially who may have been targeted
Method of delivery	How was the approach made—through suspicious activity, verbally, telephone, written, or through an informant
Content	Explicit or intangible threat, direct to target or veiled, immediate or deferred, key words and topics
Suspect demographics	Age, race, sex, incarcerated or not, group member or not, other suspects or not, subject's height, weight, eye color, known numeric identifiers (Social Security Number, driver's license number, NCIC number)
Target demographics	Age, race, sex, title, other victims
Motive	Situation related, unknown motive, irrational, habitual, ideological, or unrelated to target's official duties

concern but also key words or topics used by, or of known interest to, the subject. The latter may prove crucial in identifying anonymous subjects.

Effective threat management depends on facts, so the threat manager's second challenge is to create and maintain information channels from as many different sources as possible. Those channels have to be two-way; that is, the threat manager must also pass along to others information that he or she has gathered. The need for information underscores the need for a team approach because each member of the team has access to different sources of information.

Information flow requires information management. However designed, it should be capable of retrieving and collating specific information speedily and efficiently. Table 1.1 lists the types of variables that should be captured.

With information on these variables, the threat manager can manage current situations, cross-reference previous situations, share information on problem individuals, and create an institutional memory for his or her organization. Whatever system is created, it should be designed for easy sharing with other agencies and jurisdictions, ideally as part of formal or informal regional and national information sharing networks.

In one situation managed by the California Highway Patrol, a subject felt outraged at the official acts of a government official. He wrote several times complaining about the official to various other officials in different government agencies. Each letter crossed the threshold of inappropriateness. The recipients duly reported them to their respective agency threat managers. These various threat managers regularly shared their information and entered the reports in their databases.

Frustrated by any success with the letter writing, the subject escalated his behaviors by starting fires at various places near government buildings. At each fire site, he left cryptic graffiti messages. The threat manager searched his database for key words and topics drawn from the graffiti. From that search, he identified a likely suspect. The Highway Patrol put the suspect under surveillance and arrested the suspect as he started to light another fire.* Information feeds the threat management process.

---

* Authors' personal knowledge.

Establish Liaison with Other Agencies, Neighboring Organizations, and Institutions with Shared Interests

Once information is flowing within the organization, the threat manager should reach out to outside organizations to broaden the flow. Information flowing from as many different sources as possible allows the threat manager to link situations, subjects, relationships, and previous inappropriate behaviors by the subject. It is absolutely vital for the threat manager to reach out beyond the organization to make contact with law enforcement agencies, multiagency task forces, private security firms that provide protective services, and other relevant entities. Keeping lines of communication open with these individuals or organizations will provide intelligence information on problem individuals. The threat manager must have information coming from all sources, both inside and outside the organization. Both threat assessments and protective investigations feed on facts; both are voracious eaters. But only through information can the threat manager begin to fill in pieces of the puzzle. Information from disparate sources can link one situation to another and reveal relationships, motives, past behaviors, and previous actions of the subject.

The threat manager will undoubtedly find occasions when individuals of interest to him or her have also come to the attention of other agencies and threat managers. TSA's program manager frequently contacts agents at the Secret Service, Capitol Police, FBI, and, of all things, the National Reconnaissance Organization. The California Highway Patrol's Special Investigation Unit maintains contacts with the Joint Terrorism Task Force, local police departments, and state government agencies. Individuals who engage in inappropriate behaviors do not restrict their behaviors to one locale or one target. Employees who act aggressively at work usually act aggressively at home and probably have a history of acting aggressively in school and at various gathering places. They do not confine their bad behaviors to one venue but rather take those behaviors wherever they go.

On the evening of November 20, 2014, Myron May went to the Florida State University (FSU) campus library and began shooting at students cramming for their midterm exams. He wounded three before campus police killed him. Friends of the 31-year-old May, including his college roommate, had known for years that he suffered a mental disorder and took medication that made him "paranoid." "Those who knew Myron May, the Florida State campus shooter," one news article began, "say he struggled with a mental health disorder."* His girlfriend in New Mexico told Las Cruces Police that May's mental state "has been steadily progressing for the last several weeks and within the last couple of days it had gotten bad." May posted on his Facebook page claims that the government and others were spying on him, bugging his phone, and putting cameras in his car and at his home.* Just before May launched his attack, he left a voice mail on a friend's phone saying, "I do not want to die in vain." The message "was part of a flurry of e-mails, texts, and phone calls in which the former prosecutor laid bare his torment: He believed government 'stalkers' were harassing him and using a 'direct energy weapon' to hurt him." In one posting at a Facebook page devoted to individuals who believe they are the targets of government "handlers," May asked, "Has anyone here ever been encouraged by your handler to kill with a promise of freedom?"†

---

* Culver, J., Dobson, B., & Henry, J. (2014, November 21). Shooter identified as Florida State alum Myron May. *Tallahassee Democrat*.
† Connor, T. (2014, November 21). FSU shooter Myron May left message: "I do not want to die in vain." NBC News.com.

Many people, including police, knew May was spiraling downward, but no one knew how to help him, much less who could coordinate any assistance. Admittedly, it is quite far-fetched to expect New Mexico law enforcement to contact FSU campus police about the erratic behavior of an FSU alumni, but the point here is to note how many people recognized his mental health problems and his rapid deterioration in the weeks and days leading up to his assault. As May's situation showed, problem individuals do not act out unobserved by others. The challenge, admittedly a huge one, is to get those observations passed along to someone who knows what to do about them.

Having a liaison with another organization that may have already identified and assessed an individual who may have posed a threat to that organization in the past and now may pose a threat to the threat manager's organization gives the threat manager a great advantage in dealing with the current situation. Remember, an individual's past behavior provides the best indicator of that individual's future behavior.

Conduct Thorough Fact Finding

Protective fact finding focuses on collecting facts concerning the circumstances of the inappropriate approach and what prompted it, the characteristics of the subject, the target's relation to the subject, the subject's past behaviors, and the subject's current behaviors. The purpose is to gather enough information and evidence to support an accurate and complete reassessment of the potential risks and the best way to defuse them. We describe in detail the protective fact finding process in Chapter 2.

Use Consistent and Valid Threat Assessment Methods

After receiving the initial report of an inappropriate situation and gathering as many facts as are immediately available, the threat manager next must make an initial assessment from which to design the immediate protective response, set a course of fact finding, and begin identifying the most appropriate threat management strategies. A number of experts have developed some facile assessment tools to help the manager think through the situation. Threat managers should use these tools consistently and in the appropriate environment so that one assessment can be compared to all previous assessments. Answering the questions in the following paragraph allows the threat manager to examine what is known from a different angle. In combination, the questions provide a thorough assessment of the entire situation. Employing this approach helps the threat manager identify what is *not* known, thus giving direction to the protective fact finding.

The four assessment approaches we use address four broad but related questions. In each situation, the threat manager should always ask the following:

- What are the circumstances and context of the Inappropriate Communication or Contact?
- What are the stakes involved from the subject's point of view?
- Is the subject acting like a hunter?
- Is the subject acting like a howler?

Each of these questions focuses on different aspects of the subject's behaviors, motive, and intentions. The first question simply requires the threat manager to describe the inappropriate approach, how it was delivered, to whom it was delivered and directed, what message it says or conveys, and what may have prompted it. The second question deals with what may be at stake for the subject. It addresses how desperate or driven toward violence the subject feels. The third question seeks to determine if the subject has engaged in attack-related behaviors or behaviors common to assassins. The fourth question takes the direct opposite tack. It asks if the subject's behaviors compare similarly to the way howlers behave. We explain how to use each of these assessment approaches in Chapter 3.

Apply Threat Management Strategies Flexibly and Intelligently

The strategies for defusing the risk are best conceptualized as different options arrayed along a spectrum. Where each option falls within that range is determined by the option's effect on the subject. The spectrum reaches from discreet and passive defensive measures at one end to intrusive, confrontational acts at the opposite end. They run the gamut from doing nothing that directly affects the subject to using the authority of the law to restrain the suspect.

The threat manager should consider all of the strategies, weighing the effectiveness of each given the particular and unique aspects of the situation at hand. Each one has specific advantages and disadvantages, and each should be used only when certain conditions apply. The threat manager must determine which one offers the best chance for defusing the risk in the situation at hand at that particular moment. Once a strategy is played, the threat manager should immediately recognize that the situation has changed *precisely because a strategy has been employed.* The change requires reevaluating the situation, the assessment, and the strategy. This may result in using other strategies. That process is not endless, but often enough, it seems like it is. We describe each strategy in detail in Chapter 4.

Communicate with Potential Targets Professionally, Confidently, and Competently

The threat manager should take care, by word and deed, to reassure the target and his or her staff that the threat manager is a professional problem solver and that the responses to the incidents are under control. In implementing the appropriate protective responses, the threat manager should never increase the potential target's and the target's staff's fears by projecting the wrong attitude or sharing information that they might misinterpret. Frequent updates and open lines of communication with the protectees and their staff will help the threat manager keep them calm, attentive to instructions, and willing to follow the threat manager's lead.

The threat manager should always provide some response every time an inappropriate situation is reported. This does not mean putting a protective detail around a target every time his or her phone rings. It can be as simple as acknowledging receipt of the information or a protective response ranging from providing a personal security briefing to a full-fledged protective detail or target relocation at the maximum. We recognize that in some venues, a high-profile government official, CEO, or celebrity will, by necessity, delegate security issues to others in the organization. The threat manager should then calibrate the frequency and timing of his or her responses in coordination with the overall security efforts. In some environments, a weekly report outlining current threat issues distributed to key executives and security personnel in conjunction with immediate notifications when a high-risk situation develops will suffice. The selection of the appropriate protective response should be directly proportioned to the assessment and to the findings of any protective investigation.

Individuals targeted by inappropriate approaches often, with good reason, fear for their lives. They turn to the threat manager to allay those fears by successfully managing the subject. They expect the threat manager to act professionally and intelligently, to demonstrate that the target's security is the threat manager's highest priority. In response, threat managers need to project an image of coolness under pressure. Doing so will help calm the target and keep him or her amenable to instructions and encourage the target to follow the threat manager's handling of the situation. Many times, the target is someone accustomed to exerting power, to being the boss. These types of individuals have a natural proclivity to want to take over the situation, to, in effect, assume the role of the threat manager. This should be avoided, if not at all costs then at least at a very high cost. Targets lose all perspective except the target's point of view, which makes them incapable of making objective assessments of the situation. It also makes the confrontational strategies more attractive.

The antidote to the target dominating the response to the situation is to offer a protective response. These responses range from offering a personal security briefing to a full protective detail or target relocation. The protective response, like the threat management strategy, should be in direct proportion to the threat assessment and to the findings of the protective fact finding. The basic step of providing the target, his or her staff, and his or her family a security briefing on how to avoid encountering the subject and what to do if the subject approaches any one of them provides the threat manager the chance to project an image of professionalism, situation oversight, and reassurance. The briefing signals the target that the threat manager is aware of the risks and is taking measures to counteract them.

Of course, not every organization or institution has the resources necessary to offer a security detail or provide other types of physical security. As with everything else in the threat management process, the protective response should fit within the context of the situation. For example, TSA developed several creative responses to protect employees victimized by domestic violence. Most of those victims were security screeners working airport security checkpoints and thus exposed to the public. In many situations, TSA transferred the victim to checked baggage screening, which takes place in the bowels of the airport, away from public access. In a number of situations, TSA arranged for law enforcement officers to escort the employee from the parking lot to the terminal at the beginning of the shift and back at the end of the shift. In situations of extreme risk, TSA transferred the employee to another airport across the country. Designing an appropriate protective response depends entirely on the available resources and situational context.

Protective responses achieve two important purposes. First, security briefings inevitably improve the target's general security by reminding the target of those simple safeguards everyone should take as a matter of course. The briefing also details when and how the target should report future inappropriate approaches by the subject, even reminding the target to call 911. Second, setting up a protective response projects a positive indicator to the target that the threat manager is taking the situation with all due seriousness. It underscores the threat manager's competence, professionalism, and concern. The protective response calms the target and provides him or her proof that the threat manager is attending to their safety.

As part of the security briefing, the threat manager should diplomatically remind the target that he or she is directly responsible for his or her security. Obviously, many public officials, particularly those in high office, receive full-time security details dedicated to their safety. However, save for them, most organizations and institutions do not have the resources to hire full-time bodyguards. Many corporate executives, despite the risk, take offense at the intrusion into their private lives. Corporate security personnel at a well-known U.S. corporation, for example, warned their prominent chairman that he was at high risk of being kidnapped. After much persuasion, he finally agreed to an armored car, but reluctantly.* Threat managers must work within budgetary and personal constraints to ensure the best protective response possible.

We know of one situation in which the threat manager's response actually frightened the potential target rather than keep her calm. The target, a staff assistant to an elected official, had worked with the threat manager during previous situations. Those situations resulted in a strong rapport between the two. One day, she reported receiving an inappropriate letter from a subject well known to the threat manager and known to pose a high risk of taking action. After dealing with the situation to a successful conclusion, the staff assistant told the threat manager that this time she felt real and immediate fear for her safety and the safety of her staff and the elected official. But it was not the subject, per se, that frightened her but the threat manager's response to the situation. She described the threat manager as very tense and short with the staff member, demanding immediate information, and acting like this was something other than a routine situation. Had the threat manager maintained his calm and worked to project an image of being in control, he would not have caused the staff assistant such anxiety.* Managing the target can be every bit as important as managing the subject.

Although always implementing some protective response sends a positive signal to the target, it can also send an unnerving one at the same time. However relieved the target feels because the threat manager has arranged some security, it can also make the target even more nervous precisely because the threat manager considered a protective response necessary. The logic flows like this: "Why is this officer telling me to alter my commuting habits unless I'm really in danger." By its very nature, establishing a protective detail on a target tells the target that this situation is dangerous, even frightening. Consequently, if the threat manager determines that the risk requires physical protection, the threat manager should take the time to explain to the target that the protection is in response to a *temporary* concern that will be relieved once certain information is obtained or certain and specific things, such as the arrest of the subject, happen. By stressing the transient aspect of the protective detail that has clearly defined end points, the threat manager also prepares the target for when the time comes to bring down the security arrangements.

For those organizations and institutions that have sufficient resources to provide physical security protection for their targets during a high-risk situation, setting up a protective detail usually signals the target that his or her life is at risk. Security details should be set up under very specific guidelines. First, the threat manager should assure the target that the detail is in response to a temporary escalation in the risk and that the detail will be taken down when certain goals have been achieved. Giving the target specific reasons for

* Authors' personal knowledge.

beginning and, more importantly, *ending* the detail make removing the security far easier and less dramatic for the target. Informing the target that the threat manager is arranging for a security detail because the subject has disappeared and that the detail will be removed once the subject is located and assessed as not a risk at this time reassures the target and helps ease any qualms once the removal criteria are met.

Back in the mid-1990s, after Paul Hill assassinated an abortion doctor and his escort outside an abortion clinic in Pensacola, Florida, the attorney general ordered the Marshals Service to set up protective details at over 30 clinics across the country. It was later found out that two female staffers at the Feminist Majority office in Los Angeles selected the clinics receiving protection based on their personal concerns. Only after the Marshals Service developed precise criteria for assessing risk to individual clinics and doctors and then applied that criteria to every clinic under protection did the Attorney General allow the Marshals Service to stand down the protection. That process took nearly a year. Explaining, at the outset, the reasons for needing physical protection prepares the ground for explaining that the protection has been removed because the initial reasons have been mitigated.

Another aspect of managing the target involves information emerging from the protective fact finding. The threat manager must use discretion and common sense when sharing information with the target or the target's representatives. Sharing some information may stimulate the target's memory, allowing him or her to provide more information or the context for understanding the new information. At the same time, the threat manager needs to ensure that in sharing the information, it should be put in its full context, including the threat manager's informed assessment of the information's meaning and relevance. Telling the target about the subject's criminal history may further unnerve the target until the threat manager explains that the charges are very old and there have been no additional incidents in many years, which is actually good news because it indicates the subject may have reformed his or her behavior. Describing the information within the larger context of the situation and explaining how the new information fits into the ongoing assessment reassures the target and reinforces the threat manager's image as professional and competent.

In certain situations, information should not be shared with the target of the threat, for example, if the threat manager is unsure that the information will be kept confidential or there is a tactical reason not to share information. In general, however, sharing information helps manage the target.

Finally, above all, the threat manager must immediately and continually keep the target or the target's representatives from playing what we call the "What if?" game. Every target has an imagination, and that imagination can wreak havoc with the target's response to the situation and to changes in the situation. The "What if?" game entails the target engaging his or her imagination to conjecture deadly moves by the subject, even in the absence of any evidence of the subject heading toward those moves. What if the subject just bought a gun? What if he's in his car heading toward my house? What if he's just outside, walking toward the front door? Such questions cause great anxiety even though they are based in the target's imagination and not in fact. Fencing the target into the facts and only the facts undermines the "What if?" game. Taking and keeping charge of the situation offer the threat manager the only antidote to the "What if?" game. Keeping to the known and confirmed facts and fully briefing the target on those facts and their contextual significance keep the threat manager in control of the threat management process. As facts alone fuel assessments, they also help soothe the target's natural worries and concerns. Frequent target briefings, and keeping the target abreast of how the threat manager plans to respond and why, engenders the target's respect and confidence in the threat manager's ability to manage the situation. Targets kept in ignorance of what is going on naturally foment doubts, especially concerns about the threat manager's abilities. Targets who lack information fill that lack through the "What if?" game. Both results erode any positive relationship between the threat manager and the target. That erosion may increase the risk.

Manage Inappropriate Situations Appropriately

The initial phase of case management is the intake or triage phase. At this point, the threat manager should address the following administrative questions:

- Is this the appropriate organization to manage the situation?
- Do we have jurisdiction in the situation?
- What is the priority of this situation versus other situations being handled this time?
- Who should be notified about this situation?

Threat management situations are seldom open and shut. They begin when an inappropriate approach, not necessarily a crime, has been directed toward a target. But they have no climactic point of closing as criminal or disciplinary cases do. Even the most blatant and direct threateners can be arrested and convicted of that crime but continue threatening or, worse, plotting, from jail. An anonymous subject may direct an inappropriate approach toward a target, then never be heard from again. When can either situation be closed? Neither arrest and conviction nor time's cooling effects seem enough to support situation closure.

Threat management situations are not about investigating or solving crimes; they are about managing the behavior of an individual. Threat managers do not have a caseload of crimes assigned to them. Rather, threat managers manage problem individuals. Consequently, a threat manager's workload derives from the number of problem individuals and the severity of the problems those individuals pose.

Hence, we shy from such traditional terminology as opening or closing a threat management situation. The threat management process is neither simple nor straightforward. Tracking the stages of that process does not involve clear openings and particularly not clear closings. A situation comes to the threat manager's attention because someone reports an inappropriate approach of some kind by the subject. The approach need not be a crime, and indeed, more frequently than not, the approach is not a crime. The threat manager engages in protective fact finding while constantly assessing and reassessing the situation. He or she designs the best protective response and selects the most appropriate threat management strategy. At that point, the threat manager usually steps back to monitor the effect of the applied strategy. None of the strategies are designed to bring an abrupt end to the situation. Rather, each strategy is designed to manage the subject away from violence, to somehow defuse the risk. Unlike criminal investigations, which do enjoy an abrupt end—the arrest, conviction, and imprisonment of the criminal—managing problem subjects can extend for years. A criminal investigator's caseload consists of crimes, not criminals. A threat manager's workload consists of problem individuals who may never commit a crime. Thus, like a social worker or parole officer, the threat manager uses methods to move a subject away from an act of violence. Because of the long-term potential of threat management situations, we label the status of threat situations using the terms *active, inactive, chronic* or *habitual*, and *long-term* and define each stage as follows:

- *Active situations:* As long as the subject's behaviors point to a continued or escalating or potentially escalating risk to the target, the situation remains *active*. The threat manager may have resorted to different threat management strategies, and the results cannot be assessed as successfully defusing the risk. During this stage, the threat manager continuously makes ongoing assessments, conducts protective fact finding, hones the protective response, and applies various threat management strategies.
- *Inactive situations:* When the threat manager reaches the stage where he or she can confidently document the assessment that the subject does not pose a risk to the target at this time, the situation becomes *inactive*. At this stage, the threat manager does not have to conduct ongoing assessments, pursue leads in the protective fact finding, or apply any threat management strategies, including passive Watch and Wait. Some of the issues and ramifications surrounding the decision to inactivate a situation are discussed below in determining when is when?
- *Chronic or habitual situations:* These situations involve subjects who make repeated inappropriate approaches toward targets, frequently multiple targets, over extended periods of time, but they never escalate the risk by taking any steps beyond their preferred choice of approach. In Section II, we discuss at some length the habitual Howlers who create these long-term situations. The repeated approaches still require the threat manager to gather the initial facts and assess each new approach, but by knowing the situation involves a chronic subject, the threat manager does not need to extend the protective fact finding or change the current passive Watch and Wait strategy, provided the subject did not change or escalate his or her approach behavior from previous approaches.
- *Long-term situations:* When the threat manager assesses the situation as low risk, but steady, and the application of all the appropriate threat management strategies has produced only limited success, then the threat manager is now dealing with a long-term situation. The threat manager resorts to a Watch and Wait strategy, alternating between passive and active, or the threat manager relies on third-party monitoring or control because the subject remains of protective interest. Although both habitual and long-term situations can extend over significant periods of time, long-term situations do not necessarily involve repeated inappropriate approaches toward the target. Indeed, the situation may involve only the initial inappropriate approach, but the circumstances of the situation prohibit the threat manager from inactivating the situation because the subject cannot be assessed as not posing a risk to the target at this time. This stage is particularly effective for those subjects whose behavior suggests that they are simmering and may violently erupt months or years from now.

When Is When?

Designating a situation inactive entails steep challenges. The decision necessitates answering two extremely hard questions:

- Has enough time passed during which the subject remained inactive toward the target to conclude, with confidence, that nothing else will take place in the future?
- Does the subject, by not taking any recent action toward the target, indicate that the subject will not do anything in the future with respect to the target?

Both questions involve proving a negative; that is, no further activity means no future activity. Answering these two questions seems impossibly difficult, but crucial to managing threat management situations. Assessing the effect of any threat management strategy can be deceptive because the assessment hinges on nothing additional happening. Essentially, it involves arguing that because the subject has *not* done this or has *not* done that, the situation is inactive. Because no violence occurred—yet—the target is, and will be henceforth, safe.

Therein lies the rub. When does the *yet* become a permanent state?

In the late 1950s, Marin County, California, District Attorney William Weissich managed an arson conviction against defendant Malcolm Schlette. Schlette openly vowed revenge but first had to serve his sentence. During his incarceration, Schlette frequently discussed killing Weissich. Prison officials reported the threats to Weissich, who took the precaution of installing a steel door to his office, stashing a gun in his desk drawer, and other security measures during the remainder of his tenure as district attorney. Once he left office, however, prison officials ceased reporting to him Schlette's continued threats. Weissich let down his guard. On November 18, 1986—nearly 30 years after the trial—Schlette killed Weissich and later swallowed poison.*

Yet, the two questions addressing when is when are largely philosophical. In practice, other situations will interfere, thereby imposing a practical inactivation on those situations currently assessed as low risk or lacking in current activity. Even the most seasoned threat manager can manage only a dozen or so situations at any one time. The threat management process then closely resembles the crisis management model in which the most serious issues are addressed first.

Successful threat managers learn to set alerts on such things as significant anniversaries for the subject, such as the date of termination or the date of the final divorce decree, or noting potentially significant future events that may involve the subject. Schlette's release from prison is an example. In many situations, anniversaries or other significant dates, such as holidays, propel the subject from inaction to action. Over the years, the California Highway Patrol managed an individual who repeatedly approached an elected official, but only during the Christmas holidays. He remained quiescent the rest of the year.† To manage these tendencies, the threat manager should establish a suspense system scheduling follow-up monitoring on certain dates or time periods, such as once a quarter or half-year or right before specific dates, holidays, or subject anniversaries. Such a system saves the threat manager's time and effort while serving to check in on those subjects who, although they responded positively to the threat management strategy, may still harbor negative feelings toward the target.

* Around the nation: Grudge of 31 years ends in murder and suicide. (1986, November 20). *New York Times*.
† Authors' personal knowledge.

Summary

In this chapter, we reviewed the steps necessary for establishing a threat management process. First, the need for implementing a threat management process needs to be recognized. Next, a trained threat manager, working within a team of subject matter experts, needs to be assigned to oversee the process. Potential targets and their staffs should be trained, both as to what inappropriate behaviors they may witness to report and should avoid engaging in those same behaviors. The threat manager should create a database containing the specifics of all the inappropriate situations and individuals reported. Liaisons with other organizations and institutions should be established to share information, advice, and training. Consistent and valid threat assessment methods should be used to evaluate every reported situation. The threat manager should conduct thorough fact finding to ensure as much information is collected as possible. The threat management strategies should be applied flexibly and intelligently. The threat manager should communicate with potential targets professionally, confidently, and competently. Finally, situations requiring threat management should be managed appropriately.

Situation Analysis: When Physical Protection Fails

On July 19, 2014, a Virginia State trooper pulled Omar Gonzalez over for driving violations. While writing the ticket, the officer saw 11 firearms in the car, including an illegal sawed-off shotgun. The officer arrested Gonzalez for the weapons violation. The court later released him on bond. Two days later, officers with the Virginia State Police and agents with the Bureau of Alcohol, Tobacco, Firearms, and Explosives (ATF) searched Gonzalez's car a second time. This search uncovered a map of Washington with the White House and two other sites highlighted. The ATF agents passed the information on to the local Secret Service field office. The local agents determined that the situation did not merit further investigation or a report to the Protective Intelligence and Assessment Division at Secret Service headquarters.

Virginia's Fusion Center, a conglomerate of various law enforcement agencies—state, local, and federal—dedicated to sharing terrorism- and threat-related information, reported Gonzalez's arrest and apparent interest in the White House. The report alerted Secret Service agents assigned to the Protective Intelligence and Assessment Division. They opened their own investigation. Within a month, they had possession of Gonzalez's medical and military records. Agents from the Division also interviewed Gonzalez.

On August 25, Secret Service Uniformed Division officers noticed Gonzalez near the White House. He carried a hatchet hidden under his clothes. The officers conducted a field interview, but after deciding the hatchet did not violate DC law, they allowed him to go. The officers passed information about the incident to the White House Joint Operations Center, where a special agent ran Gonzalez's name through a protective intelligence database. He got a hit indicating that Gonzalez was the subject of an open protective intelligence case. The special agent asked the Uniform Division officers to interview Gonzalez again. The officers located Gonzalez nearby and conducted the second interview. They obtained Gonzalez's permission to search his car where they found "several empty firearms cases, four hatchets, several bottles of urine, and camping gear." Once again, the officers determined that Gonzalez had broken no laws and that he did not appear to be a danger to himself or others. They released him.

Later that evening, DC Metropolitan police responded to an anonymous tip reporting a man in a car near the White House armed with a rifle. When they arrived, they found Gonzalez in his car with the empty firearm cases. The Metro police also decided that Gonzalez had broken no laws. They left him in his car.

The next day, Uniform Division officers, under orders from their supervisor to arrest Gonzalez if he came near the White House with the hatchet, saw Gonzalez near the grounds. They interviewed him and obtained his consent to a search. They found a folding knife, but no hatchet. During the interview, Gonzalez informed the officers that he intended to leave the DC area. The officers released Gonzalez but arranged for a Secret Service unit to monitor him until he drove off, which he eventually did.

On August 27, 2 days after the hatchet incident, Gonzalez contacted the Roanoke, Virginia, Secret Service field office to inform them of his run-in with Uniform Division officers. The special agent with whom he spoke contacted the Virginia prosecutor handling the shotgun charge and informed him of the hatchet incident. The agent also attended the preliminary criminal hearing on Gonzalez's state charges.

After that, Gonzalez disappeared from the Secret Service's view for just over 3 weeks. Then, late in the afternoon of September 19, four Uniform Division officers saw Gonzalez wandering around the perimeter of the White House complex. Three of the officers recognized him from the hatchet incident. Because Gonzalez appeared to be acting normally, the officers did not approach him or report his presence to the Operations Center. An hour or so later, the officers saw Gonzalez apparently preparing to climb over the fence. They ran toward him, yelling orders to stop and get down. Gonzalez ignored them. At exactly 7:19:55 p.m., just as dusk was falling, Gonzalez climbed over the fence and jumped down on the White House lawn, then ran toward the front door. One of the officers made a brief radio report that they had a fence jumper (a fairly common incident at the White House).

Alarms sounded in the Joint Operations Center. An officer there radioed that a jumper was now on the North lawn, but the Joint Operations Center did not have the ability to override normal radio traffic, so the broadcast did not reach the Uniform Division officers stationed around the White House. Two Emergency Response Team officer-technicians stationed at the front lawn heard unintelligible radio traffic and saw other officers moving pedestrians away from the front fence. The two officers left their booth and immediately saw Gonzalez dashing across the lawn. They pointed their rifles at him as they took up pursuit, but decided against lethal force because Gonzalez appeared unarmed and the president and his family were not in residence, having left a few minutes before.

The on-duty canine officer-technician and his dog were at their post inside a van parked on the White House driveway. The canine officer had removed his radio ear piece in order to make a call on his personal cell phone. While talking on the phone, the officer noticed his colleagues running across the yard. He made a quick scan of the area and immediately saw Gonzalez running toward the mansion. Eleven seconds after Gonzalez landed in the yard, the canine officer and his dog scampered out of the van and joined the pursuit. The canine officer yelled out the required warning that he was about to release the dog. At this point, Gonzalez had almost reached the thick bushes lining the front of the White House. The canine officer gave his partner the command to apprehend the jumper, but the dog had not had the chance to "lock onto" the runner. As a result, the dog did not know which way to go.

One of the Emergency Response Team officers almost caught up to Gonzalez, but the jumper made it to the bushes. The Emergency Response Team officers, as well as the canine officer, all believed the bushes were impenetrable and that Gonzalez would be trapped there. A fourth Uniformed Division officer, on station in a car behind the canine van, heard no radio traffic about the incident and had trouble seeing anything because of his position behind the van. He did see the canine officer and the dog deploy, so he got out of his car to see what was going on. At that point, he saw Gonzalez reaching the bushes. The officer began running toward the front door.

A fifth Uniformed Division officer stationed outside the North Portico doors did not hear any radio alarms but did see colleagues running toward the house with guns drawn. In response, he drew his pistol and took cover behind a column. Just then, Gonzalez burst through the bushes and ran up the steps leading to the front door. The fifth officer aimed his pistol at Gonzalez with his finger on the trigger, but he too determined that Gonzalez was unarmed and did not pose a threat to himself or others. The fifth officer, assuming the front doors were locked, concluded that Gonzalez was now trapped on the front porch between himself, the Emergency Response Team officers, and the canine officer. He remained at the column, waiting for his colleagues to catch up.

Inside, the Uniformed Division officer stationed at the front doors heard unintelligible noise on her radio. Looking out the window, she saw the fifth officer at the column with his weapon drawn. Immediately, she got up from her chair to close and lock the front doors. She managed to close both doors, but Gonzalez shouldered through them, knocking the female officer backward. Ignoring her commands to stop, Gonzalez walked toward the East Room. The female officer tried twice to subdue Gonzalez, but he was much bigger than she was. She reached for her baton, but grabbed her flashlight instead. Throwing the flashlight down, she drew her pistol, and repeated her command for Gonzalez to stop.

Gonzalez proceeded into the East Room, then walked back down the hallway toward the grand piano deeper inside the White House. Another Uniform Division officer stationed inside the White House responded and grappled Gonzalez to the ground. Two special agents joined the struggle. Together, they subdued Gonzalez, handcuffed, and searched him, finding a folding knife on his person. They then walked him out of the house. The two Emergency Response Team officers who had chased Gonzalez to the front door remained outside. Both were unfamiliar with the White House layout. They decided to wait for backup and make a tactical entry, but by then, Gonzalez was in custody and the emergency was over.*

The Secret Service's failure to keep Gonzalez out of the White House, compounded by news of other recent security breaches, eventually cost Director Julia Pierson her job.† Yet, in fact, although an egregious perimeter breach, Gonzalez's White House intrusion never put the president, his family, or anyone else at serious risk. What Gonzalez intended to do is still a matter of considerable speculation. Given the long history of White House jumpers, Gonzalez's goal was probably to get over the fence and near the house. More than likely, he was as surprised as anyone to actually get through the front door and into the White House.

---

* The information described here is drawn from the nine-page "Executive Summary of the U.S. Department of Homeland Security Report on the White House Incursion Incident of September 19, 2014," available as a link in Schmidt, M. S. (2014, November 13). Secret service blunders eased White House intruder's way, review says. *New York Times*.
† Shear, M. D., & Schmidt, M. (2014, October 1). Julia Pierson, Secret Service Director, resigns under pressure about breaches. *New York Times*.

Issues of Interest

1. Gonzalez's successful intrusion into the White House serves as a stark reminder of the limitations of physical security, especially involving "non-lethal force scenarios such as preventing a noncompliant individual from entering the White House Mansion."* The Uniformed Division officers made their individual decisions not to fire at Gonzalez. Those decisions may have been different had the president been at home.

2. As Gonzalez proved, physical security is actually about as impenetrable as the bushes guarding the North Portico. The Secret Service put great faith in their outer perimeter security, allowing the inner security to degrade. The bushes were penetrable, the front doors were not locked, and the emergency communication system inside the front doors had been muted.† But even the outer perimeter had gaps. Gonzalez chose to scale the fence at a spot where the trident, an ornamental spike sitting atop every fence post, was missing. That gap made it easier for him to get over.

3. This entire situation underscores our firm belief about physical security. Security, which is always made up of many components, has to be effective and efficient 100% of the time. Attackers have to be effective or lucky but one time.

4. Threat management programs are necessary because physical security alone is not enough. Even if the physical security is designed perfectly, a rarity in itself, security degrades over time because nothing happens or because of a failure in implementation (lack of funding, poor training, lack of communication, inattention).

5. Threat management consists of a series of processes requiring close communication among everyone involved. Calhoun and Weston's little known Law of Communications states that the difficulties in maintaining close communications increase in direct proportion to the increase in the number of individuals and organizations involved. Trying to manage Gonzalez involved the Secret Service Uniformed Division, the White House Joint Operations Center, the Protective Intelligence and Assessment Division at headquarters, several Secret Service field offices, ATF, Virginia State Police, a Virginia court, a Virginia prosecutor, and the Washington Metropolitan Police.

    a. The Secret Service's efforts to manage Gonzalez were further hampered by its reliance on several different databases "that are not interoperable and have varying levels of accessibility, a fact that hinders timely integration, dissemination, and sharing of information." The Uniformed Division officers who interviewed Gonzalez during the hatchet incident on August 25 did not have access to some of the Service's databases containing "information that may have allowed them to change the tenor and consequences of the discussion with Gonzalez."‡

    b. The Secret Service field office failed to notify the Protective Intelligence and Assessment Division about ATF's report on Gonzalez, his firearms, and his apparent interest in the White House. In the summer of 2014, the Secret

---

* "Executive Summary," p. 7.
† "Executive Summary," p. 6.
‡ "Executive Summary," p. 9.

Service had not issued any guidance to its field offices on when to report to headquarters information about subjects who show an unusual interest in the White House.*

c. The Protective Intelligence and Assessment Division, which is responsible for classifying individuals as persons of interest, failed to alert the Uniformed Division concerning Gonzalez's "extensive protective intelligence history." Nor did the division mark Gonzalez as a person of interest for whom Secret Service special agents and Uniformed Division officers should be on guard.†

d. During the incident itself, the Service's communications systems failed at several key points, thereby disrupting the alarm about the fence jumper.* According to the Executive Summary review of the incident, "a combination of technical missteps, lack of radio discipline, improper use of equipment, and aging infrastructure contributed to communication failures" that delayed notifying several officers who might have intercepted Gonzalez before he got through the doors.*

6. The situation exemplifies a failed intervention strategy. In the month or so leading up to the incident, law enforcement contacted Gonzalez five separate times. Each time, Gonzalez exhibited behaviors associated with the path to intended violence, yet the Secret Service took no effective action. The Uniformed Division and the DC Metropolitan Police handled him using typical law enforcement standards. They did nothing because Gonzalez had not broken the law at that moment and they judged him not a danger due to mental illness. Because of all the overlapping jurisdictions, it remains unclear if any one law enforcement individual had all the available information before the actual intrusion. Without someone having a complete picture, the officers who responded to Gonzalez suffered from situational blindness.

7. Threat assessment information, which includes persons of interest, has no value unless it is shared with those who need to know the information. In this situation, the Secret Service appears to have erected several silos within its own organization. Silos are bureaucratic structures sealing off information within themselves. The field office did not pass on its information on Gonzalez received from ATF to headquarters; the Joint Operations Center did not share information with the Uniformed Division; the radios did not communicate with all the officers; the officers assigned to the Emergency Response Team had not been briefed or allowed to see the White House floor plan; the Service maintained several databases that did not talk to each other. These silos prevented a full sharing of information about Gonzalez throughout the organization. The failures were both in the design and implementation of the physical security countermeasures and in the dissemination of the threat information. Bureaucracy, turf battles, counterproductive policies, and poor management adversely affected both the physical security systems and the threat management processes.

8. Everyone involved in the great chase on the early evening of September 19 experienced what we technically call "Oh, crap" moments. The four Uniformed Division officers who recognized Gonzalez from the hatchet incident no doubt thought to

---

* "Executive Summary," p. 8.
† "Executive Summary," p. 9.

themselves, "Oh, crap," when they realized he was going to clamor over the fence. The canine officer must have thought, "Oh, crap," when he noticed the commotion of other officers chasing Gonzalez across the lawn, too late for his dog to do any good. The two Emergency Response Team officers who assumed that the bushes were impenetrable undoubtedly thought to themselves, "Oh, crap," when they saw Gonzalez reach the Portico steps on the other side of the bushes. The officer stationed at the North Portico, who assumed the front doors were locked, must have thought, "Oh, crap," when Gonzalez barged right through the doors. The female officer stationed inside the front door must have also said to herself, "Oh, crap," when reaching for her baton only to come up with her flashlight. And one can easily imagine Gonzalez, once actually inside the White House, saying to himself, "Oh, crap. What do I do now?"

Identifying Problem Individuals

2

Problem individuals create problem situations; we use the two terms synonymously. But the problem posed to the threat manager may not cross any legal threshold to become a crime. Hence, problem individuals and problem situations may not allow for a law enforcement resolution. Consequently, we purposefully avoid labeling problem individuals as suspects, criminals, or their situations as "cases." The vast majority of problem individuals shy away from actual criminal behaviors. They keep their problem behavior on the legal side of the line. The few problem individuals who cross that line may do so only at the moment of committing the violent assault the threat manager tries to prevent. Threat management is all about managing problem situations to keep them from becoming criminal violence.

Three distinct processes make up the best approach to effective threat management. The first step entails identifying the problem individual through protective fact finding and a robust reporting system. That system should encourage others to raise the alarm about any problematic behaviors they may witness. The second step requires assessing the situation to estimate the potential risk. The third step, based on the risk assessment, involves selecting the most appropriate threat management strategy for managing the problem situation. The three processes, although distinct among themselves, flow seamlessly from identifying to assessing to managing to reassessing and fine tuning, even changing, the management strategy.

As we will discuss in depth in Section II, problem individuals can be divided into two types. The vast majority are howlers, individuals who intend to cause fear to bring attention to themselves. A minority of problem individuals are hunters, who fully intend to act out violently. Either type has to be dealt with because each type presents its own problems to their targets, organizations, and society at large. In this chapter, we delve in depth into how to identify problem individuals. The two chapters that follow discuss assessment methods and management strategies for managing howlers and hunters.

Understanding Violence

The first step in identifying a problem individual's potential for violence is to understand violence itself. We understand threat management as the processes for identifying, assessing, and managing problem individuals. Likewise, we also view violence as its own process. All acts of violence fall into one of two categories. *Impromptu violence*, as its name indicates, results from a spontaneous, unplanned act that occurs in the emotional heat of the moment. *Intended violence*, conversely, culminates a planned, premeditated act. Each type of violence shares several of the same steps within each's process. Both involve developing a grievance, determining that violence alone will resolve that grievance, breaching the target's security, and actually attacking violently. Intended violence inserts two more steps into its process: researching and planning the attack and making preparations based on

25

the plan. These two steps introduce the premeditation into the process. We illustrate each process in the following diagrams. Figure 2.1 graphically describes the path to impromptu violence.

Impromptu violence tends to spiral out of control, moving quickly from grievance through ideation to breaching the target's security and attacking. Preventing it hinges on the target or an eyewitness moving quickly to defuse the emotions boiling up in the subject. Sometimes, this can be done by soothing the subject, apologizing for causing the grievance, remaining calm, treating the subject with the utmost respect, or, in some cases, acting in self-defense. Sometimes, the best strategy depends on removing the target from the situation—simply getting out of the way of the subject. In any event, impromptu violence tends to escalate quickly, with mere seconds separating grievance from attack.

Because impromptu violence is unplanned, it frequently takes on bizarre, almost comic, forms. In October 2014, for example, John Thornton checked into a Bristol, Connecticut, hotel. For reasons even Thornton may not now remember or understand, he took offense at a hotel employee mopping the floor. Thornton grabbed the mop from out of her hands and began "mopping aggressively" over the woman's shoes. When she asked him to stop, Thornton turned his back to her and pushed her into a corner. When police arrived, Thornton turned his anger on the officers, insulting and swearing at them and threatening them with bodily harm. The officers arrested him on charges of breach of peace and threatening.* Thornton did not go to the hotel intending to mop the woman's shoes. Instead, in an unplanned fit of anger, he grabbed the nearest weapon he could reach—the mop—then used it against his target. Impromptu violence mimics spontaneous combustion. It simply erupts in the heat of the moment.

In one curious incident, a woman accused of killing her husband of 8 days defended herself by essentially claiming she used impromptu violence, not premeditated murder. Almost from the moment Jordan Graham said, "I do," she began having doubts about her marriage to Cody Lee Johnson. They honeymooned at Glacier National Park near Kalispell, Montana. Graham explained to the jury that she wanted to talk about her growing doubts with Johnson but was concerned about how he would react. While hiking around the mountain, the couple "climbed down a treacherous slope" and stopped on a narrow ledge overlooking a deep ravine several hundred feet below. Graham chose that place to express her concerns to her new husband. He reacted angrily and, Graham testified, he grabbed her arm. Thinking he was going to pull her toward him, Graham admitted losing her temper and pushing him, one hand on his arm and the other on his back. "I wasn't thinking about where we were," Graham explained to the jury, "I just pushed." The jury convicted her of second-degree murder, which does not require premeditation. In her appeal, Graham claimed that her sentence of 30 years 5 months fell more in line with a first-degree murder charge. Her lawyer claimed that her admitted impromptu violence—"extremely reckless but unintentional"—warranted at most a 10-year sentence. As of this writing, her appeal remains pending.†

Intended violence is a much more methodical process where time plays not as crucial a factor as it does in impromptu violence (Figure 2.2). As with impromptu violence, the subject first develops a grievance, then comes up with the idea that a violent act is the only resolution to the grievance. At this step, intended violence introduces two additional steps not found during impromptu violence. Because intended violence is premeditated, the subject has the time to research the target and plan the violence. The planning and

---

* Connecticut man accused of "mopping aggressively." (2014). Associated Press.
† Woman guilty of pushing husband off cliff appeals. (2014). Associated Press.

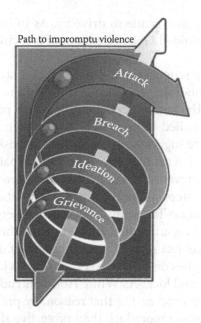

Figure 2.1 The path to impromptu violence.

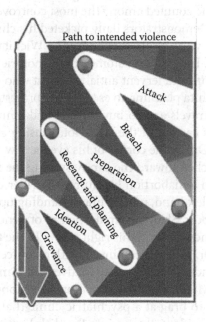

Figure 2.2 The path to intended violence.

research can be quite simple, as in the case of knowing the target intimately, thus obviating the need for research because the subject already knows the target's habits, routines, and places frequently visited. Or the planning and research can be elaborate, as in Lee Harvey Oswald's case. Oswald researched the president's motorcade route through newspaper stories, planned on using a special rifle, and planned on constructing a sniper's nest in the Book Depository. The next step along the path to intended violence is based on research and planning, to make whatever preparations the plan calls for. For Oswald, that meant sneaking the rifle into the building, using crates of books to construct his nest, cocking the rifle, then waiting for the motorcade to drive by. As in impromptu violence, the last two steps in the process of intended violence consist of breaching the target's security and attacking.

In a study of nine German school shooters and 31 "other students of concern," Meloy et al. found that 100% of the school shooters followed the path to intended violence, whereas the other students did not. The authors concluded that the path, along with a few other warning behaviors, "distinguished the school shooters from those who showed no evidence of intent to act, and were suggestive patterns for high risk cases."* Turning an intention to act violently into a violent act requires following the path from grievance to attack.

We focus in this book on preventing acts of intended violence. That prevention depends on intervening at any of the steps along the path before attack. In their book *Just Two Seconds*, Gavin de Becker, Thomas Taylor, and Jeff Marquart explain at length how security officers can physically disrupt an attempted attack in what they estimate as the 2 seconds that lapse from the time the subject reveals himself or herself until the attack is launched.[†] The Secret Service no doubt relies on the same response as its last line of defense. Doing so requires very quick reactions and luck. As White House intruder Omar Gonzalez showed, sometimes luck sides with the attacker. For that reason, we prefer earlier interventions.

In one peculiar case involving more luck than protective skill, the target saved himself through an aggressive response seconds before being shot. Until Dr. George Tiller's assassination at the end of May 2009, he counted among the most controversial and much hated abortion doctors in the country. Demonstrators daily picketed his clinic in Wichita, Kansas, and on several occasions over the years, protestors flocked to Wichita from around the nation to hold huge rallies against him. He grew accustomed to the notoriety. In August 1993, Rachelle Shannon, an Oregon housewife and fervent antiabortionist who—until then—specialized in clinic arsons, traveled to Wichita planning to escalate her protests by shooting Dr. Tiller. She held bake sales to fund her travels and to buy a pistol and ammunition. At the end of the workday, Dr. Tiller drove his car out of the clinic lot, pausing at the driveway before making the turn onto the street. Out of the corner of his eye, he saw a figure approaching on the driver's side, an arm outstretched toward the car. Assuming the figure was a sidewalk counselor attempting to hand him antiabortion literature, Dr. Tiller did as he did most evenings this happened. He raised his left hand, middle finger standing up, to brush off the counselor. At the instant he bent his elbow, Shannon fired. Instead of penetrating his chest, the bullet ricocheted off his elbow, bouncing over to his right elbow. In the two seconds between seeing Shannon and her shooting, Dr. Tiller saved himself with an obscene gesture and a lot of luck.[‡]

On rare occasions, intended violence may inadvertently morph into impromptu violence. For instance, Mijailo Mijailovie of Sweden fantasized about killing someone famous. That fantasy prompted him to brag at a psychiatric clinic that he had recently murdered someone. Six days later, he accidentally ran into Swedish Foreign Minister Anna Lindh at a department store in Stockholm on September 10, 2003. Taking advantage of the chance encounter, Mijailovie attacked the minister, stabbing her to death. The police conducted a thorough investigation but found no evidence of prior planning. Mijailovie's fantasy of

---

* Meloy, J. R., Hoffmann, J., Roshdi, K., & Guldimann, A. (2014). Some warning behaviors discriminate between school shooters and other students of concern. *Journal of Threat Assessment and Management*, 1(3), 203–211.
† de Becker, G., Taylor, T., & Marquart, J. (2008). *Just two seconds: Using time and space to defeat assassins*. Studio City, CA: The Gavin de Becker Center for the Study and Reduction of Violence.
‡ Interview of Dr. Tiller by Frederick S. Calhoun, ca. 1996.

committing an act of intended violence turned into an act of impromptu violence once a chance encounter provided him the opportunity.*

Identifying Problem Individuals

Problem individuals tend to self-identify themselves to someone. They may communicate inappropriately to the target; talk about their plans to third parties; write, text, blog, or tweet their intentions into the Internet; engage in stalking or research behavior that others witness; or otherwise bring someone's attention to themselves. Howlers crave the attention; hence, they engage in open behaviors or communications that alert the target that the target has come to the howler's attention. Those who intend to actually carry out a violent act tend toward discretion; they do not want their plans disrupted.

The trick for the threat manager is to open lines of communication with those who notice the subject. In an organizational setting, such as a business, factory, school, university, or other place bringing people together, opening communications begins with training the people there in what to look for, what to report, and to whom to report it. The threat manager needs to reach out to the staff most likely to come in contact with the subject. Those staffers include mail room staff, cleaning crews, gardeners, security guards, receptionists, personal assistants social media specialists, and others among the lower levels of the staff as they most likely work in places that bring them more into contact with other staff members and the public. Nonetheless, everyone within the organization needs to be trained and regularly retrained. New employees should receive the training as part of their orientation to the organization.

Increasingly, both hunters and howlers have taken to the Internet. Threats and threatening comments routinely appear in blog snapchats, tweets, Facebook, and in other social media conveyances. The Transportation Security Administration witnessed increasing numbers of inappropriate remarks among its security screeners posted online.[†] On October 8, 2014, the *Washington Post* reported that according to the Secret Service, more than 60% of the threats directed toward President Barack Obama are now made online. Since Obama took office in 2009, 65 people have been indicted on charges of threatening him. Daniel J. Temple, for example, tweeted "im coming to kill you" and "so I gotta kill barack Obama first." In January 2014, Temple pled guilty and a federal judge sentenced him to 16 months in prison. Two months later, Nicholas Savino received a year sentence for posting on the White House website, "President Obama the Anti-Christ, As a result of breaking the constitution you will stand down or be shot dead." At the time of Savino's arrest, police discovered three guns and almost 11,000 rounds of ammunition at his residence and in his car. The increase in cyber-threats prompted the Secret Service to issue a request for proposals for developing software that "can detect sarcasm and identify social-media influencers online" the *Post* reported.[‡]

---

* We accept here at face value the assertion that authorities conducted a "thorough investigation" but question what weapon Mijailovic used to stab the foreign minister. If it was a knife he brought with him, that would raise the suspicion that he knew she would be at the store at the time he went there. If that were the case, his assault would be an act of intended violence. Meloy, J. R. (2014). Approaching and attacking public figures: A contemporary analysis of communications and behavior. *Journal of Threat Assessment and Management*, 1(4), 256.

† Authors' personal knowledge.

‡ Ellperin, J. (2014, October 28). The new dynamics of protecting a president: Most threats against Obama issued online. *Washington Post*.

Fortunately, the most dangerous situations are also the easiest to recognize. Danger becomes most apparent at the moment of dangerousness. Someone aims a rifle in the parking lot. A woman becomes violently belligerent in the reception area. A young man shoots out the glass door at the entrance to the elementary school. A court security officer x-rays a box packed with electric wire, batteries, and a solid mass. Threat managers recognize these incidents as at the breach step along the path to intended violence. At that step, both the level of risk and the protective response become very clear. Evacuate the target from the area of risk, find and isolate the subject, and neutralize any dangerous or suspicious objects.

High-risk situations are obviously high risk. The threat manager's immediate response should be to determine where the danger originated and how imminent is the risk. Simply put, the threat manager first determines the immediacy of the threat. The best way to make that determination is to find out how the situation at hand came to be reported. A threat made by text generates one kind of protective response; a suspicious package spawns an entirely different, more urgent, reaction. Similarly, a threat manager would respond differently to an angry Internet posting directed at the chairman of the board than to an outraged stockholder shouting out his grievances during a stockholders' meeting. The difference in how the threat manager treats each instance comes from the urgency of the risk. Text messages and Internet postings do not kill; bombs and people may.

In sum, when told of a suspicious person or situation, the threat manager makes an initial assessment of the immediate level of risk. The vast majority of such situations do not constitute a clear and present danger. But that lack by no means relieves the threat manager of the responsibility to find out more facts to make more informed assessments. Most situations brought to the threat manager's attention at first appear vague and equivocal. The subject's actions and intentions are not always readily apparent. Such uncertainty requires the threat manager to sort through what is currently known and what is currently unknown. In other words, a good threat manager first begins by identifying what facts are known and what facts are unknown.

In our last book, *Concepts and Case Studies in Threat Management*, we compiled what we considered—and continue to consider still—a definitive list of 20 areas of inquiry that, when explored, provide the necessary facts for a fully formed assessment. The Need to Knows are listed below.*

1. How did the subject choose to approach the target?
2. What about the situation indicates the subject's identity and physical proximity to the target; in other words, who and where is the subject?
3. What about the situation indicates who or what the subject is targeting; in other words, who is the target?
4. What about the situation indicates the type of venue being targeted and what is it about the venue that gives insight into the subject's intent, motive, and ability?
5. What about the situation indicates whether or not the Intimacy Effect is in play; in other words, what is the nature of the relationship between the subject and the target?
6. What about the situation relates to the subject's choice of context, including the circumstances and content?

* Calhoun, F. S., & Weston, S. W. (2013). *Concepts and case studies in threat management*, p. 63. Boca Raton, FL: CRC Press.

7. Is the target currently accessible to the subject?
8. Does the subject have the ability and motivation to take advantage of any current accessibility to the target?
9. Is there a known history of previous contacts with the target or other targets by this subject?
10. Does the subject have a history of violent or threatening behaviors, including any criminal behavior?
11. What is the subject's knowledge about the target's current situation?
12. Is the subject seeking knowledge about the target and the target's current situation?
13. Does the subject's behavior indicate mental health issues, including suicidality?
14. Does the subject possess, have access to, or give evidence of a fascination with weaponry of any type?
15. Is the subject currently seeking to obtain a weapon?
16. What is the status of the subject's inhibitors, including any recent losses?
17. Has the subject exhibited controlling, isolating, or jealous behaviors toward the target?
18. Does the subject have a history of, or is currently, abusing alcohol, drugs, or prescription medicines?
19. Does the subject have any relevant medical issues?
20. Has the subject engaged in any final act behaviors?

We use these questions to guide our protective fact finding. Obviously, in any given situation or fact-finding effort, not every question will be answered or answered completely. The answers, too, are subject to change as circumstances change. As a result, as the fact finding continues, assessments must also be continuous. Assessments depend on systematic thinking through the facts and current situation, recognizing that new facts and changing situations demand new assessments.

Acting without assessing may actually increase the risk to the target. Any actions taken by the threat manager inevitably influence the target. Targets frequently link their reactions to how the threat manager responds. Overreacting can unnecessarily frighten the target; underreacting may signal the target that he or she has nothing to worry about. Managing the target can be every bit as important as managing the subject.

Simultaneously, a subject poised anywhere along the path to intended violence can be propelled further along the path by a wrong response by the threat manager because the subject usually assumes that any action—or inaction—by the threat manager is initiated and under the direction of the target. Choosing not to respond to an inappropriate communication may encourage the attention-seeking subject to escalate his or her problem behaviors. Overreacting may prompt the subject to lash back in revenge. By intelligently and deliberately assessing the known facts, the threat manager takes the time to think through the problem to craft the best protective response, identify missing "Need to Knows," and initiate appropriate management strategies.

Protective Fact Finding Compared to Criminal Investigations

Threat managers engaged in protective fact finding devote their questions to collecting facts pertaining to the circumstances of the situation; the subject's behaviors, both current and previous; and the relationship between the subject and the target. The information thus collected feeds new threat assessments, which drives a protective response and guides selecting the most appropriate threat management strategy. Like the assessments they feed, protective fact finding must be grounded in facts. The ultimate question the threat manager must answer is "Does the subject pose a risk to this target at this time?"

We emphasize "at this time" as a reminder of the fluidity of threat management and because it keeps the threat manager from making predictions. No one can see into the future. At best, we can only evaluate what has happened up to the point of the assessment. Pretending clairvoyance is a fool's game. It has no place in the threat management process. Instead, protective fact finding focuses on determining what happened to bring the current situation about. Based on those facts, the degree of risk can be assessed, protective responses designed, and the best management strategy selected.

Protective fact finding has two equal purposes. First, the threat manager collects or corroborates information to use in conducting ongoing assessments. Second, the fact finding also goes into determining the most effective threat management strategy. Once those strategies are applied, the threat manager uses more protective fact finding to gauge the effectiveness of the strategy and further assessments. This requires considerable agility in managing the threat management processes. If a particular strategy appears ineffective or, worse, if it increases the risk, then the threat manager must be ready to abandon the strategy *immediately*. Because of these dual purposes, protective fact finding can be as complex and difficult as any criminal investigation.

But protective fact finding is not a criminal investigation even though it relies on similar methods and approaches. The difference between them is profound. Criminal investigations seek to identify if a crime was committed and who committed it. They seek to bring the guilty to justice. Protective fact finding aims to *prevent* the crime from taking place. The one punishes what has already happened; the other thwarts what might happen.

Another difference between protective fact finding and criminal investigations arises from their beginning and end points. Criminal investigations usually begin with an alleged crime occurring and end with the determination either that no crime occurred or the suspect is arrested, tried, and convicted. Protective fact finding does not have such firm, obvious, initiations, and terminations. Assessments and protective fact-finding can begin with a noncriminal suspicious occurrence or the basic fact that someone is purposely bringing attention to themselves. Threat managers cannot end their protective fact finding until the threat manager can justify that the subject does not pose a risk to the target at this time. That is a daunting standard. It essentially requires proving a negative, a logical impossibility, but one faced by threat managers daily. For example, the chairman of the board's secretary reports receiving a threatening letter. But nothing happens after that; the threat manager can find no evidence indicating the letter writer has done anything toward carrying out the threat. At what point in time can the threat manager explain to the chairman that the chairman is not at risk at this time? How much inactivity obviates the threat?

Similarly, subjects who commit a crime, say by making a direct threat of physical harm, can be arrested and prosecuted, which thus brings the criminal investigation to a successful conclusion. That resolution, however, does not mean the risk has dissipated. The threat management process, including the protective fact finding, must continue until the threat manager can confidently determine that the subject no longer poses a risk at this time. Incarcerated persons frequently have outside resources. And, what if the suspect pleads to a lesser offense and either avoids jail time altogether or gets a reduced sentence? The subject may also jump bail or probation and become "at large" again. In sum, protective fact finding continues until the threat manager can confidently articulate that the subject no longer poses a risk to the target at this time—at least for the foreseeable future or until the subject takes some new action that requires new assessments, new protective responses, and new threat management strategies.

Conducting Protective Fact Finding

Protective fact finding should be conducted in a precise, orderly manner. It should proceed systematically to ensure that all sources of information are plumbed. We envision this process as a rippling effect of concentric circles moving from the target outward to issues pertaining to the subject. Fact finding should begin with collecting information about the initial situation that prompted the need for fact finding. The threat manager should immediately determine the target's location and security and then round up any information available. That information should be assessed, a protective response determined upon, and an initial threat management strategy selected. From there, the threat manager should broaden the inquiry to encompass as much information about the subject as possible. The subject's past behaviors, especially behaviors involving the target, provide excellent insights into how the subject may behave in the future. Previous acts of violence, for example, are the best indicator for future acts of violence. As new information emerges, new assessments must be made. Each new assessment requires reevaluating the current protective response and threat management strategy.

Other events or situations in the subject's life, independent of anything the target does, may enhance the risk. A subject's inhibitors—those things in any individual's life that the individual values and does not want to lose—may start toppling. Typical inhibitors include a stable family life, secure job, satisfying home, self-respect, and dignity. As the inhibitors fall, their restraining hold on the subject also weakens. Often, one falling inhibitor may cause other inhibitors to tumble, thus increasing the pressures on the subject and prompting the subject to seek relief. That relief may be in the form of a violent act.

Consequently, protective fact finding should begin by examining the relationship among the subject and the target and the situation prompting the need for fact finding, but then branch out to scrutinize what else is going on in the subject's life and circumstances. This assumes, of course, that the threat manager knows who the subject is, which, obviously, is not always the case. In reality, the threat manager can only find the available facts, always knowing that not every Need to Know will be answered, but also confident that facts—and facts only—inform each ongoing assessment.

Using the Need to Knows

The Need to Knows are organized along the concentric circles rippling out from the event precipitating the fact finding toward the subject, the subject's past, and the subject's current situation. The protective fact finding should follow answering the Need to Knows in that order to ensure a systematic look at all the relevant, and discoverable, circumstances. The Need to Knows begin with questions exploring the relationship between the subject and the target. The second set focuses on the subject's previous behaviors, both toward the target and toward others. The third set of questions looks deeper at the subject's current and past situations. That is why we find the Need to Knows so useful in conducting protective fact finding. They serve as a road map to everything a threat manager needs to make complete and fully informed assessments.

Need to Knows on the Situation Circumstances and Context

The first seven Need to Know questions examine the circumstances and context of the event that prompted the need for a protective fact finding effort. The questions are the following:

1. How did the subject choose to approach the target?
2. What about the situation indicates the subject's identity and physical proximity to the target; in other words, who and where is the subject?
3. What about the situation indicates who or what the subject is targeting; in other words, who is the target?
4. What about the situation indicates the type of venue being targeted and what is it about the venue that gives insight into the subject's intent, motive, and ability?
5. What about the situation indicates whether or not the Intimacy Effect is in play; in other words, what is the nature of the relationship between the subject and the target?
6. What about the situation relates to the subject's choice of context, including the circumstances and content?
7. Is the target currently accessible to the subject?

How the subject approached the target provides the threat manager with great insight into the subject's intentions because, in most situations,* the subject chooses how he or she makes the approach. Writing an e-mail or leaving a voice mail show that the subject intended—at the time of making the approach—to keep a physical distance from the target. Conversely, confronting the target in person or engaging in stalking behaviors puts the subject in proximity to the target, thus raising the risk to the subject. The target may react in ways unpredicted by the subject, such as physically lashing out at the subject, calling the police, snapping the subject's picture, or calling for help.

The second and third questions seem obvious but should not be overlooked because they force the threat manager to determine what is going on right now. Does the threat manager have a clearly identified subject and target or are either one ambiguous or vague? "I'm going to kill the president" specifically identifies that "I" (even if the *I*'s identity is hidden) intends to kill a specific person, that is, the president. An anonymous e-mail expressing outrage at being rudely treated at a department store and stating, "If this keeps up, somebody's going to hurt one of your employees" does not clearly identify the parties at play. Both the subject, "somebody," and the target, "one of your employees," are shrouded, suggesting that the author, at the time of composing the e-mail, had no real intention of personally engaging in violence.

---

* Information about the subject's intentions relayed by a third party or informant is not under the subject's control.

The fourth question addresses a larger context. As we wrote at length in *Concepts and Case Studies*, different venues for violence attract subjects for different reasons because of the social setting in which the violence occurs. The venue then provides the threat manager insight into the potential motive driving the subject and the type of relationship that exists between the subject and the target. By venue, we mean the social setting surrounding the subject and target. Domestic violence differs from violence against public figures because domestic violence involves intimate partners, whereas violence against public figures* usually involves strangers. Workplace violence differs from the other venues, as does violence against gathering places and violence toward symbolic or representative targets. Understanding what we call the social ecosystem in which subject and target find themselves allows the threat manager to assess motive and subject–target relationship.

The fifth question reminds the threat manager to assess the impact of the Intimacy Effect on any threats made by the subject. As we discuss at length in Chapter 9, the Intimacy Effect postulates that the greater the degree of intimacy between the subject and the target, the more likely threats of physical harm will be carried out. The sixth question expands on that, essentially prompting the threat manager to determine why the subject chose this moment in time and this place to do something that prompted the protective fact finding. Why now? Why here?

The seventh question addresses the current safety of the target. Is the target currently or potentially accessible to the subject? A letter postmarked Omaha written by an ex-husband threatening his ex-wife living in Minneapolis suggests that the target is not currently accessible to the subject but could potentially become accessible in the future. Conversely, a public figure under tight security is not easily accessible to the subject, either currently or potentially.

Need to Knows on Subject's History

The next set of questions address the subject's previous behaviors and the subject's possible previous relationship with the target.

8. Does the subject have the ability and motivation to take advantage of any current accessibility to the target?
9. Is there a known history of previous contacts with the target or other targets by this subject?
10. Does the subject have a history of violent or threatening behaviors, including any criminal behavior?
11. What is the subject's knowledge about the target's current situation?
12. Is the subject seeking knowledge about the target and the target's current situation?

The eighth question directs the threat manager's attention to the subject's current whereabouts and ability to inflict harm in relation to the target. Questions 9 and 10 ask about the subject's previous known behaviors. Howlers in particular like to harass different targets. A subject with a history of such threatening communications may well fall into that category. Previous violence between domestic partners strongly indicates the potential

---

* Remember that public figures have private, personal lives. The threat manager should not assume that because the public figure is the target, the venue is violence against public figures.

for future violence. How the subject behaved in the past, particularly in situations similar to the current one, provides the best indicator for future behavior.

Questions 11 and 12 explore the subject's past involvement with the target. How well does the subject know the target based on their actual relationship? Previous unfulfilled threats suggest that the current threat may be empty as well. Research behavior by the subject places the subject on the path to intended violence.

Need to Knows on Subject's Mental and Physical Condition

The final set of Need to Knows spotlights the subject's life circumstances, attitudes, behaviors, and mental and physical condition. They are as follows:

13. Does the subject's behavior indicate mental health issues, including suicidality?
14. Does the subject possess, have access to, or give evidence of a fascination with weaponry of any type?
15. Is the subject currently seeking to obtain a weapon?
16. What is the status of the subject's inhibitors, including any recent losses?
17. Has the subject exhibited controlling, isolating, or jealous behaviors toward the target?
18. Does the subject have a history of, or is currently, abusing alcohol, drugs, or prescription medicines?
19. Does the subject have any relevant medical issues?
20. Has the subject engaged in any final act behaviors?

Question 13 asks what is known about the subject's mental health, both currently and in the past. Suicidality is potentially serious because it indicates desperation, inevitability, and a disregard for potential ramifications of their acts. But any evidence of mental illness, including obvious clues from the situation under assessment (such as hallucinations, delusional claims, bizarre or irrational statements), should be taken into account. The issue is not simply potential mental illness. Rather, the question is whether or not any mental illness affects the subject's ability to function. Dysfunctional subjects pose less risk than functional subjects, regardless of their mental status.

Questions 14 and 15 address the subject's fascination with, access to, and familiarity with weapons, especially firearms. Weapon possession needs to be assessed in context. Long-term ownership of hunting weapons is different from recent purchase of an AK-47. But firearms are not the only weapons the subject may use. We know of one case where the husband killed his wife by spiking her drink with antifreeze.* Weapons, then, should also be assessed in context by asking to what types of weapons the subject has access. These two questions also raise the issue of how fascinated or infatuated the subject is with the idea, even fantasy, of using weapons of any sort. Evidence of a fixation with violence suggests the potential for the actual use of violence. Fantasizing about maiming or killing the target—or anyone else, for that matter—brings the subject that much closer to an actual commission of violence. The second step along the path to intended violence is coming up with the idea of using violence.

Questions 16 to 20 focus on the subject's life situation, particularly at the present time. It explores the subject's current inhibitors and any recent losses. Question 17 delves into the

---

* Nation in brief. (2005, November 5). *Washington Post*.

subject's previous negative behaviors with the target. Question 18 addresses alcohol and drug abuse, a frequent disinhibiting habit. Questions 19 and 20 focus on conditions and behaviors suggesting that the subject does not believe he or she has long to live. Terminally ill subjects obviously have nothing to lose by acting violently, whereas subjects who are disposing of their personal possessions, making out a last will and testament, or otherwise engaging in final act behaviors are also indicating that they do not intend to live much longer.

Interviewing the Subject

Without doubt, one of the best sources of information about the subject, his or her intentions, and his or her current circumstances comes from talking to the subject personally. Threat managers should never try to interview a subject without a partner. Having two people at the interview allows one of them to focus on security while the other concentrates on the subject. Other than that, we offer no set rules for where, when, and at what stage the interview should take place. Situations requiring a threat management response are far too fluid to allow for strict prescriptions. We do suggest that, when possible, the threat managers collect as much information about the subject and the subject's circumstances as possible before talking to the subject. Basic information includes the following:

- The subject's criminal history, especially anything involving violence
- The subject's mental health history
- The subject's firearms ownership
- Complete details on the situation that prompted the need for fact finding
- History of previous inappropriate conduct by the subject

This basic information will help guide the threat managers' questions and will assist in identifying tactics for the managers' safety.

The fundamental goal of interviewing the subject is to obtain as much information as possible from the subject. That information derives not just from the subject's answers to questions (which, after all, may be intentionally misleading or fabricated) but also from the subject's appearance, demeanor, and overall reaction to the interview. Much information can be drawn from simply observing the subject's behavior and reactions.

Subject interviews are not interrogations. The threat managers should do all within their power to put the subject at ease. They should be empathetic and show an eagerness to hear what the subject has to say. Subjects frequently want to unburden their feelings on anyone willing to listen to them. Because they have a grievance, they seek out individuals willing to hear their complaints. The threat manager should be that sounding board. The subject now has someone who will listen, an open invitation for the subject to pour his or her heart out.

We recommend a specific approach to conducting subject interviews. First, threat managers should avoid any acts that appear overbearing or threatening to the subject. This includes how the threat managers dress as well as act. They should project an aura of wanting to help the subject, not punish or discipline him or her. Second, threat managers should treat the subject—at least initially—with great deference and respect. Great patience is often required while the subject details his or her tale of woe. Third, threat managers must be careful not to overreact, especially if the subject engages in outbursts of emotion. Letting the subject rant provides enormous insight into the subject's grievance and his or her emotional investment in the situation. Fourth, threat managers should use their questions to keep the subject on track, usually by following a chronological approach for the subject to explain his or her view of what is going on. Finally, threat managers should carefully gauge when to shift the interview from information gathering to confronting the subject with his or her egregious behavior. Information is best gathered in a friendly atmosphere, saving until the end of the interview to confront or warn the subject of the perils to him or her from continued inappropriate actions.

Summary

Chapter 2 addressed identifying problem individuals by the inappropriate behaviors in which they engage. Once identified, the chapter described using the Need to Knows as a guide for exploring relevant areas of inquiry. It recommended collecting facts in an ever-expanding search starting from the circumstances of the situation prompting the fact finding and steadily widening the fact finding outward to collect more and more information about the subject, his or her grievance, and his or her current life situation. Finally, the chapter discussed the best approach to interviewing the problem individual, first to continue gathering information, then ending the interview with a confrontation or warning, as appropriate.

Situation Analysis: A Tragic Winters Tale

Sometime in 2009, William Gardner and Leslie Pinkston began an "on-again, off-again" dating relationship. After each "off-again" phase, Pinkston "repeatedly went back to Gardner."* They continued their bumpy dating for the next 4 years until, in January 2013, Gardner's behavior came to a head. On January 13, Gardner sent Pinkston numerous texts threatening her life. That evening, he went to her home in Winters, California, smashed out her car windows and threw a lawn chair through her front window.† Police charged Gardner with stalking, vandalism, and criminal threats. Pinkston took out a restraining order against him.‡

Two months later, in March 2013, the Sacramento County Court convicted Gardner of domestic violence.* Over the next half year or so, the relationship between Gardner and Pinkston calmed down a bit, but as Gardner's December court date for the January 13 stalking, vandalism, and criminal threat charges approached, Gardner grew increasingly nervous and aggressive. He again began sending her threatening texts, pressuring her to change her testimony against him.§ In October, a judge in Yolo County Court revoked Gardner's bail, sending him to jail. During the 24 days Gardner remained incarcerated, he placed more than 1000 collect calls to Pinkston, although it is not known if she accepted the charges on any of them.* Then, on November 15, for reasons unknown, Pinkston posted a $375 bail reassumption fee to get Gardner out of the Yolo County jail.*

---

* Dowling, S. (2014a, October 23). Witnesses to Winters murder give vivid testimony as William Gardner trial begins. *Daily Democrat.*
† Keene, L. (2014a, October 31). Gardner guilty of murder, with special circumstances. *The Davis Enterprise.*
‡ Keene, L. (2014b, January 1). Winters murder suspect heads to court in Yolo County. *Daily Republic.*
§ Keene, L. (2014c, October). Homicide case enters jury-selection phase. *Winters Express.*

Two days later, on November 17, Pinkston texted Gardner a "crystal-clear" message ending their relationship. "William," she wrote, "please stop. It's done. I'm going to be with someone else. This is my last text. Good Luck." Gardner responded, "Yup bitch, you a punk bitch. I hope you die."* Gardner's defense attorney later described his emotional state at this time as depressed, suicidal, and "in a state of utter despair."[†]

The next morning, Gardner convinced Nicole Bewley to drive him from his home in Sacramento to Winters. He carried with him a 9-mm semiautomatic pistol, which Bewley later denied knowing about it. During the drive to Winters, Gardner used Bewley's cell phone to make arrangements for his personal belongings in the event the police arrested him.*

When Bewley and Gardner got to Winters, Bewley parked her van in a parking lot near Pinkston's workplace. Gardner sat in the back seat, waiting for Pinkston to arrive at work. Pinkston, as probably was her habit, got to work in downtown Winters early. She parked her SUV on Railroad Avenue, waiting to start her workday. Gardner slipped into the backseat of her car and threw his arm across her chest, pinning her to the seat. Pinkston struggled, then managed to open the driver's door. Gardner shot her in the knee, then shot her in the head.

David Barbosa, who was in the parking lot across the street from Pinkston's car, saw the struggle and the shooting, then saw Gardner get out of the car and start walking toward him. "I froze like a statue," he testified, "I assumed he was going to shoot me." The two men made eye contact, then Gardner ran off in a different direction. After waiting a moment to make sure Gardner did not return, Barbosa ran across the street, dialing 911. He tried to comfort and reassure Pinkston, but she died in his arms.*

Bewley, again denying she knew anything about what just happened, drove Gardner away from Winters. He made it to Las Vegas where he managed to avoid arrest for 3 weeks. Las Vegas police tracked him down, then arrested him after a 6-hour standoff at a Las Vegas apartment complex. Extradited back to Winters, the Yolo County Court indicted Gardner on one count of murder with special circumstances of lying in wait and murder of a witness, stalking, and possession of a firearm by a felon.[‡§]

At trial, Gardner's defense attorney, J. Toney, disputed the lying-in-wait charge, which requires that the perpetrator launches a surprise attack. Toney admitted that his client sent numerous texts to Pinkston in the days before the shooting, telling her "he was going to kill her." Toney argued, "That's not taking somebody by surprise." The prosecutor, during closing arguments, told the jurors, "A gunshot wound to the back of the head at close range is the ultimate intentional violent exercise of power and control over another human being. She had no chance, he made sure of that." The jury deliberated for 3 hours, then found Gardner guilty of first-degree murder, lying in wait, murder of a witness, intentional and personal discharge of a firearm causing death, stalking, vandalism, and criminal threats.[¶] Just over a month later, the presiding judge sentenced Gardner to life in prison without parole.[**]

---

* Dowling, S. (2014a, October 23). Witnesses to Winters murder give vivid testimony as William Gardner trial begins. *Daily Democrat.*
† Keene, L. (2014a, October 31). Gardner guilty of murder, with special circumstances. *The Davis Enterprise.*
‡ Keene, L. (2014b, January 1). Winters murder suspect heads to court in Yolo County. *Daily Republic.*
§ Keene, L. (2014c, October). Homicide case enters jury-selection phase. *Winters Express.*
¶ Dowling, S. (2014b, October 30). Jury finds William Gardner guilty of Winters murder. *Daily Democrat.*
** Dowling, S. (2014c, December 1). William Gardner sentenced to life without parole for Winters murder. Daily Democrat.

Issues of Interest

1. This case illustrates two key elements of intimate partner violence: a pattern of dominance and control through threats and violence and the increased danger associated with the victim's attempts to end the relationship.
2. Gardner's behaviors culminating in the shooting were those of a hunter moving steadily along the path to intended violence.
    a. *Grievance:* Gardner did not want his intimate relationship with Pinkston to end, despite her efforts to break up with him. In addition, she was the prime witness against him in his upcoming trial, thus threatening him with possible imprisonment.
    b. *Ideation:* Gardner's repeated and numerous threats to kill her indicate that, from early on, he had the idea of using violence against her. Typical of domestic violence situations, as long as the threats kept Pinkston in the relationship or under his dominance, Gardner had no need to carry them out. Once Pinkston informed him that she had a new relationship with someone else, Gardner determined to take action.
    c. *Research and planning:* Gardner already knew much about Pinkston's life and routines, so he did not have to do much, if any, research. Clearly, his plan involved driving to Winters from Sacramento in time to intercept Pinkston before she entered her workplace.
    d. *Preparation:* Gardner made several preparations for killing Pinkston. He obtained a pistol and ammunition, arranged his transportation to Winters, along the way he engaged in final act behaviors by arranging for his personal possessions to be taken care of, and he engaged in a final surveillance of Pinkston from the parking lot.
    e. *Breach:* By getting into the backseat of Pinkston's car, Gardner breached what little security Pinkston had. He immediately pinned her to her seat, thereby preventing her from fleeing.
    f. *Attack:* Despite Pinkston's struggle to extricate herself, Gardner managed to shoot her first in the knee, then in the head.
3. Based on the claims of Gardner's defense attorney, his mental state at the time of the shooting was also typical of those who engage in domestic violence. The attorney described him as depressed, suicidal, and "in a state of utter despair." He was, after all, about to lose his love interest—the final straw being her announcement of having a new boyfriend. He may also have felt some relief at ridding himself of the prime witness against him in his upcoming trial.
4. Pinkston's behaviors were also typical of domestic violence situations. Toney, the defense attorney, described the relationship between Gardner and Pinkston as "on-again, off-again" from 2009 onward, but Toney emphasized that Pinkston "repeatedly went back to Gardner," a common occurrence for women caught up in a violent domestic relationship. Although Gardner was in custody for stalking her, vandalizing her property, and making criminal threats to her, Pinkston posted a $375 bail reassumption fee to get Gardner out of the county jail 5 days before he killed her. Whatever her motive for doing so—the prosecutor speculated that it was a "last-ditch effort" on her part to get Gardner to leave her alone—posting bail probably signaled to Gardner that Pinkston still had feelings for him. Also

typical of these heartrending situations, Pinkston stood practically alone against Gardner. She had obtained a restraining order, but its enforcement was erratic, nor did she have anyone she knew about to report the last threat—"I hope you die"— she received the night before the shooting. Even had she reported it to the police, who would have assessed the situation? No doubt unwittingly, Pinkston escalated the situation to its tragic end by telling Gardner she was "going to be with someone else." She probably believed that announcing a new relationship would convince Gardner that their relationship was finally over, as it would with most normal people. But for individuals like Gardner, all it meant was that if he could not have her, no one could.

5. The subject and target are (from the subject's point of view) and were (from the target's point of view) involved in an intimate personal relationship. In that context, threats have value as a positive indicator of future violence. That relationship had a history of threatening behavior on Mr. Gardner's part, with at least two incidents of violence (the January 13 vandalism and the Sacramento County domestic violence conviction).

6. Mr. Gardner appears to have had an obsessive interest in Ms. Pinkston, as evidenced by the frequent texts he sent her and the more than 1000 collect calls he made to her while in the Yolo County jail.

7. Mr. Gardner's extensive criminal history and his history of violence did not portend well for Ms. Pinkston's situation. Both were strong preincident indicators of potential violence.

8. The domestic violence venue is replete with obsessive refusals to recognize a relationship is over, threats made, and violence consummated. In these situations, the issue is about power, control, and dominance over the intimate partner. Mr. Gardner used threats and violence to keep Ms. Pinkston in their relationship. When those tactics finally failed, Mr. Gardner carried out his threats to kill her.

9. Mr. Gardner clearly represented a very high risk to Ms. Pinkston after she ended their affair. All of his behaviors leading up to that final text from her and his last text to her sounded the alarm that she was now exposed to an escalated risk. Unfortunately, no one was around to hear that alarm.

10. What was lacking in this situation, of course, was a threat manager who could make the assessment. No one but the target, Ms. Pinkston, had the overall perspective to make an assessment, but victims typically make poor assessors.

11. Finally, this situation demonstrates a central feature of situations requiring threat management. As a general rule, high-risk and low-risk situations are fairly obvious. Once a hunter steps out on the path to intended violence, his or her behaviors are easily assessed as those of a hunter, thereby escalating the risk of violence. Similarly, howlers tend to behave in ways typical of other howlers, thereby lowering the risk of violence. It is the individuals who fall in between high- and low-risk situations—those who generally have not yet decided in which direction to head— who are the most difficult to assess accurately. And as we discuss in Chapter 10, the threat manager must take care not to point those undecided individuals in the wrong direction.

Assessing Problem Individuals 3

Problem individuals who require threat management processes create situations that constantly evolve. Two distinct forces drive that evolution. The first results from the natural progression imposed by time on the course of any event, including the quirks in life resulting from circumstance, luck, accidents, untimely deaths, or some other normally occurring state of affairs. These forces are usually out of the control of the threat manager; however, he or she may be forced to react to the changes that they cause. With some prudent planning and foresight, the threat manager may be prepared for these potential changes or have safety contingencies already in place to manage them if they occur. The second force generating change grows out of the interactions among the subject, the target, the threat manager, and the dynamics of the situation itself. These dynamics are typically within the control of or, at the very least, influenced by the threat manager. Threat managers can anticipate and plan for most changes.

These two forces require conducting threat assessments from two separate angles. In this context, we define assessment as the intellectual evaluation of information, including balancing what is known against what is not known. The evaluation process uses several analytical models to facilitate the mental evaluation. These models include "instinctive evaluations" conducted while continuously monitoring events and four formal assessments conducted periodically:

1. Using the Need to Knows within the context of the situation;
2. Weighing what is at stake for the subject from the subject's point of view;
3. Applying the path to violence to ascertain if the subject is acting like a hunter; and
4. Determining if the subject is acting like a howler.

The two approaches—"instinctive evaluations" and formal assessments—integrate the threat manager's barometric instinct to changing pressures with periodic measured assessments of the current situation. The first flows with the situational currents; the second freezes the situation at a moment in time.

The first assessment approach requires the threat manager to constantly monitor the situation for any changes—positive or negative—in the level of risk. This kind of "instinctive evaluation" entails maintaining a comprehensive situational awareness sensitive enough to detect fluctuations that inevitably occur as the situation evolves. The evaluation relies on the threat manager's knowledge and instincts, honed by training and experience, to alert the threat manager to new, different, or shifting aspects of the situation. The instinctive evaluations guide immediate decision making throughout the life of the situation.

Two examples explain what we mean by instinctive evaluations. U.S. Air Force Colonel John Boyd developed a decision model he called the OODA Loop, meaning observe, orient, decide, and act. Boyd used the OODA Loop continuously throughout the dogfight. He observed, oriented, decided, then acted, repeating the process once the action was accomplished.* That is what threat managers need to do in dealing with problem individuals and the problem situations that those individuals cause. Good threat managers instinctively observe to detect changes to the situation, orient themselves by determining the impact of those changes, and decide on the best course of action, act, and then repeat the process.

When Cal Ripken, Jr., played shortstop for the Baltimore Orioles, he reacted instinctively at the crack of the bat. Within a split second, Ripken positioned himself to best contribute to the play. His action may have been to catch the ball, cover second base, backup the third baseman, relay a throw from the outfield, or get ready to run down a base runner. Whatever his response, he neither had the time, nor did he take it, to calmly assess the play to develop the most appropriate strategy. Had he done so, the play would have been over before he could react. Between pitches, Ripken no doubt took the time to assess what to do if the ball came his way, drew the second baseman off second, or flew deep into the outfield. Assessing those options informed Ripken's instinctive reaction as soon as the batter hit the ball.

Both Boyd's OODA Loop and Ripken's play rely on instinctive evaluations to determine the reaction from moment to moment. As with the threat manager, those evaluations are informed and guided by focus, training, and experience, but they are made before thought can be put into words. We are not suggesting that the threat manager act as instantaneously as the fighter pilot or the shortstop, but the process is the same. To put it another way, if a threat manager sees a gun aimed at the target, do not think: Act!

Instinctive evaluations come into play

- At the situation onset in determining the immediate resource triage;
- When monitoring resource management;
- During initial protective responses;
- Assessing significant new information and its impact on the situation immediately after the information comes to light;
- When monitoring for changes after application of an intervention strategy; and
- During ongoing target management.

Monitoring continues as long as the situation requires managing.

The second assessment approach comes into play at certain points that arise during the problem situation's natural progression. These events require more deliberate and, in some situations, more formalized threat assessments. We address those measured assessments in this chapter.

The events that usually prompt deliberate assessments include, but are not limited to, the following:

- Assessing the initial facts during the intake process for purposes of triage
- Assessing the situation anew when the instinctive evaluation determines changes to the level of risk that would change the protective response or alter resource allocation
- Assessing the situation in preparation for briefing others, such as management, colleagues, targets, or other interested parties
- As the situation is reclassified, such as designating it as active or inactive
- Assessing the effectiveness of each threat management strategy

* McKay, B., & McKay, K. (2014, September 15). The Tao of Boyd: How to master the OODA loop. *The Art of Manliness.*

Consequently, threat assessments partner continuous or ongoing monitoring of the situation as the situation evolves with deliberate assessments prompted by specific events. In effect, assessments are a process all their own.

What is a deliberate threat assessment? We approach assessments as a method of interpreting pieces of a puzzle through analyzing and synthesizing the information at hand to come to an actionable judgment. Deliberate assessments combine deductive reasoning with intuition by relying on understanding the known facts and interpreting what those facts mean in the context of the current situation. Threat managers must make assessments with due deliberation, focusing on what is currently known—the facts—without ignoring what the threat manager's previous experiences and judgment may dictate.

Assessments coldly determine how the knowns and unknowns fit into the current situation in terms of relative risk, but they also factor in how the threat manager's experiences serve as early-warning signs. The true craft of threat assessment is the threat manager's ability to recognize the relevant importance of the information within the context of each specific situation resulting in an actionable judgment. Conducting deliberate threat assessments requires asking the right questions relevant to the particular situation to see how the answers to all those questions illuminate any potential risks. They require both a scientific approach and a craftsman's sensitivity. Good threat assessments combine logical approaches, informed estimates, and reasonable deductions with a conscious attempt to understand the situation from the subject's point of view. The results are then weighed within the overall context of the situation under assessment. Deliberate threat assessments do not involve guesswork or pure speculation. They are not predictions or baseless alarms. Rather, measured threat assessments are rooted in the known facts. The threat manager then interprets those facts based on their inherent logic and the threat manager's instincts born of trained insight and personal experiences.

In one situation, the threat manager got a morning phone call from a female employee working in another city telling him that her ex-boyfriend had broken into her house and vandalized her television and radio alarm clock while she was not there. She had the day off but felt too embarrassed to call the police or tell her supervisor. For obvious reasons, the threat manager's immediate assessment of this initial report was high risk. The threat manager told the employee not to engage in any discussion, accusation, or argument with the ex-boyfriend if he should return to her house, but to immediately call 911. The employee promised to follow that advice.

Further questioning of the employee revealed that the ex-boyfriend had never used violence before, that they had broken up 2 weeks ago, and that they had two children together. The employee expressed her conviction that this was in all probability a one-time event. At the end of the conversation, the threat manager told the employee to call him that afternoon to give him a status report. The employee begged the threat manager not to tell anyone at her worksite about the situation. The threat manager declined to make any promises other than to assure her he would be as discrete as possible.

The threat manager continued to assess the facts reported to him. The threat manager's previous experiences with domestic violence situations helped him understand that he would likely not be able to convince the employee to do anything that risked embarrassing her. The threat manager also knew that the most dangerous time in a domestic violence situation occurs when the target attempts to leave the relationship. Those concerns at that moment ruled out contacting the police or getting a protective order from the court. The fact that the subject had committed the vandalism in her absence suggested that the subject .

did not intend to confront her in person. According to the employee, the subject did not have a history of violent behavior, at least in their relationship, and the breakup was fairly recent. They also had two children together, which could either suggest a strong inhibitor for him or an increase in the emotional pressures on him. The threat manager felt comfortable waiting for the employee's status report later that afternoon.

That comfort evaporated when the employee did not call or answer her phone when the threat manager called her. The threat manager's previous experiences with domestic violence situations concerned him because her silence might be the result of an assault or other altercation with the ex-boyfriend. Fully knowing her wishes not to involve her supervisor, the threat manager decided he had no choice but to call the supervisor and arrange for someone—either another employee or the local police—to check to make sure the employee was unharmed. The supervisor agreed to send one of her friends at work to her house. She further explained that the house actually belonged to the ex-boyfriend, but a judge had given her 2 weeks to live there while she found a new place to live for herself and the two children. The ex-boyfriend actually owned the television and radio alarm clock. The supervisor added that the couple was currently working out an amicable custody arrangement through the court. She promised to keep the threat manager informed of any new developments. Later, the employee's friend reported her safe, adding that she had simply forgotten to call the threat manager that afternoon. Based on this new information, the threat manager revised his initial assessment of high risk to low risk.

Over the next few days, the employee found an apartment and moved herself and the children out of the house. The ex-boyfriend moved back into his house. The couple agreed to child visitation arrangements and the employee continued reporting to work. Based on these developments, the threat manager maintained his assessment of low risk.*

And thus goes a typical threat assessment process. In the course of a single workday, the threat manager initially assessed the situation as high risk and then significantly de-escalated the assessment. That de-escalation resulted from the emerging new facts and in learning that some of the initial facts were, if not falsehoods, at least inaccurate. Even the fact that the employee forgot to report in suggested that any concerns she had for her own safety were minimal. The threat manager's experience with domestic violence situations taught him to value highly how the victim reacted to the perceived threat. Truly frightened victims usually had ample grounds for being frightened. Ultimately, the course of events sustained the changed assessment. In sum, situations evolve in various ways, some positive, some negative, and the threat manager has to account for that evolution by continuously conducting re-assessments.

Formalized Threat Assessment Approaches

We offer four different, but complementary, threat assessment approaches:

1. Based on what is known, and guided by exploring the Need to Knows, what are the circumstances and context of the current situation and the problem individual's behaviors within that situation?

---

* Authors' personal experience.

2. How does the subject perceive the situation in terms of what is at stake for him or her?
3. Is the subject behaving like a hunter?
4. Is the subject behaving like a howler?

These four questions complement each other by providing an all-around view of the situation at this time. We recommend applying all four with each assessment. The first question directs the threat manager's attention to the overall situation, while applying the Need to Knows focuses on the subject's problem behaviors within the context of that overall situation. The second question addresses the subject's goals and motivation. Based on the subject's known behaviors, what does he or she seem to be seeking to accomplish? The third question draws the threat manager's attention back to the path to intended violence, the steps along which are hunter-driven behaviors. Those behaviors are explored in greater detail in Section II. Similarly, the last question forces the threat manager to look for nonhunter behaviors, the telltale marks of a howler. Section II explicates howler attributes at length. In combination, the four questions provide a 360-degree view of the situation at this time.

1. *Based on what is known, and guided by exploring the Need to Knows, what are the circumstances and context of the current situation and the problem individual's behaviors within that situation?*

    The Need to Knows, by design, serves two extraordinary and complementary purposes. They guide the threat manager's protective fact finding by focusing attention on getting information on all relevant areas of inquiry. Far more than guidance, the Need to Knows help formulate informed assessments. They do the latter in several different ways. First, they identify what is currently known and what currently needs to be known. That measurement allows the threat manager to determine how informed the threat assessment currently is. Second, they put the knowns within the context of the situation under assessment. In different situations, specific Need to Knows may increase or decrease in importance relative to the other Need to Knows. That shifting balance forces the assessment of each situation into a unique posture. An experienced threat manager may sense that the current situation seems like one experienced before, but each Need to Know must be evaluated afresh within the circumstances and context of the current situation.

1. How did the subject choose to approach the target?
2. What about the situation indicates the subject's identity and physical proximity to the target; in other words, who and where is the subject?
3. What about the situation indicates who or what the subject is targeting; in other words, who is the target?
4. What about the situation indicates the type of venue being targeted and what is it about the venue that gives insight into the subject's intent, motive, and ability?
5. What about the situation indicates whether or not the Intimacy Effect is in play; in other words, what is the nature of the relationship between the subject and the target?
6. What about the situation relates to the subject's choice of context, including the circumstances and content?
7. Is the target currently accessible to the subject?

As explained in Chapter 2, the first seven Need to Knows focus on the general situation currently under assessment. The first question relatively, generally carries more weight within most assessments since how the subject chose to approach the target lies entirely within the subject's discretion.* That choice says something about the subject's willingness and intent. By keeping a physical distance between subject and target, the subject's behavior suggests potential low risk. Conversely, physically approaching the target signals potential high risk.

The remaining six questions focus on the current circumstances and context surrounding the situation at the time of the assessment, especially in relation to the subject and target's physical proximity to each other. Did the subject reveal his or her identity and relationship to the target? Was the target clearly identified? In which of the different venues for violence is this situation playing out? The last three questions direct attention to what is known about the current relationship between the subject and the target.

How does the information from these Need to Knows inform the threat assessment? Basically, the seven questions explore, from slightly different angles, whether or not the subject has the opportunity or is seeking the opportunity to inflict harm at this time. Obviously, those who have the current opportunity pose a high risk and those who lack current opportunity pose low risk.

8. Does the subject have the ability and motivation to take advantage of any current accessibility to the target?
9. Is there a known history of previous contacts with the target or other targets by this subject?
10. Does the subject have a history of violent or threatening behaviors, including any criminal behavior?
11. What is the subject's knowledge about the target's current situation?
12. Is the subject seeking knowledge about the target and the target's current situation?

The next set of questions brings in the subject's current and previous problem behaviors to measure the subject's present ability and willingness to cause harm. Every individual is capable of acting violently; the vast majority of us willingly choose not to. Those who have used violence in the past, those who seek out intimate knowledge of the target, and those who currently have entre to the target bear a high risk; those who have not acted violently before, those who do not ferret out personal information on the target, and those who do not have the ability to get to the target at this time pose a low risk of harm at this time.

But no accurate demographic profile exists for assessing an individual's potential risk for acting violently. Violent people populate every social stratum. Curtis Lovelace was the golden boy of Quincy, Illinois. During high school, Lovelace starred in track, wrestling, and football, earning six varsity letters and a place in the school's sports hall of fame. In college, he played center on the University of Illinois football team, becoming the team captain and a two-time all-Big Ten pick. He was also an academic all-American majoring in business. He married a former high school classmate and went to law school. After passing the bar, Lovelace took a job as an assistant prosecutor. During that long career, Lovelace also served as the Quincy school board president, sports announcer, and teacher at the local university.

* With the exception, again, of third-party or informant reports.

In December 2013, as Lovelace left his law office for lunch, Quincy police arrested him for the murder of his first wife 8 years earlier.* Even golden boys get tarnished by violence.

13. Does the subject's behavior indicate mental health issues, including suicidality?
14. Does the subject possess, have access to, or is currently seeking a weapon of any type?
15. Has the subject exhibited a fascination with weapons and/or violence?
16. What is the status of the subject's inhibitors, including any recent losses?
17. Has the subject exhibited controlling, isolating, or jealous behaviors toward the target?
18. Does the subject have a history of, or is currently, abusing alcohol, drugs, or prescription medicines?
19. Does the subject have any relevant medical issues?
20. Has the subject engaged in any final act behaviors?

The final set of questions draw attention to the subject's current *capacity* to inflict harm. They ask about the subject's mental organization, fascination with violence, access to weapons, trajectory toward violence, and current physical state.

In sum, a fully informed threat assessment addresses the subject's opportunity, willingness, and capacity to act violently. Within those broad sets of questions, each Need to Know will carry a different weight dictated by the circumstances of the situation. That weight derives from the information gleaned and not by any inherent value lying within the question itself. Not knowing of any final act behaviors carries far less weight in an assessment than knowing of actual final act behaviors. That is, determining that the subject has not engaged in final act behaviors does not necessarily lower the risk, but identifying such behaviors certainly elevates the risk. Subjects with violent pasts in similar situations probably pose a higher risk than do subjects without such a history. Each Need to Know has to be evaluated within the overall context of the situation. Gun ownership probably means less if the owner is an avid sports hunter and a lifelong member of the National Rifle Association, but it takes on greater weight if the subject recently purchased the weapon immediately after the subject lost his or her job. Good threat managers know that none of the Need to Knows exist in a vacuum. Quite the contrary, each Need to Know balances against all of the other Need to Knows.

Using the Need to Knows to guide the assessment, as well as the fact finding, provides the threat manager with a detailed view of the circumstances and context of the situation under assessment. By weighing each Need to Know afresh within the overall context of what occurred or is still occurring helps balance the information collected. The threat manager should focus on the unique attributes of each situation under assessment. In so doing, the threat manager brings a fresh, objective approach to each threat assessment.

   2. *How does the subject perceive the situation in terms of what is at stake for him or her?*
      This assessment approach requires the threat manager to try to see the situation from the subject's point of view. Glimpses of that viewpoint can be drawn from analyzing the subject's behaviors, statements, and plans, from credible associates of

---

* Suhr, J. (2014, October 12). Ex-prosecutor talk of town after murder charge. Associated Press.

the subject, or simply from the stakes of the situation itself. The approach requires the threat manager to apply empathy for the subject, that is, to try to understand what issue or grievance may be prompting the subject and how strongly the subject feels about resolving that grievance. It does not require the threat manager to sympathize with the subject or to accept the subject's version of reality as reality itself. Rather, the approach is simply an attempt to measure how strongly the subject views the situation and his or her problems within that situation.

The Stakes

What the subject may perceive to be at stake runs across a gamut of incentives ranging from ideological, personal, religious, political, or moral beliefs to financial investments, employment concerns, or emotional entanglements. All of these stakes are important to anyone; the issue here, however, is how important each one is to the subject at this time. The subject's issue does not need to be real. Delusions can be powerful motivators to prompt violent action. Individuals can become highly invested in certain issues important to them. They can value their jobs or careers, their domestic life, their political causes, or myriad other concerns. By analyzing the subject's behaviors, statements, and other evidence of the subject's personal issue, the threat manager can begin to assess how important that issue is to that subject at this time.

Two Approaches for Assessing the Subject's Stakes

We use two approaches for gaining insight into the subject's stakes and how strongly he or she feels about them. The first discerns evidence from the subject reflecting the subject's degree of emotional or mental investment in the subject's issue. Gavin de Becker developed the second approach, which he called JACA, a simple acronym standing for justification, alternatives, consequences, and ability. Each approach requires identifying and accepting the situation as the subject perceives it, regardless of whether or not the subject's perception holds up in reality.

The first approach details a spectrum of reactions to any situation. The threat manager's job is to locate where the subject currently stands along that spectrum. The range of reactions is as follows:

- *Nothing's at stake for the subject.* The threat manager finds no evidence that the subject feels any investment in the situation under assessment. He or she is behaving as if he or she has nothing to lose or gain whatever the outcome of the situation. The subject appears detached and unconcerned about any potential outcome. If the subject believes he or she has nothing at stake at this time, then that subject is less likely to act violently or inappropriately.
- *Normal acceptance.* The subject clearly has something he or she values but accepts the loss of that valuable in a nonviolent way. A wife may feel aggrieved at her husband's infidelity, but rather than resort to force, she files for divorce and is content to seek retribution through the civil proceedings. A former employee may strongly feel wrongfully terminated but proceeds to find another job or uses the union grievance process. A high school student suffers through unremitting hazing by other students but responds by gathering together with other like-minded students to form a computer

club or alternative rock band. These are normal, healthy responses to adverse situations. They indicate that the subject has moved on with his or her life and sees no value in avenging with violence whatever his or her grievance is or may have been.

- *Mild loss.* The subject may complain at length about the issue, may even leak inappropriate or intemperate remarks showing a strong investment in the issue, but the complaints do not go to extremes and do not claim the loss is greater than it actually is. Frequently, mild loss surfaces around issues involving personal pride and dignity. The subject feels rudely treated and responds with tense justifications for his or her own self-worth or self-importance. Once the subject regains his or her feelings of self-worth, the issue usually recedes into the background.

- *Much to lose.* The subject expresses an exaggerated response to the situation. The subject may appear excessively invested in the potential outcome; thus, the subject appears unusually intense about the issue. The subject may convey, at length and in volatile terms, all that is troubling him or her. Howlers frequently claim they have much to lose if the outcome of the situation does not fall in their favor. In assessing a subject's belief that he or she has much to lose, the threat manager should try to determine what is of value to the subject that is not at risk in this situation and how valuable the subject feels about those aspects of his or her life. An employee may feel outraged over a disciplinary proceeding but still shows that he or she continues to value keeping the job. This reverts back to measuring the subject's current inhibitors. Although there may be much to lose, it is not the same as losing everything.

- *Everything to lose.* Whether actually true or not, the subject clearly projects that the stakes mean everything to him or her. These subjects describe their loss in exaggerated, end-of-the-world ways that make the subject appear desperate and without hope. They show no indication that they have plans beyond the resolution of the situation, as though life ends there. They express themselves in uncompromising terms, evince great inflexibility, and insist on only one outcome. They cling to a sense of injustice, which usually means what is just and fair for them and not the societal standards of justice handed down by the judicial system. Theirs is a very personal, selfish and egotistical justice.

These subjects may start engaging in final act behaviors because they are convinced that if the situation is not resolved in their favor, they have nothing left to lose. They may associate their objectively minor situation with larger and more grandiose causes. Often, subjects with everything to lose are in situations that readily and objectively appear as having high stakes. Desperate individuals do desperate things.

In essence, this spectrum looks at the range and depth of the subject's inhibitors to determine the health and sanctity of those inhibitors at this time. But at this point, the threat manager must look beyond the current situation to assess how different outcomes may affect the subject's inhibitors. Losing a job may lead to losing a house, which may lead to divorce or separation, which may prompt increased alcohol intake, which may lead back to deciding to avenge the job loss through violence toward the former supervisor.

In one particular case that did not end in violence, the subject's emotional investment in his job prompted great concern about the potential for violence, especially the risk of impromptu violence. A few years ago, the Transportation Security Administration's (TSA's) national program manager overseeing the Workplace Violence Prevention Program was sent to a midsized airport in the northeast. One of the administrative employees had complained to a credible source that the work environment between him and the local TSA manager was so tense he feared an "explosion" would occur. The program manager and a law enforcement partner interviewed the office staff and determined that the office staff split in their loyalties between the administrative employee and the manager. All agreed that the work environment was extremely tense due to the conflict between the administrative employee and the manager. After those interviews, the team called in the administrative employee who feared an explosion. They started the interview by allowing the employee to list and describe all the issues he had with the manager. As the interview progressed, the employee became noticeably emotional and upset, raising his voice and banging his hand on the desk. He projected himself as the protector of all the other employees from the unfair working environment. Clearly, the employee had an overly zealous investment in his position and in his poor relationship with his superior. When the program manager explained who he was and why he and his partner were there, the administrative employee deflated and hastily protested that he would never resort to violence. The program manager spent some time reminding the administrative employee that it was, after all, just a job and he had a valuable life outside the workplace. The employee acknowledged that he was too emotionally invested and that, in the future, he would put the job in a better perspective.*

JACA

A number of years ago, de Becker crafted four simple questions, the answers to which give considerable insight into how the subject perceives the stakes involved in the situation. The questions require the threat manager to see the situation through the subject's eyes, to adopt momentarily the subject's version of reality. The answers to all four questions must be positive to support a high-risk assessment. Any negative answer negates the subject's potential risk. The questions are as follows:

1. Does the subject give evidence that he or she feels *justified* in resorting to violence?
2. Does the subject act as though he or she sees no *alternatives* to violence?
3. Does the subject appear to accept the *consequences* of committing an act of violence, especially bad consequences for the subject?
4. Does the subject give evidence that he or she believes that he or she has the *ability* to commit a violent act?

Violent acts, then, erupt from the combination of a deeply felt grievance justifying the violence; with no recognition of other alternatives for resolving the issue; acceptable, however unpleasant, consequences; and the confidence in one's ability to act with violence. Lacking any single one of these attributes reduces the risk of violence at this time.

Measuring what is at stake for the subject can get tricky. Subjects may perceive high stakes for themselves in ways that most people cannot understand. That perception may be shaped by mental illness, a quirk in the subject's personality, or some irrational or untenable belief on the subject's part. In August 2014, Nicolas Holzer confessed to Santa Barbara County, California, police that he had killed his father, mother, his two sons (aged 10 and 13), and the family dog. He stabbed them while they slept. When detectives asked him why

---

* Authors' personal knowledge.

he did it, Holzer told them "the killings were his destiny."* That destiny raised the stakes in Holzer's mind.

Sometimes, one's destiny can be as banal as wanting to get out of debt. Alan Hruby, a student at the University of Oklahoma in the fall of 2014, killed his parents and his sister. Now the sole heir, Hruby expected his inheritance would pay off the mounting debt he owed a Tulsa loan shark. After shooting his family, Hruby rewarded himself with a weekend trip to Dallas where he stayed at a fancy Ritz-Carlton hotel. Returning home on Monday, Hruby, according to the county district attorney, acted "very nonchalant" and "cold and callous" over the discovery of his family's bodies.† The family inheritance was all the stakes Hruby needed to commit murder.

By assessing how the subject perceives what is at stake for him or her in the current situation and by applying *JACA*, the threat manager can get another view into the subject's willingness and capacity, if not opportunity, for committing violence. Each test essentially seeks to weigh the value of the situation to the subject and how any loss or decrease in that value may prompt the subject to violence. Stakes and their internal inhibitors act as brakes; their loss acts as accelerators.

3. *Is the subject behaving like a hunter?*

We define and describe hunter behavior at length in Section II, including how recognizing such behaviors informs threat assessments and the selection of the most appropriate management strategy. We need not belabor the concept here, other than to underscore its usefulness in assessing potential problem individuals. Violence is the process of moving from grievance to action. The types of behaviors associated with traversing that path are noted here:

- *Grievance.* Behaviors associated with grievance may be such acts as expressing feelings of harm to the subject, injustice, anger, outrage, vengeance, fear, or strongly held ideological beliefs.
- *Ideation.* Behaviors indicating a subject has reached the ideation stage include the subject discussing plans and ideas for violence with others, including the target, identification with other assassins, evidence of a fixation with violence, fascination with weapons, or interest in specific anniversaries of violent events or key anniversaries.
- *Research and planning.* Behaviors include researching the target, stalking, making suspicious inquiries, gathering information about the target or the target's personal life.
- *Preparations.* Behaviors related to preparations include acquiring a weapon, assembling equipment, arranging transportation, respecting significant dates, conducting final act behaviors, and donning costumes that facilitate violence.
- *Breach.* Behaviors associated with breach are approaching the target with a lethal means or methods.
- *Attack.* Behaviors exemplifying attack are assaulting the target.

Locating where the subject is along the path to intended violence is one of the best ways to assess the subject's risk of violence. Obviously, the farther along the path, the higher the

---

* Man charged in killings of 4 family members, dog. (2014, October 15). Associated Press.
† Juozapavichius, J. (2014, October 15). Son charged with killing publisher, family. Associated Press.

risk, and the less time the threat manager has to deflect that risk. The threat manager's best bet is to block the subject at the research and planning stage or the preparation stage. These are the points along the path where the subject's behaviors become more overt and, thus, more noticeable.

In late March 2012, Allen Prue and his wife Patricia, Allen later told police, decided "to get a girl." Patricia used her computer to research "how to kidnap a girl." The couple bought a stun gun and a prepaid cell phone. As Allen confessed to the police, he and his wife "wanted somebody they could play with." For their fun, the couple picked Melissa Jenkins, a 33-year-old prep school teacher in Burlington, Vermont. On March 25, one of the Prues used the cell phone to call Jenkins at her home asking for help and claiming their car had broken down. Jenkins loaded her 2-year-old son into her car and drove out to the rural road she lived on. The Prues got Jenkins out of her car, leaving it idling on the road with the boy still inside. The next day, Jenkins' body was found in the Connecticut River. She had been strangled, beaten, and burned with the stun gun. A jury found Prue guilty of first-degree murder in October 2014.* In February, 2015, Patricia Prue pleaded guilty and was sentenced to life in prison without possibility of parole.†

The Prues' grievance was their perverse desire for somebody with whom to play. They developed the idea of kidnapping someone, researched how to do it, and then prepared themselves by purchasing the stun gun and cell phone. They lured Jenkins out of her house, then kidnapped her and essentially tortured her to death. The Prues were hunters.

4. *Is the subject behaving like a howler?*
   As with hunters, Section II delves at length into the different types of howlers and how to recognize them, so we need not repeat that here. Instead, we want to stress the importance of always asking the howler question as an off-set to asking the hunter question. It requires the threat manager to look at both sides of a problem individual's actions. That balance helps fully inform any threat assessment.

Summary

Chapter 3 discussed ways to conduct threat assessments on problem individuals or ominous situations. We recommended four distinct approaches used in combination with each other. First, we advised using the Need to Knows to assess the circumstances and context of the situation under assessment. Second, we discussed assessing what is at stake for the subject, from the subject's point of view, in the current situation. Third and fourth, we suggested always asking "Is the subject acting like a hunter?" and "Is the subject acting like a howler?" Asking both balances the assessment; using all four approaches fleshes it out.

Situation Analysis: The Disgruntled Vet

In 2008, 39-year-old Glen Gieschen enlisted in the Canadian military as an intelligence specialist. At some point during his period of service, the military inoculated Gieschen with the vaccine for H1N1—bird flu. Sometime after that, Gieschen began suffering a number

---

* Ring, W. (2014, October 22). Vermont man guilty of luring, killing teacher. Associated Press.
† Rathke, L. (2015, February 12). Patricia Prue pleads guilty to killing Vermont teacher. Associated Press.

of medical ailments, including developing multiple sclerosis (MS). He believed the vaccine caused his deteriorating health, which resulted in a medical disability retirement in 2011.*

Gieschen's retirement put his medical care under the jurisdiction of Canada's Veterans Affairs (VA). The VA took responsibility for paying Gieschen's medical expenses, but Gieschen and the bureaucracy quickly got at loggerheads over Gieschen's rehabilitation plan. Throughout 2013, Gieschen repeatedly telephoned the VA office in Calgary, Alberta, near where he and his family—a wife and daughter—lived with his parents, complaining that the VA was not responsive to his illness. Gieschen established a website and posted information about this dispute along with recordings of many of his phone conversations with the VA office. On the site, he described himself as "an internationally known spokesperson, intelligence specialist, and professional security consultant with 21 years' experience."[†]

"I am wound up very tight, and yeah, I'm not doing well because of it. It almost feels like Veterans Affairs is trying to manage my health as opposed to my doctors and specialists," he complained in one recording, adding, "I'm looking for somebody to help me do what I normally do."[‡]

The Calgary VA office occupied the seventh floor of the 22-story Bantrel Tower in downtown Calgary. In November and December 2013, Gieschen went to the Bantrel Tower where he made at least six videos as he walked the building perimeter.[‡] On a laptop, he wrote a plan entitled "to attack the offices of veteran affairs in the Bantrel Tower building." He also downloaded the building schematics showing entrances, exits, stairwells, and office locations.

At 5:47 p.m., January 8, 2014, Gieschen's wife telephoned the Royal Canadian Mounted Police (RCMP) to express her concerns that her husband may be suicidal. She explained to the police that her husband, a veteran, had just left their home armed with a rifle. Officers of RCMP responded to the parents' property and launched a search that lasted several hours before they found Gieschen sleeping in a utility trailer dressed in camouflage pants. A duffel bag lay next to him and inside police found a fully loaded .40 caliber HK semi-automatic pistol.[‡]

When RCMP officers questioned Gieschen, he admitted to suicidality. The officers promptly arrested him under the Mental Health Act. They loaded him into a police car to take him to the hospital for treatment. On the way to the hospital, Gieschen informed the officers that he had left a loaded rifle in his car, which was still parked on his parents' property.[§]

Officers of RCMP quickly located the car. Their search uncovered an arsenal containing a second HK pistol; a rifle; over a thousand rounds of ammunition; a laser sight; three jugs containing ammonia, bleach, and muriatic acid, respectively; black gun powder; smoke grenades and gas mask; body armor; 16 black sticks resembling dynamite; and materials (including gun powder) for making pipe bombs. Later, a corporal with the RCMP explosive unit built a pipe bomb using Gieschen's materials. After exploding it, the corporal concluded that it posed great danger to anyone in its proximity.[‡]

---

* van Rassel, J. (2014, November 7). Ex-soldier pleads guilty after police uncover plot to attack Veterans Affairs Office. *Calgary Herald.* Bakx, K. (2014, November 7). Calgary skyscraper attack plotter contacted Veterans Affairs for help. CBC News.
† Dormer, D. (2014, November 7). Former soldier to be sentenced after pleading guilty to plot to attack Veterans Affairs Office in downtown Calgary. *Calgary Sun.*
‡ Bakx, K. (2014, November 7). Calgary skyscraper attack plotter contacted Veterans Affairs for help. CBC News.
§ van Rassel, J. (2014, November 7). Ex-soldier pleads guilty after police uncover plot to attack Veterans Affairs Office. *Calgary Herald.*

The car also contained the video tapes Gieschen made in the fall of 2013. On his laptop, they also found a detailed plan for attacking the VA office on the seventh floor of the Bantrel Tower. The plan included Gieschen's notes from his reconnaissance of the building, which, according to the Crown Attorney, contained references to Gieschen's intention "to attack the office of Veterans Affairs in the Bantrel Tower Building." Gieschen titled one part of the plan "Risk Assessment" and another section "Walking Around the Building with IR Camera on Identifying." The plan also detailed specific actions he should take on certain floors of the Tower.*

On November 7, 2014, Gieschen pled guilty to three weapons violations.† Three months later, Judge Sean Dunnigan sentenced Gieshen to 4 years in prison, giving him credit for the time served since his January 24 arrest. In passing sentence, Judge Dunnigan described Gieschen's crimes as "chilling in their intricate planning," but the judge accepted Gieschen's remorse as authentic. During the hearing, Gieschen told the judge that he took personal responsibility for his "irresponsible" behavior.†

Issues of Interest

1. Gieschen's actions exemplify typical hunter behaviors by following the path to violence. His grievance was long-standing and deeply rooted. He believed that the VA was not treating him fairly and that it was essentially taking over his medical treatment, which he believed it was not qualified to do. That personal grievance inspired him to resolve it through violence. From the idea of violence, Gieschen moved to researching and planning his attack. His research was impressive, not only involving personally reconnoitering the Bantrel Tower but also downloading the building schematics. He also developed a written plan, including specific things he intended to do on different floors. Next, he moved to the preparation stage, collecting his weapons, bomb components, and other military accoutrements that he needed to implement his plan successfully.

2. Gieschen clearly felt emotionally invested in his plight. While serving his country, the military—from his point of view (the only one that matters when assessing such situations)—caused him to develop MS. That perceived affront quickly became compounded once he came under the auspices of the VA and his belief that the VA was balking at the cost of the treatments his medical team recommended.

3. Gieschen's grievance was long-standing and based on his belief that the government, personified by both the Canadian military and the VA, had caused him to develop MS and was now not providing him the treatment he believed he deserved. Gieschen was seeking a personal justice for his grievance and was investing significant time and energy documenting his problems, creating and updating a website, and recording conversations in this quest. His description of himself as an "internationally known spokesperson, intelligence specialist, and professional security consultant with 21 years' experience" suggests a growing grandiosity, making himself and his problems all the more important. He also evinced a growing sense of despair. "I'm looking for somebody [presumably at the VA] to help me do what

---

* Bakx, K. (2014, November 7). Calgary skyscraper attack plotter contacted Veterans Affairs for help. CBC News.
† Graveland, B. (2015, February 24). Glen Gieschen gets 4 years for firearms, explosive charges. CBC News.

I normally do," he pleaded to one VA staffer. The plea itself suggested not only Gieschen's forlornness but also his growing sense of being abandoned, first by the military and now by the VA. His subsequent reconnoitering of the Bantrel Tower and gathering equipment were reality based and consistent with a person having such a consuming grievance.

4. He began acting on his grievance in the persona that he created of an internationally known spokesperson and intelligence specialist, combined with the intelligence training he received while serving in the military. By the fall of 2013, Gieschen had transitioned from talking and thinking into action.

5. Gieschen began intelligence and surveillance operations and developed written plans for an attack on the building housing the VA offices. He memorialized his dispute through his website and on his laptop.

6. Gieschen acquired weapons, ammunition, body armor, and explosive components while exhibiting behaviors consistent with suicidality. In this situation, suicidality should be considered the wildcard. It was the one aspect of his condition that he could not control or conceal. The planning and acquisition of weapons gave Gieschen the capability to turn the violence potential of suicidality outward as well as inward; that is, he could take others with him.

7. As is typical in situations involving military veterans, Gieschen clearly used his military training to plan and prepare for his presumed intent to assault the VA offices in the Bantrel Tower. He scouted out the site, then wrote out elaborate plans for conducting this specific military operation. Even if he had no military comrades alongside him, his planning and preparations followed military protocol.

8. As is typical of many hunters, Gieschen did not reveal his plans to anyone; however, he did leak his grievance and frustration through his website and blogging, nor did he make any explicit threats directed toward his target. His frequent phone calls to the VA do not seem to have raised an alarm among the VA staff with whom he interacted. To them, he probably seemed a typical patient struggling with a bureaucracy. Gieschen, however, could not hide his worsening suicidality from his wife. By January 2014, his wife suspected his suicidality and promptly acted on that suspicion by calling the RCMP. That intervention thwarted Gieschen's plans and preparations.

9. While Gieschen had some inhibiters of a wife and family and lived with other relatives, we do not know the quality and stability of those inhibitors from his point of view. We do know his suicidality seems to have overridden the inhibitors, which can happen in any case where there are indicators of depression, hopelessness, or suicidal thinking.

10. We will never know if Gieschen was going to take the final step of breaching the building security and attacking the VA offices or other locations in the Bantrel Tower. However, he clearly had set the stage for such a violent act.

11. Canada, of course, suffers no monopoly on disgruntled veterans. To the south, the U.S. Department of Veterans Affairs, and especially its Veterans Health Administration (VHA), grapples with the problem of managing—while trying to serve—angry patients. "We are dealing with a population of Veterans that suffer from assorted mental health issues, including PTSD," a former chief of police at a U.S. VA medical facility wrote a *Washington Post* reporter, adding, "Sometimes they have drug and alcohol problems and when they feel that the VA is ignoring

them, not answering the phone, failing to return calls for assistance or there are long wait times, they get more and more disgruntled." As other members of the VA police observed, and as Gieschen proved, the VA dealt with individuals "trained in weapons and tactics, increasing the risk."[*]

12. A March 2013 report by the U.S. VA Office of Inspector General detailed the elaborate process for managing disruptive patients coming to VHA facilities. Although the report severely criticized the VHA for not following its own policies, the report nevertheless showed that VHA facilities had institutionalized Disruptive Behavior Committees throughout the system and managed a sophisticated, nationwide, Patient Record Flag database alerting VA employees to unruly patients. The mere fact that VA administrators determined that the VA needed such an elaborate bureaucratic structure to handle the problem underscores how extensive that problem is.[†]

13. When evaluating any individual, you are also evaluating his or her capability for carrying out an act of violence. When assessing military veterans, information about their length and type of service is critical. Simply put, experienced military veterans have the capacity to plan and implement violent acts that are beyond the skill level of most civilians.

---

[*] Wax-Thibdeaux, E. (2015, January 17). After fatal shooting at El Paso hospital, VA police highlight nationwide security lapses in VA's medical system. *Washington Post*.

[†] Department of Veterans Affairs Office of Inspector General. (2013, March 7). Management of disruptive patient behavior at VA medical facilities (Report No. 11-02585-129).

Managing Problem Individuals 4

We envision the threat management strategies discussed in this chapter as arrayed across a continuum ranging from the most nonconfrontational to the most confrontational. In so arranging the strategies graphically, we do not want to imply that they should be selected or applied in any particular order. The same continuum illustrates when the threat manager's intervention can usually be detected by the subject of the intervention, that is, when the strategies become confrontational. The continuum, however, is for purposes of illustration, not a guide for selecting the strategies. The threat manager should select the strategy based on its appropriateness to the situation at this time.

If, for instance, the subject committed a crime, causing his or her arrest may be the most appropriate strategy for dealing with the individual even though we consider arrest as the most confrontational of all the strategies. In the alternative, an arrest for a minor crime may be held in abeyance by the threat manager during a confrontational interview as a tactic to control future behavior. An arrest can also be delayed until the precise time that would be most effective, such as when the subject would be in the possession of a weapon—or critical evidence. Threat management is not a 1–2–3 approach, nor a by-the-book practice. The essence of good threat management is flexibility and sound judgment.

In addition to supple dexterity, the threat manager must also retain enough professional objectivity to recognize when an applied strategy may be failing. A failed strategy may be worse than no strategy at all. If one strategy does not work, switch to another one until one is found that improves the situation. The main measure of success is avoiding a violent outcome, not only violence to the target but also violence toward others, including the subject, or the public at large. In addition, the strategy must be in balance with the subject's behaviors. We avoid overkill by selecting the threat management strategy in tune with the subject's inappropriate behaviors. Subjects who write insulting letters to public officials have done nothing justifying an arrest or possibly even a visit by the threat manager or law enforcement. Indeed, arresting such a subject may create further animosity toward a target or intensify a subject's feeling of injustice. Conversely, arresting an estranged husband who violates the restraining order against him would be entirely appropriate and proportionate. Thus, threat management requires managing the subject and the situation at this time in such a way as to ensure safety to the target, other possible targets, and the public at large. All the while, the threat manager must ensure that the response remains

- Proportionate to the subject's behaviors;
- Flexible in applying different strategies when necessary; and
- Sustainable over time.

Applying any of the threat management strategies involves an intricate juggling act with many and diverse activities bouncing around at the same time.

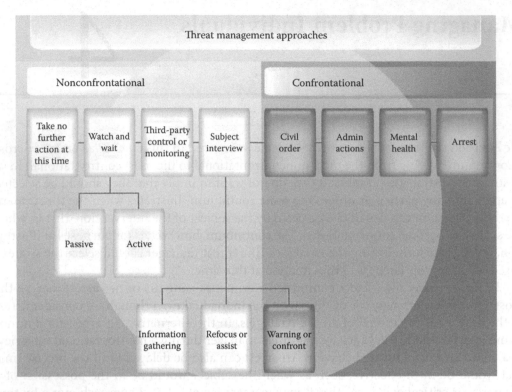

Figure 4.1 Threat management strategies.

Figure 4.1 graphically illustrates the array of threat management strategies available to threat management teams. In this chapter, we discuss each strategy in some detail, complete with observations on the advantages and disadvantages each strategy offers.

Threat Management Rules of Conduct

Threat managers need to keep constantly in mind three simple concepts when applying any of the threat management strategies. First, threat assessments have extremely short shelf-lives. They take snapshots of a particular moment in time and hence do not project far into the future. For the threat manager, this makes necessary frequent reassessments to ensure that changing conditions and new information get factored into the threat assessment process. Those new assessments may require changes to the applied threat management strategy. The simple act of applying a strategy—no matter how nonconfrontational—changes the situation. A new assessment gauging the effect of the applied strategy allows the threat manager to determine next steps.

This situational fluidity requires that threat managers avoid locking onto previous assessments. Assessing a subject as not a risk today does not mean that subject will not pose a risk tomorrow. New facts may escalate the risk; the subject's expectations may sour, spurring him or her to riskier behaviors; or the target may do something to further enrage the subject. In effect, conditions constantly change. The threat manager must embrace those changes by continuously factoring them into new assessments. Subsequent assessments may call for new threat management strategies and possible changes to the protective responses.

The second concept relates to the interaction among the subject, the target, and the threat manager. By applying a threat management strategy, the threat manager injects himself or herself into the situation. Even the strategy "take no further action at this time" affects the subject. If the subject expects some kind of response or reaction, then frustrating those expectations may prompt additional inappropriate behaviors. For example, a subject who writes an ominous letter to the target may be expecting the target to answer. If the threat manager takes no further action at this time, the subject may escalate by making a personal visit to the target. In addition, the selected strategy may not appeal to the target, thus prompting the target into behaviors potentially escalating the situation. How the subject, target, and threat manager interact profoundly affects the chemistry of the situation, both at this time and into the future. Recognizing that dynamic will assist the threat manager in gaining the necessary objectivity required to manage the situation.

Thus, in selecting any of the threat management strategies, the threat manager must carefully calibrate the impact that the strategy has on the situation, the subject, and the target. In doing so, the threat manager should consciously recognize that he or she is now on the inside of the situation looking out. By becoming part of the situation, the threat manager's own behavior prompts a ripple effect, swaying both subject and target into different behaviors. Volatility permeates both situations and subjects requiring threat management; the threat manager should approach them carefully and intelligently.

This brings us to the third concept in applying threat management strategies, the need to think through the situation diligently and wisely. The steps of the processes we discussed in Chapters 2 and 3—identifying problem individuals and assessing them—remain relatively straightforward. But applying threat management strategies offers vastly more complications. We can offer no certain guideposts, no specific rules, and only very general directions. Each situation requiring a threat management response is unique. Each has its own set of circumstances, its own context, and, ultimately, its own denouements. We can easily describe how a problem individual behaves. Section II does that quite clearly. Once identified, we offered four specific assessment tools for assessing the problem individual's potential risk. But in this chapter, we can only offer broad definitions of the nine threat management strategies and point out the strengths and weaknesses of each one. Applying them in practice opens up a whole new bag of surprises.

Two forces further complicate effective threat management strategies. Because threat management situations always involve sentient beings who act and react constantly, we call the first force *situation dynamics*. Situation dynamics evolve out of the interaction of those facts known to the threat manager, those facts unknown to the threat manager, the ongoing threat assessments of those knowns and unknowns, and the effect of the protective response. As these elements interact, they cause changes in the behavior of the subject, the target, and the threat manager, thus prompting more dynamics within the situation. We defined the situation dynamics as follows:

> the evolving interaction between the knowns, the unknowns, and the need to continuously assess each in determining the appropriate protective response at any given point in time.*

---

* Calhoun, F. S., & Weston, S. W. (2012), pp. 33–35. *Concepts and case studies in threat management.* In that book, we used the term "case dynamics, but now prefer "situation."

The principle of situation dynamics ensures that every situation the threat manager manages will always be fluid and constantly changing. Smart threat managers understand the impact of situation dynamics and prepare themselves to respond flexibly and adroitly.

We identified the second force influencing the course of events in any threat management situation as *intervention synergy*. This force is an offshoot of case dynamics in that it includes the interaction of the knowns, unknowns, assessments, and protective responses but adds an additional complicating factor—the threat manager's intervention, that is, the application of the threat management strategy. We defined intervention synergy as follows:

> the situation dynamic intensified by the stimulus of what the threat manager does or does not do in response to the threat situation.*

Note the inclusion of what the threat manager does *not* do. Not taking actions expected by the subject can be just as jolting to the situation as taking some action. Once the threat manager gets involved in the situation, he or she becomes unavoidably part of the chemistry of the situation. Intelligent threat managers recognize the principle of intervention synergy and expect its influences to affect any situation being managed. Understanding intervention synergy helps introduce flexibility and adroit threat management to every situation.

Finally, the threat manager must take into account what we term the *intervention dichotomy*. This is the potential conflict between an intervention applied by a threat manager and the effect of the intervention on the subject's inhibitors and stabilizers in their life. Interventions can be powerful tools that can affect a subject's family, livelihood, financial stability, and even the subject's freedom. The prudent threat manager will always weigh the effect of an intervention on the critical inhibitors in the subject's life and how potentially losing those inhibitors could affect the overall situation. For example, should a mentally ill and potentially violent employee be terminated, thus removing the inhibitors of both the job and the medical benefits that provide him counseling and medication? Should a threatening student be expelled from school, thereby removing the inhibitor of the school structure and access to counseling while also leaving him home alone and unsupervised during the day? Should an angry and unruly client at a social services agency be denied services due to his problematic behavior and thereby lose access to training, job placement, and counseling services that address his fundamental needs? These questions have no easy answers; however, recognizing the intervention dichotomy helps the threat manager make prudent decisions that affect inhibitors. The dichotomy also helps recognize and prepare for potential negative outcomes when inhibitors are lost due to an intervention.

We can weigh the advantages and disadvantages of each strategy, but we cannot give precise guidance on which one to use in any given situation. That guidance depends on the unique nature of each situation as it currently develops. Having thus despaired, we conclude that, although difficult and challenging, working with the threat management strategies is far from impossible. Rather, it is necessary. And that necessity is the mother of a successful threat management process.

* Calhoun, F. S., & Weston, S. W. (2012), pp. 40–41. *Concepts and case studies in threat management.*

Take No Further Action at This Time

The deliberate, informed decision to take no further action beyond identifying and assessing the subject and the situation must rest on a clearly articulable assessment that neither the subject nor the situation poses a risk at this time. It may derive from erroneous or exaggerated early reports, a misunderstanding of the subject's statements, or an initial misunderstanding of the situation as reported. In Section II, we describe a type of howler we call callow. Callow howlers simply do not understand that their behaviors are inappropriate and disturbing to the target. Indeed, they believe that their behavior is in tune with the relationship they perceive themselves to have with the target. Initial contacts from callow howlers may justify an initial strategy of take no further action at this time in hopes that the subject will stop or turn his or her attention elsewhere. Even ultimately confronting a callow subject should initially be done in an empathetic and educational manner, as though teaching the subject how best to behave. Such an approach possibly avoids inciting the callow howler into becoming a hunter.

Take no further action at this time does not resolve not knowing what to do or frustration with the situation at hand, nor should it be used by busy and distracted threat managers or those with scheduled leave. Indeed, the strategy can be a very risky selection unless the threat manager can defend its choice with facts justifying a no risk assessment. The threat manager can only justify choosing it when the threat manager can articulate why no further action is not required.

Threat managers most often invoke take no further action at this time in situations involving nonintimate subjects and targets or in group settings. Frequently, subjects troubled by some public official make inappropriate statements they have no intention of acting on. Having expressed their outrage, they feel better, which helps de-escalate the risk. In addition, the group dynamics in school or workplace or similar venues increase the chances that a statement or reported activity gets misunderstood, exaggerated, or misinterpreted. Second- and third-hand reporting always suffers greatly in accuracy.

Advantages and Disadvantages

The greatest advantage to not taking further action is that it spares time and resources that can be better applied to riskier cases. It diminishes the risk of outraging the subject, as is the case with the confrontational strategies. It also avoids insulting or angering the subject, who may believe that his or her behavior is well within the law and well within his or her rights to engage. Protecting one's innocence from organizational or government overreach can be a powerful motivator for escalating one's behavior by becoming more combative. Taking no further action in situations that pose no risk simply makes sense.

The greatest disadvantage to not taking further action is that it empowers the subject—while disempowering the threat manager—with control over what happens next. The risk here is that the next step may come as a surprise to both the target and the threat manager. To avoid this, the threat manager should carefully determine what the subject's expectations were when he or she engaged in the behavior under assessment. What did the subject want to happen in response to his or her behavior? If the subject expected a reaction and none occurs, that inaction may prompt an escalation in problem behaviors until the subject gets the desired reaction. Part of the initial fact finding, then, should focus on what is motivating the subject.

Watch and Wait

Watch and wait consists of discreetly monitoring the subject while waiting to see if he or she takes any further action toward the target. When used as an initial threat management strategy, it depends on the subject not knowing that he or she is under the threat manager's observation. It is crucial that the threat manager exercise extreme care to keep the subject ignorant of the threat manager's behind-the-scenes monitoring. If not, watch and wait can fail with very high-risk repercussions. Subjects who learn they are under some kind of observation or scrutiny simply because they expressed their opinion about the target may grow even more outraged at the intrusion into their lives. Consequently, watch and wait succeeds only as an initial strategy when the subject remains unaware that the threat manager is watching.

Unlike the other threat management strategies, watch and wait has a dual application. The threat manager can implement it as an initial strategy if the initial assessment indicates a low risk at this time. The strategy then becomes a way to maintain focus on the situation while waiting to see what the subject does next. But watch and wait also serves as an effective way to monitor how any of the other threat management strategies are working once they are employed. It allows the threat manager to gauge any changes in the level of risk to the target.

Frequently, individuals say or do things in the emotional heat of the moment, then cool down and regret their actions, recant them, or forget about them. In the public figure venue, subjects may say or do things in opposition to the public official without realizing they crossed some line that brought them to the attention of the threat manager. Raising the issue after the subject has calmed down may risk a return of the outrage. In more intimate venues such as domestic, workplace, or schools, subjects may say or do something in a fit of temper that they later feel remorse about. Watch and wait simply gives the subject time to calm down.

As a strategy for monitoring the effect of other strategies, watch and wait permits the threat manager to observe how the subject responds to whatever other strategy the threat manager invoked. For example, watch and wait allows the threat manager to gauge the effect of any administrative (usually disciplinary) action that an organization may take toward the subject. Has the subject accepted the rebuke or did it increase his or her resentment? Similarly, the threat manager may interview the subject and then provide him or her guidance with how to resolve the subject's grievance. Watch and wait allows the threat manager to see if the subject followed the guidance and if it helped resolve the initial grievance. Used in this way, watch and wait becomes the most utilitarian of the threat management strategies.

Waiting does not imply inactivity. Instead, the threat manager should ensure that the target or his or her representatives knows what is going on and knows to report any future contacts with the subject. The threat manager should also continue the protective fact finding, discreetly, of course, to further identify information bearing on the subject's current situation and grievance. As new information comes to the threat manager's attention, new assessments must be conducted. That may lead to deploying new strategies. It also means that the threat manager should take appropriate protective measures to ensure target safety.

Watch and wait can be either active or passive. Active watch and wait means the threat manager is aggressively collecting as much new information as can be had on the subject and the situation, always provided the protective fact finding is done in the background. Active also means frequent contacts with the target to ensure any subsequent interaction with the subject is immediately reported and assessed. That later interaction need not cross the threshold of being inappropriate. Passive watch and wait occurs after the threat manager has done as complete a protective fact finding as possible at this time and the decision is made to wait to see what the subject may do next. Passive watch and wait also requires close contact with the target or his or her representatives, again to ensure any subsequent contacts from the subject are immediately reported and assessed.

Used as the initial strategy, the need for absolute discretion is imperative. When used as the follow-up strategy to any of the other threat management strategies, discretion may not be necessary because the application of the other strategy alerted the subject of the threat manager's interest in the situation. As a follow on, active watch and wait may require additional contacts with the subject to verify that he or she is complying with the dictates of the other strategy. For example, subjects put under some administrative order may be required to take anger management classes to keep their job. The threat manager should monitor the subject's attendance and determine the effectiveness of the instruction. Subjects under restraining orders require the threat manager to ensure the orders are followed. For subjects who get arrested, the threat manager needs to make sure the subject obeys any bond or probation restrictions. Depending on the circumstances of the situation, watch and wait may do well as the initial strategy, but it always supports other strategies as a follow-up.

Advantages and Disadvantages

As an initial strategy, watch and wait works well with subjects who have multiple inhibitors and appear to have been venting about a specific issue involving the target. Telling a supervisor to shove off and then slamming the office door aggressively may be a one-time loss of temper. Confronting the subject after he or she has calmed down risks reinducing the temper fit. Watch and wait gives the subject time to apologize to the supervisor and for the supervisor to manage his or her employee. Escalating the response chances escalating the situation. Used as a follow-on strategy, watch and wait gives the threat manager time to evaluate the effectiveness of the other strategy.

Watch and wait is also an effective strategy in dealing with habitual howlers, those subjects who engage in low-risk behaviors toward the target over a long period of time. In general, they are communicators by a myriad of methods expressing their grievance in rude, ominous, even directly threatening communications, but the threat manager has verified their incapacity to act due to incarceration, mental commitment, or similar logistical or practical limitations. Watch and wait allows the threat manager to review future correspondence but not waste any other resources. Any change in the subject's approach to the target would, of course, prompt a new assessment and, perhaps, a different strategy.

Watch and wait works well in situations when the threat manager suspects that the subject was venting over a specific issue. Given time, the threat manager can determine if the venting was a one-time event or if the subject will continue to hold on to the outrage. The strategy also works very well when used to monitor the impact of one or more of the other threat management strategies. Its greatest advantage derives from its use of, and reliance on, time, that greatest of all healers.

Ironically, the greatest disadvantage in using watch and wait as the initial strategy also derives from its use of, and reliance on, time. Waiting is frustrating and can be nerve-wracking. The strategy keeps the threat manager from intervening in some other way. The frustration and nervousness are compounded by the uncertainty of not knowing how long to wait. Subjects have been known to create a risky situation, then disappear for months, even years, before returning to carry out the violence. For example, Charles Lee "Cookie" Thornton, who had a years-long running dispute with the city council of Kirkwood, Missouri, waited a month after losing his lawsuit before going to the regularly scheduled council meeting and killing three city officials and two police officers. Police stormed the council chamber and killed Thornton.* Shadow Yang waited 11 months before returning to his former factory and killing a former coworker, whom witnesses said he targeted. After killing Christina Wollenzien, Yang committed suicide. His motive for killing the former coworker died with him.† We know of no formula for determining how long to wait for nothing more to happen before deciding that nothing more is going to happen.

Another disadvantage to an initial strategy of watch and wait is its limitation only to low risk situations. Threat managers should never apply it as an initial strategy if the threat assessment indicates high risk. It also does not apply to situations, such as a direct threat, that are criminal. Nor should threat managers look to it when dealing with subjects who have a history of violence or mental illness. It is also ineffective against domestic violence or workplace violence where the subject and target are in close contact with each other on a daily basis. In those venues, watch and wait should only be used as a follow-on strategy.

Third-Party Control or Monitoring

The third-party control or monitoring strategy depends on locating a third party who has the ability to either control the subject or to closely monitor the subject's behavior. For both controllers and monitors, the threat manager must maintain close communications with the third party in order to keep informed about the subject. Reliable third parties are such people as mental health providers, physicians, close relatives, board and home-care providers, colleagues, or close friends. At the institutional level, reliable third parties may be found among parole or probation officers or correctional or jail personnel. One of the challenges of this strategy is to ensure that the third party remains reliable. When the relationship between the third party and the subject is professional, as with mental health providers, physicians, home-care providers, and correctional personnel, the control and monitoring may become complicated or problematic because of issues of confidentiality or because the professional may have an overwhelming caseload of other patients or inmates. Relatives may move, die, or simply may change their minds about cooperating. The strategy works only as long as the third party remains reliable. It can devolve into disaster if that reliability diminishes in any significant way.

The most effective way to implement the strategy is to take steps to ensure that the subject does not find out about the relationship between the threat manger and the third party. Its effectiveness is further enhanced if the subject accepts the control or monitoring as a natural part of his or her relationship with the third party. If the subject perceives the relationship as part of his or her life, then the subject would be less likely to blame the target for the subject being under control or monitoring. Conversely, if the subject started to suspect the target's involvement, the risk to the target may go up.

---

* Town struggles after city hall shooting. (2009, February 9). Associated Press.
† Woman shot to death at Wis. factory. (2007, September 10). Associated Press.

Understanding the difference between controlling the subject and monitoring the subject is crucial to the strategy's success. Control is best achieved in institutional settings, such as prisons, jails, or mental health facilities. Monitoring means the subject can move about freely, which means there will be periods when the subject is unmonitored. In workplace and school settings, supervisors, teachers, colleagues, and classmates are all potential monitors. Relatives, too, especially relatives living with the subject, make excellent monitors as long as they cooperate with the threat manager. In one case involving a disgruntled employee on suspension, the threat manager used a close colleague of the subject to drop by the subject's house periodically to see how he was doing during the course of the suspension. The friend confirmed that the subject was accepting the suspension well.*

Threat managers will usually find that this strategy is infrequently applied, primarily because of the lack of access to reliable controllers and monitors. Law enforcement makes better use of controllers because the police can approach correctional officers and probation and parole officers on a professional level. That kind of access to controllers presents a steeper climb for threat managers working in the corporate or private sector. Threat managers in those fields will, however, have access to monitors such as coworkers and supervisors. The third-party control or monitoring strategy does offer a way to manage subjects under the right logistical circumstances.

In a creative, albeit controversial, twist on the third-party monitor or control strategy, Federal Bureau of Investigation (FBI) Director James Comey confirmed in November 2014 that one of his agents impersonated a reporter for the Associated Press (AP) in 2007 in order to trick a 15-year-old suspected of making bomb threats to a Seattle high school. After consulting with behavioral scientists at FBI headquarters, the specialists concluded that the suspect was in all likelihood a narcissist. Based on that diagnosis, the team concluded that the young boy would respond to the chance of getting public attention. "From that behavioral assessment came the idea of this person would be the subject of a newspaper story," an anonymous FBI official explained. The Seattle FBI agent, posing as an AP reporter, asked the teenage suspect to review a fake AP story about the bomb threats. Apparently through electronic means, the agent explained to the suspect that his review of the article was necessary to ensure that the threatener "was portrayed fairly" in the counterfeit article. As hoped, the suspect agreed to review the article. When the agent sent it to him, it included malware that revealed the suspect's e-mail address as soon as he clicked on the article. Agents arrested the boy, who was later convicted in Washington State. The AP and 25 news outlets protested the FBI's tactics in this case after Director Comey confirmed the accuracy of the story.†

We are aware of similar tactics used by threat managers to gather information or form a relationship with a subject that include fake phone surveys or contests resulting in free gifts, free phone cards sent to subjects that track who they call, free software upgrades that track keystrokes, and phone calls from fake psychics that call to give free readings. Such sub-rosa tactics are probably better left to trained law enforcement officers, but the trick of posing as someone who appealed to the suspect led to a successful defusing of the risk to the high school. That, of course, is the goal of threat management. We urge threat managers to get legal advice and exercise great caution before using such methods.

* Authors' personal knowledge.
† Nakashima, E. (2014, November 7). FBI agent impersonated AP reporter in hunt for teenage suspect, director confirms. *Washington Post*.

Advantages and Disadvantages

Third-party control allows the threat manager to intervene with the subject through an established control system that the subject accepts or tolerates. From the subject's perception, the intervention derives from the subject's relationship with the third party, exclusive of anything having to do with the target. That relationship may make the subject more amenable to the intervention than it would if the subject understood that the intervention resulted from his or her interaction with the target.

Third-party monitoring opens an avenue for the threat manager to find out about the subject's thinking, attitudes, activities, concerns, and future plans without the subject knowing what the threat manager knows. Such information helps flesh out the ongoing threat assessments, thereby helping the threat manager track the subject's progress up or down the path to intended violence. Monitoring also helps uncover any changes in the subject's behaviors, plans, or life circumstances.

The greatest disadvantage of third-party control or monitoring comes from any change in the relationship between the threat manager and the third party. The third party may lose his or her institutional control over the subject, may switch loyalties, or may even start taking the subject's side. As the situation evolves and changes, the ability to control or monitor the subject may go away. For example, the threat manager can rely on a subject's supervisor to monitor the subject while still employed. Indeed, the supervisor may even be able to control the subject as long as the subject fears losing his or her job. All of that disappears once the subject no longer works at that place, whether due to termination or resignation. Similarly, school officials can monitor, sometimes even control, a student's behavior up until the moment they expel the student or the student drops out. Probationers reach the end of their probation, inmates serve their sentence, and mental health patients heal, learn to cope, or run out of medical benefits. All of these factors spell the end of the third party's ability to control or monitor the subject.

Subject Interviews: Refocus or Assist

Subject interviews straddle the line between protective fact finding and threat management. As we recommended in Chapter 2, interviews offer great potential for gaining insight into how the subject sees the current situation, what his or her plans may be, and how the subject perceives the future. That is part of the protective fact finding process. But subject interviews also provide the threat manager with the opportunity to interact with the subject to help resolve the subject's problem or refocus the subject away from the target in a more appropriate direction. In some situations, the threat manager accepts the subject's attention in the role of a sympathetic listener. The strategies of refocus or assist are subject interventions, although perceived by the subject as a positive influence on the situation or even their lives.

By refocus, we in no way mean shifting the subject's inappropriate attention from one target to another unwitting target. We consider that unethical and highly risky—not to mention undoubtedly immoral and probably unlawful. Instead, by refocus, we mean that the threat manager should stress that henceforth, the threat manager or another designated person will be the point of contact for the subject on a particular issue. When successfully done, refocusing the subject diverts his or her attention away from the target and focuses him or her on an appropriate surrogate as the person designated to resolve the subject's problems.

It requires the threat manager to convincingly show that he or she can possibly solve the subject's problems or, at the very least, provide a sympathetic ear for the subject's complaints.

By assist, we mean actually helping the subject resolve his or her problems. Frequently, subjects come up against institutions and bureaucracies with which they have never dealt and with which they have no understanding. The rules and procedures seem foreign to them, which often leads to frustration and impatience. Simply helping the subject navigate the bureaucratic maze solves the subject's problem and, in so doing, stabilizes the threat situation.

Employing the refocus or assist strategy requires the threat manager to develop a positive, empathetic relationship with the subject. Both require hearing the subject out and making an honest effort to understand what the subject's problem or issue is, and then thinking both tactically and creatively of how to address that problem or issue. It does not mean making false promises. If the subject's complaint cannot be resolved, it seriously worsens the situation by giving the subject hope that the threat manager will find some resolution. Subjects who want a million dollars should never be promised that the check is in the mail.

Advantages and Disadvantages

Using the subject interview to refocus the subject's attention away from the target and onto the threat manager or another appropriate surrogate ensures that the threat manager now has a way to monitor the subject in the future. Information gleaned from future contacts can be fed into the ongoing threat assessments. By providing a positive reception, the threat manager invites the subject to share his or her current and future concerns, frustrations, and anger. Refocus gives the subject someone to complain to at the same time it gives the threat manager a way to monitor the thinking processes of the subject. It is especially effective with subject's who have long-term problems or issues.

Using the subject interview to assist the subject works best with those subjects who have solvable problems. Typical assistance activities are doing such things as follows:

- Arranging for pro bono legal advice for subject's having legal troubles
- Obtaining proper medication for mentally ill subjects
- Acting as an intermediary between the subject and the institution or agency that can solve his or her issues
- Arranging with family members for closer supervision of developmentally disabled subjects
- Providing plaintiffs and defendants access to alternative dispute resolution services
- Coordinating with mental health providers to treat mentally ill subjects
- Working with social workers to attend to a subject's welfare needs

Refocus works especially well for those subjects who do not pose a significant risk and whose approaches are more bothersome or annoying than risky. Assisting the subject only works when the subject is receptive and it is within the threat manager's ability to affect that assistance.

The biggest disadvantage to both refocus and assist is the time investment the threat manager will have to make. By refocusing the subject, the threat manager has to carry through and allow the subject to contact the threat manager as often as the subject wants. Doing so, of course, takes time that the threat manager may better spend on other subjects or situations.

Assisting the subject also takes time and effort. It also forces the threat manager to think creatively. Problem solving requires patience, imagination, and innovation, all of which take time and can be difficult to accomplish. And, as we wrote previously, assistance works only in those situations where the threat manager actually can be of help. Neither refocus nor assist should be used in situations assessed as high risk. Neither one works with subjects who have irrational or unreasonable demands. Applying either approach ineffectively could worsen the situation and elevates the risk.

Subject Interview: Warning or Confront

Now we cross the border into confrontational strategies. Deciding to warn or confront the subject with the consequences of his or her continued actions can occur before the interview as part of the interview, strategy, or during the course of the interview if the opportunity presents itself. Either way, threat managers should be very conscious of their own safety. Warning or confronting a subject escalates the emotions of the moment, especially anger, which may prompt physical reactions from the subject. Whether planned or opportunistic, the use of both warning and confronting should be done with significant tactical awareness.

Oftentimes, subjects simply do not realize the seriousness of their behaviors. Many subjects believe they have been treated unfairly. Therefore, they reason that their search for justice excuses them; indeed, it empowers them to make their case forcibly. In his classic meditation on *Violence: Reflections on a National Epidemic,* Dr. James Gilligan observed *"all violence is an attempt to achieve justice,* or what the violent person perceives as justice" (emphasis in original).* And Gilligan's patients included regular criminals—murderers, thieves, and rapists as well as assassins and avengers. Subjects seeking justice frequently do not understand how close they teeter on criminal actions or what the consequences of taking those actions may be. Explaining in no uncertain terms what may happen to the subject if he or she continues these behaviors and warning of the potential legal or disciplinary repercussions may suffice to lead them to change those behaviors.

Confronting the subject works most effectively after the threat manager has collected enough information to support either criminal or disciplinary charges. Confronting is not about provoking the subject, rather it is presenting evidence of the subject's past behaviors that were either criminal or violated some institutional rules or regulations. Threat managers should only confront the subject when they can prove that whatever the subject did was either illegal or subject to discipline. Confronting a subject without such proof compounds the problem by revealing the threat manager as weak and ineffectual. Confronting the subject works only when the threat manager can back it up. Keep in mind that the confrontation is not about a show of force or display of toughness. It is about being smarter and in control of both yourself and the situation.

Advantages and Disadvantages

Odd as it is to say, warning the subject may actually work. Subjects on a mission of justice do not always perceive their actions in the same way everyone else sees them. Rather,

---

* Gilligan, J. (1996). *Violence: Reflections on a national epidemic* (p. 11). New York: Vintage Books.

they see themselves as just; hence, their actions must be just. One Transportation Security Administration (TSA) screener who had resigned before termination began leaving threatening and harassing voice mails on his former supervisor's telephone line, usually late at night when the screener had some certainty no one would answer. The screener was expressing his innocence and his outrage at the forced resignation. Weeks later, and clearly not understanding his phone calls as a problem, the screener applied online for a screening position and for a Federal Air Marshal position. The computer scheduled him an interview, which TSA hastily cancelled. Spouses often hope that if they could only have one last talk with their estranged spouse, they could patch things up. The spouse does not understand that his frequent efforts to contact the former wife equates to stalking. Giving individuals like these a well-communicated direct warning about their problematic behavior helps them distinguish between appropriate and inappropriate behaviors. Warnings work best with subjects who have multiple inhibitors, no criminal record or just minor offenses, no history of significant mental health problems, and who have only very recently begun their inappropriate behaviors. Frequently, warnings work well in combination with the assist strategy. The threat manager can offer his or her help, but only if the subject desists from further inappropriate approaches.

Similarly, confronting the subject may prompt admissions. Presenting the evidence against the subject may call forth a full admission of his or her behavior or it may encourage the subject to dispute some of the facts while admitting to others. The subject may want to clarify minor details, thereby affirming that he or she did what the threat manager just accused him or her of doing. "I didn't go there in February, it was March 1." Either of these responses constitutes an admission of acts that the threat manager can use to justify an arrest or discipline.

The biggest disadvantage of warning or confronting the subject is that it reveals the threat manager's hand. Now the subject knows what the threat manager knows. He or she can use that intelligence to plot future approaches. Warnings, in particular, establish a boundary between punishable behaviors and unpunishable behaviors. The subject can use that border to his or her own advantage by always going up to the border without crossing it. If, when confronting the subject, the threat manager introduces erroneous information, he or she has just strengthened the subject's hand by giving him or her deniability.

In sum, warning or confronting the subject should occur only when the threat manager is confident of his or her facts and can back up the warning or the confrontation. If there is any lack of confidence in the facts or the carry through, the strategy should be avoided and another one selected.

Civil Orders

In a precisely defined set of situations, the threat manager or the target acting on the recommendations of the threat manager can apply to a court of law to issue civil process ordering the subject to cease and desist his or her problematic behaviors and keep away from the target. Depending on the jurisdiction, these orders may be called restraining orders, stay-away orders, or protective orders.

In many jurisdictions, subjects who violate these orders may be subject to criminal prosecution. Every jurisdiction has specific requirements that have to be met when applying for the order. Each threat manager should consult with his or her legal counsel on the name and scope of civil orders available in the threat manager's jurisdiction.

Advantages and Disadvantages

Civil orders have two opposite advantages. Restraining orders are particularly effective with subjects who are law abiding and who have significant inhibitors in their lives, that is, individuals who are the least likely to be named in a civil order. Using them on these individuals effectively sends them a message that their behaviors are wrong. Often, formerly law-abiding subjects will claim that no one warned them about their actions or they will stand behind their rights. Serving them with a restraining order clearly informs them that they risk criminal penalties if they continue acting inappropriately.

We identify certain characteristics of subjects likely to obey any civil order:

- Usually law-abiding individuals
- Individuals enjoying strong inhibitors, such as good employment, satisfactory home life, or a good reputation
- Individuals who have a lot to lose independent of the current situation, such as those on probation or parole or who have a new job*

On the opposite side, civil orders work effectively for those subjects highly likely to violate the order. Issuing an order against these subjects opens the way for the threat manager to arrange an arrest once the subject violates the order. But that entails its own risks because, by definition, violations of the order occur when the subject approaches the target. Threat managers should balance using civil orders with increased risks to the target.

We also identified certain characteristics of subjects likely to violate any civil order:

- History of previous violations of civil orders
- Few or diminishing inhibitors
- Mental illness, especially command delusions or hallucinations to harm another
- Behavioral pattern of resistance to authority, for example, warrant arrest, assault on police officer, or failure to appear
- Known alcohol or substance abuse
- History of stalking behavior without a civil order in place
- Long-running dispute with the target
- History of violence
- Provocation or escalation by the target, whether intentional or unintentional*

The biggest disadvantage of civil orders is that they may actually increase the risk to the target by provoking greater anger in the subject. It strikes us as oddly illogical to seek a civil order in the hope the subject will violate it, especially when that violation entails approaching the target. As we discuss in Section II, the Supreme Court, in a 2005 case, effectively gutted enforcement of civil orders. It ruled local police have complete discretion in determining whether or not to enforce such orders.† Busy police departments can now refuse to respond to reports of violations.

To this day, obtaining civil orders remains very controversial. One side advocates using them in almost any situation, whereas the other side views them with a healthy caution that

---

* Taken from California Highway Patrol Special Investigations Unit practices.
† See pages 186–188 below.

restricts using them in all but a rare few cases. We fall in with the latter group and recommend their use in only the rarest of situations. The other disadvantage of civil orders is that they do not resolve the issue but simply begin the process of dealing with the subject over the long-term. That process also requires close monitoring. If the threat manager chooses to get a civil order, he or she must be prepared for full and immediate enforcement of any violations, even small or technical ones. A civil order that is not enforced is worse than no order at all. It tells the subject that the order is essentially powerless and that the threat manager is unable to control the subject's behaviors. Civil Orders are a risky way of trying to defuse any risk.

Administrative Actions

Administrative actions are those processes, usually disciplinary, that an institution or organization has developed to manage inappropriate behaviors through some type of punishment, sanctions, or restrictions. For most organizations, these orders are directed at employees, but they need not be restricted to only that group. The Veterans Administration hospital system has established processes for managing unruly patients, either by denying them service or strictly controlling when and where the unruly patient can receive the service. Administrative actions rely on the power and authority inherent to the institution or organization. Both the organization and the recipient recognize and accept that authority as a condition of employment or access to a particular service. For most institutions, using administrative actions becomes their favored strategy because their years of administering them have given them confidence in their use.

Since administrative actions are largely disciplinary in nature, confrontation inheres in their use. Businesses fire or suspend employees, schools suspend or expel students, and the military has different levels of discharging its sailors and soldiers. They come into play only after the subject's behavior becomes so egregious as to require discipline. Consequently, they are of little use managing subjects who do not cross the line, who act sullenly, even disrespectfully, but not outright insubordinately. Administrative actions are powerful tools that can have a significantly negative impact on the subject's life, relationships, and economic stability.

Advantages and Disadvantages

The biggest advantage in using administrative orders is that the institution or organization is comfortable with the practice. Over the years, it developed detailed policies and procedures and has used them repeatedly. In most cases, courts have vetted the administrative orders, so there is less concern over potential litigation. The recipients generally accept the policies and procedures, if not willingly, then at least begrudgingly. They can be used most effectively when the subject recognizes and accepts the organization's use of the administrative order against the subject. It is best, as well, to administer the order fairly and transparently always respecting and protecting the subject's rights.

The greatest disadvantage of relying on administrative orders is that the organization may lose any control over the subject. Particularly with terminations, the firing sets the subject free of the organization, which now has a challenge in gaining any information about the subject and his or her activities. Terminations, too, are one-shot events that address the inappropriate behaviors but do not defuse the risk. Even suspensions mean that the organization has little information about the subject during the duration of the suspension. Disciplinary acts breed resentment and feelings of injustice in the subject, only now the institution has no easy way of monitoring the subject's activities. Subjects may brood about their problems and resentment over the discipline for months, even years. In June 2003, the U.S. Postal Service forced Jennifer San Marco to take early retirement on a medical disability due to psychological problems. Nearly 3 years later, in February 2006, San Marco killed a neighbor, then returned to the postal facility where she had worked and murdered seven former colleagues, then herself. Postal authorities described it as the worst postal shooting in 20 years.* Having forced her into retirement, the Postal Service had no easy way of keeping track of her, especially for 3 years. Administrative actions may resolve the discipline issues, but they only worsen the potential risk.

Mental Health Commitments

Mental health commitments work well in managing subjects who display evidence of mental illness, especially if they are engaged in dangerous behaviors. The strategy imposes on the threat manager the responsibility for presenting to a mental health professional sufficient, compelling evidence to convince the doctor that the subject requires immediate treatment. In these days of declining government budgets, that challenge has become all the steeper as the competition for limited bed space has increased. In general, most states require proof or probable cause showing that the subject, due to a mental disorder, is now

- A danger to self;
- A danger to others; or
- Gravely disabled.

Every threat manager should consult with his or her legal counsel to determine the exact requirements in the threat manager's jurisdiction. Adopting this strategy requires understanding the symptoms of mental illness as the strategy works only for those subjects who suffer a provable mental illness and pose a danger to themselves or others.

The threat manager should document evidence of mental illness in an affidavit to present to the mental health professional. Verbal reports are far less effective. Good affidavits present precise, detailed, and specific behavioral descriptions, but always in layman's language. Offering medical diagnoses is counterproductive because they usually offend or amuse the mental health professionals.

The affidavit should follow these guidelines:

- Written, not verbal reports, are more convincing to mental health professionals.
- The affidavit should provide specific, detailed descriptions of the subject's current behaviors and any history of previous relevant behaviors.
- The threat manager need not personally witness these behaviors because probable cause can be established through credible third parties, such as neighbors, paramedics, or relatives.

* Deaths in Calif. shootings rise to eight. (2006, February 2). Associated Press. Geis, S. (2006, February 1). Ex-postal worker kills 5, then self. *Washington Post*. (Other victims died later.)

The threat management process does not end with the mental health commitment. Often, initial commitments expire in 48 or 72 hours unless the doctor determines otherwise. The doctor may decide that further time in the hospital is unnecessary or that the patient is best treated on an outpatient basis. Given the likelihood of changes in the subject's status, the threat manager needs to arrange with the staff to alert the threat manager when the subject gets back into the community. Commitments do not end the situation; at most, they allow the threat manager to employ the watch and wait strategy for monitoring the subject's response to the treatment.

The threat manager should also not assume that everything is fine once the doctor releases the subject. Frequently, patients are put on a course of medication and put back into the community to take their medicine on their own. As long as the subject continues the prescribed medication, his or her behavior may be stable. But all too often, mental health patients decide to stop taking their medicine, at which point the inappropriate behaviors return.

The following lists relevant behaviors the California Highway Patrol Special Investigations Unit has used for determining mental health commitments.

Relevant Behaviors for Mental Health Commitments

Due to a mental condition
Danger to others
Assaultive behaviors
Threatening behavior with immediate intent to harm
Subject admits to "hearing voices" instructing him or her to hurt someone
Fire setting or leaving gas turned on in the home
Engaging in dangerous behavior without regard for the safety of others, such as throwing objects, reckless driving, brandishing or random discharge of a weapon, or breaking windows
Danger to self
Actual suicide attempt
Threat to commit suicide with available means (a formulated plan increases the risk)
Hearing voices instructing the subject to injure himself or herself
Self-mutilation, burning or cutting self, or banging head
Refusing medical treatment for a life-threatening medical problem
Walking in front of cars
Leaving gas on or setting fires
Gravely disabled
Unable to provide food for himself or herself
Refuses to eat or claims that food is poisoned or altered
Claims that subject does not need to eat
Too depressed to eat, claims of no appetite
Afraid to leave room to obtain food
Unable to provide clothing
Nude or seminude in a public area
Person has disposed of his or her own clothing
Paranoid ideation that clothing is contaminated
Clothing is dirty, tattered, or inappropriate for weather conditions

Unable to provide shelter for himself or herself
  Living on the streets, but cannot explain why
  Has history of evictions without understanding why
  Living conditions are uninhabitable or pose fire or health hazards

California Highway Patrol Special Investigations Unit Practices (2005)

Advantages and Disadvantages

Perhaps the greatest advantage offered by mental health commitments is that it may get the subject treatment with his or her mental illness. In the near term, commitments give the threat manager and the target a little breathing room from dealing with the subject. In the far term, the treatment may actually succeed in treating the subject or in setting up a long-term regulation of his or her negative behaviors. Additionally, many states prohibit subjects who have been committed from gun ownership for a period of years. With subjects who display behaviors indicating significant mental illness, mental health commitments may be the only effective threat management strategy available to the threat manager.

The biggest disadvantage involving mental health commitments comes from the time, complexity, and effort involved. Gathering the necessary evidence for the initial involuntary commitment is challenging, but trying to get a longer commitment means going before a judge and presenting more evidence in the probable-cause hearing. That requires working with the state or district attorney. Time is also a factor in successful treatments. But time also gives the subject the opportunity to stop taking his or her medicines somewhere down the road. Another disadvantage to mental health commitments is the restriction on the strategy solely to those subjects who behave in ways suggesting mental illness. Treatment is for the mad, not the bad. Although the United States has lots of mentally ill citizens, they are nonetheless a minority of the population and few mentally ill persons pose a risk of violence.

Criminal Prosecutions

The strategy of criminal prosecutions is also limited, this time to subjects who actually commit crimes. Before using law enforcement resources, the threat manager should evaluate four specific considerations related to using this strategy. First, did a crime actually occur? This brings us to the crossroads where the Constitution and criminal acts intersect. The Constitution protects individuals expressing their anger, indignation, or opposition to their employers' business methods. It protects individuals complaining about government officials, whether it is the mayor or the principal of the local school. The Constitution also protects individuals who describe other individuals negatively, provided the description is factual. What constitutes a prosecutable threat? What behaviors constitute stalking?

In most jurisdictions, convicting someone for making a threat usually requires proving the subject made a credible threat (meaning the subject has the apparent ability to carry out the threat), intended to cause fear, and actually did frighten the target. Some jurisdictions recognize implied threats through a pattern of conduct or a totality of circumstances. The following guidelines may help in determining if the subject committed a crime:

- Language conveying a direct threat—"I'm going to kill you"—is usually a crime.
- Language conveying a conditional threat—"If you don't rule in my favor, I'm going to kill you"—is usually a crime.
- Language conveying a veiled threat—"Now I know why people blow up buildings like in Oklahoma City. The same thing could happen here the way you treat people"—would be considered by most jurisdictions as rhetorical and not a crime without other conduct.
- Language conveying an oblique threat—"Watch your back" or "You'll regret messing with me"—would be considered by most jurisdictions as rhetorical and not a crime without other conduct.

Being too quick in evaluating the situation without carefully examining the words communicated may result in the threat manager finding that the words actually spoken or written did not rise to the level of a prosecutable threat. The charges will then not be accepted, thus freeing the subject who is now angrier than ever before.

The second consideration involves going beyond proving a crime occurred to proving the subject committed it. Simply because a threatening letter is signed John Jones or a telephone caller claims to be John Jones or an hysterical target claims to have seen John Jones stalking does not mean the threat manager does not have to prove that the John Jones under suspicion wrote the letter, made the call, or actually stalked. In Section II, we discuss a type of howler we call the dirty trickster. Dirty tricksters essentially frame other individuals for the dirty trickster's own inappropriate approach to the target. Threat managers should always be on the lookout for these hoaxers. Establishing proof that the subject committed the crime requires the threat manager to conduct a plain, old-fashioned criminal investigation. The evidence, then, is the same as in any such investigation—fingerprints, handwriting analysis, witness testimony, or, most commonly, by the suspect's own admission. In the rush to resolve a seemingly threatening situation, this fundamental investigative step can be overlooked. The threat manager should ensure that it is not.

The third consideration requires a more delicate judgment call by the threat manager. Will the arrest actually result in the subject's confinement? What are the chances the subject will get a prompt release on bail? The threat manager can best offset this possibility by coordinating with the prosecutor to prepare a detailed affidavit for the judge or magistrate presenting all the pertinent evidence, especially that evidence related to the risk of violence posed by the subject. This information can be used to convince a judge to increase the bail or, in rare cases, deny any bail to the subject. The worst outcome is to affect an arrest, then learn that the subject made bail and disappeared. Once police arrest the suspect, the threat manager should arrange with jail officials to alert the threat manager if there is any change in the suspect's status.

If the subject can get bail, the threat manager should make every effort to convince the judge or magistrate to impose strict conditions. This allows the threat manager to exercise third-party control over the subject and his or her inappropriate behavior until the trial commences. Typical conditions include mental health treatment, prohibition on drugs and alcohol, confiscation of all weapons, authority to search the subject and the subject's home, and requiring the subject to stay away from the target.

The fourth consideration involves evaluating the likelihood of the subject plea-bargaining to a lesser offense in order to get a short jail term or, worse, a fine or suspended sentence. Heavy caseloads compel prosecutors to cut deals with defendants all the time. In this regard, threat management cases carry no immunity from such negotiations, particularly if the risk seems low. Should a plea deal occur, the threat manager should coordinate closely with the prosecutor to require the same strict conditions on any probation as for bail as part of the plea bargain.

Like mental health commitments, arrest and prosecution do not, on their own, successfully conclude a threat management situation. Even obtaining a conviction and lengthy prison sentence does not guarantee the risk has gone away. Has the threat manager determined that the subject does not have outside support willing to use violence? Additionally, the threat manager will have to monitor the subject's trajectory through the penal system to ensure that prison officials notify him or her of any change in the subject's status. Doing so represents a significant investment in resources and the threat manager's time, but time and hard work inhere in the nature of the threat management process.

Advantages and Disadvantages

The greatest advantage of arrest and prosecution, assuming both are successful, is that doing so punishes subjects who have committed crimes. The main advantage comes from society's interest in punishing individuals who commit crimes. This means, in effect, that the threat managers may have little choice in selecting this approach as a threat management strategy. Enforcing the law takes precedence.

Putting the subject in prison also severely hampers the subject's ability to approach or harass the target. It also allies the judicial system with the threat manager at the subject's expense. These are powerful advantages, but they apply only to subjects who commit crimes. Before applying this strategy, experienced threat managers first conclude whether prosecuting the suspect will be a successful intervention strategy. Again, the threat manager always asks, "Will this or any strategy make the situation better or worse?" Perhaps, the better way to put the question is, "Which of the nine strategies is most likely in this situation to make the situation better?"

Good threat managers understand that arrest and prosecution do not, in and of themselves, resolve the situation. Rather, it begins what can be a long-term process combining active and passive watch and wait. A conviction with a lengthy sentence does not, ipso facto, mean the risk is gone. The subject may have outside contacts or resources willing to assist him or her or the subject may be capable of escaping or earning early parole. The threat manager will have to establish an alert system whereby the threat manager receives notifications of any change in the prisoner's status. But still, the advantage of keeping the subject confined is a powerful one. Arrest and prosecution work best in cases where the threat manager can prove the subject committed a felony serious enough to result in a significant prison sentence.

Even prosecuting lesser crimes gives the threat manager some leverage from working the system. Misdemeanor charges provide opportunities for the threat manager to arrange for conditions of probation to use in long-term case management. However, these type charges, by themselves, do not effectively manage the risk.

Although hardly the best solution, the threat manager can go for arrest when he or she has confidence that conditions on a suspended sentence can be arranged. Such conditions establish some orderly controls on the suspect's future behaviors. They also provide a fast way for getting the subject back into custody should the subject escalate the risk to the target. For subjects known to be already on parole or probation, filing criminal charges can lead to immediate revocation of that parole or probation. It may also prompt the supervising law enforcement officer to order probation searches, drug and alcohol testing, or other controls in the terms of the subject's release.

Arrest and prosecution have several disadvantages. They are the most confrontational of all the strategies and thus risk further infuriating the subject toward the target. Failing to win a conviction opens the situation to several negative consequences. It might make the subject even more aggressive than before. Arrest and prosecution, after all, are the biggest guns in the threat manager's arsenal. The subject can easily conclude from any failure to use them effectively that he or she has beat the judicial system. Such a victory for the subject invites greater aggression.

In addition, arresting the subject alerts the subject to law enforcement's interest in him or her. Subtlety and finesse evaporate whenever handcuffs come out. Putting this strategy into play makes it nearly impossible for the threat manager to go back to less confrontational strategies. The strategy also introduces other players into the situation over whom the threat manager not only has no control but also who may have authority over the threat manager. Law enforcement and the judiciary—for reasons of their own—may brush aside any interests the threat manager has in the outcome of the situation. Nor will the system necessarily care that the target is the president of a corporation or a local big wig. From the judiciary's view, all who appear before it are equal under the law.*

Finally, because law enforcement officers enforce the law, arrest and prosecution actually restrict the alternatives open to the threat manager. If a crime occurs, the threat manager cannot debate whether or not administrative orders would work better than watch and wait or if third-party control or monitoring seems more effective than refocus or assist. Instead, enforcing the law takes precedence. But that principle effectively handcuffs the threat manager as figuratively as it does the subject literally.

Threat managers should not even consider arrest and prosecution if the threat manager cannot prove a crime committed by the subject. The strategy is also ineffective in situations involving nuisance-type violations resulting only in fines. No matter what happens, the threat manager should put in place procedures for immediately increasing the protective response in the event the criminal prosecution—for any reason—fails, thereby allowing the subject to reclaim his or her freedom without any conditions on his or her release.

Managing the Risk

In reviewing the confrontational threat management strategies, we intentionally adopted language implying our hesitancy and concern about using them. That hesitancy and concern grow out of the fact that, by their very nature, confrontational strategies increase

---

* The Supreme Court has acknowledged that Secret Service agents involved in the protection of federal officials, especially the president and vice president, enjoy more flexibility in exercising their protective responsibilities than other threat managers; see Ginsberg, concurring, in *Reichle* v. *Howards* 566 U.S. ____ (2012).

the risk. They involve the threat manager and the subject in an adverse relationship. That adversity drags the threat manager even deeper into the case dynamics and intervention synergy of the situation. That step should never be taken lightly or without fully exploring the repercussions of the action.

Always keep in mind the primary goal of any intervention. It is to manage the subject or situation at this time to increase the safety for this target, other potential targets, or the general public in a way that is proportionate to the subject's behavior in a manner that is flexible and sustainable.

Given that hesitancy and concern, we are not opposed to using any of the confrontational strategies provided the threat manager is convinced that that strategy is the most appropriate for the current situation. Given the right situation, the right time, and the right place, each strategy can effectively manage the threat. Our hesitation and concern come from accurately identifying the right time and place than from the strategies themselves. Threat management is risky business no matter which of the strategies employed—confrontational or not. Threat managers can only diminish that risk by thoughtfully, deliberately, and intelligently choosing the best strategy for this situation, time, and place. Accomplishing that alleviates our hesitancy and concern entirely.

We have described some of the advantages and disadvantages of each of the nine threat management strategies. But in doing so, we want no misunderstanding that we were offering hard and fast rules; indeed, we offered no rules at all. Threat management cases cannot be so easily bound.

At best, we can merely describe each strategy, illustrate it with realistic examples, and give its pros and cons. The threat manager must determine which one offers the best chance for managing the risk in the particular case at that particular moment. Once a strategy is played, the threat manager should immediately recognize that the situation has now changed *precisely because a strategy has been employed*. The change requires a reevaluation of the situation, the assessment, and the strategy. This may result in using yet another strategy or combination of strategies, which, in turn, require yet another reevaluation and assessment, leading to the same or another strategy. The process, we assure you, is not endless, but it often enough seems like it is.

Summary

This chapter described the threat management strategies threat managers can employ to manage a risky situation. It discussed the strategies, starting with the most nonconfrontational, then moved steadily along the spectrum to the most confrontational. But that approach was a descriptive ploy, a way to present the strategies. It is not the way the strategies should be employed. Instead, the threat manager should view the situation in its entirety and in its context and select the strategy that appears, at this time, to be the most appropriate. Take no further action at this time should be selected only when the threat manager assesses the situation as no risk. Similarly, watch and wait as the initial strategy also works only with low-risk situations. Watch and wait, though, is very effective as a follow-on when other strategies are used. Third-party control and monitoring can be effective, always providing that the third party can be trusted. Subject interviews to refocus or assist work if the threat manager can become point of contact for the target or the threat manager has the ability to assist in resolving the subject's problems.

Subject interview for warning or confrontation crosses the border into the confrontational strategies. The threat manager should warn or confront only if he or she has the ability to back up the warning or confrontation. Civil orders are especially risky, particularly after the Supreme Court's 2005 decision gutting them. Administrative orders are what organizations and institutions do best, so they will undoubtedly become the strategy of choice for those threat managers working within organizational or institutional settings. Mental health commitments are increasingly difficult because of budget cuts. They apply only to subjects clearly evincing mental health problems. Arrest, the most confrontational strategy of all, also applies only to subjects who have committed a crime that the threat manager can prove. In sum, threat managers have a wide spectrum of strategies from which to select the most appropriate for the situation confronting the threat manager at this time.

Situation Analysis: A Loser's Shot at "Redemption"

"A life of wrong turns," three reporters writing for the New York Times described it, rather generously. By any objective measure, Ismaaiyl Brinsley lived the life of a natural-born loser. Growing up from a broken home, he bounced from family member to family member around the country. He suffered from mental illness and could not hold a steady job; indeed, his arrest record—20 arrests and numerous jail sentences—prevented most job opportunities. Brinsley had frequent, near constant, run-ins with the police for petty thefts (such as shoplifting a pair of scissors, a power inverter, and a box of Trojan condoms) and other mundane crimes. He engaged in abusive short-lived relationships with women, fathering two children by separate mothers he could not afford to take care of. He even failed once in trying to hang himself. In May 2014, friends pistol-whipped him while robbing him, leaving him devastated at the betrayal. "Mr. Brinsley," the New York Times reporters opined, "seemed to be a grandstander at the end of his tether, homeless, jobless, and hopeless." At the end, he took a desperate leap toward grandiosity. Typically for him, he again fell far short.*

Coincidentally, Brinsley neared the end of that tether near the height of a nationwide controversy over several incidents of apparent police abuse. In July 2014, several New York City policemen, using a prohibited chokehold, grappled Eric Garner to the ground and held him on his stomach. He died moments later of asphyxiation. A month later, on August 9, in Ferguson, Missouri, a police officer shot and killed Michael Brown, an unarmed black teenager. Many believed Brown, hands up in the air, tried to surrender. Protests nationwide erupted, with protestors remaining in Ferguson for over a week. Property damage and looting expressed the protestors disgust. Going into the fall, other incidents of police violence kept up the anger. In South Carolina, police shot a man handcuffed and in custody in the back of a police car. In neighboring North Carolina, a policeman shot a man after ordering him to get his car registration out of the glove box. The officer fired as the man leaned into the car to retrieve the document. Police in Cleveland, Ohio, killed a young boy carrying a toy gun. Then in December, the grand juries hearing the evidence in the Eric Garner death and the one hearing the Michael Brown evidence both declined to hand up indictments. Protests flared anew.

---

* Barker, K., Secret, M., & Fausset, R. (2015, January 2). Many identities of New York officers' killer in a life of wrong turns. New York Times.

Brinsley expressed no interest in the incidents or in the protests, although many of his friends were "ardent antipolice activists." Instead, Brinsley focused on his own troubled, failed life. Now 28, he told the mother of his second child in early December that if he could not get his life together, he would kill himself. Later that month, Brinsley traveled from Atlanta to Baltimore, Maryland, to visit his sometime girlfriend, Shaneka Thompson, who lived in nearby Owings Mill. He let himself into her apartment with his key. Shortly after, he pulled out an automatic pistol and held it to his head, telling her he would kill himself. She talked him out of it, but then they got into an argument. He shot her in the stomach, grabbed her cell phone, and fled the building. Back in Baltimore, he boarded a bus bound for New York City. During the 3-hour drive, Brinsley repeatedly called Thompson's mother to find out if she still lived. He begged the mother to believe him that the shooting was accidental. But he knew, whether accidental or not, a convicted felon could not remain on the street after shooting someone. And he knew, too, that this time, he would be off the street for a very long time. The prospects of getting his life together evaporated as soon as he pulled the trigger.*

As his life seemed to crumble around him on the bus to New York City, Brinsley clung to the one positive life buoy he had remaining—his ego. Suddenly, he latched onto the antipolice protests, linking his life to the terrible injustices raining down on Black men in America. Brinsley started sending out Instagram messages to everyone he knew posing himself as the Great Avenger who would gain justice for Brown and Garner and all the other victims of police brutality. Typically for him, he misspelled Garner's name. "I'm Putting Wings on Pigs Today. They Take 1 Of Ours... Let's Take 2 of Theirs #ShootThePolice #RIPErivGardner #RIPMike Brown," Brinsley boldly broadcast.[†] Early that afternoon, the bus arrived in New York City.

Once off the bus, Brinsley took the subway to Bedford-Stuyvesant. He got off near the intersection of Myrtle and Tompkins Avenues. Walking down the street, he ran into two men. Stopping them, he asked them what gang they belonged to. He gave them his Instagram address and urged the two to follow him on it. He added that they should watch what he was about to do. Brinsley crossed the street and came up behind and on the passenger side of an idling police car in which two officers sat in the front seat. Brinsley fired four shots, hitting each officer twice in the head and upper body. Brinsley fled the scene, ending up on an elevated train platform where he finally succeeded in killing himself with a shot to the head.*

Issues of Interest

1. In analyzing instances of intended violence, we frequently see individuals whose lives are in a tailspin who connect to a high-profile social issue to which they link their violent act in a desperate effort to link their problems to some higher cause.
2. The true goal is to somehow elevate their desperate existence through association with a higher and nobler movement. In their mind, they much prefer assuming the

---

* Barker, K., & Baker, A. (2014, December 21). New York officers' killer, adrift and ill, had a plan. *New York Times*.
† Mueller, B., & Baker, A. (2014, December 20). Two N.Y.P.D. officers are killed in Brooklyn ambush; Suspect commits suicide. *New York Times*.

role of crusader or martyr to gain a spot on the front pages than being portrayed as just another petty criminal buried in the court docket.

3. In Brinsley's case, he used the antipolice brutality movement as a justification for assassinating two unsuspecting police officers in New York City, knowing full well the publicity such an assault would bring. He no doubt hoped that his final act of bravado would overshadow his previous behavior culminating with the shooting of his girlfriend.

4. Even though he perceived shooting Thompson as an accident, he knew it did not matter and that he would be sent back to prison for a very long time. Already despondent over his lack of success in life, Brinsley decided to go out in a blaze of glory. He no doubt fantasized that friends and strangers would remember his singular, selfless act of protest and not the triteness of getting caught stealing condoms or accidentally shooting his girlfriend or his failure to hang himself.

5. In the final hours of his life, Brinsley found a cause. It did not even matter if he truly believed in it or not. All that mattered was the cause put him on a higher platform that took him out of his own mundane existence and gave his death some purpose beyond failure.

6. Brinsley leaked his intentions to strangers he met on the street and through the Internet just before carrying out the act. We consider this type of leakage as a final act behavior. It should never be ignored.

Identifying the
Howlers and Hunters

Introducing Hunters versus Howlers

5

We live in a time of heightened security concerns. Magnetometers, x-ray machines, surveillance cameras, bomb dogs, explosive trace detection machines, security guards, specially treated windows, vehicle barricades, vehicle searches, and countless other physical security countermeasures have become so commonplace that they now fit seamlessly into our environment and our daily lives. Corporations have been forced to accept liability for providing their employees a secure workplace. Police officers routinely patrol public schools while school staffs conduct not just fire drills but also emergency drills to prepare students in the event of an active shooter.* Public figures and public officials surround themselves with security details. Having a bodyguard is no longer a status symbol, but a protective necessity. The emphasis on security even reaches into people's intimate lives. Nowadays, most jurisdictions no longer tolerate spousal abuse. The police response to domestic disturbance calls now requires arresting at least one of the spouses if the responding officers detect any evidence of physical injury to either spouse. Not even celebrities are immune. In April 2014, New Canaan, Connecticut, police arrested singer-songwriter Paul Simon and his wife, another singer and both Grammy winners, on domestic violence charges after the couple had a fight at their home.† Security concerns touch everyone where they live, work, and play.

The United States, indeed the entire world, reached this state of affairs partly in response to attacks from terrorists, both foreign and domestic. However, policymakers began recognizing the need for increased security more than 3 decades ago, long before the threat of terrorism reached its current level. Violence serves many masters, not just those who use it for political, religious, or ideological goals. Indeed, the increased need for good security directly results from the increased use of violence by all sorts of individuals seeking different purposes. During just 10 days in November 2005 selected randomly, several incidents occurred that illustrate the scope of the problem:

- On November 12, Christopher Millis, despondent over the breakup of his marriage, first tried to set fire to several police cars parked at a Salem, Oregon, police station, then drove to the home of a neighbor with whom he had had a long-running dispute. Arriving at the neighbor's house, Millis shot at the neighbor's car. Millis drove back into town and crashed his pickup through the front entrance of the county courthouse. He held police officers at bay for several hours before they shot him.‡

---

* During fire drills, the students leave the school. During emergency drills, they take cover in their classrooms.
† Fitzsimmons, E. G., & Cowan, A. L. (2014, April 28). Paul Simon and Edie Brickell in court over domestic dispute. *New York Times*.
‡ Rico, G., & Carboni, D. (2005, November 13). Police shooting ends Salem standoff. *Salem (OR) Statesman Journal*.

- On November 13, 18-year-old David Ludwig killed the parents of his 14-year-old girlfriend, then fled the scene with her. They drove from her home in Lancaster, Pennsylvania, to Belleville, Indiana before police identified the car and forced them to stop. He confessed to intentionally killing the parents because they forbade him from seeing their daughter. She confessed to willingly going with him.*
- On November 20, Dominick Maldonado sent a text message to his former girlfriend announcing, "Today is the day that the world will know my anger." As he entered the Tacoma, Washington, shopping mall, he telephoned police and told them to "just follow the screams" to find him. Then he opened fire, wounding six shoppers and holding four people hostage for 4 hours before surrendering. The ex-girlfriend thought he had been on Ecstasy.†
- On November 21, school officials at Northern Valley Regional High School in Old Tappan, New Jersey, closed the school for a day in response to an instant message one of their students had received over the previous weekend. The message, sent from an ex-student now living in the former Soviet Union, said, "I just bought my new Glock handgun and you better watch out." The instant messenger added, "Everybody at [the high school] ought to be careful." The message also mentioned attacking the high school. Despite the vast distance between Kazakhstan and New York, officials refused to take any chances.‡
- On November 23, Joseph Cobb returned to H&M Wagner and Sons in Anne Arundel County, Maryland. He had been fired from there a couple of weeks earlier. Upon entering the building, he ran into Raymond Himes, whom he immediately shot in the arm. Cobb then went directly to his former supervisor's office. He shouted a profanity at the supervisor, then shot him twice in the stomach. After that, Cobb left the building. Once outside, he killed himself. His two victims survived. "The incident appeared to highlight the issue of workplace violence, which began to attract national attention about 20 years ago," the *Washington Post* report of the incident noted, "It has become a major concern for advocates of worker safety."§

Neither time nor season lessened the violence. Five months later, we took another 10-day period during which various newspapers reported the following acts of violence:

- On April 9, 2006, Brian L. Patterson, beating Omar Gonzalez by 8 years, scaled the iron fence surrounding the White House and ran toward the mansion, screaming, "I am a victim of terrorism." Secret Service agents and uniformed guards gave chase with guns drawn, finally cornering him near the row of cameras set up for the daily White House news reports. "I have intelligence information for the president," Patterson told his pursuers, "I'm not afraid of you." The April 9 incident was the fourth time Patterson had gotten onto the White House grounds.¶

---

* Police: Ludwig's computer holds crime plans. (2005, November 22). CNN.com.
† Ellison, J., Frey, C., & Chansanchal, A. (2005, November 21). Shooting at Tacoma mall leaves 7 injured. *Seattle Post-Intelligencer.* Castro, H., Ellison, J., & Cat Le, P. (2005, November 22). Tacoma mall gunman warned police via 911. *Seattle Post-Intelligencer.*
‡ N.J. school shut after student threatened. (2005, November 22). Associated Press.
§ Rivera, R., & Weil, M. (2005, November 24). Former employee shoots 2 at office. *Washington Post.*
¶ Man jumps White House fence. (2006, April 9). Associated Press.

- On April 14, in Buffalo, New York, Craig Lynch, a convicted car thief living at a halfway house for recently released prisoners, killed Sister Klimczak, the nun who had run the halfway house for 16 years. Lynch had been paroled 3 months earlier. When Sister Klimczak caught Lynch in her room, he strangled and hit her. Once she was dead, Lynch borrowed a car from a relative and took the body to a shed behind a vacant house near his mother's home. He buried her there in a shallow grave.*

- On April 14 in Purcell, Oklahoma, police arrested Kevin Underwood for the first-degree murder of a 10-year-old girl. Underwood led police to a closet in his apartment where he had stuffed the body in a plastic tub sealed with duct tape. Authorities accused Underwood of killing the girl, then sexually assaulting her. Finding meat tenderizer and barbecue skewers in his apartment, the police believed he intended to eat the corpse.†

- On April 16, in Corinth, Maine, Stephen A. Marshall went to the homes of two of Maine's registered sex offenders and killed both men. Marshall got their home addresses from the Maine website listing the names and addresses of registered sex offenders living in the state. He also visited four other addresses where offenders lived, but did not find them home. Later that day, armed with three pistols, Marshall boarded a bus for Boston. Police stopped the bus just outside the city. When officers went on board looking for Marshall, he shot himself in the head. He died several hours later.‡

- On April 17 in Platte City, Missouri, police arrested two teenagers for threatening to carry out a school shooting on the seventh anniversary of the Columbine attack. The two students had told at least five classmates they intended to assault the Platte County R-3 High School. Their plan included planting explosives and bringing firearms to the school.§

- On April 18 in St. Louis, Missouri, Herbert L. Chalmers killed his girlfriend at her apartment, then drove to the local Walmart to replenish his ammunition. While reloading the pistol, he told a sales clerk he had just killed his girlfriend and was on his way to shoot his employer. The clerk alerted police, but they were too late. Chalmers arrived at Finninger's Catering Service, from which he had been fired the day before, looking for the owner. Instead, he ran into the owner's wife and daughter. After shooting them, Chalmers killed himself.¶

Jihadists hold no monopoly on acts of violence. Violence affects every social venue, from domestic settings to schools and workplaces to government facilities to public figures and officials. No social venue seems safe. Violence, too, crosses over the venues. No doubt Paul Simon and his wife have suffered stalking and harassment for being public figures, but even they have private lives into which violence crept.

Geographic location offers no immunity, either. The November and April incidents occurred in small towns and big cities, on both coasts and in between. They took place in people's homes and at workplaces, schools, even shopping malls. None had anything to do with a political, religious, or ideological agenda, but all inspired terror in their targets.

---

* Staba, D. (2006, April 18). Angel for ex-convicts is killed at halfway house she ran. *New York Times*.
† Okla. man charged with 1st-degree murder. (2006, April 18). Associated Press.
‡ Ranalli, R., & Heinz, H. (2006, April 17). Man tied to 2 deaths kills self aboard bus. *Boston Globe*; Mac Daniel. (2006, April 18). Suspect in killing wasn't screened boarding bus. *Boston Globe*.
§ MO. teens charged in school shooting plot. (2006, April 18). Associated Press.
¶ Bryan, B. (2006, April 18). Man goes on shooting spree, then kills himself. *St. Louis Post-Dispatch*.

Over the last several decades, increases in security countermeasures directly responded to increases in this type of violence, both in terms of the number of incidents and in the spread of violence to different social venues. Those responsible for maintaining security at any social venue need to understand how problem individuals behave. That includes those who intend to engage in violence. It also includes how howlers behave. The need for understanding both arises from simple necessity. Anyone who provides security will encounter both hunters and howlers. It's the nature of the beast.

Violence between individuals or groups can be either intended or impromptu. This study deals only with those who plan to create a problem, either by committing lethal violence or by threatening or harassing a particular target. It does not address impromptu violence, which requires an altogether different security response.

Although thieves commit acts of intended violence, we do not include violence related to armed robbery or thefts in our sample. Our hunters can be as greedy as any thief, but their motivations derive from other reasons, usually related to their personal needs and the social venue in which they operate. Thus, when we discuss workplace violence, we do not include armed robberies of convenience store clerks or taxi drivers. Rather, our definition focuses on acts of violence by current or former employees, vendors, customers, patients, clients, or by someone personally involved with a current or former employee, such as a spouse or intimate. The motives of these individuals, although infinitely varied, can be generalized in that the subject sees himself or herself as a victim of some real or perceived injustice or insult. That injustice may be that the subject lacks money, such as in a dispute over an inheritance, alimony, or child support, but the purpose of the violence goes beyond lifting the target's wallet or grabbing the Rolex watch. The hunters we study may well want personal gain, but they want even more that the gain be at the expense of their target. These hunters seek to right a perceived wrong.

Balancing Physical Security and Threat Management

Adequately securing against acts of intended violence cannot depend solely on physical security countermeasures. They provide only half the defense because they do little to *prevent* attacks. Instead, physical security is designed to discourage or mitigate assaults at a specific location. Magnetometers, for example, do not prohibit an individual from carrying a firearm; the machine simply alerts its operator that the person has something metallic on his or her person. Good personal protection specialists try to intercept suspicious individuals, but they rely on taking action in the last few seconds before an attack, which the hunter may have spent months planning and preparing. Surveillance cameras record what is happening, but they do not stop it. Physical security measures are like the castle walls the assailant must breach, imposing but immobile and useless once scaled.

On July 28, 2000, Aaron A. Commey, with pistol drawn, darted through the passenger security screening checkpoint at John F. Kennedy Airport in New York. The contract screeners all saw him and his pistol. They raised the alarm but made no effort to stop him. He had a gun; they did not. Police responded within the required 3 minutes, but by then, Commey had boarded a plane at Gate 33 and calmly walked into the cockpit. He held the pilot and copilot hostage for 2 hours before surrendering.* Then, as now, security screening

---

* Sullivan, J., & Kennedy, R. (2000, July 29). Armed intruder exposes limits of air security. *New York Times*.

only alerts on prohibited items such as pistols. It was never designed to prevent weapons going through it. As the *New York Times* pointed out:

> Airport security checkpoints, with their squads of guards and phalanxes of metal detectors, are considered by many passengers to be a kind of firewall, designed to stop weapons from getting anywhere near airplanes. But airline security officials have long acknowledged that the checkpoints are really meant to do only part of that job: they are supposed to detect hidden guns or bombs and provide a system for alerting armed police officers. If someone brandishes a gun and tries to force his way past, the officials said, the unarmed security officers at the checkpoints are not only unable to stop him, they are not supposed to.*

The best that physical security countermeasures can do is raise the alarm and perhaps make it more difficult for someone to bring a weapon into a secure area. But as Aaron Commey demonstrated, the level of difficulty is usually not set very high.

And what happens when someone targets the security officers themselves? On November 1, 2013, Paul Ciancia went to the Los Angeles Airport armed with a semi-automatic rifle intending to kill Transportation Security Administration transportation security officers (TSOs) manning the security checkpoints in Terminal 3. He killed TSO Gararado Hernandez and wounded three others—all unarmed—before police subdued him. The magnetometers sounded the alarm as Ciancia rushed into the secure area of the terminal seeking more TSOs, but only armed police could ultimately stop him.†

Armed security guards help, but even they have limitations. On February 5, 2001, Willie Dan Baker approached the guard shack protecting the entrance to the Navistar engineering plant outside Chicago. The company had fired Baker 6 years earlier for theft. He was due to report to prison the next day to begin serving a 5-month sentence for the crime. Carrying a golf bag loaded with an assault rifle, a shotgun, and a hunting rifle, he told the guard that he had some personal belongings he wanted to return to a friend. The guard recognized him and refused to let him in, offering instead to call the friend out. Baker pulled a .38 caliber pistol and forced her to unlock the gate, which she did. Inside the plant, Baker began firing, killing four and wounding four of his former colleagues.‡ The guard chose to remain outside the plant.

Security checkpoints manned with armed guards essentially force the hunter to start the gunfight at that location. When Jack Gary McKnight attacked the federal court facilities in Topeka, Kansas, on August 5, 1993, his first shot killed the court security officer manning the checkpoint.§ Similarly, Robert L. House also began, and ended, his October 1996 assault on the Mobile, Alabama, local courthouse by shooting at the guards manning the checkpoint at the front entrance. He killed one guard and wounded another before the guards and police returned fire and killed him.¶ Russell Weston circumvented security at

---

* Sullivan, J., & Kennedy, R. (2000, July 29). Armed intruder exposes limits of air security. *New York Times.*
† Mather, K., & Winton, R. (2015, January 2). Prosecutors to seek death penalty in fatal LAX shooting. *Los Angeles Times.*
‡ *FBI study of active shooters*, p. 22.
§ Calhoun, F. S. (1998). *Hunters and howlers: Threats and violence against Federal Judicial Officials in the United States, 1979–1993* (pp. 1–3). Washington, DC: United States Marshal Service.
¶ Curiously, the security officers at the Mobile courthouse were a kind of Barney Fife hybrid between armed and unarmed guards. The chief judge, who had responsibility for courthouse security, allowed the officers to have pistols and bullets, but no bullets in the pistols. Their response to House was delayed while they loaded their weapons. Gunman killed, guard slain in courthouse shootout. (1996, September 26). AP News Archive.

the nation's Capitol by shooting his way through the magnetometer in July 1998. Capitol police responded, but they could not prevent Weston from getting well into the building and killing two of their own.* On June 20, 2005, Perry L. Manley used an inert hand grenade to try and bluff his way past the magnetometers guarding the Seattle, Washington, federal courthouse. Court security officers contained him just at the fringes of the secure area. Police negotiated with him for 25 minutes. When Manley made "a furtive movement," police officers opened fire.[†] In planning where to position security checkpoints, one question to always answer is, "Where do we want the battle to begin?"

Allowing armed officers inside a secure area presents its own risks. On March 11, 2005, Brian Nichols, on trial and in custody for rape, overpowered the Fulton County, Georgia, deputy sheriff who was escorting him back to court. Nichols took the key to the gun locker where the deputy had stored her weapon. Armed with it, Nichols went to the courtroom. He killed the presiding judge and the court reporter. Nichols killed another deputy sheriff outside the courthouse as he escaped. The next day, Nichols killed an unsuspecting federal agent. Hours later, he surrendered to police.[‡]

Who Needs Managing?

Threat management involves managing two very different types of individuals. One group consists of hunters. They truly intend to use lethal violence to aggrieve some perceived injustice. Hunters develop a reason for committing violence, come up with the idea to do so, research and plan their attack, prepare for it, then breach their target's security and actually attack. Whatever their reason, those who intend to act violently go through the process of intended violence.

The other groups that threat managers must manage are howlers. They like to threaten and frighten with words or to express some unrequited emotional attachment, but they never follow through with any actions. In effect, howlers intend to cause fear or gain attention to themselves through threats, alarming statements, or some expression of a need to be recognized by the target. Howlers are best understood within the context of their relationship with their targets combined with what they seek to accomplish through their inappropriate communications. Those relationships are either *personal* or *impersonal*. That is, either the howler personally knows his or her target or the howler and the target are strangers to one another.

Personal howlers seek to control or intimidate their targets. They use threats, confrontations, gestures, messages, symbolic acts, and loaded references as a way of getting the target to do what they want. Frequently, personal howlers communicate in person with the target. That physical presence becomes part of the intimidation, but it ends there, with words and empty gestures, not lethal physical attacks.

Impersonal howlers usually seek to gain some kind of attention to themselves or they seek a reaction from their target. They almost always communicate from a distance. That

---

* Miller, B. (1999, April 23). Capitol shooter's mind-set detailed. *Washington Post.*
† Castro, H., & Langston, J. (2005, June 21). Child support behind courthouse shooting. *Seattle Post-Intelligencer.*
‡ Cook, R. (2005, March 27). Trial rules to be set for Nichols. *Atlanta Journal-Constitution*; Shootings, missteps hurt Atlanta's image. (2005, March 20). Associated Press.

is, howlers who focus on celebrities or public figures or individuals whom they have never met rarely confront their targets up close and in person. They prefer to keep their distance writing letters, sending e-mails, making telephone calls, texting, blogging, or using some other method that maintains a safe distance between howler and target. Since their purpose is to frighten, disturb, or get attention, they have no need to get close to their targets. Whatever their motive or social venue, personal and impersonal howlers *make* threats or other inappropriate communications, but they never actually *pose* a threat.

Both personal and impersonal howlers seek one of two outcomes with their inappropriate communications. Either they want to inspire fear and unease in their target or they want to establish or bind some relationship with the target, even if that means doing so by intimidation. We call the former *sinister* howlers and the latter *binder* howlers. Sinister howlers use threats, intimidations, and ominous communications as psychological warfare against their targets. Binder howlers express their infatuations and obsessions toward their targets. For both sinister and binder howlers, the nature of the relationships with their targets largely controls how, when, and where they make their inappropriate communications.

We use the terms *hunters* and *howlers* as shorthand for much more complex concepts. The concept of hunter refers to individuals who engage in *attack-related* behaviors. The concept of howler refers to individuals who engage in behaviors designed to unnerve or prompt emotional reactions or gain attention to themselves, but which do not culminate in violence. Throughout this study, we consistently focus on what individuals do, the actions or inactions they deliberately take. We do not offer psychological analyses, nor do we speculate about motives or driving forces. Rather, our interest focuses on the behaviors that threat managers can look for in identifying individuals who act like hunters and those who act like howlers. Behaviors are noticeable only if the observer is knowledgeable and in a position to notice them. For that reason, how the individual acts offers the best window into his or her intent.

Fortunately, a very simple rule distinguishes hunters from howlers. Hunters hunt and rarely howl; howlers howl and rarely hunt.* This simple analogy expresses a fundamental maxim of threat management: Hunters and howlers behave differently. What individuals do provides the best indicator for determining whether they plan violence or inappropriate communications. Actions distinguish hunters and howlers. Focusing on that distinction enables us to identify, assess, and manage those who hunt and those who howl.

The twin concepts apply to all venues where intended violence occurs. These include domestic situations, workplaces and schools, judicial settings, public figure assaults, hate crimes, even acts of terrorism. Think of the most notorious hunters, political murderers like Lee Harvey Oswald, random killers like Son of Sam, school shooters like Eric Harris and Dylan Klebold, terrorists like Muhammad Atta and his gang, or employees who "go postal."† Each of these hunters and their cohorts engaged in intended violence. This brief list alone amply illustrates the cross-venue nature of intended violence and those who perpetrate it.

---

* Calhoun, F. S. (1998). *Hunters and howlers: Threats and violence against Federal Judicial Officials in the United States, 1979–1993* (p. xix). Washington, DC: United States Marshal Service.
† According to a study on workplace violence within the postal service, "going postal" is a myth. See Califano et al. (2000). *Report of the United States Postal Service Commission on a safe and secure workplace* (p. 1). New York: National Center on Addiction and Substance Abuse.

Howlers, too, harass or cause fear or trouble in every venue. Sinister howlers communicate their anger and frustration in schools, on the job, and against public figures and public institutions. Binder howlers delude themselves into believing they have or should have some emotional attachment to a school or workmate or a public figure. Although howlers do not pose a risk of physical violence, they nonetheless represent a significant challenge both for their targets, who must endure their intimidations, harassments, and obsessions, and for security personnel, who must find appropriate and effective ways to manage them.

The cross-venue nature of both hunters and howlers strongly suggests that neither the target nor the setting defines who hunts and who howls. Both operate in every setting, choosing their targets for their own reasons. Threat managers need to understand that neither hunters nor howlers face restrictions within any social venue. Still, regardless of venue, howlers act like howlers; hunters act like hunters.

Consequently, threat managers must look at behaviors as the best means of identifying and assessing problem individuals, whether hunters or howlers. Managing entails controlling or manipulating the subject's future behaviors. Decades of research confirm that intended violence culminates a series of attack-related behaviors, specific actions that an individual (or group) must take to launch a physical assault. Years of experience with howlers show that they, too, exhibit their own unique traits and behaviors. Both hunters and howlers can be readily identified by analyzing what they do in terms of what is known about the distinguishing behaviors of each group. Recognizing them for who they are guides the threat management response.

Both hunters and howlers present problems for security, although in very different ways. Hunters represent serious physical risks; howlers cause mental and emotional distress. By seeing the differences between them, threat managers can better allocate limited resources while pinpointing their efforts directly on the more serious security problems raised by hunters. Although threat managers cannot ignore howlers, the problems they cause are frustrating and disruptive, not menacing. Howlers who threaten intend to instill fear in their targets. Too often, they succeed. To the extent they succeed, they compel the threat manager to expend time and resources reassuring the targets and investigating the howler. Other howlers communicate their feelings or improbable demands, sometimes romantic, toward their targets. The problem they pose grows out of the feeling of unease and distress they cause their targets. The communications of both types of howlers must be monitored in case they change. Great care, too, must be taken to ensure that no action or inaction on the part of either the target or the threat manager unintentionally turns the howler into a hunter. Consequently, successful threat management of problem individuals, whether hunters or howlers, requires flexible responses, intelligent assessments, and the intuitive ability to distinguish between those who *pose* threats from those who make them.

Purpose of Section II: Identifying the Howlers and Hunters

This part of the book offers threat managers an in-depth, practical description of how hunters behave compared with how howlers behave. That knowledge can then be applied to the threat management process for identifying, assessing, and managing problem individuals or threatening situations. This part of the book will help threat managers identify key behaviors, improve their assessments, and enhance their threat management skills.

Section II focuses on recognizable behaviors because only through recognizing the different ways hunters and howlers behave can threat managers identify those individuals posing the greatest threat and those simply making threats. The concept of hunters versus howlers is understandable enough and potent enough to equip threat managers with a way to distinguish among individuals who intend violence and those who intend only to voice their outrage or demand recognition. Making that distinction will help focus resources on those who pose the most danger, not simply those who make the most threats.

Furthermore, we go to great lengths to acknowledge differences among the different venues for intended violence. Indeed, in the Appendix, we publish an essay by Debra M. Jenkins describing in detail how the *intimacy effect* affects the value of threatening statements in the different venues of intended violence. Jenkins decided to test a hypothesis we originally made in *Contemporary Threat Management.** In that book, we suggested that the value of threats as preincident indicators of violence increased in proportion to the degree of intimacy or interpersonal relationship between the threatener and the target. Jenkins reviewed a vast number of research studies on the various venues of intended violence and concluded that our hypothesis had the support of actual research. The intimacy effect is real.

That reality means that threat managers cannot simply dismiss reports of threatening language. Rather, the threat manager must assess every inappropriate communication. Part of that assessment has to include understanding the social relationship between the threatener and the target. Do they have an interpersonal or intimate relationship? Are they strangers to each other? How does the subject perceive his or her relationship with the target? Factoring these questions into the assessment allows the threat manager to measure the influence of the intimacy effect.

Our concept of hunters and howlers rests firmly on the premise that regardless of target or setting, individuals who intend violence must engage in attack-related behaviors. The intimacy effect means only that in certain social venues, making threats can be an attack-related behavior. In other venues, it is not. In all venues, howlers merely howl. When they direct their howls at a stranger or public figure, they almost always do so from a distance. In interpersonal relationships, such as domestic settings, workplaces, or schools, sinister howlers frequently threaten or intimidate in person. However, doing so ultimately puts them at risk of carrying out the threat lest their target conclude the howler is bluffing. For this reason, the intimacy effect enhances the value of threats as preincident indicators of violence in interpersonal relationships. Fortunately, the disparate behaviors between hunters and howlers are recognizable. Once recognized and reported, the threat manager can assess them, then he or she can select the most appropriate threat management strategies to defuse the risk and deal with the subject.

In this chapter, we introduce the concept of hunters and howlers and explain the purpose of the book. Our emphasis is on providing practical, real-world concepts and strategies that threat managers can use to identify, assess, and manage both hunters and howlers.

In Chapter 6, we define precisely what we mean by the terms *hunter* and *howler.* The chapter also addresses the significant difference between merely communicating inappropriately compared with taking action in furtherance of acting violently. The chapter concludes with a discussion about howlers versus hunters.

---

* Calhoun, F. S., & Weston, S. W. (2003). *Contemporary threat management: A practical guide to identifying, assessing, and managing individuals of violent intent* (pp. 41–49). San Diego, CA: Specialized Training Services.

Chapter 7 focuses on how hunters behave. Relying on actual case examples, it plots out the path hunters must take to consummate their intent to turn to violence. The chapter reviews the process of intended violence, which we call *the path to intended violence*. It starts with grievance, then ideation, research and planning, preparations, breach of security, and attack. For each step along the path, we describe specific types of behaviors related to that step. The descriptions are not meant to be exhaustive. Human behavior is too infinitely varied to allow for that. Rather, the purpose of the chapter is to provide real-life examples illustrating what attack-related behaviors look and feel like. In addition, Chapter 7 discusses the importance of weighing the impact of the intimacy effect on hunters in the different venues. In other words, any identification of a hunter must take into account not only the individual under evaluation but also the social setting in which he or she is acting.

Chapter 8 develops a typology for understanding howlers and then defines various types of howlers and how they behave. The chapter identifies two distinct species of howlers: personal and impersonal. We further subdivide each species into either sinister or binder. Unlike hunters, both species of howlers have no set course they must follow. Consequently, they behave in more diffuse ways, although none of their actions, save their threats, are attack related.

Chapter 9 provides a kind of executive summary of the research conducted by Debra Jenkins on the intimacy effect. It quotes a number of observations she reached on the several venues of intended violence and shows how the intimacy effect works, depending on the interpersonal relationship between subject and target. Further, the chapter discusses the disconnect between the laws punishing threats and the current research on threats as preincident indicators of violence.

Chapter 10 assimilates the lessons from the previous chapters to explore such issues as identifying the rare but important instances when a howler becomes a hunter. It also describes several general principles for managing both hunters and howlers.

In support of the discussion in Chapter 9 of threats and the intimacy effect, the Appendix contains an essay by Debra M. Jenkins that reviews the research bearing on the intimacy effect. We publish it here to emphasize that the threat manager must always keep the effects of interpersonal relationships in mind when assessing threatening situations. Hunters and howlers who personally know their targets have certain advantages and disadvantages from hunters and howlers whose targets are strangers. Research shows that knowing the target personally has profound effects on such behaviors as threats, time and place of attack, and vehemence of the assault. Threats to public figures have entirely different outcomes from threats to intimates. Consequently, threat assessments must measure the interpersonal and social relationship between subject and target.

As we did at the end of each chapter in Section I, in Section II, we again present actual situation analyses to illustrate how the hunter and howler concepts apply to real-life threat management situations. In the situations presented in Section II, we follow a threat management approach, treating each situation as if it were presented to a trained threat manager. Each analysis begins with a synopsis of the relevant facts. These facts form the basis for the threat assessment. Based on that assessment, the analysis recommends a range of protective responses. It also suggests the most appropriate threat management strategies to deploy. The analysis concludes with a description of what happened once the protective response and management strategy took effect. We believe that the synopsis, assessment, protective response, and threat management strategy serve as a useful, practical template for documenting each threat management case.

Throughout the book, we strive to offer practical concepts, practical methods, and practical tools threat managers can use daily starting immediately. To be clear, we do not offer any quick fixes or easy solutions for the complex problems of managing both hunters and howlers. Instead, we present a specific approach and concise way of thinking about a very difficult and tangled issue. We believe that following this way of thinking about the issues will better equip threat managers to do their jobs, but that is not to say our ideas make that job any easier. Threats and threatening situations are never managed easily. They require much care and attention, creative responses, quick thinking, and infinite flexibility.

Summary

In this chapter, we introduced the concepts of intended violence and the various venues in which it can occur. Through numerous examples, we illustrated the widespread, cross-venue nature of intended violence and its potential impact on anyone responsible for providing security. Next, we discussed the crucial need to balance physical security countermeasures with a sound threat management process. Both are needed equally; neither fully works alone.

In addition, we broached the idea of an individual *acting like a hunter* and an individual *acting like a howler*. We further explained the importance of focusing on behaviors and subject actions as the best way for the threat manager to assess whether or not the subject at hand should be managed as a hunter or as a howler. The chapter concluded with a brief overview and synopsis of each chapter in Section II and the Appendix. Our theme has been to provide threat managers with practical ideas and approaches that they can invest in their threat management processes.

Situation Analysis: The Poacher

The Facts

In the Spring of 2003, a California Fish and Game warden caught Charles and his friend Terry poaching salmon near a fish hatchery in Northern California. At their court appearance 3 months later, a local judge fined each $1,600. The judge lectured the two men about the nature of their offense and warned them not to repeat the crime.

According to Terry, on the ride home, Charles described how offended he was by the fine and the lecture. He began talking to Terry about getting even. Over the next 2 days, Charles outlined to Terry several violent scenarios such as killing the judge by shooting him or placing an explosive device under his car. Charles also suggested burning down the courthouse, blowing up the fish hatchery dam, and poisoning the hatchery water.

On the third day, Charles sketched out a plan for building an explosive device made of pipe, gunpowder, and a thermostat as the trigger. He and Terry tested a thermostat to determine whether it generated enough voltage to set off the device. Charles again sketched out on a piece of paper the components of an explosive device, then burned the paper in the fireplace. He explained to Terry that he intended to pick up materials from construction sites where he worked and buy gunpowder discreetly in small amounts. Further, Charles talked with Terry about the steps Timothy McVeigh took to create a large explosion.

Charles asked Terry to help him on this project by going back to the courthouse to scout out the location of the power and gas entry points and to determine the best place to put an incendiary device. Charles described for Terry how they could make a crude napalm-like substance mixing gasoline, diesel fuel, and liquid detergent.

Terry contacted the Federal Bureau of Investigation (FBI). He had been a paid informant in another part of the country, so he was familiar with how the bureau worked. Terry told the agent to whom he talked about Charles' plans. The agent also learned that Charles had a criminal history including felony convictions for armed robbery, assault with a deadly weapon, and shooting into an inhabited dwelling. The FBI agent quickly arranged to polygraph Terry. Terry's answers indicated no deception.

The Threat Analysis

In cases involving informants, the first assessment to be made is the informant's credibility. Terry had been a credible informant in the past; he passed the polygraph test, and nothing in his current information casts doubt on that credibility. His information is assessed as credible. Therefore, based on the information provided by Terry to date, this assessment concludes that Charles has reached the planning and research stage on the path to intended violence. He is now ready to begin making preparations. He has a grievance against the judge for the fine and the embarrassing lecture, has decided some kind of violence will avenge him, and has begun planning his attack. His criminal history further enhances his risk because it shows he is capable of violence. Charles should be assessed as at high risk of committing some act of violence against the judge or the courthouse.

Recommended Protective Response

The judge should be located and provided a security briefing. Plans should be drawn up to put the judge under physical protection or remove him from the locality in case Charles shifts his attention back to the judge. Security countermeasures should be installed at the courthouse and evacuation plans formulated. As Charles advances farther down the path to intended violence, other security measures should be planned and available to implement.

Recommended Threat Management Strategy

The first threat management strategy to be employed is third-party monitoring through Terry as informant wearing a body wire so law enforcement agents can maintain close surveillance on Charles' planning and preparations. Once sufficient evidence exists as to Charles' final plan and preparations, but before he can implement them, Charles should be arrested. The prosecutor should then seek to keep Charles incarcerated without bail until his trial and conviction. A long prison sentence will defuse the risk Charles poses to the judge and the courthouse.

The Outcome

The FBI agents and California law enforcement accepted the recommended protective responses and threat management strategies. Terry agreed to continue as informant and to wear a body wire. During subsequent recorded conversations, Charles made it clear that burning down the courthouse would be "payback one-thousand-fold" for the grievance he had suffered from the judicial system. With Terry's help, Charles began buying road flares and gunpowder. He also finalized his plan to burn the courthouse with a napalm-like mixture of gasoline, gunpowder, and laundry detergent. On their way to the courthouse, they would stop at a gas station to purchase fuel to pour into used antifreeze containers already packed with liquid detergent. The road flares would be the igniters.

Charles set the date for Saturday night. He sheepishly explained to Terry that his live-in girlfriend would be at the hairdresser at that time, thus sparing him from dealing with her jealousy. He did not want to explain where he was going and what he was doing. Since Charles estimated that it would take nearly 3 hours to drive to the courthouse, set the fire, and drive back, he could sneak away only when his girlfriend was busy somewhere else. Her jealous reaction to his leaving the house without her caused Charles great and near-constant anxiety.

On Saturday evening, Charles and Terry left for the courthouse under both electronic and visual law enforcement surveillance. Charles announced, "Kangaroo court, here we come," as they embarked. During the drive, Charles again went over the plan with Terry. At a gas station, they bought fuel, then drove around back to pour it into the antifreeze containers already holding the liquid detergent. As they left the station, Charles said, "We're ready to rock."

The two would-be arsonists arrived at the courthouse just after dark. After circling the building a couple of times, they parked the car about 75 yards from their target. After donning latex gloves, they wiped the antifreeze jugs free of fingerprints and put open pocket-knives in their pockets. Charles intended to walk to the back of the courthouse, poke holes in the plastic containers, and throw them onto the roof of the one-story building. After letting the gasoline vaporize for a few minutes, they would light the road flares and throw them onto the roof, then run to the car and hurry back to Charles' place before his girlfriend returned.

The two men carried their incendiary devices toward the courthouse. They walked about 50 yards before the waiting law enforcement team intercepted and arrested them. The combination of Terry's testimony, the taped conversations, and the production of the incendiary devices ensured that prosecutors would have no problem keeping Charles in jail without bail. The evidence also easily secured his conviction and a long prison sentence.

Issues of Interest

The events that transpired in this case raise a number of fascinating insights into how this particular hunter behaved.

1. Like many hunters, Charles leaked his intentions to a third party. Fortunately, Terry was able to play his role as FBI informant successfully and Charles never knew until the end that law enforcement was on to him.
2. Without Terry's assistance to law enforcement, Charles' plan would most likely have succeeded. Charles would have had a strong chance of getting away with it.
3. Like many hunters, Charles did not act out in court or make any direct or veiled threats to the judge or the courthouse.

4. Like many hunters, Charles' plans began big and complicated but soon whittled down to simple and effective steps he could take based on his resources and limitations and on the vulnerability of the target.

5. Like many hunters, Charles did not want to get caught. He did many things to prevent detection and not leave evidence.

6. Like many hunters, Charles adjusted his plan to accommodate other factors from his daily life, such as scheduling the arson so as to avoid any suspicious inquiries from his jealous girlfriend.

7. Like many hunters, Charles' grievance was very personal. In similar situations, other individuals would not have been so offended or mortified as to seek vengeance through violence just because a judge fined and lectured them. Grievances, however, are hunter specific.

8. In making the threat assessment, the assessors first had to assess the credibility of the informant. In this case, the informant told the truth, but that is a rarity in threat management cases.

9. In recommending the appropriate protective responses, the assessors had to assume that Charles' focus could shift back to the judge or even to some other target, such as a fish hatchery. In addition to providing security countermeasures for the courthouse, the assessors had to be flexible enough to account for the judge or some other change in plans.

10. In recommending the appropriate threat management strategies, the assessors took full advantage of Terry's cooperation to gather sufficient evidence of criminal misconduct by Charles to ensure a conviction and lengthy prison sentence.

11. In many ways, Charles typified the way hunters behave. Like all hunters, Charles followed the path to intended violence. He developed a grievance, came up with the idea of acting violently, researched how to use the violence, made his preparations, and tried to breach the target's security. And like most hunters, he made mistakes along the way. Too often, threat managers fall prey to the belief that everything goes the way the hunter planned for it to go. Clearly, that is rarely, if ever, the case, so threat managers should be prepared to exploit the mistakes that hunters make. Charles mistakenly trusted Terry, and law enforcement took advantage of that trust. That may be the most valuable lesson the case of the *poacher* can offer.

Defining Hunters and Howlers 6

At the outset, allow us to confess that our definitions of hunters and howlers constitute something of a tautology. By definition, howlers howl and hunters hunt. Howlers never hunt because to do so would transform them into hunters. They would no longer behave the way howlers do, but instead, they would behave the way hunters do. Similarly, hunters who suddenly start howling no longer qualify as hunters; they have become howlers. Thus, the chasm separating hunters from howlers is unbridgeable precisely because crossing the bridge transforms each into the other. Hunters hunt and howlers howl because, again by definition, to behave like the other makes one the other.

Nonetheless, we find the distinction and the definition useful at a practical level because it focuses the threat manager's attention on how the subject behaves. We avoid trying to plumb the minds and motives of either group, preferring to leave that chore to forensic psychologists and psychiatrists. Rather, our approach fits the facts that threat managers confront in the order in which they confront them. The threat manager makes the determination that the subject under assessment is a howler or a hunter based on observable behaviors, not guesswork, profiles, or assumptions about what the subject is thinking or planning. The assessment derives solely from what is known about the subject's behavior and specific actions. The fundamental question the threat manager always asks is whether this subject is *acting like a hunter* or *acting like a howler* at this time.

Hunters usually show themselves by conducting research or engaging in surveillance or stalking or confiding their plans to someone or, worse yet, at the moment they breach security, by attacking. The threat manager must first manage those inappropriate behaviors away from violence or the risk of violence. In doing so, it may help to determine what motivates or drives the subject, but that knowledge is certainly not necessary to manage the subject nor is it always practically available. Indeed, in many cases, the subject's motive may be incomprehensible to everyone except the subject. Nonetheless, the subject's behaviors are both noticeable and comprehensible to the threat manager.

Howlers reveal their hand by expressing themselves to their targets or to others. In impersonal venues, the inappropriate communication is usually at a physical distance from the target, such as by mail, e-mail, telephone, or, more recently, through various social media applications. In interpersonal venues where the howler knows the target or lives, works, or studies in proximity to the target, the howler's communications are frequently made in person. Howlers' motives can be every bit as obtuse as a deluded hunter's, but because they communicate inappropriately, howlers, too, require managing.

In this chapter, we define the twin concepts *acting like a hunter* and *acting like a howler*. We illustrate each concept with numerous examples taken from experience, research, and real events. We focus on practical, observable traits and behaviors that threat managers can use to help them identify whether a subject under assessment acts like a howler or like a hunter. Chapter 7 delves deeper into the characteristics of hunters. Chapter 8 mines the behaviors associated with howling.

Take, for example, the spate of anthrax hoaxes over the past few years involving individuals who mailed envelopes filled with harmless white powder. At first blush, the threat manager might conclude that these subjects were acting like hunters. But deeper reflection suggests that, since their purpose was to frighten and alarm, not injure or kill, they actually fall within the category of howlers. Of course, as a practical matter, these howlers know that until a laboratory tests the powder, authorities cannot take the chance that the powder might be anthrax spores. As a result, with very little effort, the howler achieves the disruption and fear he or she sought by sending the powder. Still, once the lab concludes its analysis, the threat manager can recognize the behavior of a howler. Recognizing hunters from howlers will help the threat manager choose the most appropriate management strategy for each subject, whether hunter or howler.

Our purpose in this and the two following chapters is not to craft a finite checklist of identifiable behaviors, but to paint a broad picture of the ways hunters must behave and the way howlers tend to behave. The infinite variety of human behaviors prevents the creation of effective checklists, profiles, or ready snapshots. Rather, by taking the twin concepts of hunter and howler writ large, threat managers can better assess behaviors and avoid any distractions based on guesses, fears, or generalities. In confronting hunters or howlers, threat managers need to think broadly and put quirky behaviors within the context of hunting or howling.

Hunters Defined and Exemplified

The concept of behaving like a hunter applies to those individuals who act in furtherance of committing intended violence. By the term *intended violence*, we do not mean crimes of either passion or profit. Rather, intended violence involves individuals who resort to violence to resolve grievances they feel they have. It is a calculated and premeditated attempt by the hunter to achieve justice for himself or herself over some perceived injustice. That pursuit of justice, of course, is not based on the standards and mores of justice crafted by society. It is a very personal, event-specific, individually sensitive status defined by the hunter. In other words, justice in these situations is in the eye of the beholder. The grievance inspires the intention to resolve the issue through a violent act.*

Some hunters have old-fashioned motives prompting their attacks, such as a desire for revenge or for some personal gain or advantage. In February 2002, Charles Ott went to a mediation meeting at a lawyer's office in Boca Raton, Florida, armed with a pistol. He and his sister had been disputing who got the most from their parents' estate. Ott killed her, then fled. He went to his parents' former home and killed himself.† In June 2003, in Newburgh, New York, a mother and her two sons purposefully went to a third son's school so they could severely beat the teacher who had suspended him for spitting in the teacher's face.‡ In June 2004, Carl Coleman returned to the Arcadia, Louisiana, chicken plant from which he had recently been fired. A colleague saw Coleman and asked him why he had

---

* Calhoun, F. S., & Weston, S. W. (2003). *Contemporary threat management: A practical guide to identifying, assessing, and managing individuals of violent intent* (pp. 16–17). San Diego, CA: Specialized Training Services.
† Florida man kills sister, kills self. (2002, February 20). Associated Press.
‡ Mother, sons charged with beating teacher. (2003, June 6). Associated Press.

returned. Coleman replied, "I've worked hard for these people and I am going to take care of somebody." That somebody turned out to be the plant manager, whom Coleman killed before wounding himself.[*] Early one morning in late November 2014, Larry McQuilliams went on a shooting spree in downtown Austin, Texas, aiming at government buildings such as the police headquarters and the federal courthouse, firing over 100 rounds. He also tried to set the Mexican consulate on fire using propane cylinders. In an old fashioned Texas shootout, a policeman, holding the reins to two horses, shot McQuilliams. Police speculated that the shooter was an antigovernment fanatic upset over recent relaxations in immigration policies.[†] Less than a month later, Bradley Stone of Philadelphia decided to end his court fight with his ex-wife over custody of their two children by killing her and other members of her family. Stone started at his ex-sister-in-law's house, where he killed the sister, her husband, and their daughter. He then drove to his ex-mother-in-law's, where he shot her and the grandmother. He ended up at his ex-wife's house where he shot the ex-wife and her niece. Stone fled to a wooded area outside the city and poisoned himself.[‡] However inexcusable these assaults were, most people can detect a stream of logic in each hunter's actions, whether it be fighting over an inheritance, paying back a teacher or a supervisor for some perceived insult or injustice, fighting the government, or permanently ending a custody dispute.

For other hunters, their grievance makes sense only to them. In September 2000, Ronald Gay opened fire at a gay bar in Roanoke, Virginia, killing one and wounding six. He told police he was fed up with people making fun of his last name.[§] Gay did not explain how shooting homosexuals mitigated the teasing. Jose Luis Nieto of Mexico City complained for months that a preschool's daily flag raising ceremony blocked access to his house. In May 2002, Nieto's patience ran out. He drove his pickup truck into a crowd of toddlers, killing two and injuring twenty.[¶] Nieto did not explain how killing preschoolers opened street access to his house. A year later, James T. Williams, consumed with hate against anyone different from himself, burned down three synagogues and an abortion clinic in Redding, California, before murdering a gay couple.[**] Williams did not explain how such violence relieved his hatred. Colin Fisk, Martin Garcia, and Paul Chait of Phoenix, Arizona, had been friends since high school. Garcia and Chait started a business together while Fisk increasingly fed his drug habit. When Garcia tried to help him become sober, Fisk began showing up at Garcia's house armed with a weapon and threatening to shoot Garcia and his family. The Garcias obtained a temporary restraining order against him in December 2003. Five months later, Fisk killed Garcia and Chait at their office. He told police he was angry at his old friends because they had severed their ties with him.[††] Fisk did not explain how killing his former friends restored their friendship. On October

---

[*] Man fired in LA, kills boss, shoots self. (2004, June 9). Associated Press.

[†] Austin police: Man fired 100-plus rounds downtown. (2014, November 29). Associated Press.

[‡] National Digest: Police search for shooting suspect. (2014, December 15). Associated Press; Shin, P. H. B. (2014, December 23). Pennsylvania killing spree suspect poisoned himself, autopsy reveals. ABC News Good Morning America.

[§] Breaux, K. S. (2000, September 27). Gay shooting said linked to jokes. *Washington Post*.

[¶] 2 Mexican toddlers killed by truck. (2002, May 7). Associated Press.

[**] Man pleads guilty to killing gay couple. (2003, March 1). Associated Press.

[††] 2 men shot dead in Phoenix office complex. (2004, April 27). Associated Press; 2 slain at Phoenix business. (2004, April 28). Associated Press; Family had injunction on Phoenix suspect. (2004, April 28). Associated Press; Ariz. Police: Slay suspect admits drug use. (2004, April 30); Villa, J. (2004, April 29). Suspect admits link with slayings. *Arizona Republic*.

17, 2014, a 15-year-old girl stabbed her brother in their Detroit, Michigan, home while her 23-year-old boyfriend stood outside the house sending her text messages telling her what to do. Police charged the couple with plotting to kill her entire family.* These incidents of violence seem as incomprehensible as they are inexcusable.

In some situations, the incident precipitating the violence makes sense only by inquiring into the relationship, rather real or perceived, that the hunter has with the target. In March 2002, Brian Harrison of Monroeville, Alabama, fired at his girlfriend as she fled in her car because she had not toasted his bread that morning.[†] Harrison's problem, of course, had less to do with the untoasted bread than it did with his need to bend his girlfriend to his will. He wanted to dominate her and overcome her defiance. When she further challenged him by fleeing in her car, he escalated the confrontation by shooting at her. In effect, the incident boiled down to breakfast on whose terms, his or hers?

Hunting involves a process of incremental attack-related behaviors. The hunter must first decide on the prey, then research the prey's habits and habitat in order to plan the best way to consummate the attack. Once the hunter settles on a plan, the next step requires assembling the necessary weapons and equipment for carrying it out. Finally, the hunter needs to take up the hunt, culminating in the actual attack on the prey. Each of these steps in the process requires certain behaviors that can be noticeable if the people in position to notice them are trained in what to look for, what to report, and to whom to make the report.

Take, for instance, the four individuals who simultaneously detonated four homemade bombs in different parts of London's subway and bus system on July 7, 2005. For whatever their personal or ideological grievances, once they had determined to attack London commuters, the bombers began their hunting preparations. Three weeks before their attacks, three of the men explored the route they intended to take the day of the attacks. They took a practice run. One or more of them made the peroxide-based improvised explosives. They obtained ice chests and backpacks to cool, then carry, the bombs onto three trains and one bus. At the agreed-upon time, they detonated the devices.[‡] In other words, they picked their targets, researched them, prepared their bombs, then launched their attacks, all behaviors of a hunter.

Hunters do not suddenly turn to violence. Their behavior can be motivated by intense, strongly held emotions, but their attacks are not spur-of-the-moment actions. For example, Colin Fisk, who killed his two Phoenix high school buddies, had repeatedly threatened one of them over several months.[§] Many hunters, like the Unabomber, make meticulous plans based on detailed, time-consuming research. Walter L. Moody, for example, assassinated federal judge Robert S. Vance in December 1989. Moody researched the judge to obtain his home address. Further, Moody identified a friend of Judge Vance's, a fellow jurist, and found his home address. Moody constructed four sophisticated mail bombs. One he sent to Judge Vance's home, using the other judge for the return address. Judge Vance's last words

---

* Competency hearing ordered for teen in murder plot. (2014, October 31). Associated Press.
† Man faces up to 20 years for shooting. (2002, March 13). Associated Press.
‡ Rotella, S. (2006, March 6). Who guided London's attackers? Los Angeles Times.
§ 2 men shot dead in Phoenix office complex. (2004, April 27). Associated Press; 2 slain at Phoenix business. (2004, April 28). Associated Press; Family had injunction on Phoenix suspect. (2004, April 28). Associated Press; Ariz. Police: Slay suspect admits drug use. (2004, April 30); Villa, J. (2004, April 29). Suspect admits link with slayings. Arizona Republic.

to his wife were to the effect that his friend had sent him some law journals.* Moody's detailed research and elaborate planning enabled him to succeed in this part of his plan.[†]

Some hunters move quickly down the path. For example, when Clara Harris of Houston, Texas, began to suspect her husband was having an affair, she hired a detective to follow him. As the detective videotaped her husband and his consort at a local hotel, Clara unexpectedly showed up and confronted the couple. After a brief scuffle with the other woman in the hotel lobby, Clara returned to her car and deliberately drove it toward her husband as he left the hotel. While her stepdaughter tried frantically to stop her, Clara ran over her husband, circled the parking lot and ran over him twice more.[‡] This hunter needed little research or preparation and used the weapon she had at hand. Doing so allowed her to move quickly down the path. She stepped onto the path as soon as she went back to her car intending to use it as a weapon.

In sum, hunters consciously decide that violence is their only redress. They act deliberately with malice aforethought. Their violence is premeditated and planned. Further, they prepare themselves, carefully selecting their weapons, route of attack, timing, and place. They account for whatever security stands in their way and take steps to circumvent it. Finally, they move to implement their plans by launching their assaults. Although their attacks do not always go as planned, the fact that they make plans marks them as hunters.

Hunters sometimes inspire other hunters. For example, Dylan Klebold and Eric Harris planned their 1999 attack on Columbine High School for months. Six weeks out, they practiced firing the weapons they would use.[§] Although their homemade bombs failed to detonate, the pair created considerable havoc and mayhem. That horrendous event continues to inspire other students to make their own plans and preparations. Jeremy Getman actually smuggled guns and bombs into Southside High School in Elmira, New York, on Valentine's Day 2001. He confessed to police that he planned a Columbine-style attack to shoot students and teachers and toss bombs into crowds, but at the last moment, realized he could not bring himself to kill innocent people.[¶] In March 2004, an alert teacher in Malcolm, Nebraska, saw Josh Magee take a drink from a liquor flask while sitting in his car in the school parking lot. Police found him armed with a bolt-action rifle, ammunition, and 20 homemade bombs. Other students reported that Magee frequently talked about Columbine.** In December 2005, police arrested two teenagers who confessed they were planning to attack their former high school in Lancaster, California. According to the *Los Angeles Times*:

> The teenagers described themselves as Goths, deputies said. They commonly wore black trench coats, in apparent imitation of Eric Harris and Dylan Klebold. The 15-year-old had the word "hate" carved into his forearm, deputies said.

---

*   Calhoun, F. S. (1998). Hunters and howlers: Threats and violence against Federal Judicial officials in the United States, 1979–1993 (pp. 2–3). Washington, DC: United States Marshal Service.
†   Moody mailed his other bombs to the NAACP in Jacksonville, FL, a civil rights attorney in Savannah, GA, and the Eleventh Circuit Court of Appeals courthouse. The civil rights attorney was killed; the other two bombs were intercepted.
‡   Girl says she tried to stop killing. (2002, August 1). Associated Press; P.I. reports client killed husband. (2002, August 5). Associated Press.
§   CBS *Evening News*, October 22, 2003.
¶   Teen gets 8 years for guns in school. (2001, December 17). Associated Press.
**   Teenager found with 20 homemade bombs. (2004, March 19). Associated Press.

A search of their homes uncovered knives, ammunition, a gas mask, carbon dioxide canisters, and a large volume of instructions on bomb making printed from the Internet. The two boys also had photographs of Harris, Klebold, Timothy McVeigh, Charles Manson, and Lee Harvey Oswald. They planned to launch their attack on Valentine's Day 2006. Fortunately, a fellow student heard them talking about their plans—leakage—and alerted authorities.* In April 2006, police in Platte City, Missouri, arrested two teenagers for plotting an attack on their high school as a commemoration of the seventh anniversary of the Columbine attack.† That weekend, police in Riverton, Kansas,‡ and North Pole, Arkansas,§ arrested five and six students, respectively, all for plotting Columbine-style attacks on their own high schools. The fame of Klebold and Harris continue to exert a powerful appeal to some disgruntled teenagers.

In May 2014, a 17-year-old student at Will Rogers High School in Van Nuys, California, decided to settle forever a dispute he had with another student. He posted on social media a challenge to the other student to meet him in the school parking lot. After receiving an alert from a third student, school police found a pistol and ammunition in the 17-year-old's backpack.¶ Five months later, in Tallinn, Estonia, a 15-year-old student shot and killed his teacher. The student's Facebook page posted pictures of guns and scenes of war. He captioned one picture in English, writing, "Don't judge me cause I'm quiet. No one plans a murder out loud."** Strong advice from a true hunter.

Whether inspired by previous acts of violence or prompted by their own motives, hunters take actions in furtherance of acting violently. They plan, prepare, and attack, seldom making their plans out loud. Threat managers can best identify hunters by concentrating on attack-related behaviors. Actions are the best indicators of hunting activity.

Anatomy of a Hunter

Bart Ross became a hunter sometime during the winter of 2004–2005. Devastated by jaw cancer in the early 1990s, he blamed Chicago's Northwestern Hospital for the pain and disfigurement the successful cancer treatment left him with. He sought revenge through the courts, only to be frustrated and disappointed when both the state and federal courts refused to sustain him. By 2004, his court filings in the Northern District of Illinois federal court gave ample testament to his burgeoning hatred of the way the judicial system had treated him. After nearly a decade of seeking judicial support, in the summer of 2004, Ross filed another federal lawsuit against Northwestern Hospital. His self-prepared filing accused the court of abiding in his torture, compared the judicial officials to Nazis, and demanded that the court grant him restitution from all that he had suffered from his medical treatment.†† In the fall of 2004, Judge Joan Lefkow dismissed Ross' case.

In February 2005, Ross fell so far behind in his house rent that he knew he faced eviction. Unemployed and out of hope, he abandoned the house and lived for 2 weeks in his van. His self-eviction served as the last straw. Ross researched his prey, made his plans, and

* Ricci, J. (2005, December 17). 2 teens jailed in alleged plot for Columbine-like attack. *Los Angeles Times*.
† MO. teens charged in school shooting plot. (2006, April 18). Associated Press.
‡ Students say rampage was rumored at school. (2006, April 22). Associated Press.
§ 6 Alaska students held in alleged plot to attack school. (2006, April 23). Associated Press.
¶ Mom charged after teenage son brings gun to school. (2014, October 15). Associated Press.
** Tanner, J. (2014, October 27). Student, 15, shoot, kills teacher in Estonia. Associated Press.
†† McCarthy, B. (2005, March 14). Lefkow killer tracked in '99. *Chicago Tribune*.

put his preparations in order. Early in the morning of February 28, 2005, he broke into the basement of Judge Lefkow's home determined to wait for her to return from work that evening. As is the lot of both men and mice, Ross' plan went awry. Around midmorning, Judge Lefkow's husband went to his basement office and stumbled onto Ross, who shot him. Ross then executed the other occupant of the house, Judge Lefkow's mother.*

For the next 2 weeks, Ross eluded police while apparently stalking other judges who had held against him. When a policeman pulled him over in West Allis, Wisconsin, to ticket him for a broken taillight, Ross immediately shot himself in the head. Police investigators found among his possessions a suicide note confessing his guilt and a list of other judges and their home addresses. One of those on the list lived near West Allis.*

Significantly, Ross never threatened Judge Lefkow. He expressed his frustration with the judicial system inappropriately in his court filings. Instead, Ross chose to further express his dissatisfaction with the system through violence. He became a hunter.

Howlers Defined and Exemplified

The concept of *howler* describes those individuals who communicate inappropriately, ominously, even threateningly, or who communicate emotionally, but who never act violently. The only behavior a howler engages in is howling. Howlers are great communicators. How howlers choose to communicate inappropriately is largely controlled by their actual (not perceived) relationship with their target. Personal howlers, who have an interpersonal relationship with their target, essentially use that relationship, and the knowledge gained from it, to further their purposes. If, for example, they seek to control their target, they resort to threats, gestures, symbolic actions, or loaded references in order to prey on what they know of their target's fears and concerns. They confront the target, engage in harassment, and otherwise do their best to convince or cajole the target into behaving as the howler wants. In effect, personal howlers are classic bullies, all bombast and bravado on the outside but cowards on the inside.

Impersonal howlers, who have no personal relationship with their target, find their method of communicating inappropriately constrained by their lack of access to the target. For example, impersonal howlers frequently have no way of knowing at any single moment exactly where the target is. Often, all the howler has is an address or phone number. Their lack of personal familiarity forces them to communicate from a distance using such methods as letters, telephone calls, texts, and various social media outlets. If these howlers decide to bridge the distance by approaching the target, they stop howling and start hunting.

Some howlers are sinister, some are binders. Sinister howlers make threats, either direct, veiled, or implied. Binders express inappropriate or unreciprocated emotional feelings toward their targets or they want some connection with their targets. They may not actually know the target, or the target could be an acquaintance or former intimate. The crucial element for binders is that their emotions are expressed inappropriately and the target does not return the feeling.

---

* Dardick, H., & Sadovi, C. (2005, March 11). Decade of despair boiled over to paranoia. *Chicago Tribune.*

Both species of howlers let their targets know exactly how they feel, what they want to do, and how they hope to do it. But they never get beyond the wanting and hoping. They may appear untoward, even menacing, but the appearance is fooling. With some howlers, the initial communication satisfies them and the target never hears from them again. With other howlers, communicating becomes an addiction. They often make numerous communications and expand to multiple targets.

In the summer of 2005, New York Yankees baseball star Derek Jeter received a letter warning him that if he continued to date white women, he would be "shot or set on fire." The threatener sent the letter to Yankee Stadium. According to a Federal Bureau of Investigation agent investigating the case, the wording of the letter closely resembled language in 60 other letters sent over the previous 3 years to prominent black athletes and public figures. Recipients included Supreme Court Associate Justice Clarence Thomas, Miami Dolphins football player Jason Taylor, and the parents of tennis player James Blake. The law enforcement officers investigating the case firmly believed all the letters came from one individual. None of those threatened suffered any kind of attack. When the howler upgraded his communications to e-mails, police tracked him to a computer in public library in Cleveland, OH.* On May 15, 2008, David Tuason pleaded guilty to sending the letters. He explained that, years earlier, his girlfriend left him for a black man.* Communicating is easy; shooting someone or setting him or her on fire presents a considerably more difficult challenge. Sending 60 letters to a diverse population of prominent black men over a 3-year period, especially sending them to publicly available addresses like Yankee Stadium, without ever following up the threat with action strongly suggests the work of an impersonal howler. The written word, however frightening its expression, never killed or physically injured anyone. In this case, the howler conditioned the threat on the recipient's doing something, that is, to stop dating women of a certain race. At the same time, the threatener took no personal risks. Tuason hid in anonymity, mailing the letters from Cleveland, Ohio, and carefully avoiding leaving any clues that might reveal his or her identity. For the howler, the letter itself fulfills his or her purpose. In this case, Tuason made a racist political statement and tried to instill fear in the baseball player. For the sinister howler, that is more than enough.

Impersonal howlers who make threats prefer to frighten, disturb, or pester their targets while avoiding any risk to themselves. Hence, they communicate in ways designed to do that. They write, e-mail, telephone, fax, page, or go on social media, all methods that allow them to keep their distance from their targets. Yet, they use gruesome, disgusting, even terrifying descriptions of what they want to do to the target. During the year 2000, Eric J. Temple threatened President Bill Clinton and candidate George W. Bush, as well as three federal prosecutors. In one letter to a prosecutor, Temple warned, "When I come for each of you individually, I'm going to cut your heads off, rip your eyes out, and cook your bodies for a holiday meal." Temple also promised to blow up the White House with a nuclear bomb.† Being told that you will be shot or set on fire or eaten can be disquieting, especially if you have no way of identifying or recognizing who will make the assault. These types of howlers count on that. They want their targets unnerved. They engage in primitive psychological warfare, using as weapons threatening words or violent images describing violent fantasies. But words and images are their only weapons. To succeed, they depend

* Jilted lover behind threats to black men. (2008, May 17). Associated Press.
† Man gets prison for threats to Feds. (2002, February 5). Associated Press.

on enlisting the assistance of their target's own imagination to further feed the fear. They fail whenever their target remembers the childhood adage about sticks, stones, and words.

Impersonal howlers who profess romantic bonds with their targets tend to become love obsessed. These types of howlers live in a delusional world where they envision an interpersonal relationship with someone they may never have met and, when it involves a celebrity, they probably never will meet. The communications from these binder howlers express in great detail their fantasies and emotional connections with the targets. Although frustration at not seeing their feelings reciprocated may ultimately transform them into sinister howlers, binders disturb their targets by the creepiness of their delusions and their unrequited, obsessive desire to have an emotional connection with the target.

Threat managers can best identify howlers by concentrating on how the subject chooses to communicate inappropriately, what the purpose of the communication or message is, and what is known of the subject's relationship to the target. Although it is impossible to prove a negative, the threat manager also needs to determine whether the subject has engaged in any other attack-related behaviors. Because of the impossibility of proving a negative, assessing howlers is far more difficult than assessing hunters. One can never be sure that a particular subject has not engaged in research or preparation behavior simply because the threat manager can only assess the known facts he or she has. The unknown cannot be assessed. Ironically, then, one can have a high confidence level that one is managing a hunter, but less confidence that one is dealing with a howler. Ultimately, it boils down to experience and good judgment.

Anatomy of a Howler

RF, a federal prisoner confined to the federal Bureau of Prison's Springfield, Missouri, medical facility, frequently howled. He spent most of his days composing lengthy letters to federal judges all across the country. He mailed the letters, all of them filled with threats and recriminations and angry, irrational ramblings, to any judge he could think of or for whom he could get an address out of the prison library's *Judicial Staff Directory*. He described in lurid detail how he would cut the judge's head off, then stuff the judge's arm into the neck hole. He promised to rape wives and daughters, then kill them too. His tone was angry and relentless, as though nothing would stop him. Nothing, that is, except prison bars.

Most of the judges had never met RF, nor did RF know them, know what their caseloads were, or even what their decisions had been. He threatened them because they were judges. As RF once explained to his doctor, he would not know what to do with himself all day if he did not have his letters to write. RF threatened judges as a hobby.*

The Effect of Space and Time on Howling

The development of the written word enabled individuals to communicate with each other over distances and time. Subsequent technological inventions, such as the telegraph, telephone, fax, pager, e-mail, texting, Internet websites, Facebook postings, Instagram, Twitter, and blogs, enhanced distance communications. People no longer had to be within hailing distance to converse. Physical proximity became irrelevant. Instead, people could express

---

* Calhoun, F. S. (1998). *Hunters and howlers: Threats and violence against Federal Judicial officials in the United States, 1979–1993* (p. xix). Washington, DC: United States Marshal Service.

their ideas, give word to their emotions, espouse their opinions, report their news, or make themselves heard from miles away. Distance no longer impeded communicating.

These advances in communicating had an unforeseen effect. They facilitated howling. Communicating at a distance allowed individuals freer vent to their emotions and their feelings, unhindered by the social decorums that control personal interactions. In other words, people communicate differently when doing so over a distance rather than face-to-face. A simple test proves the point. Any sampling of office e-mails clearly shows that people express themselves more forcefully behind the safety of their computers than they do in meetings or during face-to-face encounters with colleagues. E-mails somehow liberate people to express their opinions much more unequivocally, even forcefully. The same applies to other forms of distance communications.

In January 2006, Deborah Howell, the ombudsman for the *Washington Post* charged with representing the readership's interests at the paper, published an article commending the *Post* for breaking the story on lobbyist Jack Abramoff's shady and illegal dealings with Congress. In passing, Howell mentioned that Abramoff gave campaign donations to both Republicans and Democrats alike. In fact, Abramoff never gave directly to any Democratic candidate, but he did encourage his clients to give money to both parties. Howell's literal mistake raised such a firestorm of e-mailed criticism, much of it vulgar and sexist, and some of it threatening, that the *Post* temporarily closed its website to further electronic abuse.*

E-mailers and bloggers across the country called Howell a liar, an idiot, a "right-wing whore," and a number of other personal epithets family newspapers simply do not print. "Yes, the WAPO [*Washington Post*] needs an enema, and Howell should be the first thing that gets medicinally removed," one reader wrote. Another added, "Howell is simply a paid liar. How this creature endures itself is something I don't understand. What a piece of flotsam." However, when Howell responded to one reader who accused her of being a fool with a lack of integrity, the reader ended up offering her a sheepish apology. "I took some time and read an interview (online) with you, among other things," the reader wrote. "When I finished, I shuddered a little bit because it made me think I may be exhibiting an attribute that in others I despise. My e-mail to you was a cheap shot at your integrity and for that I am sorry."*

Howell speculated that perhaps the "anonymity" of the Internet "emboldens e-mailers to conduct a public stoning." Yet, most of the e-mailers could be identified by their e-mail addresses; many even signed their names or included contact information. Anonymity was far less a factor than the distance communication combined with the speed of communicating electronically. Her readers reacted angrily to her column and vigorously typed out their opinions on their individual keyboards, no doubt drawing great satisfaction from hitting the "Send" button. Howell did not realize it, but she had stumbled into a hornet's nest of partisan impersonal howlers.*

As Howell found out, impersonal howlers take full advantage of the new freedom offered by distance communications. It empowered them. It allowed many howlers to determine how they communicated, what they communicated, when they communicated, and to whom they communicated. Communicating from a distance even allowed each howler to choose how much personal information he or she would reveal. Distance communications also freed howlers to express themselves in stronger, even blunter, terms. They could now say or write what they really thought without worrying about dealing

---

* Howell, D. (2006, January 22). The firestorm over my column. *Washington Post*.

with their target's reaction. In their multitude, they could even temporarily close down the *Washington Post's* Web site.

Since Howell's experience in 2006, the use of social media to scold single individuals has grown exponentially. When law professor Lisa McElroy inadvertently sent her law class an e-mail containing a link to a porn site, the slip went viral across the Internet. Complete strangers inundated McElroy and her school's e-mail and websites with condemnations, threats, and ridicule. As McElroy described it, their "schadenfreude was irresistible."* McElroy fell victim to a new Internet phenomenon known as "public shaming," what Ron Jonson describes as the electronic equivalent of putting the town idiot in the public stocks.

Mass public shamings have become so commonplace that Ronson published a book in 2015 describing the phenomena. *So You've Been Publicly Shamed* describes dozens of incidents where public and private individuals suffered written attacks on Twitter, Facebook, and other media for innocent—if also idiotic—postings those individuals put on their Twitter, Facebook, or other media accounts. Justine Sacco, for example, tweeted her 170 Twitter followers while journeying to South Africa for a family vacation. Just before boarding at Heathrow for the last leg of the trip, she tweeted, "Going to Africa. Hope I don't get AIDS. Just kidding. I'm white." Eleven hours later, when the plane landed, Sacco learned that she and her last message were "the number one worldwide trend on Twitter." Over 1 million people responded to her racist, but obviously silly, tweet. The responses were sexist (many expressing a hope that she would get raped) and hate filled. The attacking tweeters also went after her employer, who reacted by firing her from her job. Even a year later, Sacco had not fully recovered from the ordeal of her public shaming.[†]

Not even the president of the United States can escape the shaming phenomenon. On May 18, 2015, President Barack Obama sent out the first-ever presidential tweet, using the account "@POTUS." "Hello, Twitter," Obama wrote, "It's Barack. Really! Six years in, they're finally giving me my own account." The majority of the recipients responded positively, but a significant number responded with "racist, hate-filled posts and replies," according to the *New York Times.* Jeff Gullickson of Minneapolis posted the famous Obama "HOPE" campaign poster, doctored to make it appear with a noose around Obama's neck and the word "Hope" changed to "Rope." The accompanying message read, "#arrestobama #treason we need 'ROPE FOR CHANGE.'" Gullickson's reply prompted two Secret Service special agents to visit him the next day. The speed of the Internet, combined with the protection gained by sitting behind a computer rather than confronting someone personally, offers an irresistible way to scold and humiliate anyone unfortunate enough to make a mistake—or even go—on social media.[‡]

In general, personal and impersonal howlers approach their targets quite differently. Personal howlers may communicate from a distance or in person. They often make verbal threats or inappropriate statements directly to their target. Spouses spit out threats to each other during the heat of emotionally charged arguments. Some workers intentionally intimidate or disturb their colleagues or supervisors by talking frequently about weapons or what would happen if they had a weapon with them at that moment. Schools are full of bullies who use words and gestures to frighten their fellow students. Even when

* McElroy, L. T. (2015, April 24). After a public shaming, reclaiming my dignity. *Washington Post.*
† Ronson, J. (2015). *So you've been publicly shamed* (pp. 51–68). New York: Riverhead Books.
‡ Davis, J. H. (2015, May 21). Obama's Twitter debut, @POTUS, attracts hate-filled posts. *New York Times.*

communicating from a distance, personal howlers will frequently use some personal information about the target or they will use symbols or loaded references they know the target will understand. For personal howlers, proximity to their targets and personal knowledge about their targets enhance their ability to frighten, control, or disturb.

Impersonal howlers have a high likelihood of communicating inappropriately from a distance. Because they do not know their target, they may only have a publicly available address. Their lack of insider knowledge about their target limits their reach. Their ability to charm, frighten, or disturb the target is bound by what is publicly available or observable. They may use deductions and guesses about where their target may be or what the target may be doing, but their communications do not have the same level of specificity personal howlers have.

For example, an impersonal howler may deduce that the head of a company has an office at the company's headquarters. A personal howler would know what floor and which corner the office is located. An impersonal howler may read in the tabloids that Madonna has children. A personal howler knows the children's names, where they go to school, who their friends are, and what games they play. The relationship between the howler and the target greatly influences both the content and the method of delivery of the howler's inappropriate communications.

The vast majority of impersonal howlers choose to do their howling in writing or over the telephone. Since sinister howlers do not actually intend to carry out their threats, making them from a distance ensures the howler's safety. People tend not to threaten other people in person unless they are prepared to back up the threat or, as with personal howlers, they know the target well enough to have confidence in the target's reaction. Telling persons face-to-face that you intend to kill or harm them inevitably causes them to react. That reaction may well imperil the threatener physically, a situation impersonal howlers prefer to avoid. Impersonal howlers also tend to shy away from expressing their emotional attraction to some stranger directly and in person, assuming, of course, that they can get physically close to the object of their affections. In most cases, they cannot. Writing or telephoning gets them in contact. Impersonal howlers, whether sinister or binder, prefer to do their howling from afar. Distance is the great liberator. It frees them to say their piece without risking an immediate response from their target.

Impersonal howlers enjoy greater freedom for their delusions and obsessions by writing them out, not actually acting them out. Advances in technology merely offer howlers more choices in how they decide to communicate from afar. Impersonal howlers write letters, make telephone calls, send e-mails, use texts, post their views on websites and in blogs, send Instagrams, mail harmless gifts or packages, leave graffiti, or use some combination of these means of communicating. However the impersonal howler communicates, it is almost always from a distance and the communication itself poses no harm, however frightening, distressing, or disturbing its message.

Communicating from a distance also emboldens the howler's imagination. They imagine a target's response to the communication rather than actually observe it. This plays much better than reality. Imagined responses always exceed the howler's expectations because, after all, the howler wants them to. If the purpose of the communication is to instill fear in the target, then the howler will imagine the fright created in the target. If the purpose is to attract the target emotionally, then the howler's imagination will conjure that. Whatever the howler wants, his or her imagination will supply it far better than reality will.

For example, one particular howler became fixated on a female Hollywood celebrity. He began sending e-mails discussing the meaning of her movies and how her characters tied in with symbols from the Bible, other movies, and other actors. Frequently, he wrote lengthy missives exploring in detail various themes he had developed. One day, this howler noticed that a website devoted to the celebrity had been slightly revised. Coincidently, the revision corresponded to a theme he had recently been discussing in his e-mails. The howler immediately concluded that this change indicated that the celebrity had received his messages and was now sending him a coded answer. It cheered him to believe that she read his e-mails.* The response he imagined her to have was much better than the reality. Fan club staff, not the celebrity, managed the website. She was not even receiving his e-mails. Howlers, however, do not let reality get in their way.

In a study of 3,096 inappropriate communications directed toward federal judicial officials, Frederick S. Calhoun found that 92% of the communications were specious, that is, empty in the sense that no action was taken to approach or attack or imperil the judicial official. In 4.1% of the cases, a suspicious escalation occurred but fell short of violence. In 3.9%, some violence took place, although not always against the judicial target.† When Calhoun analyzed the inappropriate communications by method of delivery, he found that 96.6% of the written communications and 96.7% of the telephone communications were specious. In comparison, only 41.9% of the cases involving suspicious activities and 80.6% of the verbal communications were specious. The findings were statistically significant (see Table 2.1).‡

Calhoun concluded that the method of delivery used by the subject when communicating with federal judicial officials served as a strong preincident indicator of whether the subject is a hunter or a howler. Taken together, these results clearly show that those who do not intend to act violently toward federal judicial officials communicate with those officials in writing or over the telephone, both of which keep a distance between the subject and the target. Conversely, those who do intend to act violently toward federal judicial officials engage in suspicious activities or make their inappropriate communications verbally in person. Significantly, none of the three federal judges assassinated since 1979 was threatened by his assassin. Calhoun concluded:

> The method of delivery was, in effect, the threatener's signature. It most reflected his style and personality, his drive and motive, his intent and purpose. Those who wrote or called interposed some physical distance between themselves and their victim. They were howlers, baying out their outrage from atop the canyon walls, well protected from any response of the victim. Those who spoke their threats to some court official or, worse, those who assaulted or attempted to assault their victim went beyond mere howling to hunt. As the method of delivery strongly showed across 3,096 threats, the howlers rarely hunted; the hunters rarely howled.‡

Keeping a distance is, perhaps, the truest mark of the impersonal howler. But distance has other repercussions marking impersonal howlers. Because they feel safely away from their targets, these howlers tend to express themselves more straightforwardly and explicitly unless disguising their meaning makes the inappropriate communication more

---

* Authors' personal knowledge.
† Calhoun, F. S. (1998). *Hunters and howlers: Threats and violence against Federal Judicial officials in the United States, 1979–1993* (p. 56). Washington, DC: United States Marshal Service.
‡ Calhoun, F. S. (1998). *Hunters and howlers: Threats and violence against Federal Judicial officials in the United States, 1979–1993* (p. 66). Washington, DC: United States Marshal Service.

chilling or attractive. Sinister howlers frequently make direct, detailed threats. They offer elaborate descriptions of the death or injury that will befall their targets. The public shamings of Howell, McElroy, and Sacco each contained threats and wishes for gruesome punishments for the offenders. Binder howlers describe their fantasies and daydreams in intimate detail. After all, the descriptions are symptomatic of the howler's desperate need for a relationship. Both types of howlers avoid vagueness and elliptical references in favor of straight talk. Hunters, by comparison, usually choose not to communicate at all once they go on the hunt.

Even among intimates, where threats serve as strong preincident indicators of future violence,* the threats do not always correspond in time with the act of intended violence. The threatening statements usually precede the violence by hours at least and usually by days or weeks. Once the spouse or coworker decides to resort to violence, he or she usually quits threatening, moving from talking about violence to acting violently.†

For the threat manager, one of the best clues to a subject's intentions can be derived by the method of delivery used by the subject to communicate with the target. Because the subject chooses how to communicate, that choice alone gives great insight into what the subject may be planning to do, at least at the moment he or she drafted the communication. Subjects who choose distance communications tend to be howlers. Conversely, subjects who engage in suspicious activities or who communicate inappropriately in person or face-to-face with their target tend to be hunters. Although the threat manager should always factor all the known facts into the assessment, the subject's method of delivery should be treated as one of the more significant factors.

Consequently, as a rule of thumb, when a howler directs his or her inappropriate communication toward a target the subject does not personally know and the target enjoys a position of power, authority, or status, the subject most likely will do so from a distance in order to minimize risk or exposure to the subject. Conversely, when the howler intends to intimidate, control, or cause fear in an intimate or acquaintance, those communications are as frequently achieved in person as they are over a distance. Personal howlers do not fear the consequences of their sinister communications because they know their targets and thus have confidence in predicting the target's reaction. The different means of communicating between personal and impersonal howlers represent one of the outgrowths of the intimacy effect.

Hunters versus Howlers

The key to understanding hunters versus howlers lies in the difference between acting and talking. Threatening someone is a behavior, but alone, it is not a behavior that lends itself to carrying out the threat. Threats are actually promises of some *future* action. Many are conditioned on the target's doing or not doing something; others are deferred in time, and some are veiled (sometimes to the point of obtuseness). The Cleveland howler, for example, warned Derek Jeter that dire things would happen *if* Jeter did not stop dating white women. Presumably, the burden of avoiding being shot or set on fire now fell on Jeter and his choice of dates. Many prisoners condition their threats by explicitly postponing the promised action

---

* Jenkins, D. M. When should threats be seen as indicative of future violence?, Appendix.
† We deal here with intended violence, which is planned and premeditated. During impromptu violence, threats can occur simultaneously with the violent act.

until they get out of prison. Other threats warn of terrible events perpetrated by someone else, sometimes a vague deity, superior being, or alien. Despite their variety, threats are only one form of behavior. Carrying them out requires a whole different set of actions.

In some venues for violence, especially those in which an interpersonal relationship exists between the hunter and the target, hunters frequently engage in the behavior of threatening their intended target. Most domestic violence cases are scarred by repeated threats. But that behavior occurs amidst a spiraling escalation of attack-related behaviors. The hunter threatens his or her spouse but also stalks him or her, makes plans to attack, obtains the necessary weaponry, and ultimately attacks.

The threats occur within a web of activities all designed to control the behavior of the spouse, to somehow convince him or her not to leave the relationship and, especially, to do the threatening spouse's bidding. Because of the intimate relationship, the threat itself may be clear only to the target.

For example, police in California responded to a domestic relations complaint in a small town outside Sacramento. When they arrived at the residence, they determined that the husband had hit the wife. The officers immediately arrested and handcuffed the husband. As they led him out the front door, the husband turned back to his wife and said, "Don't worry, honey. When I get out, we'll go to Las Vegas." The officers noticed that the wife reacted fearfully, visibly shaken by the innocuous promise. After putting the husband in the back seat of the patrol car, one of the officers returned to interview the wife. She told him that a year earlier, while visiting Las Vegas, the husband had beaten her so severely she ended up in a hospital. Because she understood the husband's reference and it instilled fear in her, prosecutors obtained a conviction against the husband for making the threat using symbolic language.* Understanding the controlling nature of domestic relation threats helps explain why violence so frequently results after a targeted spouse resists the control, such as through obtaining a judicial restraining order.

Howlers howl; hunters hunt, even if sometimes the hunt entails threatening the target. Threats, then, must be assessed not only within the context of the intimacy effect, but also by what other actions are taken. Threat managers need to recognize the differences between hunters and howlers and invest those differences into their ability to identify problem individuals and to assess their risk. Doing so promises the best way to make clean, persuasive, supportable assessments. Knowing how hunters act offers the best insight into the most practical ways to manage individuals of violent intent. Similarly, understanding the way howlers behave will help inform how they should be managed. Threat managers cannot afford to ignore either hunters or howlers, but how they manage each varies according to circumstance and context.

Although howlers can become hunters, doing so requires that they stop howling and start hunting. In essence, they change their behavior so that they are no longer acting like howlers. They step out on the path to intended violence. Usually, these individuals suffer what we call the *last-straw syndrome*. That is, something happens to trigger the howler into taking up the hunt. Some aspect of the situation changes, either through some reaction by the target or a significant change in the subject's life circumstances. Whatever the cause, the individual now feels a compelling grievance that only violence can assuage. Howling no longer suffices.

---

* Heisler, C. J. (2004). The law of threats. In *Investigation and prosecution of stalking and related crimes* (p. X-3). Sacramento, CA: California District Attorneys Association.

Summary

This chapter defined the twin concepts of *hunter* and *howler*. It described hunters as those individuals who engage in attack-related behaviors to further their intention to carry out an act of violence. It defined howlers as individuals who communicate inappropriately, ominously, even threateningly, or emotionally but who never take action to implement their ideas. The chapter offered several examples of hunters and howlers and stressed that each is identified by specific behaviors. The chapter also explored the effects of space and time on impersonal howlers, especially the growing phenomenon of "public shaming" through social media. Throughout, the chapter emphasized the importance of looking at how problem individuals, whether hunter or howler, behave and the actions that they take as the best indicators for assessing them. Finally, the chapter concluded by stressing the importance of distinguishing hunters from howlers and adopting threat management strategies applicable to each.

Situation Analysis: The Payoff

The Facts

Oliver has worked for a corporation for 17 years. His personnel file shows that 3 years ago, his annual performance rating dropped from above average to average. The next year, it declined again to below average. Last year, he received a poor performance rating. In July, the corporation initiated the process to terminate Oliver. The termination took effect August 24.

Between July and August, several of Oliver's coworkers complained about his belligerent attitude toward them. A female coworker reported that Oliver demanded that she not walk past his cubicle and if she did, he would see to it that she would not be walking for long. A male coworker told his supervisor that Oliver frequently glared at him and on several occasions went out of his way to jostle the worker as they crossed paths in the central hallway. The human resources staff members who worked on Oliver's termination reported that he told two of them that they would regret the way they were treating him. The staff members requested the presence of security officers during Oliver's exit interview. The interview and Oliver's departure from the corporation went smoothly.

Oliver called his human resources contact demanding that he receive his cash payment for unused leave immediately. The contact explained that processing leave claims could take as long as 90 days. Oliver replied that that was unacceptable. He explained that he had been offered a position out of state and needed the cash payment to cover his moving expenses. Oliver warned that if he did not receive the payment soon, he would return to the company and "wake people up" to his problem. Oliver subsequently telephoned several times a day demanding his money. His human resources contact described the calls as angry and threatening. The contact reports that he fears for his safety.

The Threat Assessment

Although Oliver has acted in a threatening manner in the past and has made ominous statements, he has no history of acting violently. Rather, he uses intimidation against coworkers as a way to keep them off balance. His current telephone calls indicate that he is trying to use the same intimidation behavior to compel his human resources contact to expedite his unused leave compensation. Security has no record that Oliver has returned to the company facility, nor has security received any report that Oliver has been seen in the area. At this time, based on the known facts, we assess Oliver as a howler with a low risk of resorting to violence. More than likely, he will continue to use telephonic intimidations short of violence.

Protective Response

Security officers should be briefed on Oliver's intimidations and shown his photograph. They should also be instructed not to let Oliver on the premises. Oliver's human resources contact and former supervisor and coworkers should receive a security briefing on measures they can take to enhance their personal security. They should also be advised to report any communications or contacts they may receive from Oliver.

Threat Management Strategy

Oliver is an excellent candidate for the refocus-and-assist strategy. Because he claims to have a new job out of state and needs the cash from his unused leave balance to pay for his move, getting him that payment should be expedited. Helping him get out of state and into a new job will build up his inhibitors, thus decreasing the chances of his acting violently. Helping him get into a new job will also refocus him to the future and away from his bad experiences with his former employer.

Outcome

Oliver's belligerent and intimidating demeanor fostered considerable resentment among his coworkers and human resources staff. That resentment caused the staff to drag their feet processing his unused leave compensation. When members of the threat management unit requested that the claim be expedited, they were told that human resources had lots of priorities. Oliver's claim was not at the same level as their other demands. The threat managers took the issue to the department head but were again rebuffed with the explanation that Oliver hardly deserved any special treatment.

At that point, the head of the threat management unit approached the corporation's chairman and chief executive officer. They had developed a professional relationship based on a number of inappropriate communications directed at the chairman in the past. When the head of the threat management unit explained the situation, the chairman immediately telephoned the director of human resources and ordered that Oliver's check be cut that day.

The threat management team personally delivered the check to Oliver and used the visit to confirm his intention to leave the state for his new job. They also asked for his future contact information so they could check up on him if necessary. Three days later, the team confirmed that Oliver had moved out of his apartment and was on his way out of state. Two weeks later, the team confirmed that Oliver was working at his new job.

Issues of Interest

Oliver's situation illustrated a number of unusual aspects of contemporary threat management:

1. Although we do not advocate rewarding intimidating behaviors, in some cases, getting the subject what he or she wants solves the problem both for the subject and for the threat manager.
2. Threat managers need to remember that they are facilitators as well as security professionals. By cutting through the bureaucracy and getting Oliver his check, the threat managers effectively deflected Oliver from intimidating corporate staff and refocused him on starting his new job.
3. The individuals whom Oliver targeted with his intimidations became so upset and resentful of his interaction with them that they deliberately slowed down the process for delivering his check. In other words, their resentment toward him blinded them from seeing that by helping him, they also helped themselves get rid of him. It took an objective threat management approach to see the solution that had been staring them in the face. Even then, it took high-level intervention to get the check cut.
4. The head of the threat management unit was able to use his contacts from previous threat management cases to facilitate applying the threat management strategy. Such networking can be enormously useful in addressing future cases.
5. Threat management is as much social work as it is investigative or security. Threat managers need to be innovative and flexible in determining the most effective management strategies. Their assessments, too, need to take into account not only how the subject is behaving, but also what the subject appears to be seeking.

Understanding Hunters 7

Hunters act. They engage in *attack-related* behaviors, that is, they do things in furtherance of their plan to commit violence. If, for example, a plan entails sending a mail bomb to a target, then the hunter collects the necessary materials, constructs the bomb, researches the target's mailing address, addresses the package, applies the postage, and mails it. Hunters who decide to use a firearm must determine the target location, obtain the weapon, load it, carry it to the attack scene, then get close enough to the target to fire. These hunters engage in noticeable behaviors. They expose themselves to being identified as hunters.

What Hunters Do

Attack-related behaviors are best conceptualized as steps hunters must take to carry out acts of premeditated violence. We call this concept the *path to intended violence*. To review, essentially, the stepping stones consist of the following:

1. *Grievance*, which is the motive or reason compelling the hunter to act.
2. *Ideation*, which requires actually settling upon the idea that violence is justified and necessary.
3. *Research and planning*, which means going beyond the idea to actually figuring out how to consummate the violence.
4. *Preparation*, which involves obtaining the necessary equipment, such as weapon of choice, and taking any other actions required to initiate the plan.
5. *Breach*, which entails initiating the plan by circumventing the target's security (however primitive or sophisticated that may be) to launch the attack.
6. *Attack*, which is the actual physical assault.

Because attack-related behaviors essentially define an individual as a hunter, the threat manager should always keep in focus what the subject is doing to identify him or her as a hunter.

Our description of the assorted behaviors associated with each step is not definitive, merely illustrative. Human behavior manifests itself in an infinite number of ways that defy compilation into a shopping list of actions. In general, hunters behave in ways that are conducive to how they have chosen to hunt. Mail bombers do things differently than snipers. Hunters who do not expect to survive their attacks, who indeed wish to die during the attacks, engage in different behaviors than do hunters who want to escape after their attacks. As we describe and illustrate the various behaviors along the path to intended violence, our purpose is not to capture all possible behaviors but to suggest the kinds of activities threat managers should be alert for.

Our approach is neither psychological nor sociological. We have no pretense of under-standing what goes on inside the head of a hunter. *Why* each hunter acts the way he or she does is unique to each and, in fact, may never be fully known or understood. Many people have put forth various theories to explain why Lee Harvey Oswald shot President John F. Kennedy. Indeed, the inability to understand Oswald's grievance has fueled the innumer-able conspiracy theories spawned over the years. The only thing of which we are sure is that Oswald had a grievance that led him to come up with the idea of violence. Thus inspired, he then researched, planned, and prepared for his attack. As the motorcade turned into Dealey Plaza, Oswald was in position to breach the president's security and launch his attack by squeezing the rifle's trigger. Traveling that path required him to act. He bought the rifle, built the sniper's nest in the book depository, smuggled his equipment inside, took up position in time to snipe on the motorcade, fled the building, and hid out in the movie theatre. Ultimately for our purposes, why he took those actions is less important than observing and understanding what those actions indicated. His behavior indicated that a hunter was on the prowl.

The same holds true of Jack Ruby. Maybe he shot Oswald to avenge the lost president or to ensure Oswald's silence or because he thought Oswald the personification of the devil. Whatever propelled him, at some point that weekend, Ruby decided on violence, obtained a pistol, researched where the police would take Oswald, got himself into position to breach the police perimeter, then shot Oswald as he walked past with his police escort. Like Oswald, Ruby took his reasons to the grave.

Rather than psychological, our bent is more practical. It revolves around actions, behaviors, and other things hunters do. Dietz et al. compared individuals who had inap-propriately approached members of Congress with those who only wrote inappropriate letters to Congressmen. The approachers, of course, acted like hunters; the nonapproach-ers, like howlers. The study uncovered some fascinating differences in how hunters and howlers behave. It identified 10 factors statistically associated with approaching a member of Congress, all of them behaviors. Hunters

- Wrote repeated letters.
- Provided identifying information.
- Telephoned in addition to writing.
- Closed letters appropriately.
- Expressed themselves politely in their letters.
- Took the role of special constituent.
- Cast the member of Congress in a benefactor role, including the role of rescuer, benefactor, or potential benefactor.
- Repeatedly mentioned love, marriage, or romance.
- Expressed a desire for face-to-face contact with the member.
- Expressed a desire for rescue, assistance, valuables, or recognition.*

These characteristics can be summarized in a couple of broad generalizations distinc-tive of hunters. First, the Dietz team found that hunters change their behaviors. They write,

---

* Dietz, P. E., Matthews, D. B., Martell, D. A., Stewart, T. M., Hrouda, D. R., & Warren, J. (1991). Threatening and otherwise inappropriate letters to members of the United States Congress (p. 1463). *Journal of Forensic Sciences, 36.*

then telephone, then approach. Second, and more importantly, hunters want something more than the reaction that their communication causes. They want the Congressman's help, assistance, marriage, or affection. The letter or phone call is a means to some other end, not an end in itself. Perhaps that explains the study's finding that "subjects who sent inappropriate letters that contained no threats were significantly more likely to pursue a face-to-face encounter."* Those who hunt members of Congress know they will not get what they want with threats. Other actions work better.

Dietz et al. also conducted a similar comparison among those who inappropriately approached a Hollywood celebrity compared with those who merely communicated inappropriately in writing. The team found that those who sent a total of 10 to 14 communications (not more and not less) to a particular celebrity were most likely to approach. In addition, celebrity hunters

- Corresponded for a year or longer.
- Expressed a desire for face-to-face contact with the celebrity.
- Announced a specific time when something would happen to the celebrity.
- Announced a specific location where something would happen to the celebrity.
- Made repeated mentions of entertainment products.
- Telephoned in addition to writing.
- Sent letters from two or more different postmarks.†

Like the Congressional hunters, celebrity hunters actually wanted to meet the celebrity. They changed their behaviors from writing to telephoning to approaching. They saw a future relationship of some sort beyond the letter writing and they planned accordingly. For celebrity hunters, the inappropriate communications were only one means to their ends. The letters were not ends in themselves. Secret Service researchers also found that individuals who intended to use violence against public officials avoided threatening those officials. The researchers once interviewed a man who had stalked President George H. W. Bush with the intention of assassinating him. "Why," they asked him, "did he never threaten the president?" The man responded incredulously, "Why would I threaten the president; I really wanted to kill him. If I had threatened him, you guys would have arrested me before I could carry out my plan."‡

As Dietz found, hunter behaviors are observable if the threat manager knows what to look for. Making those observations raises another key issue. Because the threat manager cannot see everything, he or she should train those who are in a position to notice suspicious activities on what to look for and to whom to report. The training should be extended not only to potential targets but also to their staffs, families, and associates. These individuals then serve as the "Doppler radar" for alerting the threat manager about potential problem individuals, suspicious events, or inappropriate contacts.

---

* Dietz, P. E., Matthews, D. B., Martell, D. A., Stewart, T. M., Hrouda, D. R., & Warren, J. (1991). Threatening and otherwise inappropriate letters to members of the United States Congress (p. 1466). *Journal of Forensic Sciences*, 36.
† Dietz, P. E., Matthews, D. B., van Duyne, C., Martell, D. A., Parry, D. H., Stewart, T., … Crowder, J. D. (1991). Threatening and otherwise inappropriate letters to Hollywood celebrities. *Journal of Forensic Science*, 36, 208.
‡ Author's conversation with Robert Fein and Bryan Vossekuil, ca. 1996.

In sum, threat managers must train themselves to see the world and the people who populate it differently. Threat managers must recognize all the myriad attack-related behaviors that comprise the path to intended violence. They must piece together seemingly unrelated reports or incidents or behaviors that, taken as a whole, portray a hunter. Why is that person asking questions about schedules? Who is that guy watching our building? What did the caller mean by the statement, "People have limits on how much they're persecuted?" When did that suspicious bag appear on the sidewalk? Where did the protestors go? By using the concept of the path to intended violence, threat managers can sharply focus their thinking and analyses to spotlight hunters when they first appear.

In reviewing the six steps along the path to intended violence, we use Paul Hill's odyssey as a prime example of how an individual moves along the path. Hill, a former Presbyterian minister turned car detailer, husband, and father of three, began his trek to attack on March 10, 1993. He reached the end of the path 16 months later, on July 29, 1994. Nearly a decade after that, the state of Florida executed Hill for two cold-blooded murders.

On Grievances

On March 10, 1993, Michael Griffin assassinated Dr. David Gunn, purportedly to keep Dr. Gunn from performing any more abortions in Pensacola, Florida. Paul Hill had recently moved his family to Pensacola. Although never particularly active in the antiabortion movement before Gunn's murder, the killing converted Hill into an active, vocal proponent of the so-called "justifiable homicide" doctrine espoused by violent, radical antiabortionists. These ideologues argued that saving a fetus justified killing the doctors and their staffs who performed abortions. Five days after the shooting, Hill appeared on the Phil Donahue Show *opposite Dr. Gunn's son. He defended Griffin's act.* Ironically, Hill initiated his proselytizing at about the same time that Griffin began denying he had killed the doctor. A jury ultimately convicted Griffin.*

For the next 16 months, Hill enjoyed periodic spurts of publicity for his defense of justifiable homicide. In addition to appearing on Donahue, *he also appeared on ABC's* Nightline *and talked to interviewers from a host of other media outlets.* Hill always carefully prefaced his remarks with the caution that he had no intent to actually harm a doctor, but he approved and encouraged anyone else who might. He also came to see himself as a better representative than Griffin of the violently radical wing of the antiabortion movement. In Hill's mind, Griffin's cries of innocence and charges of conspiracy diminished the importance of acting violently "in defense of the unborn." As a former Presbyterian minister, Hill believed he had more stature than Griffin.† Surely, his words carried more credibility than Griffin's act.*

In his spare time away from working as a car detailer, Hill began demonstrating at the Ladies Center clinic.* Pensacola police arrested him several times for trespassing and disturbing the peace. Although some of the veteran protestors originally viewed him skeptically, over the course of those 16 months, Hill rose to some prominence within the Pensacola-based antiabortion community. But time also had the effect of thrusting other issues onto the front pages and the talk shows. Hill and his radical cause became old news. Hill shrouded his grievance with religious and moral convictions against abortion, although his desire for infamy undoubtedly also influenced his actions.

---

* "Who Is Paul Hill?" author unknown, http://www.armyofgod.com/PaulHillindex.html.
† Hill, P. (1999, June). Why I shot an abortionist (pp. 1–2). Retrieved from http://www.armyofgod.com/Paul Hillindex.html.

Grievances, like the ideation that may follow, involve a state of mind, not necessarily discernable behaviors. That means that each hunter gets to choose whether to reveal his or her particular grievance. In contrast, for example, when hunters reach the research and planning step, they engage in behaviors requiring them to act in public where those actions are noticeable. The activities include information gathering, surveillance, suspicious inquiries, drawing maps or diagrams, making lists, and creating diaries or blogs. Neither grievance nor ideation necessarily entails such overt, observable activities.

Individuals may choose to express their grievances in a variety of different ways. Hill took his public and sought as much media attention as he could get. Other hunters write letters, make telephone calls, or talk about their problems with anyone who will listen. On August 24, 2001, Louis W. Joy III told a friend he was despondent because his estranged wife had obtained a restraining order against him. Joy's despondency was compounded with humiliation when police officers escorted him through his own house to collect his things. The next day, Joy flew his plane into the house, destroying it and killing himself. The coroner ruled the crash deliberate.*

Often, the subject's fixation on the problem strikes others as obsessive. The subject appears singularly focused on the grievance. His or her behavior concerning the issue comes across as intense, unbending, emotionally exaggerated, and fixated. Clinic workers at Ladies Center became concerned enough about how intense Paul Hill acted that they began videotaping his protest activities.† Somehow, for them, he stood out from the other protestors. Reid Meloy, studying approachers and attackers on public figures, developed a concept he coined "intensity of pursuit" by which Meloy meant that the more intensely a subject communicated with the target, the more likely the subject would eventually approach or attack that target.‡ Paul Hill's behavior in the weeks leading up to his attack grew increasingly more intense. Augustin Garcia of Hackensack, New Jersey, considered Gladys Ricart his wife, even though they had never bothered with getting married. For most individuals, that problem would have been mooted after she broke up with him, but Garcia refused to acknowledge the end of the affair. Throughout the summer of 1999, Garcia kept the faith that they would reunite. Although he later claimed ignorance of her wedding plans to another man, he drove to her house on September 26, 1999, with a pistol in his briefcase and extra bullets in his coat pocket. He crashed the wedding and killed her.§ Individuals who obsess over their grievances are only a step away from accepting violence as the only way to solve their problems.

Grievances come in all shapes and sizes. In September 2000, Sophal Prom killed her coworker, Darlene Adams, because Prom could not keep the pace that Adams set on the Prestige Display and Packaging assembly line.¶ In December of that year, former Georgia Sheriff Sidney Dorsey and two other men killed Dorsey's successor, who had beaten him in a hotly contested election.** In April 2002, Peter B. Mehran killed the man who lived in the apartment below him because the neighbor had complained about how loud Mehran played

---

* Pilot dies as plane hits house in N.H. (2002, August 27). Associated Press.
† Authors' personal knowledge.
‡ Meloy, J. R. (2011). Approaching and attacking public figures: A contemporary analysis of communications and behavior. In C. Chauvin (Ed.), *Threatening communications and behavior: Perspectives on the pursuit of public figures* (pp. 75–102). Washington, DC: The National Academies Press.
§ Man guilty of murdering girlfriend. (2001, October 22). Associated Press.
¶ Edwards, J. (2001, December 14). Woman sentenced for killing co-worker. *Cincinnati Enquirer.*
** Arrests made in slaying of Ga. Sheriff. (2001, November 30). Associated Press.

his music. Notes found in Mehran's car indicated that he planned the killing and intended to escape. During the shooting, however, Mehran managed to shoot himself as well as his neighbor. Both died.* A month later, patrons at a bar in a small town in Pennsylvania challenged Jon McClure's claim that he had fought in the Gulf War. Outraged that anyone would question his war record, McClure went home, retrieved a shotgun, and returned to the bar. He killed three people and wounded one. The next day, he killed himself rather than surrender to police.[†]

On October 16, 2014, Scott Peters got into a domestic dispute at his home in Holiday Hills, Illinois. Peters appeared so emotionally invested in the dispute that he shot two sheriff's deputies who responded to the scene.[‡] On February 10, 2015, Chapel Hill, North Carolina, police arrested Craig Hicks on charges of murder. The family of the three victims labeled the incident a hate crime because the victims were Muslims of Arab descent. Investigators, however, soon came to believe a fight over parking spaces at the apartment complex where the shooter and the victims all lived probably motivated Hicks because they shared a history of fighting over the limited spaces. According to Karen Hicks, the suspect's wife, Hicks championed individual rights and believed everyone was equal—unless, apparently, someone dared take his parking space.[§] Grievances grow from individual peculiarities; they need not be either objectively rational or even understandable by the reasonable man, just persuasive to the hunter.

Lots of people get shown up by coworkers, but they do not react violently. In every election, one side always loses, but the losers rarely go shooting after the winner. Neighbors complain about each other all the time without resorting to violence to resolve their disputes. Barroom arguments may lead to brawls, but rarely do they end in shotgun blasts. Most domestic disputes do not end in attacks on the police. Neighbors usually find places to park. Yet, all these grievances led to violent outcomes. Like beauty, the importance of any particular issue lies in the eye of the beholder. One person's grievance is another's minor annoyance.

By 1992, Robert Mack had worked at General Dynamics for over 20 years. Then his performance started to fall off. He began going absent without leave. When he did show up for work, his productivity fell well below that of his coworkers. In response, his supervisor suspended him for 3 days. While Mack stayed home, the supervisor, acting in consultation with union representatives, decided to dismiss Mack. Management and the union representative cosigned a letter to Mack informing him that he had been fired and setting a date 3 weeks away for him to meet with the supervisor and the union representative to finish the termination proceedings.

Robert Mack took offense, but not at the termination. He knew his job performance had declined. However, the way the company informed him about it deeply offended him. After 20 years on the job, they wrote him a letter rather than telephoning or facing him in person. The letter bothered him so much that every time he closed his eyes to rest, the letter appeared in his mind, bursting into flames. If only someone had called him, had

---

* Dispute over music leaves two dead. (2002, April 2). Associated Press.
† Three killed in PA. bar shooting. (2002, May 1). Associated Press.; PA. cops: Gunman argued over past. (2002, May 2). Associated Press.
‡ Deputies shot, suspect on the loose near Chicago. (2014, October 16). Associated Press.
§ Katz, J. M., & Perez-Pena, R. (2015, February 11). In Chapel Hill shooting of 3 Muslims, a question of motive. *New York Times*; Kaplan, S. (2015, February 12). Alleged Chapel Hill killer described as neighborhood troublemaker, obsessed with parking and noise. *Washington Post*.

shown just a little of a personal approach, he would have been all right with the company's decision. He held the company accountable, he explained later, because it dehumanized everything. According to Mack, General Dynamics bore the blame for what he did. On the day scheduled for his meeting with the supervisor and union man, Mack took with him a rifle. He shot both men in the head, killing one and severely wounding the other.*

The General Dynamics tragedy illustrates the peculiarity about grievances. Each grievance is highly unique and personal to the offended individual. At first glance, any rational explanation for Mack's motive would be that the company fired him after 20 years on the job. But that was not what prompted Mack. He knew his work performance had fallen off. He knew he had gone absent without leave. In sum, he knew the company had sufficient reason to terminate him. He simply objected to how his supervisor and the union representative handled the termination.

Grievances are individually peculiar things. In 1988, for example, a Mafia don went on trial for a host of crimes. Throughout the proceedings, the don sat stoically. He evinced no anger or personal feelings toward the prosecutor even though he faced the prospect of spending the rest of his life in prison. Even after his conviction, the don held no grudge. One day, however, the don overheard one of the assistant U.S. attorneys speculating about seizing the don's wife's fur coat as an illicitly obtained asset. Infuriated at this perceived insult to his wife, the don let a contract to have the prosecutor killed.†

It matters less what the particular grievance is than how emotionally invested the individual is with the issue. Eric Harris complained to his diary that classmates did not invite him to join their various activities. "I hate you people for leaving me out of so many fun things. You people had my phone, and I asked and all, but no no no no no no don't let the weird looking Eric come along." He and Dylan Klebold attacked their high school in Columbine, Colorado, killing a dozen fellow students and a teacher. In describing their plan, Harris confessed, "I want to leave a lasting impression on the world."‡ Other school shooters have felt equally embittered over what they considered personal slights from their classmates, although not all were quite as grandiose in their ambitions as Harris and Klebold. By any objective, rational standard, not being invited to after-school social events hardly warranted shooting up the school. Except, of course, it mattered enough to Harris and Klebold.

In March 2004, two second-grade boys hid a .22-caliber revolver and a box of bullets in the playground sandbox. They intended to kill a fifth-grade girl because she had teased them. Fortunately, another student reported the two boys, and authorities disrupted their plan.§ Yet, who has not been teased in school? Most students respond with teasing of their own. With these two boys, the teasing assumed a grave importance that went well beyond how most students deal with schoolyard taunting.

The individualized nature of grievances means that the threat manager needs to look for direct evidence for the motive and avoid deducing what it might be. Grievances are highly personalized to the individuals holding them. They simply cannot be ascertained by any "reasonable man" approach, test, or deduction. By any objective standard, individual

* Fired worker kills one man, injures another at plant. (1992, January 24). United Press International.
† Calhoun, F. S. (1998). *Hunters and howlers: Threats and violence against Federal Judicial officials in the United States, 1979–1993* (p. 3). Washington, DC: United States Marshal Service.
‡ CNN.com, December 5, 2001.
§ 3 arrested in plot to shoot classmate. (2004, March 18). Associated Press.

grievances can appear unreasonable, illogical, even goofy. Indeed, any review of violent incidents frequently leaves one wondering how such a petty or trivial or bizarre issue could result in carnage. Unfortunately, no "objective standard" applies to individual grievances precisely because they are so subjective. What matters is not how important the issue is, but how important the subject perceives the issue to be.

Consequently, trying to identify individuals who may intend violence by trying to deduce their possible grievances rarely works. Just as importantly, it may send the threat manager in the wrong direction because the tendency is always to apply the rational man approach. Looking for reasonable motives is an unreasonable approach to threat management. Among school shooters, for example, perhaps only Peter Odighizuwa had the most readily understandable motive for killing three of his professors and wounding three students at his law school in western Virginia. A day earlier, Odighizuwa had been suspended over his failing grades. Even so, lots of students fail without turning to violence. Only Odighizuwa can really know why his suspension spawned a violent result. Violence is rarely understandable to anyone but the perpetrator.[*]

The highly individualized nature of grievances makes it exceedingly difficult, if not impossible, to try to identify potentially violent people by first ascertaining what their particular motives are. Although having a grievance is the first step on the path to intended violence, rarely can it be the first step in identifying the violent individual. On February 28, 2005, someone broke into Judge Lefkow's basement window and killed her husband and her mother. News reports immediately focused suspicion on Matthew Hale. Based solely on motive, he seemed a likely enough suspect. Judge Lefkow had presided over his criminal trial some years earlier. She found him guilty. More importantly, he had subsequently been convicted of conspiring to assassinate her. It seemed clear to everyone that he had ample motive, that is, revenging his criminal conviction and finishing his interrupted plans to have her killed.

Yet, despite these strong motives, Hale had a slight problem in terms of his ability to go after the judge. He had no assets and was kept in solitary confinement until his sentencing, his only visitors his mother and father.[†] It is hard enough to contract a killing when one has the funds and the freedom to find an assassin. Indeed, when Hale tried the first time, he ended up contracting with a Federal Bureau of Investigation informant, which is what landed him in jail and solitary confinement. Convincing someone to do it for free while you languish in prison presents extraordinary difficulties.

Bart Ross took his grievance over a civil lawsuit through the rest of the steps to intended violence and launched his attack. Compared with Hale, Ross's issue hardly attracted attention. But it was important to him. He had invested enough emotion in his complaint that it had become an obsession. Acting violently against those in the judicial system seemed the only resolution for him. Hale may have had plenty of motive, but Ross had motive and ability, and he had created his own opportunities.

The Lefkow case raises an interesting point about grievances and their use in identifying individuals of violent intent. Precisely because grievances are so personal to the individual, they offer little value as a means of identifying violent intent. Indeed, as with the

[*] Kunkle, F., & Timberg, C. (2002, January 17). Dean, 2 others fatally shot at rural Virginia Law School. *Washington Post*.
[†] Dardick, H., & Sadovi, C. (2005, March 11). Decade of despair boiled over to paranoia. *Chicago Tribune*; MCarthy, B. (2005, March 14). Lefkow killer tracked in '99. *Chicago Tribune*.

Lefkow case, focusing first on who reasonably has the most logical grievance can be, and frequently is, misleading. Too many threat management cases show that linking grievance to violence does not support the reasonable man test. Too often, people's objections are entirely irrational, many even *unreasonable* to anyone but the subject.

Although grievance is the first step along the path to intended violence, it cannot be the initiating point for threat management. For example, many Americans oppose abortions and pray for the procedures to stop. The vast majority of these people do not follow the path taken by Hill. Similarly, everyone at one time or other feels aggrieved about something, but by far, most people do not let that issue, hurt, or slight propel them to violence. Consequently, identifying that someone has a grievance does not mean, ipso facto, that the individual will resort to violence. Grievance is the first necessary step, but feeling aggrieved does not unalterably commit the aggrieved individual to any future acts. Other steps must follow.

In addition, many individuals embarked on the path to violence keep their grievance secret. Revealing it pinpoints the target, which the subject may not want to happen until he or she is ready. Subjects intent on violence do not want too much information getting out and used against them. Kevin Cruz made no contact with his former company until November 3, 1999, when he walked into an office at the Northlake Shipyard in Washington State and fired 11 rounds, killing two people and wounding two others. According to press reports, "prosecutors believe he harbored a grudge because he was fired soon after the company's insurance company cut off his benefits for a work-related injury, saying he wasn't really hurt."* Because grievances are personal, they are easy to keep secret. They reside in the subject's head, which means that revealing them is entirely at the subject's discretion.

Some subjects initially announce their grievances in legal, proper, ways. They file lawsuits, initiate complaints, or make protests. They feel, like both Hill and Ross, that they have pursued every legitimate option open to them, but all without success. That continued failure, as well as an ultimate inability to recognize more or different options, moves the subject forward to violence, almost as a last resort. The complete frustration caused by feeling powerless and unheard pushes these subjects onto the path to intended violence.

But when it comes to grievances, the threat manager knows one certainty. Once an individual comes to attention because he or she has reached a later stage along the path, that individual first had a grievance. The steps along the path are sequential. Grievance always comes first. Once the threat manager identifies a subject as a potential hunter, the protective investigation can determine what the subject's issue really is. Knowing the motive helps inform the threat assessment. The threat manager can assess the subject's emotional investment in the grievance. Obviously, the stronger the investment, the higher the risk.

Once someone is identified through other means as potentially contemplating violence, then determining what that grievance is can be extraordinarily useful in assessing the risk he or she poses. Had law enforcement officers identified Ross, checking his court filings and past behaviors would have shown them the depth of his emotional investment in his civil case against Northwestern University Hospital. They would also have found how desperate he felt because of the wrongs he believed he had received from the judicial system in general, Judge Lefkow in particular. The intensity of his feelings clearly would have led to an assessment that he posed a significant risk. We know this to be true because

---

* Shipyard shooter guilty of 2 deaths. (2002, February 11). Associated Press.

5 years earlier, Ross came to the attention of law enforcement officers assigned to the state's attorney general's office. After investigating him and interviewing him, the officers concluded that he posed a significant risk.* Before he could act out, his attention shifted to seeking relief through the federal courts. That led him to Judge Lefkow.

In sum, threat managers need to understand the subject's grievance, but that understanding usually comes after the subject comes to their attention for other actions related to other steps along the path to intended violence. That understanding plays a crucial role in the assessment and management stages of threat management, but rarely in the identifying phase.

On Ideation of Violence

On July 21, 1994, an idea struck Paul Hill like a thunderbolt. For nearly a year and a half, he had expressed his grievances over abortion. He had preached the need to take lives in order to save others. He had demonstrated at the local clinic to show his opposition, but until July 21, he openly avowed that he would not personally turn to violence. On that day, he reached his personal Rubicon. He decided it was time to go beyond talking and demonstrating to action. He later remembered detailing a used car and wondering who would be the next attacker on an abortion doctor. Suddenly, "the idea of acting myself struck; it hit hard.... I began to consider what would happen if I were to shoot an abortionist. My eyes were opened to the enormous impact another such shooting in Pensacola would have."[†]

Interestingly, at this moment of personal epiphany, Hill's language began to incorporate shades of violence: "The idea of acting myself struck; it hit hard." He added, "I realized that many people were still reeling from the previous shootings. A second punch, in the same spot, would continue a chain reaction."[‡] The idea of violence found expression in violent terms.

Still, Hill later confessed, "the decision was agonizing." He would forfeit his wife and family and undoubtedly spend the rest of his life in prison. Yet, once he crossed that great divide between grievance and ideation, he felt better for it. "When I went from debating whether to act, in general, to planning a particular act, I felt some relief." Having taken the biggest step, deciding on violence, the other steps seemed far less challenging. According to Hill, once he crossed to ideation, "I felt that the Lord had placed in my hands a cup whose contents were difficult to swallow, but that it was a task that had to be borne."[§]

Hill chose to keep his ideation a secret lest someone try to stop him. Still, he admitted that during the 8 days between the time the idea struck him and the attack, he remained withdrawn and preoccupied. On a family outing to the beach, Hill felt detached. "I enjoyed watching them through eyes unknown to them—like a man savoring his last supper."[¶] He knew he could keep his secret from his wife only so long. If he did not act soon, while she and the children were away on vacation, "she would almost certainly develop suspicions later, and my plans would be spoiled for fear of implicating her."[**] Still, Hill took great pains to hide his emotions and give no clues as to the terrible thing he intended to do. On that hot Florida day, while cleaning a used car, Hill reached the second stop along his personal path to intended violence.

* Dardick, H., & Sadovi, C. (2005, March 11). Decade of despair boiled over to paranoia. *Chicago Tribune*.
† Hill, P. (1999, June). Why I shot an abortionist (p. 1). Retrieved from http://www.armyofgod.com/Paul Hillindex.html.
‡ Hill, P. (1999, June). Why I shot an abortionist (p. 3). Retrieved from http://www.armyofgod.com/Paul Hillindex.html.
§ Hill, P. (1999, June). Why I shot an abortionist (p. 5). Retrieved from http://www.armyofgod.com/Paul Hillindex.html.
¶ Hill, P. (1999, June). Why I shot an abortionist (p. 4). Retrieved from http://www.armyofgod.com/Paul Hillindex.html.
** Hill, P. (1999, June). Why I shot an abortionist (pp. 3–4). Retrieved from http://www.armyofgod.com /PaulHillindex.html.

As Hill's experience showed, the second step along the path to intended violence requires crossing something of a watershed in the subject's trajectory from grievance to attack. Arriving at the decision that violence offers the only resolution to the subject's issue is a great leap forward along the path. In many ways, ideation requires the biggest step of them all. The vast majority of people suffering some sense of injustice do not cross that great divide to seeking violence. Perhaps only the actual attack demands as much fortitude and determination as deciding to do it.

Like Hill, many hunters choose to keep their decisions secret. Still, ideation can be detected through the hunter's observable behavior. Because reaching ideation is such a watershed, crossing it can result in changes in demeanor or behavior. After July 21, Paul Hill acted preoccupied, distracted, even troubled. Jack McKnight, who attacked the Topeka, Kansas, federal courthouse, refused to talk about the future beyond prison with either his lawyer or probation officer.* Having received a 10-year sentence for growing marijuana, McKnight's ideation included his own suicide. He knew he had no future. Other hunters may seem resolved, perhaps even relieved that the deciding point has passed. For those hunters who have loudly and frequently proclaimed their grievance, a lapse into silence may point to ideation. Indeed, *any* change in behavior may indicate a decision.

Bolder hunters may act more expressly. They may communicate inappropriately with their targets or, like Hill, use more violently expressive language. Their attention may focus on particular dates or anniversaries or court appointments. Some hunters take their inspiration from media reports of major acts of violence or by the examples of iconic assassins such as Lee Harvey Oswald, Sirhan Sirhan, or John Hinckley. Harris and Klebold clearly served as role models for succeeding generations of school shooters. For example, Adam Lanza, who killed more than two dozen individuals at Sandy Hook Elementary School in December 2012, greatly admired—to the point of obsession—the Columbine killers.[†]

Hill saw himself as a step above Griffin. Arthur Bremer, who shot George Wallace, felt like the man who shot Archduke Ferdinand in 1914, thus setting off the chain of events that culminated in World War I.[‡] Secret Service researchers interviewed a woman who was preparing to kill President George H. W. Bush. She had become fixated on John Wilkes Booth, even going so far as to buy the same model Derringer that Booth had used to shoot Lincoln.[§] Such obsessive attention to particular details can signal that the hunter has decided to prepare for the hunt.

Some subjects, when considering violence, communicate in grandiose ways, associating their grievance to some larger issue or campaign. The subject is not involved in a simple insurance dispute but has taken on a widespread conspiracy between the judge and the insurance company lawyers. The old saying that people can measure their power and importance by the power and importance of their enemies certainly applies to many hunters. Paul Hill believed his act of murder would spark a nationwide revolution. Edward

---

* Calhoun, F. S. (1998). *Hunters and howlers: Threats and violence against Federal Judicial officials in the United States, 1979–1993* (pp. 107–108). Washington, DC: United States Marshal Service.
† Sedensky III, S. J., State's Attorney, Office of the State's Attorney Judicial District of Danbury. (2013, November 25). Report of the State's Attorney for the Judicial District of Danbury on the Shootings at Sandy Hook Elementary School and 36 Yogananda Street, Newtown Connecticut, on December 14, 2012 (p. 3).
‡ de Becker, G., Taylor, T., & Marquart, J. (2008). *Just two seconds: Using time and space to defeat assassins* (p. 24). Los Angeles: Gavin de Becker Center for the Study and Reduction of Violence.
§ Secret Service Presentation, National Sheriff's Association Threat Management Seminar, February 2000.

Lansdale, who, in October 2000, shot to wound the woman who had accused him of molesting her, believed his story would be sold for a movie or a *60 Minutes* investigation. Ismaaiyl Brinsley, the loser, sought redemption for his misled life by killing two New York City policemen. He framed the killings as a protest for alleged police brutality nationwide. For these hunters, their adversaries loom large.

Hunters have also been known to communicate or act ominously, although short of explicit threats of violence. Lansdale told his daughter and her mother he would be dead in 2 weeks from an unspecified disease. He gave his car to the mother and added his daughter's name to the title of his house.*

In the fall of 2001, a high school girl warned her favorite teacher that a handful of the girl's friends were plotting to harm both students and teachers. School administrators at the New Bedford (Massachusetts) High School had heard other rumors about the plot. The information allowed them to forestall it.†

For intimates who become hunters, their point of ideation may coincide with their making explicit threats of harm or death toward their target. They almost take pride in announcing that they reached the ideation stage, often in very graphic language. Over the course of a year, Steven Lancaster repeatedly sent ominous, threatening notes to his estranged wife, Janice: "I'm ready to go any time to lay my body to rest and [I am] not going to be the only one." He told their children he was "going to kill your mother stone dead." On January 3, 2000, Steven killed Janice, then himself.‡

Shortly after David Reza was fired from the San Onofre Nuclear Generating Station in 2001, he began making threatening phone calls to former supervisors and other employees. "He said he had lots of guns and he was going to come back and shoot them," a sheriff's office spokesman reported. Reza spoke the truth. When police arrested him for the threats, they also carried out a search of his residence and a rented storage locker. They found more than 250 firearms, including assault rifles, tear gas, hand grenades, thousands of rounds of ammunition, and a container of explosive powder.§ Reza wanted his fellow workers to know he was coming.

Although not all hunters directly threaten their targets, many communicate their plans to someone else—a phenomenon now called "leakage." During the last week of October 2005, William Freund posted messages on an online forum describing his intention to launch a "terror campaign" using his newly purchased Remington 870 shotgun. "It's the synthetic Kind [sic] so IT [sic] looks very modern and is super heavy to whack people with," he posted. The operators of the website tried to contact Freund's parents but decided against alerting law enforcement out of concern that the young man had enough problems already. On Saturday, October 29, Freund donned a dark cape and a paintball mask and went prowling through his neighborhood armed with his shotgun. He killed two neighbors, fired at another house, and tried to shoot a third neighbor, but the Remington jammed. Freund then went home and killed himself.¶

---

* Calhoun, F. S., & Weston, S. W. (2001). *Defusing the risk to judicial officials: The contemporary threat management process* (pp. 3–5). Alexandria, VA: National Sheriffs' Association.
† Ferdinand, P. (2001, December 27). Shaken but unharmed, Mass. School says 'the system worked.' *Washington Post*.
‡ St. George, D. (2000, August 27). Murder in the making: Those who knew Janice Lancaster saw bits and pieces of a family tragedy. She saw more and struggled to change it. *Washington Post*.
§ Calif. man arrested for threats. (2002, January 9). Associated Press.
¶ Yoshino, K., Tran, M., & Berthelsen, C. (2005, November 2). Threats online: Is there a duty to tell. *Los Angeles Times*.

Sirhan Sirhan told his garbage collector that he intended to kill Robert F. Kennedy. Liam Youens maintained an Internet blog where he discussed his plans to kill Amy Boyer. He consummated those plans on October 15, 1999.[*] Harris and Klebold also posted their violent musings on a website.[†] Several months before McKnight shot up the Topeka courthouse, he said to a friend, "What I ought to do is kill all those bastards," apparently referring to the people in the justice system who were sending him to prison for 10 years.[‡] Mike Bowers wrote California governor Gray Davis in 1999 to complain about Bowers' treatment at the Atascadero State (mental) Hospital in San Luis Obispo County. Bowers also made a number of delusional statements, commented on the fall of the Soviet Union, and claimed to be the leader of the new world order. On January 17, 2001, he crashed his 80,000-pound truck into the California Capitol, burning himself alive, but injuring no one else.[§] Ismaaiyl Brinsley sent out Instagram messages claiming his intent to avenge the deaths of Michael Brown and Eric Garner, whose name he misspelled.

The signs indicating a subject has reached ideation tend to be expressive indicators such as dramatic changes in behavior, inappropriate communications with violent themes, threats, references to violence, or descriptions of themselves as martyrs to a larger cause. The clues consist of any indications that the subject has begun thinking about violence in general or acting out violently in particular. But ideation, as its name indicates, is about ideas, and ideas can be very closely held by the person having them. Fortunately, the remaining four steps along the path to intended violence require overt, observable behaviors.

In sum, the threat manager should look for changes in behavior, references to violence, threats to intimates or colleagues, obsessive attention to details related to violent acts, or undue interest in other acts of violence as indicators that a hunter may be emerging. Unfortunately, the absence of these behaviors does not provide counter-indications that the subject is not a hunter. As Paul Hill demonstrated, hunters are perfectly capable of keeping their ideas to themselves.

On Research and Planning

Paul Hill had several things to take into account in devising his plan to kill an abortion doctor. First, Hill knew that the doctor came to Pensacola every Friday. Second, he wanted to get the assassination over with while his wife and children were out of town on vacation. That gave him only a brief window of opportunity. Knowing her travel plans, Hill reckoned that "I would have the remainder of the day she left, and all of Thursday, to prepare to act on Friday—eight days after the idea first struck me."[¶] As part of his research, the day after reaching his decision, Hill went to the clinic to protest. He described discovering a crucial piece of information. Normally, Hill arrived at the clinic before any other protestors. On this morning, exactly a week before his attack, another protestor had beaten him to the scene: "After discrete questioning, I learned he had been there when the abortionist had arrived, about 7:30…. I discovered that the abortionist

[*] Barry, E. (1999, November 29). Killer's dreams bared on the Internet/N.H. man took to web to boast and to stalk. *Boston Globe*.

[†] Erickson, W. et al. (2001). *The report of Governor Bill Owens' Columbine Review Commission* (p. 17). Denver, CO: Governor's Office.

[‡] Calhoun, F. S. (1998). *Hunters and howlers: Threats and violence against Federal Judicial officials in the United States, 1979–1993* (p. xvii). Washington, DC: United States Marshal Service.

[§] Authors' personal knowledge.

[¶] Hill, P. (1999, June). Why I shot an abortionist (p. 3). Retrieved from http://www.armyofgod.com /PaulHillindex.html.

had arrived prior to the police security guard. This information was like a bright green light, signaling me on." His wife's vacation schedule, combined with the doctor's work schedule, determined the date Hill would attack. His research gave him the timing of it. Since he already owned a shotgun, he knew what weapon to use. Next, he needed a plan.*

Hill used the information he had to plot out what he would do. The following Friday, he would arrive at the clinic before 7:30 a.m. After that, "my plan was to carry the shotgun from my parked truck to the front of the abortion clinic in a rolled-up poster board protest sign. I would leave the concealed shotgun lying on the ground until the abortionist drove past me into the clinic parking lot."†

Nonetheless, Hill later confessed, "in spite of my careful plans, the morning of the shooting was not easy."† Researching, planning, even preparing are nothing compared with actually acting out violently.

By its very nature, intended violence requires forethought and premeditation. That leads to some degree of research and some degree of planning, though both the research and the planning can be quite simplistic or elaborate. The Unabomber conducted sophisticated research in picking his targets, then in custom-building bombs designed to arouse the target's curiosity to ensure that he or she opened the package. In contrast, Sirhan Sirhan's plan was simplicity itself. He researched Kennedy's itinerary, hid in the kitchen closet, and shot the Senator as he walked past.

Research and planning entail overt behaviors. Hunters may need to conduct surveillance of the target, which requires them to go to some physical location for their observations. Arthur Bremer, for example, attended public rallies where President Nixon appeared and even followed him on a trip to Canada. During each public appearance, Bremer studied the Secret Service's security arrangements in hopes of finding a way to circumvent them. When that proved too difficult, he switched targets. A few weeks later, he shot Governor George Wallace.‡ Walter Moody researched Judge Robert Vance's personal life. He found out the judge's home address and gleaned some insights into who the judge's friends were. After constructing his mail bomb, Moody used as the return address the home address of a fellow judge.§ For both Moody and Bremer, their research required travel, making inquiries, and looking up information.

For some hunters, the research can be simple. William Strier shot attorney Jerry Curry six times outside the Van Nuys, California, courthouse on Halloween 2003. Curry represented the professional trustee who controlled a large trust fund set up for Strier after an automobile accident. The trustee had refused to release some funds Strier wanted. As Curry came out of the courthouse, Strier approached him and asked, "Are you Mr. Curry?" When the attorney affirmed his identity, Strier pulled his pistol and opened fire.¶ Mark Bowers, who crashed his tractor-trailer into the California Capitol, first circled the capitol

* Hill, P. (1999, June). Why I shot an abortionist (p. 3). Retrieved from http://www.armyofgod.com/Paul Hillindex.html.
† Hill, P. (1999, June). Why I shot an abortionist (p. 5). Retrieved from http://www.armyofgod.com/Paul Hillindex.html.
‡ Laucella, L. (1998). *Assassination: The politics of murder* (p. 309). Los Angeles: Lowell House.
§ Calhoun, F. S. (1998). *Hunters and howlers: Threats and violence against Federal Judicial officials in the United States, 1979–1993* (pp. 2–3). Washington, DC: United States Marshal Service.
¶ Curry, J. (2003, November 7). Interview by K. Couric. The *Today* Show.

complex, presumably looking for the most direct route that would allow him to get up plenty of speed.[*]

Other hunter behaviors indicating research and planning include information gathering; asking suspicious, personal, or detailed questions; and conducting research on the target or places frequented by the target or places scheduled for the target to visit. The planning may involve drawing maps or diagrams, making up a schedule, or keeping a diary. Bremer maintained a diary; Paul Hill had a personal schedule to keep. In early 2004, six students at the Laguna Creek (California) High School conspired to attack the school with guns and bombs. Alerted by a concerned parent, police searched the homes and found one antique .22. They also found a hand-drawn map of the school cafeteria. One of the students confessed that the plan included breaking into a local hardware store and stealing the firearms they needed.[†]

The plan need not be elaborate. In June 2001, Dominic Culpepper decided to kill Frank McCool because the 16-year-old had stolen a half-pound of his marijuana. Culpepper arranged for two other teenagers to lure McCool to Culpepper's home. Once there, Culpepper beat McCool to death with a baseball bat.[‡]

Oddly, the planning may take into account the hunter's personal issues. Hill wanted to murder the doctor while Hill's family was out of town on vacation. Charles the Poacher planned to firebomb a courthouse in California on the one night a week his jealous and possessive girlfriend had her hair done.[*] Being henpecked restricted his hunting.

In sum, the threat manager should pay special attention to any behavioral indicators that someone is conducting research on a target. Research and planning require overt, noticeable behaviors. Indeed, this is the stage where threat managers are most likely to identify suspicious subjects. That identification is crucial to threat management because without it, there can be no assessment and no opportunity for managing.

On Preparation

Paul Hill wanted to ensure nothing went wrong with his plans to kill the doctor on the one Friday his wife and children would be out of town. He took his shotgun to the firing range to practice. He later wrote: "One particular obstacle arose to test my determination. While practicing with my shotgun at a nearby gun range, it began to jam. A local sporting goods store had a handy replacement: a 12-gauge Mossberg shotgun with a shortened barrel and an extended magazine. It was called 'The Defender.'"[§] Hill clearly wanted to ensure that his weapon would not fail him.

Hill also engaged in another act of preparation common to those hunters who do not expect either to survive or escape after their attack. When he and his family went to the beach the Saturday before the Friday shooting, Hill used the occasion to say a silent good-bye to his wife and children. He remembered that afternoon feeling proud to be a father playing with his children in the surf: "They enjoyed their father's attention. I took them one by one...in water over their heads as they clung to my neck. As I carried and supported each child in the water, it was

---

[*] Authors' personal knowledge.
[†] Stanton, S., Bazar, E., & Kolber, M. (2004, February 11). Plan to attack school alleged. *Sacramento Bee.*
[‡] Teen convicted in fatal beating. (2002, February 14). Associated Press.
[§] Hill, P. (1999, June). Why I shot an abortionist (p. 5). Retrieved from http://www.armyofgod.com/Paul Hillindex.html. Curiously, subsequent revisions of Hill's account deleted the description of these preparations.

as though I was offering them to God as Abraham offered his son." Unbeknownst to his family,
Hill used the beach excursion as a final act of being together because he knew that prison would
soon separate him from them. He continued with other final-act behaviors up to the moment he
left to drive to the clinic. When Friday came, Hill rose early to prepare for the day by spending
"time in prayer and Bible reading."† Although his resolve started to weaken that morning, he
forced himself to go forward.*

Preparations involve putting things together and getting ready for the assault. Hunters
at this step engage in such behaviors as obtaining their weapon of choice, making sure it
works, assembling the necessary equipment, arranging their travel to the attack site, cos-
tuming, conducting final acts, or observing significant dates. In effect, they ready themselves to implement their assault plans.

Getting the weapon of choice ready is most important. When California police arrested
David Reza for making terroristic threats against his former supervisors and coworkers at
the San Onofre nuclear plant, they discovered he had amassed an arsenal of weapons and
explosives large enough to equip a small army.‡ Six weeks before Harris and Klebold shot
up their high school, they took the weapons they planned to use into the mountains and
practiced firing. Friends videotaped them.§ When Augustin Garcia drove by his former
girlfriend's house, he carried with him a handgun, with extra ammunition in his coat
pocket. Garcia's defense lawyer claimed that the shock of her imminent betrothal threw
Garcia into a violent rage, but his preparations for shooting her convinced the jury otherwise.¶ In all these instances, and in every instance of intended violence, hunters prepared
their weapons before the attacks. In making those preparations, they risked exposure.

Not all hunters hunt with firearms. Their choice of weapon can therefore complicate
their preparations. In February 2002, Gene Hodler tried to bring to an end his long-running
court dispute with his ex-girlfriend over several hundred thousand dollars they had
amassed together as day traders. Hodler rigged a pipe bomb to the turn signal on her car.
The explosion severely burned her feet and legs.** That attack required Hodler first to make
the pipe bomb, then wire it to the turn signal, both fairly elaborate preparations that also
risked exposure. Jordan Graham chose a simpler method of murder. She pushed her newly
married husband off a mountain ledge at Glacier National Park.††

Other hunters prefer toxicants. Vincent Hall of Fairfield, California, put insecticide
on his ex-girlfriend's lipstick and antidepressant medication. She tasted "something foul"
when she tried to bite her antidepressant pill in half.‡‡ Seven Denver fifth graders repeatedly
put pills, glue, lead, and chalk in another student's water bottle and sodas. The perpetrators
explained they did not like the victim and wanted to hurt her.§§ Elisa McNabney used horse

---

*   Hill, P. (1999, June). Why I shot an abortionist (p. 4). Retrieved from http://www.armyofgod.com/Paul
     Hillindex.html.
†   Hill, P. (1999, June). Why I shot an abortionist (p. 5). Retrieved from http://www.armyofgod.com/Paul
     Hillindex.html.
‡   Adler, J. (2002, January 10). Fired nuclear worker had arms cache, police say. *Washington Post*.
§   CBS *Evening News*, October 22, 2003.
¶   Man guilty of murdering girlfriend. (2001, October 22). Associated Press.
** Fla. man charged in pipe bomb blast. (2002, March 15). Associated Press.
†† Woman guilty of pushing husband off cliff appeals. (2014, October 24). Associated Press.
‡‡ Man accused of poisoning lipstick. (2002, July 18). Associated Press.
§§ Police: Students tried to poison girl. (2003, January 17). Associated Press.

tranquilizer to kill her husband,* whereas Ann Kontz used arsenic on hers.† James Keowin, well known in Missouri as a radio talk show host, killed his wife by spiking her Gatorade with a chemical constituent of antifreeze. She had found out he had lied about enrolling in Harvard Business School.‡ Ryan Furlough, at the time of the incident a Maryland teenager, put cyanide in a romantic rival's soda, killing him.§ In all of these toxic murders, the hunter first had to obtain the poison of choice and put it into something the victim would ingest, both acts of preparation someone might have noticed.

Securing the weapon may be the most crucial step, but it is still only part of the preparations that hunters make. Depending on the plan, they may need other equipment. Hunters who choose to attack with bombs first have to make or obtain the explosive device, then prepare to deliver it. In 1993, Jack McKnight spent over 40 hours constructing two dozen pipe bombs. On August 5, he personally delivered the bombs to the Topeka, Kansas, federal courthouse.¶ Christopher Bishop, knowing that his ex-wife worked in the Apex Supply Company mailroom, mailed two bombs to the company address. His ex-wife opened the first package and suffered minor burns on her face and hands when the bomb detonated. Another employee inadvertently opened the second package upside down so that the force of the explosion was directed away.** Bishop and McKnight, like all bombers, had to acquire their bomb-making equipment, assemble the bombs, and prepare them for delivery. Those activities exposed them to discovery.

Many plans require the hunter to arrange to get himself or herself to wherever the victim is. This can be simple, as when Hinckley took a cab to the Washington Hilton,†† or it can be more complicated, like Oswald's building his sniper's nest in the book depository where he worked. The Unabomber traveled from his Montana cabin as far away as the California coast to ensure the postmark on his mail bombs could not be traced back to him. The travel itself exposes the hunter to other people, thus posing the risk that someone may notice him or her.

Hunters also engage in final-act behaviors. In 1999, Mark Barton killed his wife on Wednesday, his two children on Thursday, and on Friday shot up two day-trading places where he had lost his life savings. On his way to the stock centers, he first went to his attorney's office and executed his last will and testament.‡‡ In the weeks before Lansdale's assault on his accuser in the Yreka courthouse, he spent several hours making audiotapes addressed to his sister in which he told her his reasons and justifications. He also encouraged her to sell his life story to a television movie producer for $10,000 (another grab for grandiosity).§§ On his last night alive, Jack Gary McKnight videotaped three messages to his in-laws. He asked his father-in-law to poison some trees the two men had planted on

*   Woman arrested in husband's death. (2002, March 19). Associated Press.
†   Kontz, A. M., murderpedia.org.
‡   Nation in brief. (2005, November 8). *Washington Post*.
§   MD. teen convicted of first-degree murder. (2004, May 18). Associated Press.
¶   Calhoun, F. S. (1998). *Hunters and howlers: Threats and violence against Federal Judicial officials in the United States, 1979–1993* (p. xviii). Washington, DC: United States Marshal Service.
** Police probe two bomb explosions. (2001, July 19). Associated Press.
†† Clarke, J. (1990). *On being mad or merely angry: John W. Hinckley and other dangerous people* (p. 6). Princeton, NJ: Princeton University Press.
‡‡ Authors' personal knowledge.
§§ Calhoun, F. S., & Weston, S. W. (2001). *Defusing the risk to judicial officials: The contemporary threat management process* (p. 4). Alexandria, VA: National Sheriffs' Association.

McKnight's farm. The next morning, McKnight killed his dogs before setting off for the Topeka federal building.* Sometimes, the final act brings complete finality.

In sum, the threat manager should take very seriously any evidence that the subject is preparing his or her attack. The preparations stage is the last step before the actual assault is launched. This is the point where the hunter begins implementing his or her plan of assault. It is also the last chance the threat manager has to intervene prior to the hunter's breaching security.

On Breach

Hill did not drive directly to the clinic. Instead, he "decided to drive past it first, to see if everything looked normal (I was concerned that someone may have become suspicious and called the police)."[†] A police car passed his truck going the opposite way, which startled him, so he drove farther on to make sure the squad car kept going. He turned the truck around, parked it, hid the shotgun as planned, and took up his post to await the doctor's arrival. As the moment approached, he began praying that the doctor would arrive before the police. "God heard my prayers," Hill wrote, "and the abortionist arrived prior to the police guard." Even then, Hill still had some security to breach. The doctor was escorted by James Barret, a retired general who had "vowed to shoot first and not miss," Hill claimed.[†] While Barret parked the truck, Hill retrieved his shotgun and walked down the clinic drive. "When I lifted the shotgun, two men were sitting in the front seats of the parked truck; Jim Barret, the escort, was directly between me and the abortionist."[†] With the shotgun aimed and ready to fire and the targets unaware of his approach, Hill had breached the doctor's last line of defense.

Breaches offer precious little time for security officers or targets to react. The famous Zapruder film shows Oswald's shots occurring within a time span of under 4 seconds. On November 1, 1950, Oscar Collazo and Griselio Torresola tried to shoot their way into Blair House to assassinate President Harry Truman. Secret Service agents blocked their way. The ensuing gunfight lasted less than 40 seconds, during which the combatants fired as many as 31 shots.[‡] Adam Lanza killed 20 first graders, 6 adults, and himself at Sandy Hook Elementary in less than 11 minutes.[§] For hunters who choose surreptitious assaults, such as poison or bombings, the time between breach and attack shrinks even more. For example, when Judge Vance opened the package sent by Moody, the explosion was practically instantaneous with his ripping open the package. Breach leaves precious little time for security to provide its defenses.

In sum, breach offers the threat manager one last chance to thwart the hunter. But as last chances go, breach allows little or no time to respond. It can be done but is expensive because it requires having sufficient bodyguards and other security countermeasures. That requires considerable training and infrastructure support. In the end, too, it relies on luck.

---

* Calhoun, F. S. (1998). *Hunters and howlers: Threats and violence against Federal Judicial officials in the United States, 1979–1993* (pp. xvii–xviii). Washington, DC: United States Marshal Service.
† Hill, P. (1999, June). Why I shot an abortionist (p. 6). Retrieved from http://www.armyofgod.com/Paul Hillindex.html.
‡ Hunter, S., & Bainbridge, J. Jr. (2005). *American gunfight: The plot to kill Harry Truman and the shoot-out that stopped it* (p. 3). New York: Simon & Schuster.
§ Sedensky III, S. J., State's Attorney, Office of the State's Attorney Judicial District of Danbury. (2013, November 25). Report of the State's Attorney for the Judicial District of Danbury on the Shootings at Sandy Hook Elementary School and 36 Yogananda Street, Newtown Connecticut, on December 14, 2012 (p. 2).

On Attack

As Hill walked down the clinic drive, he began firing. The first blasts killed the escort, who sat between Hill and his target. Hill emptied the shotgun into the driver's side of the truck, then reloaded as he walked around to the passenger side. He emptied the shotgun on that side as well, killing both the escort and the doctor and severely wounding Barret's wife, who was taking cover in the backseat. "When I finished shooting," Hill reported, "I laid the shotgun at my feet and walked away with my hands held out at my sides, awaiting arrest."* The police arrived quickly and took Hill into custody. Nearly a decade later, the state of Florida executed Hill by lethal injection.

Hill exemplified all the steps a hunter has to take along the path to intended violence. He acquired a grievance, came up with the idea of resolving that grievance through violence, researched his target and planned his attack, made preparations, breached the doctor's security, and attacked. Along the way, he engaged in observable behaviors. Once at ideation, his demeanor changed. His research required asking suspicious questions, such as did the police arrive before the doctor. His plan involved using his shotgun, so his preparations required practicing with it at the firing range. When the shotgun did not work, he purchased a new one. He also engaged in a few final-act behaviors, such as saying a silent goodbye to his family. At the clinic, he breached security by hiding the shotgun rolled up in a protest poster in the bushes along the clinic fence. Once the doctor and his escorts arrived, Hill retrieved the gun and began his fateful walk down the clinic drive.

Hill apparently even realized that his behaviors might have aroused suspicions. He reported that he worried that someone might have become suspicious and contacted the police, so he drove past the clinic to make sure all was clear. Clinic employees, although clearly unaware of Hill's murderous plans, did pick him out from among the other protestors as someone particularly to be concerned about. They had alerted police and frequently videotaped him to show he trespassed on clinic property. Police had arrested him for the trespassing. The clinic got an injunction against him to prevent him from getting too close to the clinic. But without a trained threat manager, no one recognized Hill as a hunter, so no one employed any threat management strategies to divert him off the path to intended violence.

In sum, if the subject reaches the attack step along the path to intended violence, both the threat management process and the physical security countermeasures failed. The threat management process depends on three crucial phases: *identifying* an individual who intends to act violently, *assessing* how far along the path to intended violence the subject has traveled, and *managing* the subject off the path. That process cannot begin at breach or attack. Thus, it is crucial that the identification occur much earlier, preferably at the research and planning step. For this reason, threat managers need to cultivate and promote a solid reporting process so that potential targets, their staffs, and their families know what to be aware of, what to report, and to whom to report it. Reporting inappropriate communications or suspicious behaviors allows the threat manager to initiate the threat management process.

---

* Hill, P. (1999, June). Why I shot an abortionist (p. 6). Retrieved from http://www.armyofgod.com/Paul Hillindex.html.

The Undetectable

We know of one extreme, and therefore exceptional, situation during which the hunter remained completely undetected—indeed, undetectable—until the moment he breached the target's security. Adam Lanza suffered from mental illnesses his entire life. Early on, his mother chose to accommodate his various symptoms rather than treat the underlying causes. Lanza's teachers, school psychologists, and the Connecticut mental health system eventually went along with the mother's insistence that everyone placate Lanza's "eccentricities." Ultimately, Lanza's high school teachers facilitated an early graduation for him at the end of his eleventh grade, no doubt hoping that in doing so they ridded themselves of a problem student. Instead, they allowed his mental state to fester and eventually permitted him to become someone else's problem, with tragic consequences.[*]

In the years, months, weeks, and, finally, days leading up to Lanza killing his mother while she slept in her bed, then killing 20 first graders, 6 adults, and himself at Sandy Hook Elementary School in New Town, Connecticut, we have been unable to detect a single point where anyone with the necessary authority could have identified his hunter-like behaviors and somehow intervened. Lanza's grievance grew out of his mental illness, a symptom of which was an obsessive fascination with mass shootings, especially school shootings. For example, Lanza maintained a spreadsheet detailing each shooting, including the number of victims.[†] That fascination undoubtedly prompted him to seize the idea for his violent act. He occasionally communicated with peers who shared his interest in such events, but he never expressed any interest in committing one himself. In the last months of his life, Lanza literally isolated himself from the world. He effectively sealed himself in his bedroom and refused to communicate with anyone, including his mother with whom he lived, except by e-mail. He developed anorexia—his corpse weighed only 112 pounds—so he had little risk of running into his mother in their kitchen.[‡] His self-imposed seclusion made his behaviors impossible to observe, much less manage.

His unique situation also did not require engaging in many public hunter-like behaviors. Years earlier, his divorced parents, trying desperately to find some activity to share with him, taught him how to shoot and bought him weapons. Lanza had no need to acquire the weapons he used as he already owned them. His mother taught him to drive and got him a car, the same car he used to drive himself to the nearby elementary school, nor did Lanza need to scout out the school because he had attended it as a youth. For Lanza, what we describe below as the "last-straw syndrome" appeared to occur when his mother announced her intention to sell the house and move to either North Carolina or Washington State. Although Lanza agreed to the move, it meant taking him from his sanctuary. That he ultimately could not abide.[§]

Lanza did engage in all the requisite behaviors along the path to intended violence. All killers do. Lanza just did it in a way that would have been near impossible to discern by anyone other than his mother who was facilitating the isolation. As the Office of the Child

---

[*] Report of the Office of the Child Advocate, State of Connecticut. (2014, November 21). Shooting at Sandy Hook Elementary School (p. 8) (hereinafter cited as "Child Advocate Report").

[†] Sedensky III, S. J., State's Attorney, Office of the State's Attorney Judicial District of Danbury. (2013, November 25). Report of the State's Attorney for the Judicial District of Danbury on the Shootings at Sandy Hook Elementary School and 36 Yogananda Street, Newtown Connecticut, on December 14, 2012 (p. 3).

[‡] Child Advocate Report, pp. 45, 102–3.

[§] Child Advocate Report, pp. 103–5.

Advocate noted in its report, too often during Lanza's short life, his mother, his schools, and the Connecticut mental health system not only failed treating his mental illness, they also actually facilitated that illness by accommodating his demanding, mentally ill life-style.* Had any of those individuals or institutions taken a more aggressive approach to treating him appropriately, Lanza could have been diverted from what fate condemned him to. Indeed, those accommodations allowed him to take the path to intended violence deep in the shadows, unobserved, unassessed, and unmanaged. His self-imposed—and accommodated—isolation made him undetectable to anyone with the authority to intervene.

Summary

This chapter reviewed the various types of behaviors in which hunters engage when they take up the hunt. All hunters have grievances or reasons for deciding that violence will resolve their issues. That grievance may be reasonable only to the hunter, but it nonetheless provides the hunter's motivation. Second, all hunters must decide that violence is the only option available to them. Simply put, subjects must come up with the idea of using violence to settle their problem. Third, all hunters must research and plan how they will commit the violence. The research and planning can be complex and sophisticated or they can be straightforward and simple. Fourth, all hunters must prepare their attack according to the dictates of their plan. They must arm themselves, build their bomb, obtain their poison, entice their target to a cliff ledge, or otherwise get themselves ready for the attack. Fifth, all hunters must breach their target's security, again according to the dictates of their plan. That security can be as tight as that surrounding the president or as lax as that for targets who protect themselves. Sixth, and finally, all hunters must summon the courage to actu-ally attack once the security is breached.

Acting violently is not a simple matter. Threat managers can use the various behaviors associated with each of these steps to help identify individuals of violent intent, assess their actual degree of risk, and manage the subject away from violence.

We ended the chapter acknowledging one special case that allowed the hunter to proceed from grievance to attack completely unobserved; indeed, more than that, no one in Newtown, Connecticut, even had the capability of observing Adam Lanza until he breached the school's security and went on his deadly rampage. Yet, Lanza's situation seems altogether extreme, requiring nearly complete isolation up to the moment that he shot his way into the elementary school. Fortunately, that very extremity makes Lanza's situation unique.

Situation Analysis: The Nonaccidental Tourist

The Facts

Jay e-mailed a large corporation's public complaint center in February. In the e-mail, he expressed his belief that a prominent public figure under Secret Service protection had

* Child Advocate Report, p. 45.

been poisoned. The content of the rest of the e-mail had nothing to do with the corporation's business or responsibilities. Jay described himself as a homeless person living on Social Security disability benefits. He claimed to live in a homeless shelter in a large Northwestern city. Jay believed that the government was trying to control his mind and that the other men living at the YMCA tried to rape him. Based on the inappropriate reference to the public figure, the implied delusional disorder, and the references to violence, the staff of the complaint center forwarded the e-mail to the corporation's threat management unit.

The Threat Analysis

Although Jay's e-mail contains an inappropriate reference to a Secret Service protectee and includes allegations of violence committed against himself, Jay expresses no intention to take any action beyond sending the e-mail, nor did the e-mail give any reason to conclude that Jay believes he has a personal relationship with the Secret Service protectee or with anyone affiliated with this corporation. In addition, Jay's e-mail contains no mention at all of this corporation's staff, facilities, or mission. Based on the impersonal nature of his relationship with the Secret Service protectee, the sinister aspect of his reference to the person, and his choice of making a distant communication, Jay is assessed as a howler at this time. Based on the facts under assessment, he is considered a very low risk to this corporation's staff, facilities, or business.

Protective Response

The corporation's threat management unit should forward Jay's e-mail to the Secret Service. In addition, Jay should be flagged in the contact center's computer database to ensure that any future communications, whether inappropriate or not, will be forwarded to the threat management unit for assessment. The corporation should not respond in any way to Jay's e-mail.

Threat Management Strategy

Based on the low-risk assessment, the corporation should adopt a passive watch-and-wait strategy toward Jay. Any future communications from him, whether inappropriate or not, should be monitored to determine any changes in theme, tone, or method of communication. Although Jay's interests at this time have no relation to the corporation's staff, facilities, or mission, his choice to e-mail the corporation an inappropriate communication requires that future communications, whether inappropriate or not, be assessed by the threat management unit. All future communications should be immediately forwarded to the appropriate law enforcement agencies such as the Secret Service.

The Outcome

Jay continued to e-mail the corporation's complaint center an average of one communication a day. The e-mails continued to express his objections to mind control by the government and he continued to complain that he was the victim of violence at the shelter. In one series of e-mails, Jay described how he followed a young schoolgirl on a bus. The threat manager forwarded those e-mails to the police department where Jay lived. A police officer interviewed the manager of the shelter to verify that Jay lived there and to find out more about him. On the basis of the information obtained from the shelter manager, the police officer determined that Jay was suffering from some mental illness but that he did not pose a risk to anyone else, including young school children.

The corporation's threat management unit continued to monitor and forward Jay's e-mails. In an e-mail in early May, Jay discussed a man who had the same last name as Jay who taught at a small college in a mid-Atlantic state. Jay claimed that the professor was his brother, whom he held responsible for murdering Jay's other family members, including their younger siblings. The threat management unit contacted the college police department and forwarded the e-mails to the chief. The police chief informed the threat management unit that the college had had communications from Jay in the past. He also stated that the college professor was no relation to Jay. Every time Jay brought up the professor in subsequent e-mails, the threat management unit forwarded the e-mail to the police chief.

In August, Jay announced his intention to take a vacation, traveling the country via a Greyhound AmeriPass, which allowed him 30 days' unlimited travel throughout the continental United States. As part of his itinerary, he planned to visit his "brother" in order to "confront" him. Suddenly, for reasons unknown, Jay became a hunter. He started acting. Each day, Jay would arrive by bus in a different city, go to the library to send an e-mail, then spend the night at a local homeless shelter. His direction of travel took him eastward toward the college. The threat management unit was able to obtain Jay's state department of motor vehicles photograph and forward it to the campus police chief. The chief confirmed through Greyhound that Jay was traveling aboard its buses, then arranged to have a city police officer meet the bus when it reached the college town. The officer identified Jay, asked what his business was, then sternly warned him not to set foot on the campus grounds or try in any way to approach or confront the professor. Jay denied sending the e-mails and promised not to go near the campus or the professor. Two days later, Jay resumed his bus tour of the country. Several months later, he stopped e-mailing the corporation.

Issues of Interest

The events that transpired in this case illustrated a number of important lessons for threat managers:

1. Simply because Jay never referred to the corporation's staff, facilities, or business did not mean that the corporation's threat management unit could ignore his e-mails once it determined that Jay had communicated inappropriately. Jay's choice to send his e-mails to the corporation complaint center put a responsibility on the corporation to assess and monitor those e-mails. This was not so much the unit's looking for new work as having new work imposed upon it.
2. Although Jay's inappropriate interest in the Secret Service protectee, the schoolgirl, and the college professor had no relationship to the corporation's staff, facilities, or business, the threat management unit had a responsibility to determine which law enforcement agency had jurisdiction and to alert that corporation of Jay's inappropriate interest. In this case in particular, not alerting other law enforcement agencies would have put the college professor at risk.

3. Whenever an organization opens itself to receiving communications from the public, it must be prepared to manage inappropriate communications.

4. For months, Jay acted as an impersonal, sinister howler. He communicated from a distance, made inappropriate comments about his targets, but took no action beyond sending the e-mail. In August, however, his demeanor and method of communication suddenly changed. Instead of complaining about his "brother's" past activities, Jay decided to "confront" the brother. He also acted in furtherance of carrying out that decision by buying the bus pass and traveling across the country. What prompted that change from howler to hunter may never be known because Jay gave no reason for it. It may have been as simple as Jay's seeing a Greyhound bus advertisement. For whatever reason, the transformation from howler to hunter resulted in a dramatic change in Jay's behavior from sending e-mails to sending e-mails while traveling toward the college town.

5. Neither hunters nor howlers need rational motives for their actions, provided their actions make sense to them. Jay suffered a delusion that he had a brother and that the brother had committed crimes, including murder. Jay acted on the delusion by attempting to "confront" the brother.

6. Once Jay turned to hunting, the threat management strategy had to be reassessed and changed from passive watch and wait to confronting him with a warning.

7. Finally, Jay amply illustrates a fundamental fact about threat management and the hunters and howlers it manages: Both hunters and howlers may cross jurisdictional lines. Because they may cross jurisdictions, threat managers need to be prepared to coordinate and cooperate with different organizations and agencies, even to the point of seeking out the appropriate entity and establishing a new relationship for sharing information and managing the subject.

Understanding Howlers 8

Unlike hunters, who are best understood by analyzing their attack-related behaviors, howlers are defined by their relationship to their targets, then by what they seek to accomplish through their inappropriate communications. We classify howlers into one of two broad types, then categorize them into two groups and several subgroupings within each type. The typology derives from the nature of the relationship—real or as perceived by the howler—between the howler and his or her target. The groupings depend on what the howler intends or seeks to accomplish. For both types, of course, the communication, however delivered, is the end game. Using these categories will help the threat manager accurately assess the subject, factor in the *intimacy effect*, and identify the most appropriate management strategy.

Little research has as yet been done to further our understanding of howlers and how they behave. The following discussion relies on those few studies and also on our experiences in managing howlers. We also received insights and suggestions from Gavin de Becker, who undoubtedly has worked with more howlers than anyone in the field of threat management. Ironically, although less studied than hunters, howlers compose most of the workload for any threat manager. Researchers should pay more attention to them.

Howler Categories

Personal howlers know their targets. They may have an intimate relationship with them or they may work or go to school with them, live nearby, or attend the same social functions. This type of howler may also communicate inappropriately with an organizational entity, such as a business, school, or government agency. But the communication is spawned by the howler's current or former relationship with that business, school, or government agency. The howler may have worked there, attended classes, or had personal dealings with the agency. The degree of familiarity between the personal howler and his or her target spans the spectrum from casual acquaintance to current or former intimate, but the distinguishing feature of personal howlers is that they personally know their targets. They use that knowledge to inform their communications.

Impersonal howlers do not know their targets. They communicate inappropriately with public figures such as government officials, celebrities, or individuals who happen to make the news, such as lottery winners. Impersonal howlers may also target organizations such as government agencies, businesses, or institutions, but not because they have had personal dealings with the agencies, businesses, or institutions. Rather, they are drawn by the targets' prominence, authority, or symbolic representation. The Central Intelligence Agency frequently receives inappropriate communications or contacts with no indication the howler has targeted any particular person who works there. Similarly, airlines, courthouses, schools, and abortion clinics all suffer bomb threats. Whatever their target, the distinguishing feature of impersonal howlers is that they have no personal familiarity with the person or entity to whom they address their inappropriate communications. Consequently, their communications are marked by the absence of any personal knowledge about the target.

By analyzing what personal and impersonal howlers seek to accomplish through their inappropriate communications or contacts, they can be categorized into two large groupings, each of which has several subgroupings. Both personal and impersonal howlers have either a sinister intent or they intend to bind themselves in some way to their target. *Sinister* howlers want to scare their targets. *Binder* howlers want some kind of interpersonal relationship, usually intimate, with their targets.

Sinister howlers make explicit threats or use disturbing, ominous, even frightening language. They provide graphic descriptions and express themselves in angry, violent terms. They pose themselves as relentless, unbending, and uncompromising. Their motives vary, but they are united in seeking to instill fear in their targets. Their purpose is not to cause physical harm; it is psychological. Sinister howlers prey on their targets' emotions. They try to manipulate their target's imagination. They hope that the target will believe all the terrible actions the howler threatens. Their success depends on how much the target believes.

Binder howlers believe they have or they want an interpersonal relationship with their target. Personal howlers who seek a bind actually know their target and may, in fact, have had a relationship that the target no longer wants. Impersonal howlers who desire a relationship do not personally know their targets but may have seen or heard of them, usually through the media.

Beyond that, differences begin to emerge between sinister and binder howlers depending on whether they fall into the personal or impersonal types. Figure 8.1 organizes the howler groups according to their purposes or motives.

The range of motives shown by these groupings underscores the attractiveness that making threats or communicating inappropriately holds for certain individuals. With the possible exceptions of habitual and copycat howlers, the other types all seek to solve some problem between themselves, the target, or, in the case of dirty tricksters, a third party. The problems, of course, are unique and personal to each howler, but that makes them no less real to the howler and, through the communication, to the target.

Howlers of all stripes seek their goals through communication. By giving expression to their anger, hatred, desire to kill or maim, or emotional frustration with the target or the world, the howler accomplishes his or her goal. He or she may communicate once or multiple times, but each communication is an end in itself. For this reason, the threat manager must take each communication with fresh seriousness. Each one offers new insights into the howler's current state of mind. Any changes in demeanor, focus, or complaint need to be assessed in light of everything the threat manager knows about the howler.

Recognizing which type and group to which the howler belongs allows the threat manager to make informed decisions about how to manage the subject. It also allows the threat manager to look for warning signs that the subject may be near a flash point that might transform the subject into a hunter. This is especially possible among personal howlers, but it can happen with any of them. Clearly, the threat manager must avoid any management strategy that might induce such a transformation but must also be alert to any other influences affecting the howler.

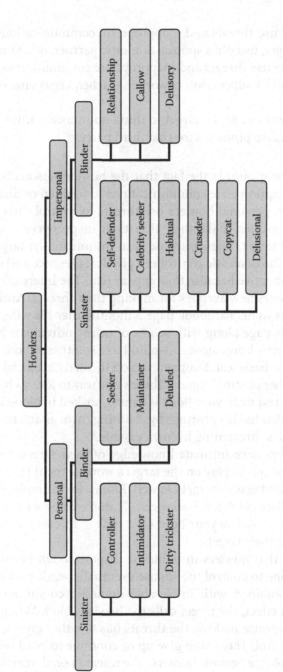

Figure 8.1 Howlers grouped by motive or purpose.

Personally Sinister Howlers

Our research and professional experiences suggest that sinister howlers who personally know their targets can be grouped into three distinct groups:

1. *Controller* howlers use threats and inappropriate communications to control the behavior of the target, usually a spouse, domestic partner, or a family member.
2. *Intimidator* howlers use threats and inappropriate communications to intimidate their target, typically a supervisor, coworker, teacher, classmate, or others within their social group.
3. *Dirty trickster* howlers want the target to think an innocent third party made the threat in order to cause problems for that third party.

What distinguishes these groups is the fact that the howler personally knows his or her target and intends the inappropriate communications to frighten or disturb the target.

In domestic settings, personal howlers use threats to control their intimates. Unlike most howlers, controllers often make their threats or inappropriate communications in person, directly to their target. Their purpose is to intimidate the target to bend him or her to the howler's will. The domestic controller's physical presence and access to the target make the threats more effective because they appear real. The Internet's social media connections have given howlers new avenues for making their threats. Anthony Elonis began adding threatening posts to his Facebook page 5 months after his wife, Tara, left him. He knew she would visit his page along with scores of other individuals he had befriended. "If I only knew then what I know now…I would have smothered your ass with a pillow. Dumped your body in the back seat. Dropped you off in Toad Creek and made it look like a rape and murder." Another posting began, "There's one way to love ya but a thousand ways to kill ya. I'm not gonna rest until your body is a mess, soaked in blood and dying from all the little cuts." Elonis defended his postings by claiming them as art, no different from the rap singer Eminem's lyrics threatening his own ex-wife.[*]

Because these howlers have intimate knowledge of their target, they can easily customize their communications to play on the target's worst fears. If the couple has children together, the offspring can become targets as well. Elonis, for example, suggested their son "should dress up as a Matricide" for Halloween. "I don't know what his costume would entail though," he posted, "Maybe your head on a stick."[*] In effect, controllers use everything they can to subdue their targets.

One of the reasons that howlers in domestic disputes often become hunters is that the ability of threats alone to control the spouse eventually weakens. Over time, repeated threats, especially if combined with intolerable domestic conditions, lose the desired impact on the target. In effect, the target calls the howler's bluff. When the threats fail to control the spouse, the spouse making the threats has to either give up or escalate his or her actions to regain control. Those who give up or continue to howl remain howlers, and those who escalate to violence become hunters. The research on domestic violence strongly supports the increased potential for violence when a spouse leaves an abusive relationship. A spouse who leaves is in effect forcing the howler either to put up or shut up. Debra

* Bazelon, E. (2014, November 25). Do online death threats count as free speech. *New York Times Magazine.*

Jenkins found that the lethality of domestic violence increased significantly if the victim had already physically left the relationship.*

For example, Tom dominated his wife, Anne. He used threats and physical intimidation to bend her to his will. He tracked the mileage on her car, always demanding to know where she had been and to whom she had spoken. Fearing that she could not support herself, Anne put up with the threats and domination in return for Tom's financial support, even though he gave it grudgingly. She felt trapped; he felt in control.

In assessing the situation, the threat manager recognized Tom as a controller who would remain a howler as long as Anne did what he told her to do. The threat manager reasoned that as long as Anne subdued herself to Tom's demands, then the threats worked and Tom had no need to escalate toward violence. Indeed, it would be counterproductive for him to carry out the threats because what he really wanted was the control. The threat manager strongly cautioned that as soon as she left the relationship, she should seek protection at a shelter or other place where Tom would not be able to find her. Once she left, the threat manager recommended keeping close tabs on Tom in order to identify any attack-related behaviors on his part. Evidence of any of these could be used to support an arrest or civil order against Tom. The terrible quandary facing Anne, of course, was either to live with the threats and controls or leave and risk having Tom decide to make good on his promises of violent retribution.

Thus, threat managers can recognize inappropriate communications from controllers by their

- Focus on a spouse, intimate partner, or family member;
- Delivery in person to the target or the ready availability of the target to the controller;
- Use of intimate knowledge about the target; and
- Insistence on controlling the target's behavior.

Threat managers should also keep in mind that as the value of the threats diminishes over time, the subject may be tempted to take violent action to reassert control. Violence may also result if the controller loses control over the target.

Similarly, *intimidators* in workplaces or schools use fear to control coworkers and supervisors or classmates and teachers. They use threats and intimidating demeanors to convince their colleagues to do what the intimidator wants or to leave the intimidator alone. Supervisors who fear their subordinates cannot effectively supervise. Coworkers who fear a colleague tend to avoid that colleague, even if it means handling the colleague's work. The same holds true for teachers and fellow students. Like controllers, intimidators engage in face-to-face confrontations with their targets because they are thrown together in the workplace or schoolyard. They also use their access and personal knowledge of their targets to exploit weaknesses for their own advantage.

Threatening incidents at schools appeared to increase after the well-publicized school shootings that occurred across the last half of the 1990s. A much harsher law enforcement response greeted the increase. For example, on March 15, 2001, two second grade boys in Irvington, New Jersey, folded a sheet of paper in such a way that it resembled a handgun.

---

* Jenkins, D. M. Appendix—When should threats be seen as indicative of future violence? Threats, intended violence, and the intimacy effect.

Eight-year-old Hamadi Alston stood up at his desk, pointed the paper gun at his classmates, and said, "I'm going to kill you." Police arrested both boys for making terrorist threats.* Eight days later, 18-year-old Benjamin Ballard of Portland, Oregon, sent an instant message indicating there would be "a lot of bodies" at Edgemont High School in Greenburgh, New York. Despite the cross-continent distance between Ballard and the school, the Federal Bureau of Investigation arrested Ballard for making a threat and school officials closed the school. Ballard said he was making a joke, but howlers rarely get a laugh.†

Also, like controllers, intimidators eventually reach a crossroads when their threats and intimidating demeanors begin to lose their ability to instill fear in the targets. At this point, the intimacy of the relationship cuts both ways. The targets know the howler as well as he or she knows them. If the intimidations drag on long enough, the targets may eventually challenge or ignore the bully. At that point, the intimidator has to back his or her intimidations by becoming a hunter, changing tactics, or retreating.

For example, Mitch used his 6-foot-6-inch height and 280-pound weight to physically intimidate his coworkers at an accounting firm. Although he never explicitly threatened anyone or did anything else that might prompt disciplinary or termination proceedings, he had his coworkers thoroughly cowed. He delegated his work to them, then signed his name to the final products. His immediate supervisor knew of the intimidations but felt too concerned for her own safety to report the problem up the chain of command.

The threat manager recognized Mitch as an intimidator who would remain a howler as long as his intimidations worked. She recommended a dual management strategy combining administrative orders and a variation on target transfer. The threat manager suggested that the identity of the coworker who reported Mitch to senior management be closely guarded and that Mitch receive a transfer under some routine bureaucratic guise to another division. The supervisor of the new division should be briefed about Mitch's inappropriate behaviors. If Mitch tries to use intimidation in his new position, he should quickly be brought to task and told that the behavior is unacceptable. Continued intimidations could then be handled as part of the firm's disciplinary process.

Thus, threat managers can recognize inappropriate communications from intimidators by their

- Focus on supervisors and coworkers or teachers and classmates or similar interpersonal relationships;
- Purpose to frighten or discomfit their targets;
- Use of personal knowledge of the targets;
- Delivery in person or accessibility of the target to the intimidator; and
- Insistence on using intimidation to influence target behaviors or organizational decisions.

Intimidators closely resemble controllers and both closely resemble schoolyard bullies. How much of their controlling and intimidating are bluff and how much is serious ultimately determine whether they will remain howlers or become hunters.

Both controllers and intimidators frequently make their threats in person to their targets. Eventually, the controlling threats and intimidating behaviors wear thin to the target.

---

* Nation in brief. (2001, March 22). *Washington Post*.
† Nation in brief. (2001, March 27). *Washington Post*.

The target begins to ignore or challenge the controller and the intimidator, forcing both to show what they are made of. Because they are involved in interpersonal relations with their targets, neither the controller nor the intimidator can hide behind distance. Consequently, the intimacy effect also affects the subject. Threats early on carry weight in influencing the target, but that weight ultimately wears off. As the veneer strips away, both the controller and the intimidator reach a point where they have to retreat completely or begin hunting. Unlike other howlers, they do not have the safety distance provides.

For example, Steven Lancaster threatened his wife, Janice, for over a year. A week after she obtained a temporary restraining order against him, he carried out his threats by killing her and himself.* In early September 2001 in Sacramento, California, Burns Security suspended Joseph Ferguson after his ex-girlfriend, also a Burns employee, complained that he had vandalized her car. Over the course of the next week, Burns threatened his former colleagues and made videotape boasting that he had "put on a hell of a show." Burns added that "I giveth and I taketh away, that's how it goes in… life." Burns also claimed that he wanted to outdo Nikolay Soltys, who, in August 2001, had killed six of his family members in Sacramento, California.† On September 9, a week after his suspension and the beginning of his threats, Burns began killing. Over the next 2 days, he came within one murder of matching Soltys' body count before police came for him. Four of his five victims were employees of Burns Security. After a 40-minute car chase with police, Ferguson killed himself.‡ Interpersonal relations between the subject and the target can quickly blur the line between hunters and howlers.

Some personally sinister howlers seek to get a third party in trouble. These *dirty tricksters* disguise themselves as that third party, hoping that their threats will get the third party arrested or disciplined. Typically, dirty tricksters have some interpersonal dispute with the third party. For example, an ex-husband will forge his ex-wife's name on a threatening letter to a government official. The purpose is to have the ex-wife arrested and jailed for making the threat. In other cases, the dirty trickster may pose as a concerned citizen or informant trying to pass on disturbing information about the innocent third party. They employ poison-pen communications. Their real target is the third party, not the person threatened.

For example, John J. Donovan Sr. proved the ultimate dirty trickster. Donovan is a self-made millionaire, executive mentor, and business consultant. The *New York Times* dubbed him the "Johnny Carson of the training circuit" because so many Fortune 500 companies hire him as a speaker.§ Unfortunately, Donovan could not get along as well with his own family. For several years, he and his five children engaged in various legal squabbles and accusations. Donovan accused his offspring of trying to force him off his 68-acre estate. They accused him of molesting one of the daughters and harassing the other children through frivolous restraining orders. In all, the family filed 17 lawsuits against each other.§

Then, on December 16, 2004, Donovan called 911 from the parking lot of his company, Cambridge Executive Enterprises, to report two men had shot him several times. When officers responded, they found Donovan wounded in the left side, a window shot out of a car parked in the parking lot, and spent .22-caliber cartridges scattered across the asphalt.

---

* George, D. S. (2000, August 27). Murder in the making: Those who knew Janice Lancaster saw bits and pieces of a family tragedy. She saw more—and struggled to change it. *Washington Post*.
† Booth, W. (2001, August 31). Police catch man sought in killing of six relatives. *Washington Post*.
‡ Slaying suspect commits suicide. (2001, September 11). Associated Press.
§ Millionaire indicted for claim he was shot. (2006, May 4). Associated Press.

Donovan told the officers that as he emerged from the building to go home for the evening, two men who sounded Russian fired four or five shots at him. Most of the bullets were deflected by the large belt buckle he was fortuitously wearing. One bullet passed through his left side but did not strike any organs. Later in the investigation, Donovan told police that his son James arranged for the shooting.*

Although the police initially accepted Donovan's account, they grew suspicious after determining that the surveillance camera that covered the parking lot was not working the night of the incident. They also learned that Donovan was an experienced shooter who had been issued a concealed weapons permit. Undoubtedly, the police also must have been a bit skeptical about the bullets striking Donovan's belt buckle. No doubt someone on the police department assessed Donovan as a dirty trickster, especially after he accused his son of orchestrating the assault. On May 4, 2006, the Middlesex County (Massachusetts) district attorney obtained an indictment against the elder Donovan on charges of lying to police and filing a false police report. Donovan strenuously denied the charges. A judge found him guilty in August 2007.† Ironically, when news reporters interviewed Stuart Madnick, a former business partner of Donovan's, Madnick told them he was "not shocked" about the charges. "I learned over the years never to be surprised, particularly with him. That's what makes him so interesting," Madnick said.*

Thus, the threat manager can recognize inappropriate communications from dirty tricksters by their

- Use of explicit threat language or actions with specific information on who supposedly sent the threat or committed the acts;
- Lack of an issue or complaint with the target of the inappropriate communication by the dirty trickster; and
- Insistence on implicating the third party.

The key to understanding dirty tricksters is their method of drawing attention to someone else in order to get that person into some kind of trouble.

Personal sinister howlers differ from their impersonal counterparts in the ease with which they can transition from howler to hunter. The intimacy effect greatly facilitates that change. Because personal howlers know their target and observe their target's responses, they are less able to imagine or fantasize about the target's reactions. Conversely, impersonal howlers cannot so easily gauge how their targets respond. Thus, their imagination and fantasies have free rein. In effect, sinister personal howlers are more grounded by reality; impersonal ones are not.

Personally Binding Howlers

Binder howlers who know their targets can be categorized into three groups:

1. *Seekers* try to establish an intimate relationship with their target despite the target's continued rejection of the seeker's attention.

---

* MacQuarrie, B. (2006, May 5). Star entrepreneur staged attack on himself, DA says. *Boston Globe.*
† Tech guru guilty of false shooting claim. (2007, August 17). Associated Press.

2. *Maintainers* insistently try to reestablish a former intimate relationship with their target, but the target wants to end the relationship.
3. *Deluded* binders suffer from a delusion that they have had or should have an intimate relationship with a target.

Personal binders do not intend violence against their targets as long as they remain convinced they have a chance to establish or maintain a personal relationship with the target. In that stage, killing the target would be self-defeating. The danger of violence comes when the personal binder realizes that he or she has no hope of that much-desired personal relationship.

Seeker binders usually become infatuated with a fellow student, coworker, neighbor, or relative and persistently try to initiate a closer relationship with that individual. Seekers communicate in a variety of ways. They may write letters, call on the telephone, or leave gifts or messages where they know the target will be. They frequently have considerable difficulty accepting rejection. Indeed, they easily convince themselves that with just a little extra effort, the target will have a change of heart. One more gift or another e-mail or a quick conversation will prove to the target that the seeker's feelings should be reciprocated.

Seekers frequently confuse themselves with suitors. They fail miserably at understanding that suitors do not press their suit once their object says no. Instead, seekers confuse persistence with romance. By not accepting the no, seekers go way beyond pressing their suit to pushing the limits of acceptable behavior in whatever social venue they find their target. Their approach to their target borders on, even crosses over into, obsession.

Threat managers frequently encounter seekers in workplaces or schools or any place where people spend long periods of time together in a common setting. Seekers frequently get accused of sexual or physical harassment. They represent a particular problem in workplaces because not only does their own job performance suffer from their distraction, but they also distract the target and, quite frequently, their own and the target's coworkers.

For example, toward the end of the school year, Julie, a high school junior, reported that her science teacher, Mr. Jarvis, had been making sexual innuendos to her, asking personal questions, and inviting her to eat at his lunch table and see him after school. Julie felt uncomfortable with the approaches and wanted to be transferred out of his class. After the transfer was made, Jarvis continued his unwanted pursuits. However, at no time did he cross any moral or ethical line in his dealings with her. Instead, he carefully remained within professional boundaries and did not give adequate grounds for disciplinary action. In that respect, Jarvis was smart.

The threat manager recognized Jarvis as a seeker who had become infatuated with one of his students. Fortunately for both, Jarvis had not yet done anything to support disciplinary action. The threat manager assessed this as a positive indicator that Jarvis felt inhibited about not risking his career. The threat manager recommended that Jarvis be transferred to another school on the other side of the school district. He should also be cautioned about further efforts to contact or approach the student. If that should occur, the threat manager advised that the school would then have sufficient cause to move against him using administrative orders.

Thus, threat managers can recognize inappropriate communications from seeker howlers by their

- Focus on a specific individual who has rejected or ignored their advances;
- Expressed desire for a closer relationship over the target's objections; and
- Persistent attempts to contact the target.

The key to seekers is that they have never had, and never will have, a positive relationship with the target because the target does not want one.

A close cousin to seekers is the howler who insists on maintaining a relationship that the target considers over. *Maintainers* closely resemble seekers in their behaviors, except they have actually had a personal relationship with the target. Maintainers can use their intimate knowledge of the target and the target's habits to inform their campaign to re-win the target. Unlike most seekers, maintainers do not necessarily belong to the target's organization. They may not be coworkers, fellow students, or someone else involved with the threat manager's organization. For example, the maintainer may work somewhere else but appear at the target's worksite as part of the effort to reestablish the previous relationship. Because maintainers know more than seekers about the private life of their target, they can exploit that personal knowledge. They can pursue the target at the target's home, workplace, school, church, or relatives' or friends' places. They are every bit as persistent as seekers, but their approach is considerably more knowledgeable.

As with seekers, the persistence of the maintainer disrupts not only the target's life but also the target's colleagues, friends, and relatives. Maintainers cannot take no for an answer, so they keep coming back. Indeed, getting a no often emboldens them to escalate their pursuit. Because they know the target so well, they can convince themselves that the target does not really mean the rejection.

For example, in February, Rhonda broke up with her boyfriend, Joe. Two weeks later, Joe began leaving her long voice-mail messages and flooding her corporate e-mail account with messages begging her to give him another chance. Despite her repeated rejections, Joe remained undaunted in his efforts to change her mind. Rhonda moved out of her apartment into another one, changed her phone number and e-mail address, and took other precautions to ensure that Joe would not find her new residence. However, she was unwilling to give up her job and promising career with the talent agency.

The threat manager recognized Joe as a maintainer who would continue his pursuit of Rhonda as long as he could get messages through to her. The threat manager recommended that building security be provided his photograph. He also advised the company to try a variation of the monitoring strategy by changing Rhonda's e-mail and telephone number but leave her old mail and number active so Joe's messages and e-mails could be monitored for any changes in his demeanor. The threat manager took responsibility for monitoring Joe's messages using a passive watch-and-wait strategy. As long as he remained a maintainer who expressed himself through telephone calls and e-mails, he would also remain a low risk of violence.

Thus, threat managers can recognize inappropriate communications from maintainer howlers by their

- Focus on a specific individual with whom they have had a positive personal relationship in the past, but which the target wants to end;
- Detailed familiarity with the target, especially the target's personal life;
- References to past times together, including coded or symbolic threats or inappropriate references; and
- Use of multiple methods of communicating with the target.

The key to understanding maintainers lies in their obsessive inability to accept the target's decision to move away from their previous relationship.

Deluded personal howlers suffer from a psychological delusion that they have or should have a closer personal relationship with the target than they actually have. Those deluded howlers who fixate on a fellow worker or some other acquaintance differ from seekers and maintainers based on their mental instability. Both seekers and maintainers know that the object of their pursuit is rejecting them; they simply believe that persistence and their inherent charm will win the day. Deluded howlers do not recognize the rejection because it does not enter their mind set. They fervently believe that they have a relationship that simply does not exist.

For example, Kathy J. first came to the threat manager's attention as a deluded personal binder. Two years later, she returned as an impersonal delusory howler. In 2002, sheriff's deputies responded to a call about a suicidal person armed with a pistol. When they arrived at the reported address, they found Kathy, clearly distraught, lying in bed and holding the gun to her head. A female deputy patiently built up a rapport with Kathy and managed to talk her into putting down the gun. Once Kathy surrendered, the deputies took her to the local mental hospital for evaluation.

Although the female deputy treated the incident simply as part of her job, Kathy convinced herself that the two had a much more personal relationship. She began writing the deputy letters, thanking her and expressing a desire to meet the deputy socially. At first, the deputy simply ignored the letters, but that did not stop Kathy. Indeed, in addition to the letters, Kathy began sending the deputy e-mails through the sheriff's website. The letters and e-mails became increasingly amorous and fanciful. Kathy wrote about fictitious dinners and dates between them. After several months of distance communication, Kathy appeared one night at the sheriff's office. She waved down a deputy who happened to be leaving. Kathy explained that she was the female deputy's girlfriend and asked the deputy to deliver the take-out dinner she had brought for the deputy.

The threat manager assessed Kathy as a deluded personal binder. Because all of the communications and the approach had been directed to the sheriff's office, the threat manager recommended giving the deputy a personal security briefing as the best protective response. The threat manager also recommended dual threat management strategies. First, the deputy should get a restraining order prohibiting Kathy from approaching her at any time. Second, the threat manager recommended arranging a third-party monitoring through Kathy's mother, whom the sheriff's office knew could be depended on based on her response to Kathy's mental commitment after the suicide attempt. Kathy still had enough inhibitors, including a good job. The restraining order worked. Through the mother, the threat manager monitored Kathy's obedience to the order and eventual loss of interest in the deputy.*

Threat managers can recognize inappropriate communications from deluded personal howlers by their

- Focus on a relationship that does not and never did exist;
- References to that nonexistent relationship;
- Evidence of being deluded or out of touch with reality; and
- Persistence in pursuit of the object of their delusion.

Deluded howlers live in a fantasy world of their own creation. Their obstinacies derive from that unreality.

---

* Authors' personal knowledge.

Impersonally Sinister Howlers

Howlers who do not know their targets but communicate with them in sinister or ominous ways can be grouped into six categories:

1. *Self-defender* howlers feel that a target or an organization has attacked them and, therefore, the howler needs to defend him or herself.
2. *Celebrity-seeking* howlers direct their threats and inappropriate communications to public figures or other celebrities precisely because of the target's public status.
3. *Habitual* howlers like to make threats as a hobby.
4. *Crusader* howlers use threats to advance some personal cause.
5. *Copycat* howlers are inspired to make threats and inappropriate communications by news reports of acts of violence or threatened acts of violence.
6. *Delusional* howlers suffer a mental delusion compelling them to threaten their target.

In many cases, the sinister howler feels under attack and is lashing back in anger or despair. These *self-defenders* feel imposed upon by something they believe the target has done or is about to do to them. More precisely, the self-defender perceives that he or she has suffered some injury or indignity through some fault of the target. In fact, self-defenders may risk losing their jobs or face prison or be embroiled in a divorce or child custody dispute. They may have been bullied or teased at school or passed over for promotion. Whatever the insult or injury, they feel it very personally. The wound goes deep into their egos.

Self-defenders seek to solve their problem through instilling fear in the target. If they can scare the target away or scare the target into doing what the self-defender wants, then the self-defender's problem will go away. His or her ego will be repaired. Consequently, communications from self-defenders tend to make a complaint or reference an issue or dispute. They talk about their particular problem, usually in great detail. They are desperate to be heard, for being heard exonerates them from making the threat. Self-defenders are specific in what they want and how they want it done. They rarely accept any responsibility for their personal situation or problems. They blame their targets entirely, which serves to increase their wrath. Self-defenders reason that if the target caused the problem, then the target must fix it. They seek both justice and restitution, but on their terms only.

Because self-defenders express a specific complaint, they tend to be the howlers most likely to communicate only once. Many of them make their complaint inappropriately but feel better for having gotten it off their chest. They then get on with their lives. Given the American emphasis on freedom of expression, many self-defenders may not even realize they have communicated inappropriately.

For example, Jonathan W. owned his own business, had a wife and three children, and played a prominent role in his church and community. One day, a customer slipped and broke his arm at Jonathan's business establishment. The customer sued, claiming negligence on Jonathan's part. The costs of the lawsuit escalated enough that Jonathan finally had to dismiss his attorney and begin representing himself. When he failed to follow court procedures and decorum, the judge personally rebuked him. The next day, Jonathan called the judge's chambers and asked to speak to the judge. When told the judge was unavailable, Jonathan replied, "Tell the judge to show me some respect. This is my life we're talking about and if he takes mine, I'll take his." Jonathan then hung up the telephone.

The threat manager who assessed Jonathan's inappropriate communication recognized him as a sinister howler seeking to defend himself against a perceived insult from the judge. The threat manager factored into the assessment the inhibitors in Jonathan's life, especially his family, home ownership, and standing in the community. Given that Jonathan's message was to demand future respect from the judge, the threat manager recommended adopting a passive watch-and-wait strategy to see if Jonathan's outburst was a one-time occurrence. Had Jonathan insisted on something else, such as an apology, retribution, punishment, or a disciplinary action against the judge, the threat assessor would have recommended that a threat manager interview Jonathan. The interview could start as a friendly effort to assist him but, if necessary, could end with a warning to avoid future inappropriate communications. But because that did not occur, the threat manager settled on a passive watch-and-wait management strategy.

Having expressed his anger at the judge, Jonathan calmed down. He returned to court and successfully avoided any additional admonishments from the judge. He also won the lawsuit. Jonathan never tried to contact the judge again.

Thus, threat managers can recognize inappropriate communications from self-defender howlers by their

- Focus on a specific issue, complaint, or dispute affecting them;
- Desire for the target to rectify the situation;
- Use of threats or ominous references to frighten the target into acting;
- Refusal to take personal responsibility for their conduct as it relates to the dispute; and
- Insistence on a resolution according to their terms.

Because self-defenders are issue specific, they direct their inappropriate communications to those whom they hold responsible for their situation. They do not send out bulk communications or direct them to individuals not involved in the dispute. They feel empowered by their threats even though their situation reveals their impotence. If they had the power to effect the change, they would not need to threaten or communicate inappropriately.

What marks impersonal sinister howlers is their lack of information about the target. The Secret Service once had a case of an individual who clearly demonstrated his complete lack of personal knowledge about his target. This subject threatened to kill presidential candidate and then Vice President George H. W. Bush. The howler addressed his threatening letters to President Ronald Reagan at the White House, not the Naval Observatory, where the vice president lived. When Secret Service agents tracked down the threatener, they asked why he addressed the letters to President Reagan when his actual target was the vice president. The howler explained that he knew the White House address was 1600 Pennsylvania Avenue, but he did not know the vice president's address. Thus, it was easier for him to send the threats to the president, presumably hoping the president would be kind enough to forward them along.*

Celebrity-seeking sinister howlers focus on public figures or celebrities precisely because the targets are famous. The threat or inappropriate communication may have been inspired by something the celebrity did or it could be directed at the celebrity simply because he or she is well known. Hundreds of celebrity howlers threaten the president of the United States every year, sometimes because they disagree with his policies but more

* Secret Service training presentation, Newark, NJ, January 2000.

often just because he is the president. Other politicians, such as governors, mayors, and members of Congress also receive inappropriate communications both because of their public stance on issues and because of the positions they hold. Similarly, actors and other public figures become the targets of celebrity howlers. They too are targeted both for what they do or say and for the personae they project in the media.

Celebrity-seeking howlers obviously focus on their chosen public figures. Their communications may contain explicit threats, but they may also make ominous comments, suggestions, or proposals. Generally, too, celebrity-seeking howlers evince little knowledge of their targets beyond what is popularly available. Some action by the public figure may attract the howler's attention. Typically, however, the celebrity-seeking howler addresses the celebrity because the celebrity is famous. The howler envies that fame and tries to steal some of it by communicating with the public figure. It is not the celebrity's stance on the issues of the day or how he or she behaves or what he or she does that enrages the celebrity-seeking howler. Rather, the howler objects that the celebrity is famous instead of the howler.

For example, Tom Q. became obsessed with a male movie star after the star appeared in an action film in which he was portrayed as having near superhuman strength and stamina. Tom completely bought into the movie's premise and the star's feats and did not seem to understand the power of special effects. Instead, he repeatedly wrote the star claiming that he, Tom, could do everything the star had done in the movie. He challenged the star to fight him, then explained in great detail how he would overpower the star and show the world how much stronger he was.

The threat manager assessed Tom as a celebrity-seeking impersonal howler who made all his communications through letter writing. The letters never showed any evidence of detailed knowledge about the star. Quite the opposite, the letters all indicated that Tom thought the star was, in reality, the character he had played in the action movie. The threat manager recommended maintaining the star's current level of security as an appropriate protective response and monitoring Tom's subsequent communications for any change in theme, knowledge, or tone.

Thus, threat managers can recognize inappropriate communications from celebrity-seeking howlers by their

- Focus on the celebrity as a celebrity or on individuals portrayed in the media, or on fictional characters in a movie or on television;
- Lack of personal knowledge or information not reported in the media about the public figure;
- Expressions of animosity due to the celebrity's fame, fortune, popularity, or position of power and influence; and
- Perception that the howler is equal to or better than the howler's opinion of the public figure.

Because celebrity-seeking howlers are attracted to fame and power, they may focus on one particular public figure or more than one. Their interest may shift from target to target, either because the public figure's public position shifts or simply because a different celebrity attracts the howler's attention. For example, former presidents receive far fewer inappropriate communications than they did while in office or than their successors receive.

A profound indignation over the celebrity's fame or power undergirds the celebrity-seeking howler's inappropriate communications. These howlers do not profess their love for the celebrity nor their delusions of sharing their lives together. Sinister celebrity-seeking howlers are jealous. By threatening the public figure or communicating in disturbing, ominous ways, the howler imagines bringing the celebrity down a few notches by the fear and trembling the communication causes. In essence, the communications somehow validate the celebrity-seeking howler's sense of self-worth.

In other cases, sinister howlers simply enjoy the act of making explicit threats. They have no ulterior motive other than scaring their targets or, more precisely, imagining the fear their communications cause. These *habitual* howlers howl repeatedly, frequently to multiple targets who have no connection other than being targets of these communications. For habitual howlers, the act of communicating is just as important as the message they are trying to get across. Most of the time, they do not know their targets personally. Instead, they find them in business directories, by reading news stories, or by sending "To whom it may concern" type messages to particular organizations, businesses, or government agencies.

For example, doctors obviously work at Veterans Administration (VA) hospitals, so it is easy for howlers to address their communications to "Head of Surgery" or "Chief Oncologist" or some other title typically associated with a VA hospital. Large corporations have chairmen and presidents. Reproductive health care facilities have doctors, nurses, and patients. Courts have judges, prosecutors, and clerks. Cities have mayors, states have governors, and the United States has a president. All of them are easy targets for letter writing. For habitual howlers, the self-satisfaction comes in composing the threatening communications, then imagining the reactions they will cause.

Many habitual howlers are inmates confined to prisons or mental health facilities, or even prison mental wards. Inmate howlers, whether incarcerated or institutionalized, make threats as a way of getting attention. Bored or frustrated with their incarceration or institutionalization, and with plenty of time on their hands, they direct their communications generally at public officials or individuals featured recently in the news. By threatening a government official, they invite an investigation. The investigation usually includes law enforcement officers interviewing the inmate. That interview breaks the monotony of life in a prison or mental health facility. It gets the inmate attention, thus confirming that he or she is important and cannot be ignored.

For example, in December 2002, Rodney Yoder, an inmate at a maximum security mental hospital in Illinois, admitted sending over 100 threatening letters to judges, a staff assistant to a U.S. senator, and other public figures in 1995 and 1996. Yoder hoped the letters would get him reassigned from the hospital to a federal prison. That would give him a fixed release date. At his recommitment hearing in 2002, Yoder assured the jury that he never carried out the threats he mailed. He promised the court he would not do so if he was released from the hospital. The jury voted to recommit him for at least another 6 months.[*]

A good threat assessor would have recognized Yoder as a habitual howler because of the number of inappropriate communications Yoder sent. The threat assessor would have recommended a third-party control strategy using the mental hospital staff to control and monitor Yoder's future attempts to communicate inappropriately. That contact with the hospital staff would have also ensured that the threat manager would be alerted to any changes in Yoder's status.

---

[*] Man who threatened judge recommitted. (2002, December 5). Associated Press.

Thus, threat managers can recognize inappropriate communications from habitual howlers by their

- Focus on making voluminous communications, frequently to multiple, unrelated targets or to public figures or individuals recently featured in the media;
- Lack of expressed personal motive or complaint for making threats to the particular target;
- Emphasis on threatening or violent references;
- Markings that the communication was sent from a prison or institution, such as an envelope stamped "legal mail" or showing an institution's return address;
- Indications of mental illness in the writing; and
- Insistence on making multiple threats as a means of getting attention.

Simply put, habitual howlers like to make threats. They send their communications to multiple targets over long periods of time. They have no specific complaint or issue, find their targets in public directories or by good guessing, and make no effort to draw any connection between them. They communicate inappropriately solely for the purpose of communicating inappropriately.

In one bizarre case beginning in the early 1990s, CD was incarcerated in a state penitentiary. U.S. Marshals overnighted some federal prisoners in the state facility while en route to the federal penitentiary to which the prisoners had been sentenced. That night, CD fell in love with one of the federal prisoners, but the next morning the marshals took their prisoners away. CD determined that committing a federal crime was his ticket to get into the federal prison system and reunite with the object of his affection. Because he was already in state prison, his ability to commit such a crime was severely limited to most activities except writing threatening letters to federal officials. He began a long campaign of mailing threatening letters to federal judges, prosecutors, and individual marshals.

After confirming CD's incarceration, the threat manager assessed him as a howler who would continue making baseless threats in order to be tried and sentenced in federal court. The threat manager recommended prosecuting CD for the threats. Unfortunately for CD, the courts determined that his punishment for being convicted of making threats would commence at the conclusion of his state sentence 20 years hence. CD got the attention he sought, just not in the way he wanted it.*

Crusaders howl as a way of advancing some cause they perceive as larger than themselves. They threaten political or social opponents in the hope of disrupting the target's operations, business, or social activities. They use threats to persuade their opponents to abandon their views or adopt the howler's. Crusader howlers are specific in their choice of targets. They go after individuals who represent some political or social cause opposed by the crusader. Religious, moral, or political beliefs motivate them, which allows them to justify the threats as a necessary evil in a larger war. In their minds, the purity of their motives justifies the extremity of their tactics.

For example, Clayton Waagner violently opposed abortions and those who performed them. He expressed his opposition in religious and moral terms. At one point, he toyed with the idea of killing abortion providers, but he could never quite work up the courage to attack. Instead, he settled on a unique way of howling. Inspired by the anthrax letters

* Authors' personal knowledge.

addressed to two U.S. senators and several newscasters in the fall of 2001 that resulted in the deaths of five people,* Waagner tried a howler-style variation of the tactic. "In October of 2001," he explained, "I mailed fake anthrax to 500 abortion clinics. In November of 2001, I Federal Expressed another 300 fake anthrax letters. The white powder I used was harmless, but tested positive for anthrax." Inside each envelope, he also included a brief letter explaining that whoever opened the letter had just been exposed to anthrax. Waagner calculated that his letters resulted in "3,940 clinic closure days, and the disruption of nearly 20,000 scheduled abortions. According to abortion clinic numbers, 5,000 or more babies are alive today because of my act of 'Domestic Terrorism.'"† Waagner now crusades from a prison cell.

Had a trained threat assessor evaluated Waagner's anthrax letters, he would have recognized a crusading howler based on Waagner's targets, all reproductive health care facilities. The best threat management strategy for handling Waagner was arresting him because his letters did break the law and disrupt dozens of clinics and their personnel. Once arrested, the threat management strategy would change to third-party control and monitoring, in this case by the prison staff.

Thus, threat managers can recognize inappropriate communications from crusaders by their

- Focus on political, moral, or social issues;
- Presenting their issue as larger than themselves;
- Portraying themselves as part of a larger group or collective (which usually does not exist); and
- Insistence on justifying their behavior by how they perceive the importance of their particular issue.

Crusaders have causes. They use threats and inappropriate communications to advance those causes. In effect, they believe that the importance of their issue outweighs everything else. It also excuses their behavior.

Finally, a portion of sinister howlers are *copycats*. They hear or read about some incident, usually an instance of violence, and use that as the inspiration for their threats. This usually happens in the immediate aftermath of some well-publicized tragedy. The copycat then refers to the event as part of the threat or ominous communication. In early March 2001, Charles "Andy" Williams killed two and wounded 13 at his high school in Santee, Califronia.‡ Over a month later, 18-year-old Patrick A. Smith of Maryland e-mailed two high school girls in California. One of the girls attended Williams' high school. Smith wrote, "I'm finishing what Andy started and this time its going to work." Police arrested Smith for making the threat.§ Copycat howlers follow the news.

For example, in the week or two after Timothy McVeigh bombed the Murrah Federal Building in Oklahoma City, Oklahoma, law enforcement agencies throughout the country received reports on threats against government buildings. Some were straightforward

---

* http://en.wikipedia.org/wiki/2001_anthrax_attack.
† Waagner statement, http://www.armyofgod.com/ClayWaagnerMainPage.html.
‡ Adler, J., & Booth, W. (2001, March 6). 2 Students die in Calif. shootings; 13 are injured; Classmate, 15, is held. *Washington Post*.
§ MD. Man pleads not guilty to school threats. (2001, April 25). *Washington Post*.

bomb threats. Others specifically referenced the Oklahoma bombing, saying that the same thing would happen to the building targeted by the threatener. Law enforcement had to take each threat seriously because hunters can be copycats, too. Yet, the threat assessor who assessed these multiple bomb threats recognized the threateners as copycat howlers because none of the threats resulted in an actual bombing. Instead, the threat assessor determined that the threateners also wanted to use the horror generated by the Oklahoma City bombing to cause fear in their targets. As a result, the threat manager recommended arresting anyone caught making a copycat threat. In lieu of that, all that could be done was to watch and wait for the infamy of McVeigh's action to fade in the public's and the copy-cat's collective memories.

Similarly, for weeks after Ismaaiyl Brinsley killed two New York City policemen on December 20, 2014, hundreds of threats to New York Police Department (NYPD) officers came through telephone calls to 311 and 911, as well as online postings and tips on various social media sites. Many of the threats mimicked the Instagram messages Brinsley posted on his way to shoot the two officers. On December 31, for example, someone posted to Twitter: "Let the piggies come. I got guns. Time to start shooting cops." By January 1, 2015, police had arrested 21 individuals for making such threats. All were copycats.*

The NYPD Deputy Commissioner of Intelligence and Counterterrorism explained how his department assessed these threats. First, they divided them into angry speech, hate speech, and a threat "where someone is indicating they intend to act." The Deputy Commissioner described the results of the department's investigations, saying, "What we've found in a number of these are, you've got dangerous people with serious criminal records, some of whom possessed weapons, who are making these threats. And in other cases we've found guys who are big and bad over the computer but when the cops knock at their door, they are reduced to tears, saying they were drunk and never really meant anything by it."* Howlers specialize in being big and bad over the computer.

Thus, threat managers can recognize inappropriate communications from copycats by their

- Focus on recent well-publicized acts or threats of violence;
- Nonviolent use of past well-publicized tactics that resulted in violence or threat of violence; and
- Insistence on benignly attempting to copy someone else's act of violence or threat of violence.

Copycats get their inspiration from the news. They want to wrap themselves in the aura of an actual hunter without going through the necessary steps of taking up the hunt. By referring to someone else's violence, these howlers try to piggyback on the fear the previous violence caused. They ride into infamy on the coattails of the actual hunter.

Finally, some impersonal sinister howlers suffer from some mental disorder that compels them to threaten or harass their target. They may perceive the public figure as the devil or some evil force. Many *delusional* impersonal sinister howlers feel threatened by the public figure or, at a more grandiose level, these howlers may feel the public figure poses some danger to the community at large, perhaps even the entire world.

---

* Baker, A. (2015, January 1). Man threatened to kill officers, authorities say. *New York Times.*

One delusional impersonal howler believed that he and a female gospel singer loved each other even though they had never met. He knew of her feelings toward him through the messages she sent him in her song lyrics and by the way she looked at him from the pictures on her album covers. He sent her an average of five letters and packages a day, plus scores of e-mails. When the singer's management staff began returning the letters and packages unopened and then blocked his e-mails, he convinced himself that she had been corrupted and had become the devil's consort. His love turned to hate. His e-mails took on an ominous tone. He made references to an ending, as though the singer would bring on the end of the world. He expressed a desire to stop her, to make a last goodbye, and to be present at the end. Throughout, however, the writer maintained his distance and continued to communicate only through e-mails.*

Thus, delusional sinister howlers can be recognized by their

- Focus on some imaginary or unreal perception of the public figure;
- Belief that the public figure represents a threat to the howler or to others; and
- Insistence that the public figure is someone other than who the public figure really is.

Impersonally sinister howlers vary in their motives and purposes. Some believe they are defending themselves; others try to bask in a celebrity's glow. Habitual howlers make threats almost as a hobby. Crusader howlers promote some cause. Copycat howlers use references to the acts of hunters to cloak themselves in the hunter's act. Delusional howlers live in their own made-up worlds.

Knowing impersonally sinister howler traits, motives, and purposes enables the threat manager to recognize that the communication under assessment came from a howler, indeed, from a particular type and category of howler. That understanding and knowledge will help the threat manager select the most appropriate strategy for handling that particular howler. Just because howlers do not escalate to violence does not mean that the threat manager does not have to manage them. Sinister howlers create fear and disrupt the lives of their targets. They must be managed in order to mitigate or offset that fear and disruption. As each of our examples showed, threat managers have a variety of strategies to use in managing howlers.

Impersonally Binding Howlers

Many impersonal howlers try to bind themselves to strangers, almost always public figures or celebrities. These types of binders use the target and their perceived or desired relationship with that target to escape the banality of their own lives by essentially stealing or borrowing the more exciting life of the target. Failures on their own, they lust after the public figures success. We classify these impersonal binders into four types:

1. *Relationship* binders look to the public figure for a relationship. They seek to become a lover, relative, or friend to the target, even if at a distance, and feel somehow incomplete if that relationship does not materialize. Relationship binders frequently see themselves through their pretended relationship with the target. They have little sense of self-worth beyond that relationship.

* Authors' personal knowledge.

2. *Delusory* binders suffer a mental illness that results in their convincing themselves that they have a binding relationship with their target. They believe that the public figure sends them messages through his or her activities or they believe destiny will bring them and the public figure together.

3. *Callow* binders simply do not realize how inappropriate their communications with the target are. They convince themselves that they have a binding relationship with the target, and therefore, this is the way people in a binding relationship act.

4. *Relationship* binders draw great satisfaction simply from communicating with the target. The communications forge the relationship. Binders are happy with the long-distance communication because it gives them a connection to their target, nor does receiving a response from the target matter much to the relationship binder because they still have the relationship through their communications.

   Impersonal binders look beyond the dreariness or boredom of their own lives to find fulfillment in someone else's life. Seeking that fulfillment explains why so many impersonal binders focus on public figures or celebrities. People in positions of power or glamour give the appearance of transcending mundane existences.

For example, a state senator began receiving numerous overfamiliar letters and cards. All were signed the "U.S. Ambassador to Singapore." The alleged ambassador also sent a package containing a plaque and a written commendation. Through liaison with other agencies, the threat manager identified the sender as a 60-year-old woman who had used other titles in the past to communicate with public figures and send them bogus awards. Her pattern was to begin numerous and intense communications with a target, then lose interest, presumably to move on to another target. Her communications, although clearly efforts at personal relationships, had never escalated or turned sinister.

The threat manager assessed the woman as a relationship binder seeking to ingratiate herself with the state senator. He recommended adopting a passive watch-and-wait strategy of monitoring subsequent communications from her. Given her past behavior, she would soon enough lose interest in the state senator, probably to move on to another target.*

Thus, threat managers can recognize inappropriate communications from relationship impersonal binders by their

- Focus on a public figure, especially the exciting or glamorous aspects of the public figure's activities;
- Expressed desire to continue communicating with the public figure as though those communications formed a bond between them;
- Claims to be the best or closest or top supporter or defender of the target; and
- Insistence on believing that the binder and the target have a true connection.

Relationship binders want a friend, someone in whom they can confide or share. They find such relationships among the famous and the well known.

Delusory binders step beyond reality in believing they have a personal, even intimate relationship with the target. They believe that their target responds to the binder's communications by sending coded messages in speeches, songs, performances, even by secret

---

* Authors' personal knowledge.

looks in photographs or film footage. The delusion is usually tenacious and the binder refuses to accept any reality that challenges the delusion.

For example, 2 years after Kathy J. began obeying the restraining order to keep away from the female deputy who had talked her out of a suicide attempt, she became an impersonal delusory binder. When the local city police department, in an effort to recruit more female officers, posted the photographs and biographies of its highest ranking female officers, Kathy took notice. One of them was a deputy chief. Kathy began sending the deputy chief e-mails to her work account and leaving voice mails on the chief's office telephone. All the phone messages were left late at night when Kathy had some assurance no one would actually answer the phone. In the e-mails and phone messages, Kathy talked about how she had seen the chief's photograph on the police website. Kathy immediately felt a special kinship with the chief. She knew they were destined to have a love affair. Over time, the e-mails became more sexually explicit, including fantasies involving the chief's law enforcement equipment, especially her handcuffs.

When the local newspaper published a story on the deputy chief that mentioned her children, Kathy began talking about her plans to form a family with the chief and the children. That discussion alarmed the chief, who then referred the case to the threat manager.

After checking with his threat-manager colleagues in other jurisdictions, the police threat manager learned about the previous personal delusion toward the female sheriff's deputy. The police manager contacted the sheriff's threat manager to share information. Because the initial strategy of obtaining a restraining order and setting up a monitoring through Kathy's mother had worked, the two threat managers agreed to expand those controls to cover the police deputy chief. Once again, Kathy obeyed the restraining order. From the mother, the threat managers learned that Kathy had turned her attention to the deputy chief after breaking up with her girlfriend. Once she developed a new relationship, her interest in the police and sheriff's personnel would quickly fade.*

Thus, the threat manager can recognize inappropriate communications from delusory impersonal binders by their

- Focus on a nonexistent reciprocal relationship between the binder and the target;
- Claims that the target is sending messages or signals through the target's work, appearances, or other improbable means;
- Insistence that the target feels toward the binder as the binder feels toward the target; and
- Evidence of possible mental illness in their behavior.

Delusory impersonal binders usually enjoy their delusions without trying to actually live them. They communicate from a distance and rarely engage in approach behavior.

Callow binders are generally too unsophisticated to realize the inappropriateness of their communications. They have a naive and innocent approach to the world. Infatuated with the target, they express themselves in ways they think lovers always do. They cannot fathom that their communications might be misunderstood and their intentions misinterpreted. If confronted, they frequently act shocked or horrified that anyone would take offense at what they did or how they communicated.

---

* Authors' personal knowledge.

For example, an entire group of individuals banded together by a common hobby became callow impersonal binders. Shortly after Arnold Schwarzenegger took office as governor of California, the value of his autograph skyrocketed among autograph seekers. One autograph club came up with the idea of making a contest out of it. Through their website, they offered bragging rights to the first member who could get Governor Schwarzenegger's signature.

The members took the game seriously. Because the governor had a law enforcement security detail, getting physically close to Schwarzenegger meant getting past the security. Club members began crashing events, sneaking into places where the governor was scheduled to appear, and lining the route through which he had to walk to get to his next location. Although all the members wanted was his autograph, their efforts disrupted the security.

The threat manager recognized the members as aggressive autograph hounds. She realized they were callow impersonal binders intent on winning the club's game. As an appropriate protective response, she recommended that the security detail treat the members sternly. Her recommended threat management strategy was to persuade the club to call off the game, thus refocusing the members on their regular pursuits. Once the club announced an end to the game on its website, the efforts of the club members stopped.*

Thus, threat managers can recognize inappropriate communications from callow impersonal binders by their

- Focus on presuming the target will accept or respond to their communication;
- Nonviolent motivations or intentions; and
- Insistence on acting on their presumptions.

Frequently, callow binders can be quite stubborn in contacting the target, but with the right persuasion and approach, the threat manager can, if necessary, convince them of the error of their ways.

Impersonal binding howlers try to fill some gap in their lives. They believe that their binding with someone else, whether stranger or acquaintance, will fill that void. The emptiness can be oppressive enough to compel the impersonal binding howler to turn sinister or, worse, take up the hunt. Consequently, how the threat manager manages these individuals is crucial. Making them feel rejected or left alone compounds the problem that drove them toward seeking a relationship in the first place.

What Howlers Want

Howlers want something very different from what hunters want. Howlers use their communications to cause a reaction, to frighten or enamor, to upset or provoke. They have no need to do anything beyond speaking, writing, or calling, even if they speak, write, or call repeatedly. They never intend to take any action in furtherance of their inappropriate communications. For the howler, communicating is sufficient. It results in the end they seek. Hunters, by comparison, want a more tangible result. They intend to take violent action to rectify their issues. For them, justice is expressed in force, vengeance in blood, affection in approaching.

* Authors' personal knowledge.

Sinister howlers seek fearful reactions from their targets. They communicate to frighten or disturb. As a result, and as odd as it sounds, the target actually invests the threat with whatever value it ultimately has. For the howler, how the target reacts to his or her threat or, just as importantly, how the howler imagines the target to react is the primary goal. Making the threat is sufficient.

Sometimes, sinister howlers strike gold. On December 2, 2005, Javier Rodriquez of Connecticut had a court date related to driving violations. Because the court had suspended his driver's license, he decided not to drive himself. Unfortunately, he could not find anyone to take him. To get out of this predicament, Rodriquez walked to a telephone booth near his home and placed five telephone calls to various locations across the state. During each call, Rodriquez claimed that bombs had been placed in courthouses and judicial buildings all over the state. In response, all 45 state court buildings were evacuated and searched, including the one at which Rodriquez was scheduled to appear. After police traced the bomb threat calls to the pay phone, they compared the names of nearby residents to the names of people who were scheduled to appear in court and did not show up. That led them to Rodriquez.[*] He caused plenty of panic, which was the purpose of his phone calls. Unfortunately for him, the scheme did not keep him out of court.

Dietz et al. compared individuals who had inappropriately approached members of Congress with those who only wrote inappropriate letters to congressmen. The approachers, of course, acted like hunters, the nonapproachers like impersonal howlers. The Dietz team found that "subjects who sent threats to members of Congress were significantly *less* likely to pursue a face-to-face encounter with him or her."[†] More tellingly, Dietz et al. found the following types of threats were characteristic of those who made no effort to approach, that is, the howlers

- Threatening any kind of harm toward any public figure;
- Threatening to kill any public figure or those around a public figure;
- Indicating that a threat would be executed by the subject or his agent;
- Indicating that a threat would be executed by someone other than the subject or his agent;
- Making any direct threat;
- Making any veiled threat;
- Making any conditional threat; and
- Making any implausible threat.[‡]

The team concluded that the presence of a threat in a communication to a member of Congress "appears to lower the risk" toward the congressman.[‡]

As we discussed in Chapter 7, Dietz and his crew concluded that those who approached members of Congress generally wanted something fairly tangible, like the congressman's

[*] Associated Press, December 3 and 6, 2005.
[†] Dietz, P. E., Matthews, D. B., Martell, D. A., Stewart, T. M., Hrouda, D. R., & Warren, J. (1991). Threatening and otherwise inappropriate letters to members of the United States Congress (p. 1466). *Journal of Forensic Sciences, 36.*
[‡] Dietz, P. E., Matthews, D. B., Martell, D. A., Stewart, T. M., Hrouda, D. R., & Warren, J. (1991). Threatening and otherwise inappropriate letters to members of the United States Congress (p. 1463). *Journal of Forensic Sciences, 36.*

assistance with a problem. Not so with howlers. They saw congressmen entirely differently, so their communications strove for a completely different effect. Howlers

- Wrote in cursive;
- Took an enemy role, including the role of assassin, persecutor, and condemning judge;
- Cast the congress member in an enemy role, including the roles of persecutor and conspirator;
- Attempted to instill fear in the member;
- Attempted to provoke upset in the member;
- Attempted to instill worry in the member; and
- Made threats.*

These impersonal howlers saw achievement in the communication itself. They used it to instill fear or provoke upset or cause the congressman to worry. The howlers achieved what they wanted through writing or calling. They needed do no more. Unlike hunters, they had no need to communicate in different ways. They had no need to be nice or solicitous. Most importantly, they had no need to approach. Their imagination provided them plenty of images of scared, upset, and worried congressmen. The howlers fully succeeded in their purpose simply by writing their letters.

Dietz et al. also conducted a similar study on those who communicated inappropriately with Hollywood celebrities. For celebrity howlers, like their congressional counterparts, writing inappropriately was the end game. Celebrity howlers

- Used tablet-like paper;
- Provided their full addresses;
- Expressed a desire to marry, have sex with, or have children with the celebrity;
- Enclosed commercial pictures;
- Attempted to instill shame in the celebrity;
- Indicated a sexual interest in the celebrity;
- Mentioned other public figures repeatedly; and
- Mentioned any kind of sexual activity.†

Unlike celebrity hunters, celebrity howlers did not change their method of communicating. Rather, they used their letters to express their intimate fantasies. As with congressional howlers, celebrity howlers sought a reaction from the celebrity through the communication itself. They showed no interest in accomplishing or doing anything else. For them, it sufficed to describe their sexual and romantic fantasies without the trouble of acting them out.

Unlike congressional howlers, celebrity howlers showed no strong correlation between threatening and not approaching. Rather, Dietz et al. found that "the presence or absence

* Dietz, P. E., Matthews, D. B., Martell, D. A., Stewart, T. M., Hrouda, D. R., & Warren, J. (1991). Threatening and otherwise inappropriate letters to members of the United States Congress (p. 1463). *Journal of Forensic Sciences*, 36.
† Dietz, P. E., Matthews, D. B., van Duyne, C., Martell, D. A., Parry, D. H., Stewart, T., ... Crowder, J. D. (1991). Threatening and otherwise inappropriate letters to Hollywood celebrities. *Journal of Forensic Science*, 36, 208.

of a threat in the communications is no indication whatsoever of whether a subject is going to pursue an encounter."* Although the relationship between explicit threats and not approaching was much more pronounced among congressional howlers, celebrity howlers nonetheless fit the mold of individuals who achieved their goal through writing inappropriate communications. The writing was an end unto itself, not a means to some other objective. Perhaps significantly, members of Congress attracted more impersonal sinister howlers while celebrities caught the attention of more impersonal binder howlers. That difference no doubt helps explain the different findings on threats.

In sum, what howlers want is achieved through the act of communicating inappropriately. Both personal and impersonal howlers, both sinister and binder, serve their purposes through their communications. What they want is the reaction, real or, better yet, imagined from the target. Sinister howlers of every stripe seek to cause fear or disquiet in their targets. Binding howlers hope their communications will spawn a relationship with the target. For all howlers, the act of communicating suffices.

Impersonal howlers, whether sinister or binder, generally prefer to keep their distance from their targets. They rely on distance communications to get their inappropriate communications across. They let these communications do all the work. They design their letters, phone calls, faxes, e-mails, or whatever to cause the desired reaction from the target. Even better, once an impersonal howler launches a communication, he or she is then free to imagine that reaction. Thus, no matter what really happens, the howler always believes he or she succeeded in getting the result sought. Doing anything more risks letting reality intrude.

Summary

Chapter 8 analyzed howlers. It typed them by their relationship to their targets and categorized them by what they sought to accomplish. Personal howlers know their targets; impersonal howlers do not. Sinister howlers seek to inspire fear in their targets; binder howlers try to establish some kind of relationship with their target. We categorized sinister personal howlers into three distinct groups. The groupings centered on what the howler intended his or her howling to accomplish, such as controlling the target, intimidating the target, or playing some dirty trick on a third party. Personal binder howlers may seek a relationship with someone they know, try to maintain a relationship their target wants to end, or respond to some delusion the howler has that makes him or her believe he or she has a relationship with the target.

Impersonal sinister howlers fell into five groups: self-defenders, celebrity seekers, habitual, crusaders, and copycats. Impersonal binders divided into relationship, delusory, and callow. After defining and illustrating each type, including some of the threat management strategies appropriate to each, we examined what howlers want and how what they want differs from what hunters want.

---

* Dietz, P. E., Matthews, D. B., van Duyne, C., Martell, D. A., Parry, D. H., Stewart, T., ... Crowder, J. D. (1991). Threatening and otherwise inappropriate letters to Hollywood celebrities. *Journal of Forensic Science, 36*, 208.

Situation Analysis: The Snitch

The Facts

In December 2006, a prisoner serving a life sentence at a state penitentiary without possibility of parole approached a guard. The prisoner claimed he had information concerning a plot by a particular gang to kill a prominent state elected official using explosives. The prisoner claimed his source was a civilian employee at the prison who belonged to the gang. According to the prisoner, this civilian employee had told him about the plot. Corrections officers assessed the informant as credible and passed the information to the state threat management unit.

At the time, the state was roiled by media frenzy over the impending execution of a world-famous gang member. The governor of the state was receiving a lot of attention because he had not yet announced his decision on whether to commute the prisoner's execution to a life sentence. Along with the media attention, the governor also received an increased number of threats and other inappropriate communications.

The Threat Analysis

Any case deriving its information from an informant first requires assessing the informant's credibility before assessing the potential threat. However, given the controversy over the upcoming execution, the information from the prisoner could represent leakage of an actual plot. Given the current pressure generated by the execution, the threat management unit's assessment was to treat the case as a potential high risk until an aggressive protective investigation determined the prisoner's actual credibility. The unit would reassess the potential threat based on the findings of the protective investigation.

Protective Response

The threat management unit recommended that the commander of the governor's security detail be notified of the potential threat. In addition, the governor's public schedule was to be reviewed to determine whether any security adjustments were necessary.

Threat Management Strategy

Based on the urgency of determining the informant's credibility, the threat management unit should deploy agents to interview the prisoner and, once his or her identity was established, interview the prison civilian employee accused of being the source. Polygraphs or voice stress analyzers should be used on both individuals. New information should immediately be fed back to the threat assessors for their revised assessments.

The Outcome

A team of threat managers was immediately dispatched to the state prison to interview the informant. The managers learned that the prisoner had never been an informant in the past. During the interview with the prisoner, he claimed that a prison male nurse gave him his daily insulin injection. The nurse, knowing that the prisoner's son produced rap music, expressed to the prisoner his desire to record some rap songs the nurse had written. The prisoner agreed to write a letter of introduction for the nurse to take to the prisoner's son.

Once the prisoner wrote the letter and the nurse delivered it, the nurse became friendlier and more at ease with the prisoner. According to the prisoner, the nurse's discussions started turning around violence and the nurse's need to establish his "street cred." The nurse confided to the prisoner that he knew of a plot to kill an elected official using explosives. The prisoner, worried about his son's connections to the nurse, passed the information on to prison officials. The threat managers evaluated the prisoner's demeanor and command of the facts as sincere and firm, thus giving him some credibility. The prisoner also agreed to take a polygraph examination. The managers scheduled it for the next morning.

The threat managers determined through prison personnel files that the nurse had worked at the prison for 5 years. He had a good record with positive evaluations and no disciplinary problems. The nurse was on his regular day off and could not be located at home. Due to the urgency of the situation, the threat managers set up a surveillance post at the residence to await the nurse's return.

When the nurse arrived home that evening, the threat managers requested to interview him. With some hesitation, the nurse agreed. During the interview, the nurse admitted that he gave the prisoner his daily insulin injections. He also confirmed that the prisoner had written a letter of introduction to the prisoner's son about the nurse's rap songs. The nurse adamantly denied any knowledge or information about an assassination plot.

At this point in the interview, the threat managers adopted a tougher, more interrogatory style of questioning in order to increase the pressure on the nurse. After about 45 minutes of grilling the nurse, he began to cry and offered to confess what really happened.

According to the nurse, he and the prisoner had talked about the nurse's interest in rap music. The prisoner had written the letter, which the nurse delivered. The nurse established a relationship with the rap producer, who expressed interest in the nurse's songs. At the son's request, the nurse agreed to carry a letter back to the father, along with some cigarettes and a lighter. The next day, he delivered the items to the prisoner.

A few days later, the prisoner told the nurse that the prisoner's son wanted to see the nurse. When the nurse met with the son, the son gave him a small amount of marijuana to take back to the prisoner. The nurse objected, but the son reminded him that he had already violated prison rules and the law by passing the letter and cigarettes to the prisoner. After delivering the marijuana to the prisoner, the prisoner ordered the nurse to meet with his son regularly and smuggle packages from the son to the prisoner. If the nurse did not comply, the prisoner threatened to turn him in to prison authorities. He would lose his job and probably end up in prison himself.

Several months passed during which the nurse made a few more deliveries. The nurse took advantage of a promotion to a supervisory position to schedule other nurses to give the prisoner his daily injections. The prisoner sent him a note ordering him to resume giving the shots himself. If not, the note warned, the nurse would be sorry. The nurse continued to avoid the prisoner. After a while, he convinced himself the ordeal was over. The nurse readily agreed to a polygraph examination that night. The examiner determined that the nurse's answers were nondeceptive.

The next morning, the prisoner refused to go to the scheduled polygraph test. He claimed that he had received "hard looks" from other prisoners. He did not want to be labeled a snitch.

Based on the new facts derived from the expedited protective investigation, the threat management unit's threat assessors assessed the allegation of a plot against an elected official as not credible and, hence, low risk. The assessors determined the prisoner was a personal howler using dirty trickster tactics against the nurse in order to punish the nurse for no longer serving as a private courier.

Issues of Interest

The events that transpired in this case illustrate a number of important lessons for threat managers, especially pertaining to information from informants:

1. All informants, but especially inmate informants, need to be treated with great caution and skepticism. They can appear very sincere and convincing, and as in this particular case, elements of their story can be verifiably true.
2. Informants can also be very manipulative and mercenary in generating their information.
3. In all cases involving an informant, the informant's credibility about all aspects of his or her story should be assessed before assessing the informant's allegations.
4. The use of polygraph examinations or voice stress tests is the best way to verify the informant's credibility about all aspects of his story.
5. Other issues, political or social, may escalate the priority of a threat case. In this case, the pending controversial execution of a gang member had an impact on both the resources available to the threat management unit and the pressure to quickly resolve the case.
6. Other law enforcement agencies may deem the informant reliable, but the threat manager has to make his or her own determination about that credibility.
7. Highly developed interview and interrogation techniques are essential to the threat manager's ability to get to the truth. In the instant case, those skills prevented a threat case from going out of control.
8. In social venues susceptible to the leakage phenomenon, such as schools and workplaces, the source of the leak should be treated as an informant whose credibility needs to be established.
9. In sum, individuals who pass along derogatory information about other individuals should not be automatically accepted as credible. Whether in workplaces, schools, or prisons, informants must first be assessed for credibility before their information or allegation is assessed.

Working with the Intimacy Effect and the Law

9

For too many years, threat managers and the laws that proscribed threatening communications focused almost exclusively on explicit threats. Cases were not opened until, or more likely unless, the subject explicitly threatened the target with physical harm. The law punished only threateners and attackers, not stalkers or harassers or those who prepared themselves to act violently. This emphasis on threatening communications had the unfortunate effect of spotlighting sinister howlers, leaving the hunters well hidden in the shadows.

Over the past decade or so, research studies and practical experience began convincing threat managers to see threats as only one behavior among a full panoply of other attack-related behaviors engaged in by hunters. Contemporary threat management discounted the previous overriding emphasis on threats and shifted its focus to attack-related behaviors. Threat managers began to understand that hunters posed a threat while howlers merely made threats. Each, hunter and howler, had to be managed, but the strategies for doing so for each differed radically.

Research, combined with experience, sometimes bitter experience, suggests that the relationship between threats and actual violence has to be understood within the context or venue in which it occurs. Threats are relative, for their predictive powers very much depend on the relationship between the subject and the target. To explain this phenomenon, we hypothesized that the value of threats as preincident indicators of violence increased in proportion to the degree of intimacy between the subject and the target. We called this hypothesis the *intimacy effect*. It postulates that threats have value as an indicator of future violence the more interpersonal or intimate the relationship between the target and the threatener. The opposite also holds; that is, threats have limited to negative value as indicators of future violence when the subject and target have no interpersonal relationship. Threat managers can work with the intimacy effect by factoring it into their assessments and their selection of management strategies.

Consequently, when assessing threats, the threat manager must always ask the following:

- What is this threat intended to do?
- What is the social setting or venue in which the threat occurred?
- What is the relationship, real or perceived, between the threatener and the target?

If the threatener seeks to control a spouse or intimidate coworkers, supervisors, fellow students, or teachers, then the value of the threat increases. If, instead, the subject aims only to instill fear in strangers or uses the threat to gain attention or makes repeated, empty threats, or uses the threat to express complete frustration or anger at some bureaucratic process or system beyond his or her ken, then the value of the threat as a preincident

171

indicator of future violence decreases. Taking into account the intimacy effect, then, goes a long way toward assessing specific threats.

At the same time that research and threat management discounted the importance of threats as preincident indicators among strangers, lawmakers, especially at the federal level, toughened up the penalties for making such threats. Conversely, even though the research showed that the intimacy effect increased the value of threats in interpersonal venues, the Supreme Court dealt new laws mandating law enforcement responses to domestic disputes a grievous blow by ruling that police departments have wide discretion in enforcing temporary restraining orders such as those commonly issued in domestic situations.* As a result, research and the law fell largely out of sync.

This chapter first summarizes research conducted by Debra M. Jenkins to test the intimacy effect hypothesis against the research on domestic and workplace violence, school shootings, and attacks on public figures. Jenkins found that the research on the various venues of intended violence supported the hypothesis. Next, the chapter addresses the significant gap between the intimacy effect and the focus of federal laws and recent court decisions. Finally, the chapter examines recent state efforts to bring their statutes into line with the research. Although federal laws and court decisions essentially contradict the research, state legislatures seem to be taking a much more realistic approach to confronting intended violence. Perhaps, in time, the federal approach will catch up with the states.

Working with the Intimacy Effect

The Appendix presents a research essay written by Debra M. Jenkins summarizing the current research on the relation between threats and the major venues of intended violence. Jenkins has reviewed studies focusing on violence toward public figures, workplace colleagues, school officials and students, and current and former intimates. She concluded that the research supports the principal tenet of the intimacy effect even though no primary research has yet been done on the effect.

Rather than summarize Jenkins' summaries, we refer the reader to her work. Here, we quote from a number of observations Jenkins reached regarding each of the major venues and on intended violence in general. In addition, we strongly endorse her recommendation that the intimacy effect become the subject of some primary research to further refine our understanding of it. Much of the research Jenkins reviewed focused on some other topic, with threats addressed as a secondary or even tertiary issue.

Jenkins observed the following.

Violence against Public Figures

Public figures are attacked without first being threatened in most cases studied.
There is little motivation to threaten a public figure if violence is the desired outcome.
Consequently, the research shows that threats are not good preincident indicators for violence against public figures.

---

* We discuss further in the chapter the significance of this case for managing domestic disputes *Castle Rock* v. *Gonzales*, 545 US 748 (2005).

Violence against Workplace Colleagues

Threats are more prevalent among coworkers than from other sources in the workplace.

Workers suffer attacks of greater lethality from coworkers than from clients.

Most threat assessment professionals believe that threats among coworkers are important in determining level of danger.

Consequently, the research suggests that the intimacy effect may apply in coworker workplace violence.

Violence against School Officials and Students

Researchers are conflicted about how important threats are in the assessment of potential violence in the school venue.

Threats of violence in the school venue may more likely be in the form of "leakage."

Leakage supports the intimacy effect hypothesis because it occurs within interpersonal settings.

Violence against Domestic Intimates

Threats of violence are common among intimate partners.

It is possible to discern intended violence from impromptu violence in the domestic venue.

Separation of an intimate couple may trigger more lethal intended violence.

Female intimate partners are less likely to threaten before a violent attack.

Control motive is prevalent in male intimate–partner threats.

Loss of control may prompt male intimate–partner attacks.

Intimate partners who are severely or lethally violent are likely to have made previous threats of violence.

The research on threats and violence in the domestic violence venue supports the intimacy effect.

General Observations

Threat assessors may be able to evaluate direct threats differently depending on familiarity of victim and target.

There is a stronger relationship between threats and intended violence in the domestic violence venue than in the public-figure violence venue.

The enforcement of laws against threats of violence is less likely in the domestic venue than when directed toward public figures.

If threat assessors wait for direct threats to occur against public figures, they may be misdirecting their attention away from real dangers.

Within the domestic violence venue, the separation of intimates may be the most lethal stage of the relationship.

Workplaces and schools provide social environments of familiarity where threats and talk of violence before an attack are common.

In workplaces and schools, due to leakage, others are likely to know or suspect an attack is likely or imminent.

Research drawn from the various venues for intended violence supports the intimacy effect hypothesis that the value of a threat as a preincident indicator increases in proportion to the degree of familiarity between subjects and targets.

Based on Jenkins' findings and observations, we envision threats as occurring along an interpersonal continuum in which the value of the threat increases in direct relation to the intimacy of the interpersonal relationship. Figure 9.1 illustrates this progression. Where the two lines join, threats carry the greatest weight because that is the intimate–partner social setting. Where the two lines diverge at the greatest distance, threats carry little weight as preincident indicators because that is the stranger-to-stranger social setting in which neither subject nor target knows—or even think they know—each other.

Using the relationship continuum allows the threat manager to envision the value of threats within the social context in which they occur. We do not mean by this that all threats directed at intimate partners ultimately lead to violence. Rather, the research suggests that a higher proportion of threats between intimates ultimately do result in violence, especially when compared with threats to public figures. The intimacy effect should serve the threat manager as a crude barometer for measuring the pressure that threats bring to the different venues of intended violence. Sometimes that pressure rises to the level of hurricane force. At other times it is no greater than a mild spring day.

In all the years we have spoken on the intimacy effect, someone always asks, "How do we gauge the intimacy effect when there is no relationship, but the threatener believes (either mistakenly or delusionally) that there is a relationship?" The prudent answer to that question is to always assess the relationship from the subject's point of view. If he or she strongly believes a relationship exists, take any threats as a positive indicator of future violence.

Yet, having urged the threat manager to work with the intimacy effect when assessing threats, we hasten to emphasize that the threat manager's attention should always be on the subject's behaviors, of which making or not making a threat is one of many. The intimacy effect suggests that threats between intimates should be taken seriously. The hypothesis does *not* imply that threats always precede violence between individuals who know each other. Hunters individually decide if engaging in threat behaviors precedes violence. Again, both research and experience show that how an individual acts best determines whether he or she is a hunter or a howler. Hunters engage in behaviors that promote their hunting; howlers engage in behaviors conducive to howling.

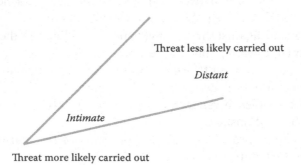

Figure 9.1 The intimacy effect from intimate to impersonal.

Ironically, of course, the ability of the threat manager to discount the value of a threat because of the impact of the intimacy effect in no way means that the threat can be ignored or shelved. After all, making a credible threat against another person violates state, sometimes even federal, laws. The threat manager may know for a certainty that he or she is managing a howler. At the same time, the threat manager cannot allow the howler to break the law with impunity. For corporate threat management teams, school officials, mental health professionals, and others outside the law enforcement community, this situation raises a host of new challenges. Used creatively and innovatively, these situations also open up a host of opportunities for intelligently managing both hunters and howlers.

Two cases illustrate how the twin concepts of acting like a hunter and acting like a howler, combined with measuring the intimacy effect, enhance the accuracy of the threat manager's assessments. Psychologist Reid Meloy boldly asserted, "threats are not that big a deal." He based that conclusion on a review of research, most of which dealt with either threats to public figures or stalking cases.* Meloy did not take into account threats among intimates that culminated in violence. But he did describe a case study that dramatically showed how acting like a personal howler seeking control, when combined with the intimacy effect, can transform the howler into a hunter.

According to Meloy, a case in Colorado involved a husband who physically and sexually abused his wife over the course of a decade. Whenever she expressed a desire to leave, he would respond, "If you do, I'll bag you," by which he apparently meant put her in a body bag. After 10 years of threats and abuse, the wife finally left, thus ending the howler's control over her. Her departure turned the husband into a hunter. Within a week of her moving out, the husband decided to kill her, developed a plan to do it that depended on his personal knowledge of her workday, assembled his weapons, and went to the supermarket where she worked.

When she arrived, the husband shot her in the back. He chased her into the store, killed her, and also killed the store manager. He left the store and drove his van to the highest point in the parking lot and waited for police to arrive. He killed the first officer on the scene but eventually surrendered after law enforcement officers returned his fire.†

Rather than discount the threats because they occurred repeatedly for nearly a decade without being carried out, threat managers familiar with the hunter-and-howler concepts and the intimacy effect would understand that the husband was a controller. For most of the decade, his threats successfully kept his wife from leaving him. Because the threats worked, he had no need to carry them out. Indeed, carrying them out would have defeated his determination to keep her in the relationship. When finally she did pack up, the threat manager would have recognized that the intimacy effect indicated that the risk of the threats being carried out was higher once the husband lost control over his wife. At the point of her departure, the threat manager would assess the husband as a high risk for carrying out lethal violence.

In Meloy's defense, he did recognize that in cases involving stalking of private individuals, "Articulated threats appear to have a positive and significant relationship to violence

---

* Meloy, J. R. (2000). *Violence risk and threat assessment: A practical guide for mental health and criminal justice professionals* (p. 161). San Diego, CA: Specialized Training Services.
† Meloy, J. R. (2000). *Violence risk and threat assessment: A practical guide for mental health and criminal justice professionals* (pp. 161–162). San Diego, CA: Specialized Training Services.

risk, but the correlation is weak."* But the correlation is not measured simply between public and private figures. Rather, the correlation scales along the degree of intimacy between subject and target. Public figures have intimates and acquaintances, thus making them subject to the intimacy effect, too. The lethal formula in Meloy's case study combined a personal howler who sought to control an intimate, but who eventually lost his control over her. That combination correlates very well with the risk of violence.

The second case study involves an impersonal howler who habitually made threats. In 1986, Scott L. Rendelman was a 31-year-old accountant living with his wife and children in Rockville, Maryland, a suburb of the nation's capital. When he invested a client's $283,000 in gold without the client's permission, law enforcement charged him with 15 counts of embezzlement. The court sentenced him to 4 1/2 months in prison. "The first thing that happened was that I lost everything," he remembered 15 years later when he finally got out of jail. "The credit card people started suing me. The mortgage people came after the house. My wife took the kids and divorced me." Finally, the appellate court upheld his conviction.[†]

Rendelman's first threat was as an impersonal self-defender objecting to the appellate judges' ruling. Those threats got him a 10-year prison sentence. Within the first 6 months, Rendelman essentially gave up on life. "And after 6 months they'd ground me down. I had absolutely no desire to get out. I was ashamed. I didn't want to face my family again, and I had absolutely nothing to go back to," he later remembered. He found he actually preferred prison life. "You didn't have to pay bills. They did your laundry for you. Brought you your meals—room service. And I didn't have to show my face and be ashamed," he admitted. As a result, he became an impersonal habitual howler. Every time his sentence drew near closing, he sent threatening letters to public officials, including presidents George H. W. Bush and Bill Clinton and the governor of California.[†] He signed himself "GRM," which stood for Government Rehabilitated Motherfucker.[‡]

Threat managers familiar with the hunter-and-howler concepts and the impact of the intimacy effect would recognize Rendelman as an impersonal, habitual howler who communicated in writing from a distance. He did not know his targets, but he threatened them repeatedly and did so for his own benefit and enjoyment. The intimacy effect would discount the value of his threats as preincident indicators of violence. Consequently, the threat manager would assess him and his threats as low risk.

Ultimately, the judge who presided over Rendelman's last threat case saw that enough was enough. He refused to send him back to prison. "The court wants to take Mr. Rendelman finally out of the nightmare that he's been living for the last 15 years," the judge explained. Instead, the judge ordered Rendelman to serve a year at a halfway house where he would be required to find a job and begin paying rent. "That letter writing is over," Rendelman told a reporter. "I just did it from prison basically because I didn't want to be released." Significantly, however, he added, "Now, though, if they did send me back to prison, that's when I'd start writing again."[†]

Rendelman kept his word. Once released from the halfway house in Sacramento, he apparently returned to Maryland, where he sent threatening letters to the client he had

---

* Meloy, J. R. (2000). *Violence risk and threat assessment: A practical guide for mental health and criminal justice professionals* (p. 166). San Diego, CA: Specialized Training Services.
† Wiley, W. (2002, February 15). Threatening letters turned short term into 15 years. *Sacramento Bee*.
‡ Authors' personal knowledge.

originally embezzled from demanding that the former client pay him $100,000 in restitution. He also threatened the client's attorney. The state arrested Rendelman for extortion, then convicted him of those charges in 2005. From the Maryland prison, he began sending threatening letters to the prosecutor, the judge, several federal judges, President George W. Bush, and Bush's White House staff. "When I get out," Rendelman wrote Assistant State's Attorney Carol Crawford, the prosecutor, "I will hunt you down. You must die. Death! Death! Death!" He warned the state judge "When I get out I'll tie a rope around your neck and hang you from the ceiling of your chambers." Both state officials testified that Rendelman's letters to them caused them fear and resulted in each of them taking security measures. Federal prosecutors brought charges and a jury convicted Rendelman of writing the threats. A federal judge sentenced him to 15 years in prison, adding a recommendation that the Federal Bureau of Prisons closely monitor Rendelman's correspondence.*

By the time of Rendelman's 2007 conviction for threats, he had spent 22 of the last 25 years in prison, the vast majority of that time for making threats.† Those few of his victims that he knew, he encountered them only in court in their official capacities. The other targets—the president, the White House staff, several federal judges—remained strangers to him. Significantly, and in support of the intimacy effect, Rendelman never took action beyond writing letters to carry out his threats. As the reporter who covered his release to the Sacramento halfway house in February 2002 noted, Rendelman "made a hobby of sending threatening letters to public officials."‡ His reaction to the prison experience transformed Rendelman into a habitual howler.

The value of the intimacy effect lies in its filtering the results of the research on intended violence. Because most of that research has focused on public figure threats, the lessons of the research for threat managers became skewed. Rather than dismiss direct or veiled threats out of hand, the intimacy effect requires the threat manager to inquire into the nature of the relationship between the threatener and the target. That inquiry alone will go a long way toward making the threat assessment an informed, knowledgeable, and defensible analysis. By also applying the twin concepts of acting like a hunter and acting like a howler, the threat manager further enhances the threat assessment by focusing on the subject's behaviors. The concepts of hunters, howlers, and the intimacy effect foster the best assessments.

Applying Federal Law

While the research on domestic and workplace violence, school shootings, and attacks on public officials uncovered the influence of the intimacy effect, Congress tightened up the federal response to explicit threats directed at federal officials. At the same time, the Supreme Court made a half-hearted effort to apply its concept of *true threat* as an exception to First Amendment rights of free speech. Because the Supreme Court failed to define the concept, individual circuit courts of appeal developed and applied their own definitions. Not surprisingly, that resulted in considerable confusion among the circuits. Federal law

---

* Castaneda, R., & Londogo, E. (2007, December 15). Man guilty of threatening state judge and prosecutor. *Washington Post*; Castaneda, R. (2008, April 22). Man gets 15 years for threat letters. *Washington Post*.
† Castaneda, R. (2008, April 22). Man gets 15 years for threat letters. *Washington Post*.
‡ Wiley, W. (2002, February 15). Threatening letters turned short term into 15 years. *Sacramento Bee*.

and federal court decisions drifted far away from what the research on intended violence was finding out about threats and attack-related behaviors.

For example, federal law makes it a crime to threaten a federal judge. Yet, in over 3,000 threatening communications directed toward federal jurists between 1980 and 1993, no individual who threatened a federal judge ever actually attacked that judge. That pattern continued over the next 14 years. One could argue then, as Dietz did with members of Congress, that judges who receive threats are relatively safe from the person making the threat. Conversely, the three federal judges who were assassinated were never threatened by their assassins.* Nor did Bart Ross explicitly threaten Judge Lefkow or her family or any of the other judges on his list.

Perhaps, Congress intended the law punishing threats to insulate federal judges from frightening, disconcerting communications so they could better focus their attention on the cases before them. However, if Congress passed the law criminalizing threats as a way for law enforcement to enhance security for federal jurists, it missed its mark. The only security against actual assaults that federal law affords federal judges is the law punishing such assaults, but that seems precious little consolation.

So, too, with the laws securing the president. Congress made it a crime to threaten the president or to assault the president, but that was all. Every year, the Secret Service arrests scores of individuals who utter threats against the incumbent. But in the service's own research on 43 individuals who attacked a public figure in the United States, none threatened their target beforehand. Indeed, the researchers felt so strongly about discounting the value of threats they concluded that the belief that threats precede violence was a "myth."† If Congress intended to provide law enforcement with tools to *prevent* presidential assassinations, it again missed its mark.

Take the case of Steven Baldwin, presidential threatener. On July 20, 2005, Baldwin mailed two packages to the White House. One had a label declaring "Biological Weapons Enclosed." The other label said, "Letter Bomb!" Secret Service agents did not assess either package as actually posing a threat to the president. Rather than arrest Baldwin, the investigating agents simply warned him to stop sending threatening mail to the president. Clearly, the investigators assessed Baldwin as more of a pest, a howler, than someone who really posed a risk to the president. In the summer of 2005, the Secret Service did not even bother prosecuting him for sending the packages with the threatening labels. That would change as soon as Baldwin's behavior became even more disruptive.

The warning worked for nearly 6 months until December 14, when Baldwin again sent a package addressed to President George W. Bush. This time the package label read "Brace For Impact, I've Read Your Fortune & The Signs Are Not In Your Favor." The mailroom x-ray showed a possible improvised explosive device inside the package. This prompted the White House mailroom to shut down for nearly 2 hours until investigators determined that the package held a cell phone wrapped in wires.

This time, Baldwin had gone too far. The brouhaha over the December package inconvenienced the mailroom and the Service. Consequently, Secret Service agents arrested him several weeks later. The charges they filed against him revealed just how serious a threat

---

* Calhoun, F. S. (1998). *Hunters and howlers: Threats and violence against Federal Judicial officials in the United States, 1979–1993.* Washington, DC: United States Marshal Service.
† Vossekuil, B., & Fein, R. (1998). *Protective intelligence and threat assessment investigations: A guide for state and local law enforcement officials* (p. 6). Washington, DC: National Institute of Justice.

they thought he posed: making a false threat using biological weapons, making a false threat using explosive materials, and threatening the president.* Clearly, the Secret Service used the law to help it manage a howler. But does that enhance the security of the president? The service reacted to the disruption of the offense, not any actual danger posed by Baldwin's actions.

Congress has also not offered its own members any better security than it has offered the judiciary and the presidency. As with presidents, judges, and other federal officials, Congress made it a crime to threaten or assault members of Congress. Yet, research conducted 25 years ago by Dietz et al. showed a statistically significant relationship between threatening a member of Congress and *not* approaching that member. Dietz et al. described the finding as particularly "robust."[†] One could almost argue that a public official is better off in terms of personal security if the subject threatens him or her. Unfortunately, the law has taken little notice of what the research found.

The Supreme Court further muddied the legal waters surrounding threats by creating a new category it called "true threats." Although the definition of a true threat remains murky, it seems to require the courts to balance expressed threats with the First Amendment by evaluating the threatening statement within the context of everything that happened as well as what the subject intended, where and how the threat was communicated, and any reasonable reaction of the recipient. In *Watts* v. *United States*, which dealt with the threat to the president statute, the Supreme Court recognized that

> The Nation undoubtedly has a valid, even an overwhelming, interest in protecting the safety of its Chief Executive and in allowing him to perform his duties without interference from threats of physical violence. … Nevertheless, a statute such as this one, which makes criminal a form of pure speech, must be interpreted with the commands of the First Amendment clearly in mind.[‡]

In the instant case, Watts, while attending an anti-Vietnam War rally in 1966, told a small group of his fellow protestors on the grounds of the Washington Monument that "if they ever make me carry a rifle, the first man I want to get in my sights is L.B.J."* The majority on the Court held that the statement was more political than threatening, pointing out that Watts' audience laughed at the comment. The Court added almost off-handedly that "the statute initially requires the Government to prove a true 'threat.'"* The Court offered no clarification of exactly what it meant by that term.

Over 20 years later, the Supreme Court tried to clarify the meaning of true threats. In *R.A.V.* v. *St. Paul, Minnesota*, the Court explained:

> And the Federal Government can criminalize only those threats of violence that are directed against the President, see 18 U.S.C. 871—since the reasons why threats of violence are outside the First Amendment (protecting individuals from the fear of violence, from the disruption that fear engenders, and from the possibility that the threatened violence will occur) have special force when applied to the person of the President.[§]

* Seattle man charged with threatening Bush. (2006, January 13). Associated Press.
† Dietz, P. E., Matthews, D. B., Martell, D. A., Stewart, T. M., Hrouda, D. R., & Warren, J. (1991). Threatening and otherwise inappropriate letters to members of the United States Congress. *Journal of Forensic Sciences*, 36, 1466.
‡ *Watts* v. *United States*, 394 U.S. 705 (1969).
§ *R.A.V.* v. *St. Paul, Minn.*, 505 U.S. 377 (1992).

R.A.V. seems to imply that "true threats" are those not protected by the First Amendment because of the need for "protecting individuals from the fear of violence, from the disruption that fear engenders, and from the possibility that the threatened violence will occur."* More confusing still, *R.A.V.* had nothing to do with the president. It involved several teenagers who planted a burning cross in the yard of an African-American family. The St. Paul trial court convicted *R.A.V.*, one of the youths, of violating a city ordinance that "prohibits the display of a symbol which one knows or has reason to know 'arouses anger, alarm or resentment in others on the basis of race, color, creed, religion or gender.'"* The Supreme Court found the ordinance in violation of the First Amendment. Ironically, in the two cases addressing threats, the Court found in favor of the individuals convicted in the lower courts of violating statutes prescribing threatening communications.

The closest anyone on the Court has yet to come to articulating a definition of true threat occurred in a 1975 concurring opinion written by Justice Thurgood Marshall, with Justice William O. Douglas joining. The majority opinion rested on a technicality and did not address the merits or the meaning of true threat. George Rogers, a local Shreveport, Louisiana, "town drunk," showed up at a coffee shop one morning and began expressing his opposition to President Richard Nixon's planned trip to China. He told several patrons and a waitress or two that he was Jesus Christ and had privileged information that the Chinese had a bomb that they might use against the American people. Rogers told his unwilling audience that he intended to go to Washington to "whip Nixon's ass" or "kill him in order to save the United States."†

Rogers became enough of an irritant that someone summoned the police. The arresting officer asked Rogers if he had threatened the president. Rogers replied, in part, "I'm going to Washington and I'm going to beat his ass off. Better yet, I will go kill him." Rogers added that he would have to walk because he did not like riding in cars. The police did not arrest him on any local charge, but they did refer his statements to the local Secret Service office. The Secret Service promptly arrested him for threatening the president.†

"This sad set of circumstances," Marshall wrote, "resulted in a five-count indictment under the 'threats against the President' statute, 18 U.S.C. 871 (a)." At trial, the jury found Rogers guilty. Rather than overturn the conviction on a technicality, as the majority voted to do, Marshall and Douglas wanted to address the breadth of the threat statute. They found that the lower courts interpreted the statute to mean applying an "objective" literal interpretation to the words uttered. That is, if the communication carried a threat on its face, then the subject had violated the threats-against-the-president statute. Marshall believed that balancing the statute against the First Amendment required delving deeper to determine whether the person making the utterance actually *intended* to make a threat. "Statements deemed threatening in nature only upon 'objective' consideration will be deterred only if persons criticizing the President are careful to give a wide berth to any comment that might be construed as threatening in nature," Marshall opined, "and that degree of deterrence would have substantial costs in discouraging the 'uninhibited, robust, and wide-open' debate that the First Amendment is intended to protect." Marshall explained:

> I would therefore interpret 871 to require proof that the speaker intended his statement to be taken as a threat, even if he had no intention of actually carrying it out. The proof of intention would, of course, almost certainly turn on the circumstances under which the statement was

* *R.A.V.* v. *St. Paul, Minn.*, 505 U.S. 377 (1992).
† *Rogers* v. *U.S.*, 422 U.S. 35 (1975).

made… Under the narrower construction of 871, the jury in this case might well have acquitted, concluding that it was unlikely that Rogers actually intended or expected that his listeners would take his threat as a serious one. Because I think that the District Court's misconstruction of the statute prejudiced petitioner in this case and may continue to do mischief in future prosecutions brought under 871, I would reverse on this ground.*

Clearly, the Supreme Court sympathizes with fools and drunks, but it has yet to fully distinguish between true threats, either to presidents or private citizens, and free speech.

A number of commentators have expressed grave reservations about the lack of clarity from the Supreme Court regarding the definition of true threats, especially given the chasm between the law and the research. Their commentaries, especially those concerned with the lack of guidance in the school venue, further illustrate the continued disconnect between the research findings on intended violence and the judicial findings on threats. These commentators argue that until the gap between the law and the research closes, threat managers will find themselves frustrated by the demands of the federal courts.

Jennifer E. Rothman asserted that the Supreme Court's silence on clarifying the definition of true threats has resulted in "unaddressed confusion" among the lower courts. Some circuit courts focus on the intent of the person making the threatening communication; other circuits focus on an objective interpretation of the communication by a reasonable person, usually the recipient.[†] Thus, an individual who intended to make a threat may be acquitted in some circuits if his or her target did not reasonably infer that a threat had been made. In other circuits, subjects who did not intend their communication as a threat could be convicted if the target reasonably interpreted the communication as threatening. Justice Marshall's fear of continued "mischief" has been realized. The Supreme Court has not taken any opportunity to rectify the different approaches.

As a solution, Rothman proposed a three-part test for determining a communication a true threat. First, the subject intended to make a threat. Second, the subject indicated that the subject or some specific confederates of the subject would carry it out, as opposed to some unnamed or unidentified parties carrying it out. Third, would a reasonable person understand the communication as a threat?[‡] If the communication passed all three tests, the subject had made a true threat. Failing any single test negated the validity of the threat.

Scott Hammack believed that the problem of no clear definition or approach has been compounded by advances on the Internet. After citing a number of incidents involving threatening communications on the World Wide Web, Hammack observed, "These cases illustrate how the Internet amplifies the effects of threats and the need for courts to understand the full impact of this new technology. The courts' two traditional approaches to true threats, the subjective speaker test and the objective listener test, both fail to deal with on-line threats effectively."[§]

Hammack predicted that the very elements that make the Internet, such a strong source of information and exchange of ideas also lend themselves to hate mongers and would-be terrorists. "The features that make the Internet an ideal free speech forum, such

---

* *Rogers* v. *U.S.*, 422 U.S. 35 (1975).
† Rothman, J. E. (2001). Freedom of speech and true threats. *Harvard Journal of Law and Public Policy*, 25, 286.
‡ Rothman, J. E. (2001). Freedom of speech and true threats (pp. 333–5). *Harvard Journal of Law and Public Policy*, 25, 286.
§ Hammack, S. (2002). The Internet loophole: Why threatening speech on-line requires a modification of the courts' approach to true threats and incitement (p. 95). *Columbia Journal of Law and Social Problems*, 36.

as the large and transient audience, rapid exchange of information, anonymity and low cost of access, also serve to magnify threatening speech," Hammack observed, adding that "these features also allow clever speakers to exploit a gap in the courts' threats approach by using incitement to create the same effect as a threat."* Hammack believed that if the courts continued their current muddied approach to true threats, it "will allow the Internet to become a prominent weapon of terror, while simultaneously permitting the restriction of benign speech."* Instead, Hammack proposed a hybrid approach that would take into account what the subject intended to communicate and how the target reacted to it.*

The Supreme Court's muddled approach to true threats has drawn the ire of legal researchers interested in the spate of school shootings that has received so much media attention over the past two decades. School shooters, researchers have found, tend to talk about their plans for violence with their fellows. This phenomenon has been labeled by FBI researchers on school shootings as "leakage."† "In each of the recent school yard slayings," Lisa Popyk wrote on November 10, 1998, "somebody read the class assignments that ended up being rants on violence and death, someone heard the threats or saw the weapons. Some even helped form the plan. And yet no one spoke up or tried to stop them."‡ For example, in a shooting at the Bethel, Arkansas, high school in 1997, a crowd of students, one equipped with a video camera, knew about the plan and congregated on the second-floor balcony to watch when Evan Ramsey, the shooter, arrived. Although leakage is not entirely the province of school shooters, the phenomenon has attracted the attention of legal commentators interested in developing a coherent approach to true threats in schools.

These scholars have criticized the courts for not addressing leakage. "Recent court cases suggest that the courts are largely out of touch with the real needs of threat assessment and of the schools' necessary response to stop violence," Sara E. Redfield wrote. "Specifically, the courts fail to recognize the vital difference between a threat made and a threat posed."§ She could as easily have applied this analysis to any and all of the venues for intended violence. Redfield became so enamored of the FBI's proposed assessment process for students that she recommended that the courts use the same process for determining whether a student had made a true threat. The suggestion would require the courts to take into account the sociological climate at the school, the psychological profile of the accused student, and family relationships and dynamics in judging the accused.§ That judicial approach probably risks more harm than the current ill-defined definition of true threat. Although Redfield correctly distinguishes between someone who makes a threat from someone who poses a threat, making that distinction should be left to trained threat managers, not jurists.¶

Lisa M. Pisciotta proposed a simpler, but no less unrealistic, solution. She would give considerable deference to school officials and how they handled the student. However, Pisciotta's approach risked running directly up against the Supreme Court's traditional concern with granting broad protection to the First Amendment. Pisciotta observed that

---

* Hammack, S. (2002). The Internet loophole: Why threatening speech on-line requires a modification of the courts' approach to true threats and incitement (p. 102). *Columbia Journal of Law and Social Problems*, 36.

† O'Toole, M. E. (2000). *The school shooter: A threat assessment perspective* (pp. 16–17). Quantico, VA: Critical Incident Response Group, National Center for the Analysis of Violent Crime.

‡ Popyk, L. (1998, November 10). Killers gave plenty of warning signs. *Cincinnati Post*.

§ Redfield, S. (2003). Threats made, threats posed: School and judicial analysis in need of redirection. Retrieved from http://www.law2.byu.edu/jel/v2003_2/Redfield.htm.

¶ Mohandie, K. (2000). *School violence threat management: A practical guide for educators, law enforcement, and mental health professionals*. San Diego, CA: Specialized Training Services.

> School administrators across the country have begun to implement zero-tolerance policies when dealing with threatening behavior by students. Administrators are suspending, expelling, and even having students arrested for discussing and planning acts of violence against their teachers and schools…. In response to these zero-tolerance policies, civil rights and First Amendment groups have zealously advocated the free speech rights of censored students.*

Because of the leakage problem, Pisciotta would have the courts dismiss the constitutional issues and back the school administrators. She argued, "As courts attempt to draw this line in the context of student threats, they must remember that adolescents are still learning responsibility, civility, and maturity, and consequently need to grow into their constitutional rights." Rather than emphasize individual freedom, she urged the courts to acknowledge that "educational professionals must be granted ample discretion in order to regulate and punish student threats and keep America's schools productive and safe."† Because the few Supreme Court cases that have addressed threatening communications have all revolved around protecting First Amendment rights, Pisciotta's approach probably has little chance of being judicially accepted.

In 2015, the Supreme Court again shied away from providing clear guidance on what constitutes a "true threat" and what standards trial courts should apply in determining the nature of threatening communications. The case involved Anthony Elonis, a self-described wanna-be rap artist. Using the *nom de rap* "Tone Dougie," Elonis began posting on Facebook explicit threats toward his wife shortly after she left him in 2010, taking their two children with her. Elonis also posted threats to kill coworkers at the amusement park where he worked; bomb a police station; kill kindergarten students at one of the nearby elementary schools; and, after an FBI agent interviewed him about his postings, he threatened to slit her throat and turn her into a ghost. Throughout these lyrical threats, Elonis inserted references to the First Amendment and claims that Tone Dougie's raps were fictional rants providing Elonis therapy and a vent for his anger over his marital problems. All of the potential targets—his ex-wife, coworkers, and the FBI agent—testified that the threats put them in fear for their lives. Elonis's supervisor fired him because of the posted references to attacking the amusement park.‡

At trial, the judge instructed the jury that if they found that the threats would put a "reasonable person" in fear, then the jury should find Elonis guilty of making interstate threats in violation of federal law. Nine of the country's 11 Circuit Courts of Appeal apply that same standard.§ The judge did not offer the jury any instructions as to weighing the defendant's mental state or intentions at the time Elonis wrote his posts. The jury convicted Elonis.

"Elonis's conviction cannot stand," Chief Justice John Roberts, Jr., wrote for the seven-justice majority.¶ "The jury was instructed that the Government need prove only that a reasonable person would regard Elonis's communications as threats, and that was error."** In a mind-numbing discussion of when to apply a defendant's "mental state" at the time of the

---

* Pisciotta, L. M. (2000). Beyond sticks and stones: A first amendment framework for educators who seek to punish students' threats (pp. 637–48). *Seton Hall Law Review, 30.*
† Pisciotta, L. M. (2000). Beyond sticks and stones: A first amendment framework for educators who seek to punish students' threats (pp. 669–70). *Seton Hall Law Review, 30.*
‡ *Elonis* v. *U.S.*, 575 U. S. _____ (2015), pp. 1–17.
§ *New York Times* Editorial Board. (2015, June 1). The court and online threats.
¶ Justice Samuel Alito wrote separately, concurring in part and dissenting in part.
** *Elonis* v. *U.S.*, 575 U. S. _____ (2015), p. 16.

crime, using as precedents mostly obscenity cases, Roberts concluded that the jury should have considered Elonis's mental state at the time he posted his rap lyrics. Roberts dismissed the "reasonable person" standard, noting that it "is a familiar feature of civil liability in tort law, but is inconsistent with 'the conventional requirement for criminal conduct—*awareness* of some wrongdoing.'"* In overturning Elonis's conviction and returning the case to the lower courts, the majority opinion gave those courts no guidance as to how a jury should inquire into Elonis's "mental state" at the time of the crime. "Wrongdoing," Roberts quoted from precedent, "must be conscious to be criminal."† The majority deferred to the lower courts to craft a way for making that determination in situations involving threats across interstate borders, including the Internet.‡

Perhaps taking a clue from state legislatures (see below discussion on working with state laws), in 1996, Congress addressed the issue of interstate stalking. Interestingly, the federal Interstate Stalking Punishment and Prevention Act does not require evidence of a credible threat as proof of stalking. Instead, the law requires proof that the subject traveled between states "with the intent to kill, injure, harass, or intimidate another person" or to put that other person "in reasonable fear." The law, then, directly addresses hunters who travel between states. In 1999, Congress amended the law to include cyberstalking.§ Although the statute moved away from the threat requirement, it still poses a challenge to prosecutors by making them prove that the defendant specifically intended to injure or instill fear in the victim. It does not allow for imputed knowledge, that is, that the stalker knew or should have known that his or her actions would result in injury or fear. Rather, the prosecutor has to prove the stalker specifically knew the impact and effect of his or her actions.¶ That requirement poses a tough standard of proof.

With the possible exception of the federal antistalking statute, federal law and court decisions have produced the curious result that individuals like Steven Baldwin will be convicted of false threats, even though no one believed he actually posed a threat to the president, while laws addressing attack-related behaviors go largely unwritten. Undoubtedly, Justice Marshall would find Baldwin's case an equally "sad set of circumstances" as those he addressed in *Rogers* v. *U.S.* In effect, federal laws and court decisions do a fine job policing howlers, but threat managers will find them of little value in managing hunters. Even in the sensitive venue of school violence, the Supreme Court has yet to balance the First Amendment against the leakage phenomenon. Based on past decisions, threat managers can probably expect little help when it finally does. In the federal arena, the disconnect between the law and its interpreters and the research on intended violence remains a wide and thus far unbridgeable chasm.

---

* *Elonis* v. *U.S.*, 575 U. S. _____ (2015), p. 13.
† *Elonis* v. *U.S.*, 575 U. S. _____ (2015), p. 16.
‡ During oral arguments, much was made of the fact that rap star Eminem published lyrics threatening to kill his ex-wife. In his separate opinion, Justice Alito proposed an interesting distinction between Elonis's threats and Eminem's. Alito wrote that no one took Eminem's threats seriously because he obviously wrote them to sell records and concert tickets. Elonis wrote his for therapy and venting knowing that his targets would see the postings. See 575 U.S. _____ Opinion of Alito, J., p. 6.
§ Briggs, K. M. (2004). Federal stalking laws. In *Investigation and prosecution of stalking and related crimes* (pp. XV-1–XV-23). Sacramento, CA: California District Attorneys Association.
¶ Briggs, K. M. (2004). Federal stalking laws. In *Investigation and prosecution of stalking and related crimes* (p. 6). Sacramento, CA: California District Attorneys Association.

Working with State and Local Laws on Threats and Domestic Violence

Whereas the U.S. Congress and U.S. courts have failed to marry the law with current research findings, state legislatures and state courts, especially in California, have taken the lead in doing just that. State laws proscribing threats usually require four elements of proof. First, the communication must, in fact, contain a true threat. Second, the person making the communication must intend to make a threat. Third, the threatener must have the apparent ability to carry it out. Fourth, the threat must instill reasonable fear in the recipient. Case law has interpreted apparent ability broadly enough to cover individuals incarcerated or institutionalized. Across the country, individuals who intentionally threaten someone else with harm break state laws.

Making threats illegal helps threat managers in certain venues, especially among intimates and acquaintances, but it only targets howlers in other venues involving threats to strangers. These laws offer effective ways to police intimate partner violence, as well as violence in schools and workplaces. They are mostly ineffective in enhancing a target's security in settings involving threats among strangers. Indeed, they may even offer a false sense of security in those settings because they essentially police howlers, not hunters. The laws against threats have yet to cleanly shift their focus from what individuals communicate to what they do. Until that shift occurs, the law puts howlers at risk, not hunters.

In contrast to the U.S. Congress and the Supreme Court, the California legislature has crafted a clear, straightforward definition of what the anti-stalking law calls "credible threats." California courts have enhanced that definition through their interpretations of it. According to the statute, a credible threat is

> a verbal or written threat, including that performed through the use of an electronic communication device, or a threat implied by a pattern of conduct or a combination of verbal, written, or electronically communicated statements and conduct made with the intent to place the person that is the target of the threat in reasonable fear for his or her safety or the safety of his or her family and made with the apparent ability to carry out the threat so as to cause the person who is the target of the threat to reasonably fear for his or her safety or the safety of his or her family. It is not necessary to prove that the defendant had the intent to actually carry out the threat. The present incarceration of a person making the threat shall not be a bar to prosecution under this section. Constitutionally protected activity is not included within the meaning of "credible threat."*

The most important breakthrough made by the statute was to invite the courts to infer a credible threat through the subject's behavior, not based simply on what the subject communicated in writing or verbally. For example, according to Raymond Armstrong, the appellate court upheld a stalking conviction based on an inferred credible threat derived from the subject's bizarre behavior. The courts can also infer the existence of a credible threat through the context of the subject and victim's previous or current relationship, including a lack of any interpersonal relationship.†

---

* Armstrong, R. S. (2004). Stalking law: The statute and its interpretation. In *Investigation and prosecution of stalking and related crimes* (p. IX-2). Sacramento, CA: California District Attorneys Association.
† Armstrong, R. S. (2004). Stalking law: The statute and its interpretation. In *Investigation and prosecution of stalking and related crimes* (pp. IX-2–IX-3). Sacramento, CA: California District Attorneys Association.

The statute's requirement that the threat put the target "in reasonable fear" allows prosecutors to enumerate all the reasons the target felt fear, including previous acts of violence by the subject, criminal convictions, and any untoward incidents in the subject and target's relationship. The court ruled, for example, that Steven Spielberg reasonably felt fear for himself and his family from the man who took action to kidnap him, even though Spielberg was in Europe and the stalker (and hunter) was in Los Angeles in the custody of the police when Spielberg learned about the plot.* Such expansive interpretations of the antistalking statute gave California threat managers and law enforcement considerable leeway in managing stalkers.

The problems that stalking and threat laws run up against are the constitutional protections of free speech, not to mention the post-*Castle Rock* issue of police discretion. State and federal laws criminalizing threats and threatening behaviors try to overcome these protections by usually requiring proof that the offender, by word or deed, intended to cause fear in the victim and that the words or deeds did in fact cause actual fear. This usually boils down to showing that the offender had opportunity and means and that the target knew it. The "crime" has become the causing or instilling of fear in the target. Ironically, that is precisely what sinister howlers aim to do.

Fortunately, the evolution of both laws and court interpretations addressing domestic violence and stalking has begun a clear trend toward taking behavior into account. Beginning in the 1980s, states began passing mandatory arrest laws to address what many viewed as a crisis in police nonenforcement of domestic abuse crimes, especially the nonenforcement of restraining orders. "Because these cases were considered non-criminal," Sack observed, "police assigned domestic violence calls low priority and often did not respond to them for several hours or ignored them altogether."† To combat this inattention to a growing national tragedy, states mandated that police must arrest a spousal abuser. "Many states enacted mandatory arrest statutes under which a police officer must arrest an abuser when the officer has probable cause to believe that a domestic assault has occurred or that a protection order has been violated," a column in the *Harvard Law Review* noted.‡ The statutes were purposefully designed to remove all police discretion in the matter.

Both the laws against domestic violence and the reason prompting the courts to issue restraining orders addressed subject behaviors. Domestic violence entails threats, subjugation, hitting, pushing, strangling, and other forms of physical attacks used by hunters. Restraining orders seek to stop harassing, stalking, threatening, disrupting, and approaching, again all tactics used by hunters. Threats, state legislatures began to understand, were but one type of behavior used by the abusive spouse to control the abused spouse. By addressing all the behaviors, the states turned their laws toward hunters, at least hunters caught under the spell of the intimacy effect.

Unfortunately, perhaps ultimately even tragically, in a 2005 decision, the Supreme Court dealt a crippling, perhaps fatal blow, to the legislative efforts to mandate police enforcement of temporary restraining orders in domestic-abuse cases. The majority reached its decision in the face of a particularly horrific example of how violent domestic

---

* Armstrong, R. S. (2004). Stalking law: The statute and its interpretation. In *Investigation and prosecution of stalking and related crimes* (p. IX-3). Sacramento, CA: California District Attorneys Association.
† Sack, E. J. (2004). Battered women and the state: The struggle for the future of domestic violence policy. *Wisconsin Law Review*, 1663.
‡ Developments in the law: Legal responses to domestic violence. (1993). *Harvard Law Review*, 106, 1498, 1537.

disputes can be. Simon and Jessica Gonzales, who shared three daughters aged 10, 9, and 7, initiated divorce proceedings in 1999. During the process, the husband made suicidal threats and engaged in sufficient erratic behavior that the court obliged Jessica's request for a temporary restraining order. The court granted it on May 21. When it was served on June 4, it became permanent. The order excluded Simon from the family home and prohibited him from "molesting or disturbing the peace of Ms. Gonzales and their three daughters." The order allowed Simon to take the girls every other weekend and for 2 weeks each summer. Upon reasonable notice and with Jessica's consent, Simon could also take the girls out to dinner one night a week.*

A few minutes after 5:00 p.m. on Tuesday, June 22, Simon kidnapped the three girls while they were playing in the yard. He had not discussed with Jessica taking the girls to dinner. When Jessica discovered their absence, she immediately sensed that Simon had taken them. She called the police to report the possible violation of the restraining order. Castle Rock police officers responded, interviewed Jessica, and told her they could do nothing to enforce the order and for her to wait until 10:00 p.m. for the children to return. If they were not back by then, the officers instructed her, she was to call the police.*

At approximately 8:30 p.m., Jessica reached Simon on his cell phone. He told her he had taken the girls to Elitch Gardens, an amusement park in Denver. Jessica immediately called the Castle Rock police to report that she had confirmed Simon's violation of the restraining order. She pleaded with the police to find and arrest Simon at the amusement park. Again, the officer refused to enforce the order and advised Jessica to wait until the magic hour of 10:00 p.m.†

Shortly after 10:00 p.m., Jessica called the Castle Rock police station to report the girls still missing. This time, the officer advised her to wait until midnight. A little after midnight, Jessica called again, but again the police refused to act. In fact, it turned out at trial, the Castle Rock police had a policy and custom of not enforcing restraining orders in domestic disputes despite the state legislature's efforts to mandate that enforcement. Jessica went to her husband's apartment complex where she reported to police that he and the girls had not returned. The police dispatcher promised to send a patrol car, but none ever came. Jessica went to the police station at about 1:00 a.m. An officer interviewed her, but took no report. The officer again made no attempt to enforce the restraining order or to find the three children.†

Simon had not told his wife that, in addition to taking the three girls to the amusement park, he had also purchased a semiautomatic pistol and ammunition. At around 3:20 a.m., he pulled his truck into the Castle Rock police station, got out, and opened fire on the building. Police officers returned fire, killing Simon. The officers found the three girls in the cab of the truck, all dead from gunshot wounds.†

Despite the fact that the standard language on the back of the restraining order specifically instructed "law enforcement officials" that "YOU SHALL USE EVERY REASONABLE MEANS TO ENFORCE THIS RESTRAINING ORDER" and despite the legislative history of the Colorado statute giving a clear showing that the legislature intended to make enforcement mandatory in domestic dispute situations, the United States Supreme Court

---

* *Jessica Gonzales* v. *City of Castle Rock* et al., 10th Circuit Court of Appeals, Number 011053 v 2 (April 29, 2004).
† *Gonzales* v. *Castle Rock*, 366 F. 3d. 1093 (2005).

held in a 7-to-2 ruling that enforcement of the order was discretionary for the police, not mandatory. Because the police could enforce it as they chose, the majority concluded that Jessica Gonzales "did not, for purposes of the Due Process clause, have a property interest in police enforcement of the restraining order against her husband."*

However, one reads the *Castle Rock* majority opinion, it strikes us as dumbfounding that any court would rule that lawful court orders are at the discretion of the police to enforce, especially in a case in which the Castle Rock police made the choice more out of laziness and bad habit than any legitimate law enforcement rationale. In consolation, the Court observed that when Simon violated the restraining order, he gave Jessica Gonzales "grounds on which he could be arrested, criminally prosecuted, and held in contempt."† The Court stayed silent on the issue of how she could effect that arrest given the apparent lack of interest by the Castle Rock police officers and Simon's eventual suicide by cop. Had Simon survived his shootout with police, violating the restraining order would have been the least of his legal troubles.

Even more disturbingly than this rather callous response, the Court simply refused to take seriously the Colorado legislature's efforts to address domestic violence through mandatory police responses. "We do not believe that these provisions of Colorado law truly made enforcement of restraining orders *mandatory*," the majority agreed.* Apparently, it all depended on what the definition of "shall" is. Rather, the Court pointed to a long tradition of deferring to police discretion in the face of riots, mayhem, and difficult decisions of when to arrest or not. That attitude may have a profoundly negative effect on the two-decade long effort by state legislatures to get local police departments to take domestic violence seriously. That alone makes *Castle Rock* a notorious setback for preventing intended violence between intimates.

Castle Rock bodes to become just as big an impediment to state stalking laws as it seems to be for restraining orders precisely because one strategy for controlling stalking behavior relies on temporary restraining orders. However, most states make stalking a crime, thus raising anew police discretion in how to enforce it, that is, if the *Castle Rock* precedent in terms of police discretion applies. Given how broadly stated the majority's opinion stretches, it may well have value as a precedent with antistalking laws.

State Stalking Laws

Beginning in the early 1990s, antistalking laws have developed from the diverse experiences of high-profile celebrities and victims of domestic violence. The stalking issue received national attention after Robert John Bardo first stalked, then murdered, actress Rebecca Schaeffer in 1989. His love–obsession for her innocent character in the television series *My Sister Sam* turned to hatred and disgust when she made her film debut in *Class Struggle in Beverly Hills*, in which her character had a love scene. As a direct result of Bardo's assault, the California legislature passed a law defining a stalker as "someone who willfully, maliciously and repeatedly follows or harasses another victim and who makes a credible threat with the intent to place the victim or victim's immediate family in fear of their safety." The

---

* *Town of Castle Rock, Colorado* v. *Gonzales*, individually and a next best friend of her deceased minor children, Gonzales et al. 000 U.S. 04-278 (2005).
† *Gonzales* v. *Castle Rock*, 366 F. 3d. 1093 (2005).

stalker must engage in two separate incidents to show a "continuity of purpose" and thus give credibility to the threat. By 1993, every state had enacted antistalking laws.*

California, because Bardo killed Schaeffer there, led the way in 1990. Its antistalking law requires three elements of proof. First, the subject must willfully, maliciously, and repeatedly follow or harass the target. Second, the subject must make a credible threat. Third, in making the threat, the subject must have intended to instill fear in the target or the target's family.† The first element clearly focuses the law on activities in which hunters engage. Although hunters and stalkers are not synonymous, many stalkers easily cross over to the hunt. A stalker who intends to somehow convince his or her estranged spouse to renew their relationship is not a hunter who intends lethal violence. But when that stalker becomes convinced the spouse will not return and, therefore, should suffer, the stalker becomes a hunter. Many celebrity stalkers seek some sort of relationship with the celebrity, perhaps romantic, but at least nonviolent (from the stalker's point of view). Once rejected or, more precisely, once the stalker realizes or understands the rejection, then the celebrity stalker may decide to punish the celebrity for that transgression. At that point, the stalker becomes a hunter.

Robert Hoskins' case illustrates the ease with which stalkers can become hunters. On three separate occasions, Hoskins gained entry to the singer and actress Madonna's private residence by climbing over the wall surrounding the house. Hoskins wished only to express his undying love for the star and to ask her to marry him. Each time security guards shooed him away, however, his love turned and he threatened to kill her. On the second approach, Hoskins told the security officer that if Madonna did not marry him that evening, he would "slice her throat from ear to ear." The guard encouraged Hoskins to leave. As he walked down the road, Madonna rode past him on her bicycle. Hoskins did not recognize her.‡

Seven weeks later, Hoskins again scaled the wall. When a security officer confronted him near the swimming pool, Hoskins lunged for the officer's sidearm. After a brief scuffle, the officer shot the stalker twice. Hoskins survived and was convicted of a number of offenses, including stalking. While awaiting sentencing, Hoskins scrawled all over the walls of his cell "I love Madonna" and "Madonna loves me." After the jail guard chided him for the graffiti, Hoskins blamed Madonna for writing it. When he got out of jail, he promised the guard, he intended to "slice the lying bitch's throat from ear to ear." During an interview with Los Angeles Police Department psychologist Kris Mahondie, Hoskins explained that he was in love with, and had impregnated, a spirit that had inhabited Madonna's body. The spirit had since left Madonna and gone to another celebrity. Once he served his 10-year sentence, Hoskins intended to take up his pursuit of the spirit wherever it then resided.§

---

* Armstrong, R. S. (2004). Stalking law: The statute and its interpretation. In *Investigation and prosecution of stalking and related crimes*. Sacramento, CA: California District Attorneys Association. http://www.franksreelreviews.com/shorttakes/shaeffer/shaeffer.htm.

† Armstrong, R. S. (2004). Stalking law: The statute and its interpretation. In *Investigation and prosecution of stalking and related crimes* (p. IX-1). Sacramento, CA: California District Attorneys Association.

‡ Mahondie, K. (2004). Stalking: A 21st century perspective. In *Investigation and prosecution of stalking and related crimes* (pp. I-13–I-14). Sacramento, CA: California District Attorneys Association. Names obtained from http://crimemagazine.com/stalkers.htm. Mahondie, a psychologist for the Los Angeles Police Department, described the case without mentioning anyone's name, but the facts he relates exactly match Hoskins' case.

§ Mahondie, K. (2004). Stalking: A 21st century perspective. In Investigation and prosecution of stalking and related crimes (p. 14). Sacramento, CA: California District Attorneys Association.

Hoskins swiftly and repeatedly went from undying love for Madonna to wanting to kill her. In doing so, he exemplified the thin line separating stalkers from hunters. Indeed, stalking is an attack-related behavior in which many hunters engage as they go down the path to intended violence. What separates the two, hunters from stalkers, is their purpose and intent. Stalkers seeking romance do not become hunters until rejection convinces them to kill. As Hoskins amply showed, that intention can shift from romance to murder and back in a revolving cycle that ends either through threat management intervention or tragedy.

One of the fundamental problems the laws against stalking run up against is that, short of the attack itself, most attack-related behaviors do not involve criminal conduct. Although some states have tried to address hunter-type behaviors with stalking laws and criminal-trespass statutes, these laws, like the original California statute, usually also require some type of credible threat to make them enforceable. Legislators have found it nearly impossible to craft legislation prohibiting what for everyone else are legal activities, that is, buying a weapon, searching the Internet, asking questions, or expressing negative feelings toward someone. Adding to the law a requirement for a threat seems to be the only way to balance the subject's rights into the stalking elements of proof. Many hunters use that requirement to their advantage.

Nonetheless, the states have made great progress toward dealing with hunter behaviors, certainly more than the U.S. Congress. California's use of behaviors to substantiate credible threats should serve as a model for other states to follow. More importantly, threat managers will find useful tools hidden among the state laws addressing threats, threatening behaviors, and stalking. Making use of these laws, especially in combination with other management strategies, simply enhances the threat manager's ability to manage both hunters and howlers.

Summary

This chapter summarized research conducted by Debra M. Jenkins to test the reliability of the intimacy effect hypothesis. Jenkins found that the research on domestic and workplace violence, school shootings, and attacks on public figures supports the hypothesis. Unfortunately, federal laws and court decisions have not taken the research into account. Fortunately, state legislatures are beginning to shift their focus away from just punishing threats and toward punishing threatening behaviors.

Situation Analysis: A Mother's Help

The Facts

Several years ago, a woman placed an ad in the local newspaper to sell her dog. Two days later, she received a telephone call from a man who identified himself as Richard J. After a brief conversation, Richard told her he had decided not to buy the dog. Instead, Richard brought up a current statewide controversy involving a major international corporation headquartered in their city. Richard told the woman that if the controversy was not resolved the right way, the chairman of the corporation, who was well known throughout the state, "will be dead." The woman reported that Richard seemed to get more agitated as he talked.

A day later, the woman mentioned the phone conversation to a friend. The friend encouraged her to contact the local police. The next day, police investigators contacted the security office at the corporation. Because the corporate security officers had worked with the police on previous situations, both agencies had developed a good rapport. The police investigators told the security officers that Richard J. had no criminal record or registered weapons.

Two days later, the corporate threat manager and his partner interviewed Richard at Richard's residence. They learned that Richard was 41 and living at his mother's home. He worked at a minimum wage job and seemed "slow" in his mental capabilities. He told the threat managers that he was under the care of a nearby mental health clinic.

Richard admitted making the statement about the corporate chairman. He had listened to a talk radio program discussing the issue and talking against the corporation and its chairman. Richard stated he was merely summarizing the talk radio discussion in his conversation with the woman selling her dog.

Threat Assessment

Based on the facts known at this time, Richard is assessed as a celebrity-seeking howler who poses little risk of violence to the chairman or the corporation. In talking over the telephone to an uninvolved third party, Richard got carried away by controversial rhetoric that culminated in a veiled threat to a public figure. He gave no evidence of any personal knowledge about the chairman or the corporation beyond what he heard on the talk radio program. The fact that he receives counseling from a mental health clinic on an outpatient basis suggests that he has mental problems that may be contributing to his outburst. At present, there is no evidence that Richard has engaged in any attack-related behaviors. Instead, he has focused on espousing his opinion over the telephone to a stranger.

Recommended Protective Response

Because the issue continues to receive a lot of controversial publicity, the security office, as a precaution, should issue a bulletin with Richard's picture to the corporate security officers who patrol the building. The chairman's personal assistant should also be briefed to determine whether the chairman should be briefed. The chairman's upcoming schedule includes two nearby speaking engagements, so security officers should accompany the chairman to those two events.

Recommended Threat Management Strategy

Richard's inappropriate reference to the chairman dying may constitute a prosecutable threat. The district attorney should be consulted about the possibility of having Richard arrested and tried. In the meantime, and as an alternate strategy, a passive watch and wait would be appropriate to determine whether Richard will continue his inappropriate interest in the chairman. In addition, the report of the inappropriate communications should be given to the mental health clinic treating Richard.

The Outcome

The district attorney declined to prosecute Richard, so corporate security adopted the passive watch-and-wait strategy. They also passed the report to Richard's mental health clinic for his counselor's information. Although receptive to receiving the report, the clinic staff maintained a neutral attitude and refused to discuss Richard's case with the threat manager.

Four months later, Richard called the city unemployment office seeking assistance for job training. During two telephone calls within 30 minutes of each other, Richard brought up the chairman and used angry, profane language describing how the chairman should be dead. Officials at the unemployment office reported the calls to the police department. Investigators shared the report with the threat manager. Because the district attorney had already ruled that wishing the chairman's death was not a criminal act, the threat manager decided to interview Richard again, but this time to arrange for Richard's mother to be present. The threat manager also passed on the new report to the mental health clinic.

With his mother sitting next to him, Richard's demeanor during the second interview was very meek and cooperative. The mother told the threat managers that Richard was supposed to be seeing his counselor at the mental health clinic, but she suspected that he was not going. She also informed them that Richard had been drinking before making the two calls to the unemployment office.

The threat managers arranged for third-party control over Richard through his mother. She agreed to take him to his appointments at the clinic. She also forbade him to drive his pickup truck because of his drinking. She promised to allow him to drive only if he obeyed the rules of going to the clinic, not drinking, and not making inappropriate telephone calls.

Over the next several months, the threat manager kept in periodic contact with the mother to ensure the third-party control was working. The controversy involving the corporation and its chairman abated and no longer received any media attention. After 6 months, the threat manager put Richard's case in inactive status.

Issues of Interest

Several of the issues involved in the case of this howler raise interesting insights, such as the following:

1. Prosecution in threat management cases can be problematic because of differences of opinion between the prosecutor and the threat manager.
2. The threat manager was prudent to discuss the case with the district attorney before swearing out a warrant. Had Richard been arrested first and then let go by the district attorney, he may have been more difficult to manage. Because the threat manager had assessed Richard as a howler, the threat manager had other strategies to employ.
3. The threat manager shared the report on Richard's inappropriate comment with the staff at the mental health clinic treating Richard in order to alert his counselor to Richard's problem behavior. Although mental health professionals are bound to respect patient confidentiality, they are not restricted from receiving information about their patient's behavior. Prudent threat managers know to make full use of this one-way communication.

4. The threat manager first employed a passive watch-and-wait strategy but escalated it to third-party control when Richard again communicated inappropriately.

5. Finding a trusted third party to control the howler can be an effective strategy. The mother's use of the pickup truck as a reward for good behavior acted as an inhibitor for Richard. Because the good behavior included going to mental health counseling, Richard's underlying mental health issues received treatment.

6. Threat managers need to apply threat management strategies flexibly and innovatively. When the threat manager lost the option of having Richard arrested, he had already decided on a fallback strategy. When that strategy ultimately failed, the threat manager identified a trusted third party to use as a control over Richard. Ultimately, time, the abatement of the controversy, and Richard's continued mental health treatment allowed the case to go inactive.

7. When employing third-party controls, the threat manager needs to keep open good lines of communication to monitor how the controls are working. Using third-party controls does not mean passing the problem individual on to someone else. Rather, it means working with the third party to manage the problem individual.

Working with the Hunter, Howler, and Other Concepts 10

Chapters 7 and 8 portrayed hunters and howlers, respectively. For hunters, we focused on the types of behaviors in which they engage as they traverse the path to intended violence. Because crossing the path requires engaging in noticeable activities, the threat manager should always be alert to any reports suggesting attack-related behaviors. Because of that emphasis on behavior, our description of hunters zeroed in on the actions they take rather than discerning the reasons prompting those behaviors. This approach mirrored the reality that threat managers confront. Frequently, the threat manager will receive reports describing suspicious behaviors without any clue concerning the subject's motive. Although the threat manager knows with certainty that the hunter has a grievance, the hunter may not choose to reveal exactly what that grievance is. As a result, threat managers often must manage the hunter without knowing what prompted the hunt.

For howlers, we described various categories in which howlers seem to fall. We could as easily have categorized hunters; indeed, they too fall into most of the same categories as howlers. James Kopp, for example, killed Dr. Bernard Slepian because Slepian conducted abortions. Kopp was a *crusading* hunter. Similarly, Mark Chapman, who assassinated John Lennon, was a *celebrity-seeking* hunter. Jack McKnight, who killed one and wounded two during his assault on the Topeka, Kansas, federal court, acted out of revenge for his arrest and imminent imprisonment for growing marijuana. He was a *self-defending* hunter. Dennis Rader, the notorious "BTK"* serial killer from Wichita, Kansas, killed 10 people between 1974 and 1991. He was a *habitual* hunter. Spouses who intend to kill their mates do so when the other spouse does not bend to their will. These spouses are *controllers*. Similarly, workplace violence frequently involves *intimidators*. Thus, the categories clearly apply to both howlers and hunters.

But while such categorizations work well for understanding howlers, they can be distracting when dealing with hunters. First, determining to which category a hunter belongs may not be so clear until the latter stages of the case. Howlers tend to self-identify their categories upfront through their communications. Because hunters may not communicate anything, their motives may take the threat manager longer to discern. In the meantime, the hunter continues to engage in attack-related behaviors to which the threat manager has to respond. Although the threat manager knows with certainty that the hunter has a grievance, because grievances come first on the path to intended violence, the particulars of that individual grievance may not be so clear until fully investigated.

Second, the category into which the hunter falls is less important than identifying which stage along the path to intended violence the hunter has reached. Whether self-defender, crusader, controller, intimidator, personal or impersonal, those who hunt ultimately have to engage in attack-related behaviors. Hunters in different categories do not necessarily behave or communicate differently. When Chapman shot Lennon, the act

* BTK stood for "bind, torture, kill" and was Rader's pseudonym for himself.

differed very little from Kopp's shooting Slepian 20 years later. Both hunters aimed and fired. Moody and the Unabomber may have had different designs for their bombs, but they nonetheless made them in such a way as to be conveyed through the U.S. mails. Ultimately, acts of violence and their outcomes resemble other acts and outcomes. Thus, we did not categorize hunters even though we recognize that many of the howler categories easily apply to them.

In this chapter, we discuss ways in which threat managers should manage both hunters and howlers. First, we present an untested hypothesis explaining the phenomenon of when a howler becomes a hunter. Although this transition frequently occurs among intimates and acquaintances, it remains relatively rare in cases involving strangers. That raises a serious, and as yet unanswered, question about the influence of the *intimacy effect*. Can we take lessons learned from the transition from howler to hunter among personals and apply those lessons to any such transformation among impersonals? For the second edition, we have added a brief review of some other concepts that affect—positively and negatively—the threat management process. Finally, we offer an overview of some general principles threat managers should follow to manage both hunters and howlers.

Working with the *Last-Straw Syndrome*

Throughout this book, our mantra has been that hunters hunt and howlers howl, a distinction that both distinguishes them and identifies them. By definition, hunters cannot be howlers and howlers cannot be hunters. But that definition is somewhat tautologous: Howlers cannot be hunters because by taking up the hunt, they cease to be howlers. Only hunters engage in attack-related behaviors. Consequently, once a subject who had previously acted like a howler embarks on the path to intended violence, the subject becomes a hunter. Similarly, hunters cannot be howlers because, once they start acting like howlers, they simply cease to be hunters. Only howlers communicate inappropriately without taking additional actions. Thus, by definition, hunters and howlers stand apart.

Setting those semantics aside, as a practical matter, howlers can become hunters. Some howlers reach a point where something happens to propel them across the line to take up the hunt. Something tips them across the great divide that separates howling from hunting. We call that tipping point the *last-straw syndrome*.

Consider these ten examples:

1. Thomas Wendt began threatening to kill his ex-wife and himself during their divorce in 2000. He continued making threats after the divorce became final. Vicki Keller-Wendt repeatedly asked police to protect her. "I don't know what you can do to make him leave me alone and make me feel a little safer," Keller-Wendt wrote to a judge pleading for a restraining order against Wendt. The judge granted the order but included a ludicrous condition prohibiting Wendt from using a firearm for anything but hunting. That meant he maintained possession of his three firearms. Still, Wendt did nothing more than continue to threaten her; he took no action to implement his threats, that is, until the last straw fell. In March 2002, Wendt waited outside the Mount Pleasant, Michigan, courthouse for his ex-wife, her niece, and a friend of his ex-wife. He knew they were scheduled to testify against him for violating the restraining order. When they arrived, he shot them

to death.* Keller-Wendt's pending testimony against him proved to be Wendt's last straw.

2. Ronald Taylor believed whites persecuted him. Unemployed and receiving disability checks for mental illness, Taylor spent his days writing about how much he hated whites, Jews, and homosexuals, but like every howler, Taylor took no actions to express his hatred physically, that is, until March 2000, when he broke his door. He called his landlord to have it fixed but grew impatient when the maintenance workers did not come immediately. When the two workers arrived, Taylor attacked one of them. When the other worker tried to pull Taylor away, Taylor shot him in the chest. Taylor then went on a rampage through his Pittsburgh neighborhood. He ended up killing three men and wounding two others. All his victims were white. For Taylor, the last straw came when two white men took too long to fix his door.†

3. Joseph Wesbecker's printing company refused to follow his doctor's advice and change his job of operating folding machines. Instead, the company put Wesbecker on permanent disability leave. Over the next 13 months, Wesbecker threatened company officials. "This guy's been talking about this for a year," one company employee stated. "He's been talking about guns and *Soldier of Fortune* magazine. He's paranoid and he thought everyone was after him." Still, Wesbecker did not approach the plant until something, whether an official notice or a paranoid delusion, made him believe the company was going to cut off his disability benefits. On September 14, 1989, Wesbecker returned to the plant armed with an AK-47, two MAC-11 machine pistols, two handguns, a bayonet, and thousands of rounds of ammunition. At first, he went to the upper floors of the building looking for bosses and supervisors. When he could not find anyone in management, he began shooting former coworkers randomly, killing 7 and wounding 15 before taking his own life. The last straw that propelled Wesbecker from making threats to actually attacking was his belief he was about to lose his benefit stipend.‡

4. The John Jay College of Criminal Justice expelled Dabrium Jones in 2000 because he had harassed a professor after receiving a failing grade. Harassing, of course, is what howlers do. Hector Ortiz, the dean of students, indicated to Jones that he might be readmitted after completing a counseling program. Jones went to the college on August 28, 2001, expecting to resume classes, but the dean refused to enroll him. The next day, Jones came back to the school armed with a knife and hunting for Ortiz. He found the dean in a hallway and began stabbing Ortiz in the torso and neck. The rejection was the last straw for Jones.§

5. By February 1993, Michael Griffen had suffered a world of hurt. His marriage was failing; one daughter had severe and expensive neurological problems; his job was boring; and his self-esteem had fallen. After stumbling into the local anti-abortion movement, Griffen became convinced that God wanted him to assassinate Dr. David Gunn, who came into Pensacola every Tuesday to perform

---

* Alleged courthouse gunman arraigned. (2002, March 6). Associated Press.
† Shooting spree murder trial begins. (2001, November 1). Associated Press.
‡ Worker on disability leave kills 7, then himself, in printing plant. (1989, September 15). Associated Press; In killers disorder, cycles of elation and depression. (1989, September 16). Associated Press; Survivors of shooting and gunman's relatives ponder sad riddles. (1989, September 17). Associated Press.
§ Ex-student accused of stabbing dean. (2001, August 29). Associated Press.

abortions. On four separate occasions, Griffen, armed with a pistol, encountered Dr. Gunn but could not bring himself to shoot the doctor. Instead, he warned Dr. Gunn that God wanted the abortions to stop. On March 10, 1993, Griffen went early to a scheduled antiabortion demonstration. Having worked the night shift the night before, Griffen decided to go home as soon as he saw Dr. Gunn arrive. He walked down an alley behind the clinic just as Dr. Gunn drove up. Griffen walked past the car with the doctor sitting in the front seat. When Griffen reached the trunk, he heard what he thought was a gunshot. Spinning around, Griffen pulled his pistol and saw the doctor now out of his car. Thinking someone had already killed Dr. Gunn, Griffen fired four times into what he thought was a corpse. The autopsy and physical evidence showed Dr. Gunn had received four gunshot wounds. All the bullets came from Griffen's gun. The last straw that turned Griffen from a howler into a hunter was the sound of Dr. Gunn's slamming the car door shut.*

6. For about a year, Christopher Millis and his next-door neighbor, Gary Hurd, engaged in angry disputes about cutting trees and complaints about Millis to the homeowners' association. Hurd called the police on Millis 10 times, but the disputes never turned violent. Over the same year, Millis' life started falling apart. He lost his job, then around Thanksgiving, he and his wife agreed to get a divorce, although they decided to wait until after the holidays and continued living together with their six children. On Friday night, November 11, 2005, Millis and his wife got into a last argument and he kicked her out of the house. Early the next morning, Millis got up, drove to the Keizer, Oregon, police station and began pouring gasoline on the officers' personal cars. He set fire to two cars before Officer Carrie Meier pulled in to go to work. Millis fled with Meier in pursuit until Millis fired two shots at Meier's car. Millis then drove back to his neighborhood where he fired seven shots at Hurd's two pickup trucks. "As soon as I heard it, I thought it was him," Hurd remembered. "I'm not surprised at all." Millis changed vehicles and literally drove his pickup truck into the Marion County Courthouse front door. He held police at bay for 3 hours until a SWAT team member wounded him. For Millis, the fight with his wife turned into his last straw.†

7. William Strier, suffering severe back pain from an automobile accident, wanted to use insurance monies he received in a trust fund to cover the costs of a back operation. The trustee refused to release the money. She apparently failed to convince Strier that the refusal was in his interest because giving him the trust money would disqualify him from California Medicare. Outraged, Strier telephoned the trustee and threatened to kill her if she did not give him the money he needed. Distance communications, of course, are the mark of a howler. The trustee and her attorney, Gerald Curry, scheduled a hearing for October 31, 2002, to ask the court to replace the trustee and to approve their fees so they could withdraw them from Strier's trust funds. The judge approved both requests. When Curry left the courthouse, Strier approached him, asked if his name was Curry, then began shooting him. Curry took cover behind a tree as Strier shot him five times in the shoulders and

* Griffen, M. (1996, February 14). Interview.
† King, T. (2006, August 30). Marion courthouse plunger gets 16 years for courthouse rampage. Salem-News.com.

arms. Knowing the trustee and her attorney could draw from his trust fund when he could not served as Strier's last straw.[*]

8. Tacoma, Washington, Police Chief David Brame dominated his wife even more than he controlled his department. While keeping complete control over police promotions and policies, Brame gave his wife $100 every 2 weeks for groceries and household expenses. He monitored her car mileage and made her explain any trips outside the house. Every morning, he made her weigh herself in his presence so he could track any weight gains. When they fought, as they increasingly did, he sometimes choked her and threatened her. In what became a pattern, the day after a fight, he would send her flowers signed, "Your secret admirer." Returning home that evening, Brame would use the flowers and note to accuse his wife of having an affair. That would bring on another fight. He pressured her to agree to have sex with him and a Tacoma policewoman (who was resisting his unwelcome advances). He told her she would be dead before she got any of his retirement benefits in a divorce. He also reminded her that their marriage vows included "until death do us part." On February 7, 2003, Brame aimed his service weapon at his wife's face and calmly mentioned that "accidents happen." But Brame held back from escalating the violence. At the end of February, his wife left him and filed for divorce. When he tried to fight it, she filed court papers detailing the choking incidents, the threats, and the sexual pressure. Still Brame controlled himself until the allegations of abuse, threats, and sexual aberration became public on April 25, 2003. That public humiliation proved Brame's last straw. On Saturday, April 26, Brame took the couple's two children on various errands. Although he normally did not carry his weapon while off-duty, that day he did. Seemingly by chance, he ran into his wife in a strip mall parking lot. Leaving the kids in his car, he approached his wife's car. First he shot her in the head, then himself. He died that day, she lived a week longer.[†]

9. In 1986, Janet Geisenhagen sued her neighbor, Curtis Thompson, because she claimed Thompson's dog had bitten her 6-year-old son. Thompson won the lawsuit, but the experience engendered a bitter hatred toward the Geisenhagens. For years, Thompson would drive by their house very slowly, glaring through the car window. The Geisenhagens complained repeatedly to the police, but Toulon, Illinois, was a small town and the police simply advised, "You know he's crazy, just ignore him." In 1999, Thompson chased after a Geisenhagen employee driving a van. Thompson sped past the van, blocked the road, and jumped out of the truck with a hammer. Although he did not strike the employee, police arrested Thompson for assault. Found guilty, the judge sentenced Thompson to 25 days in jail and 2 years' probation. He also ordered Thompson not to have any contact with the employee or the Geisenhagen family. Once he served his sentence, Thompson increased the number of times he drove past the Geisenhagen house. But though his behavior was certainly threatening, Thompson was never violent against his neighbors. In

---

[*] Curry, G. (2003, November 10). Interview. The *Today* Show; CNN, October 27, 2005.
[†] Modeen, M. (2003, May 2). Brame references troubled evaluators. *Tacoma News Tribune*; Mulick, S. (2003, May 2). Police recount the Brames' fatal encounter. *Tacoma News Tribune*; Harden, B. (2003, May 5). Tacoma murder case's revelations shake city. *Washington Post*; Robinson, S. (2005, May 11). Inside David Brame's police department. *Tacoma News Tribune*.

March 2002, the last straw fell. After Thompson failed to appear in court on an unrelated assault charge, a deputy sheriff went to arrest him. Thompson managed to get the deputy's pistol and shoot him. He hopped in the squad car and drove to the Geisenhagen house. He broke in and killed both the husband and the wife. He fled the scene but was ultimately stopped at a police roadblock and wounded.*

10. Russell Weston suffered severe delusions involving conspiracies, aliens, time travel, and the very real refusal of the federal government to allow him to cross federal land to dig for gold in Montana. He traveled to Washington to visit the Central Intelligence Agency because he needed to give its director an important message about the Ruby Surveillance System. In Jefferson County, Montana, Weston came to the attention of both the Secret Service and the local sheriff, but his inappropriate comments never gave either agency sufficient cause to arrest him. In 1996, after 7 weeks in a Montana mental hospital, Weston moved back to Illinois to his parents' house. In July 1998, local police tried to serve a warrant on one of the Westons' neighbors. Hearing the police, the neighbor killed himself. Police found drugs in the house, which brought in the federal Drug Enforcement Administration (DEA). DEA agents plastered federal "No trespassing" signs on the neighbor's house. Seeing the signs, Weston told his father federal commandos were coming to get him. That belief proved the last straw. Weston drove to Washington. He knew the Ruby Surveillance System was kept on the first floor of the U.S. Capitol. On the afternoon of July 24, 1998, Weston shot his way into the Capitol, killing a Capitol policeman at the magnetometer and shooting it out with another Capitol policeman in the majority whip's office. The second policeman died but managed to severely wound Weston.†

Although hardly a scientific sampling, these 10 incidents give a flavor of the variety of last straws that can transform a howler into a hunter. Like grievances, to which they contribute, last straws are unique to the individuals burdened by them.

Sometimes, the target creates the last straw that tips the howler into becoming a hunter. In August 1971, Ed Taylor began writing friendly, supportive letters to Los Angeles radio traffic pilot and popular commentator Jim Hicklin. He addressed the letters to Hicklin's home. Hicklin allowed himself to get annoyed at the fan mail. He hired private detectives to track Taylor down and make him stop.

Two detectives paid Taylor an unannounced visit and warned him to stop writing. Unfortunately, the warning had the reverse effect. It turned Taylor into a sinister howler. Rather than quit writing Hicklin, Taylor began sending the radio personality angry, accusatory letters demanding an apology. He also wrote the general manager of Hicklin's radio station and the Federal Aviation Administration (FAA) demanding that the former fire Hicklin and the latter take his pilot's license. Then Taylor took action, although lawful. He filed suit against Hicklin. And he continued to write, but the tone and themes of the letters escalated into more and more sinister language, with references to violence and more allegations, including a letter to FAA claiming Hicklin had flown his helicopter close to Taylor's house on a "strafing mission."

---

* Ill. Slay suspect said to have grudge. (2002, March 26). Associated Press.
† Hull, A. (2001, January 23). A living hell or a life saved? Capitol shooter's untreated madness fuels legal and ethical debate. *Washington Post*; CBS *Evening News*, July 25, 1998.

The court dismissed Taylor's lawsuit and FAA made clear it would not do anything about Taylor's allegations. Taylor, convinced he needed to defend himself, bought a pistol. Hicklin, in turn, made his own escalation. He asked the district attorney's office to stop Taylor from harassing him. Investigators interviewed Taylor, which gave him a chance to present his complaints to someone in authority. Or so he thought. Several days later, the district attorney's office dropped the last straw. Prosecutors had him arrested for misdemeanor libel. Not only did police officers arrest him, but they also arrested him in front of his elderly mother. That made Taylor's grievance involve both the perceived injustices done him and also the indignity of having his own mother witness the final injustice.

That final grievance, the indignity of the arrest, tipped Taylor to the next step, the idea that violence alone would resolve his problem with Hicklin. From that step along the path to intended violence, Taylor moved quickly and easily. Again, Hicklin helped by providing Taylor with information about his private plans. He talked on his radio show about an upcoming vacation cruise he and his wife would be taking on the cruise ship *Italia*, sailing April 2, 1973. Simply listening to Hicklin's radio program provided Taylor the research he needed to plan his attack. On launch day, Taylor boarded the *Italia*, found Hicklin's cabin, and shot him to death in front of Hicklin's wife and the friends who had come to wish the couple bon voyage.*

Not everyone who takes up the hunt first endures a last straw. Still, the last straw appears to occur frequently enough that threat managers need to remain sensitive to the possibility. Last straws or, more specifically, the subject's reaction to a triggering event constitute simply one more behavior the threat manager should be on the lookout for. If the threat assessor has no evidence that a last straw has fallen, then that lack should have a neutral effect in assessing the chance of lethal violence since the syndrome does not always occur. However, if the last-straw syndrome does come into play, it should have a profound and powerful impact on the threat assessment.

Threat managers need to be sensitive to the last-straw syndrome for three important reasons. First, they should be prepared to exploit last straws that transform hunters into howlers. Finding a hunter's weakness or hesitation or second thought, the threat manager can use that information to tip the hunter toward howling. Second, in dealing with howlers, threat managers should take note of any change or new circumstance that might portend a last straw event. Third, and most importantly, threat managers should exercise special care to never create or become a last straw.

The last-straw syndrome does not occur in every case for every howler. But when it does occur, threat managers need to be able to recognize it, or at least recognize that a straw has fallen. Frankly, that is easier than it appears on its face. Regardless of what the last straw may be, it prompts the former howler to take up the hunt. That means a significant change in behavior. Thus, the threat manager can identify the last-straw syndrome through the subject's changed behavior.

Threat managers should interpret change as broadly as possible. Changes can take the form of new, *attack-related* behaviors or they can simply arise from the sudden cessation of previous, non-attack-related behaviors. The change can come from circumstances unrelated to the reason the howler is howling. Sudden losses, such as loss of a job or a place to

---

* de Becker, G. (1997). *The gift of fear: Survival signals that protect us from violence* (pp. 140–146). New York: Little Brown and Company.

stay or loss of a loved one, can serve as a last straw. When managing howlers, any changes the howler makes should be taken seriously.

As a final note on the last-straw syndrome, it does not belong exclusively to howlers. Frequently, a last straw type of event launches hunters to take up the hunt. For example, teenager Kip Kinkle never openly talked or threatened or made any howling communications. He clearly thought about violence and showed a great interest in firearms, even to the point of collecting several guns without his parents' knowledge. But beyond fantasies and daydreams, he did not have any specific plans to use the weapons. Kinkle's last straw occurred when his high school expelled him for having a stolen pistol at school. Too embarrassed to tell his parents of this latest problem in a long list of adolescent trouble-making, Kinkle found it easier to kill both parents when they came home. The next day, he drove himself to school at lunchtime armed with a semiautomatic rifle, two pistols, and a knife. He killed 2 students and wounded 25 others before classmates tackled him.* For Kinkle, fear of his parents' reaction to his latest troubles proved to be his last straw, and one that launched him on the path to intended violence.

Other Concepts Influencing the Threat Management Process

A number of other concepts have important roles in how the threat management process plays out. We explored many of these in *Concepts and Case Studies in Threat Management*, but they bear a brief repeating here precisely because of their influence—both positive and negative—in managing either hunters or howlers. In any situation that requires applying the threat management process, experienced threat managers find themselves caught up in the ebb and flow of the constantly changing circumstances of the situation itself. Indeed, simply initiating the process creates a rippling effect throughout the entire situation. And, too, the threat manager needs to manage the information generated by the situation with extreme vigilance. Keeping too close a hold can be as fatal as too much broadcasting of the information. Finally, the current economy and its spawn of severe budget cutbacks in both the public and private sectors hogties most threat management programs by restraining the threat manager's choice of available management strategies.

We call the rippling effect that courses across every problem situation the *case dynamics* inhering at the heart of the situation. Anytime a subject takes some action directed at his or her chosen target, that action prompts a reaction from the target. In addition, the subject fully expects a reaction, although the expectation and the actual reaction do not necessarily match. Thus, the action of one and the reaction of the other combine into a new situation that leads to new actions by the subject and new reactions by the target. The situation, in sum, remains dynamic and ever changing.

The case dynamics become further activated by the introduction of the threat management team and the initiation of the threat management process. Now the situation has three players—the subject, the target, and the threat manager. This creates what we call an *intervention synergy* within the situation. As in a chemical reaction, each player bounces off the other players, oftentimes in unexpected and unplanned ways. Consequently, the threat manager needs to maintain an acute self-awareness throughout the course of the situation. The manager must recognize the dynamics between the subject and the target

---

* http://www.pbs.org/wgbh/pages/frontline/shows/kinkel/kip/cron.html.

and the synergy created by his or her own intervention. The threat management process contains many moving parts colliding together and bouncing into each other. This sounds complicated because it is.

Information remains the coin of the realm in the field of threat management. Yet, too often, that currency gets debased in the way organizations and threat management programs use it. Every bureaucracy, big or little, wants to separate itself from other organizations, protecting its own sources. That may be a good business practice in certain circumstances, but it can prove fatal in trying to manage a threatening situation. Good threat managers understand the need to avoid erecting information *silos* and *bunkers*. Silos get built when individuals and entities within and among organizations fail to share information, especially information pertaining to suspicious or troublesome individuals. Bunkers arise when individuals or organizations focus solely on their own needs, their own security, thereby turning a blind eye to any weaknesses in the security of other individuals, organizations within the same community or the public at large. Threat managers can best tear down these silos and bunkers through the judicious sharing of information within the threat manager's community.

Finally, current economic conditions create significant problems for any threat management program. Governments, both federal and local, have severely cut back on the services they provide. These budget shortfalls have affected the provision of mental health and police services and the ability of the judiciary to handle its cases. Corporate organizations have also suffered diminished resources that have also shrunk the resources devoted to budding threat management programs. Threat managers must learn to work through these cutbacks creatively and imaginatively. There are no other choices.

Managing Hunters and Howlers

In Chapter 4, we briefly summarized the various threat management strategies that threat managers can use in dealing with both hunters and howlers. In the situation analyses at the end of each chapter, we showed how those strategies can be applied in real-life situations. The situation analyses also offered a working format for writing a threat assessment. As the situation analyses illustrated, we recommend starting the assessment with an objective, straightforward statement of the known facts. The summary should avoid adjectives, adverbs, speculations, opinions, or interpretations. Instead, it should stick strictly to the facts.

After summarizing the facts, the threat assessor should explain the threat assessment based on those facts. The assessment, obviously, is the assessor's opinion and interpretation of those facts. The assessment should be directly related to the facts. It, too, should avoid any speculations beyond the known facts. At the same time, the assessment should make clear that any new evidence or change in circumstances by the subject will need to be reassessed. The assessment should also explicitly state that the threat manager based it solely on the facts known at the time. Threat assessments have notoriously short shelf lives. New facts, new behaviors, or new circumstances should always prompt a reassessment.

On the basis of the threat assessment, the threat assessor should make a detailed, specific recommendation for the most appropriate protective response. This can be as simple as giving the target a quick briefing on personal security measures or it can be as complicated as arranging a security detail to physically protect the target or moving the target to a secure location. The recommended protective response should always match the assessment.

Finally, the threat assessor should recommend the most appropriate threat management strategies for managing the subject. This can be a single strategy or a combination of strategies. Like the protective response, it should be completely in sync with the assessment.

10 Guidelines for Managing Hunters and Howlers

We conclude our discussion of understanding hunters and howlers with 10 general guidelines concerning the effective management of both subjects. These can serve as a set of guiding principles that threat managers will be well advised to embed in their threat management programs.

1. *Always assess and manage the subject by keeping in mind the context and circumstances in which the subject acts.*

    Subjects involved in threat management cases frequently follow their own logic and live in their own world. Conventional reality may hold little meaning or relevance for them. Consequently, the threat manager has to assess what the subject believes from the subject's point of view, then design the management response in such a way as to exploit the subject's reality and perceptions. For example, if a former intimate gives evidence of believing that the previous partner will come back or still participates in their relationship, the threat manager must gauge the strength of that feeling, then find ways to wean the subject off of that perception. This could involve third-party monitoring, target transfer to the threat manager, or strict enforcement of a civil restraining order (*Castle Rock* notwithstanding). If, to cite another example, a former employee feels unjustly treated, the threat manager must understand why the subject believes that, then adopt a threat management strategy aimed at rectifying that sense of injustice. Both the assessment and the management have to address how the subject, whether hunter or howler, sees the world. This is not to say the threat manager buys into the subject's delusions; it merely requires the threat manager to take them into account. The threat manager should also keep in mind that the subject's sense of mistreatment may be rooted in reality.

2. *Always determine the impact of the intimacy effect within the context and circumstances in which the subject acts.*

    Twenty to 30 years ago, threats played too prominent a role in determining whether or not to open a case. Without an explicit threat, threat managers felt perfectly comfortable essentially ignoring the problem individual. Then research on public figure attacks prompted a whiplash-like reaction that caused a complete discounting of threats as preincident indicators of future violence. Different researchers called threats "no big deal" or described their relationship to future violence as a "myth." But this cookie-cutter approach did not take into account the different social venues in which threats and violence occurred.

    The best approach appears to require reaching a balanced median. Taking into account the intimacy effect seems to achieve that balance. Threats to intimates and acquaintances have great value as preincident indicators. Threats to strangers have little or no such value. Knowing the impact of the intimacy effect and how it applies to the case at hand will help the threat manager select the best management strategy. For example, if the case involves previous intimates with a history of domestic violence, the threat manager should consider employing more aggressive polices, such as confronting and warning or, if appropriate, arrest. On the other hand, if the subject appears to be an impersonal celebrity-seeking romantic howler focused on a public figure, the threat manager might consider a passive watch-and-wait strategy to monitor the subject's future inappropriate communications. Because the research shows that the intimacy effect links threats to violent outcomes through social venues, the threat manager should always incorporate it into the assessment and management strategy.

3. *Always be prepared to reassess the situation once a threat management strategy is applied, new information comes to light, or the subject acts again.*

   Threat assessments and, sometimes, threat management strategies have short shelf-lives. Because assessments can be made only on the facts known at the time of the assessments, new facts require new assessments. Similarly, because the application of a management strategy alters the chemistry of the case simply by being applied, that change requires a new assessment, which may lead to a new strategy. Applying the strategy also causes an action–reaction situation. Once the threat manager acts (even if that action is the watch-and-wait strategy), the subject will react. That reaction requires a new assessment and, possibly, a new strategy. For this reason, the threat manager will find the watch-and-wait strategy, either passive or active, a very useful follow-on strategy in most cases. Recognizing that threat management is a dynamic process will help the threat manager make continuous assessments and refinements to the management strategies employed.

4. *Always avoid causing or allowing a last straw to fall.*

   Threat managers cannot prevent every last straw, but they can certainly consciously avoid dropping one. Many last straws are unique to the subject. In those situations, the most the threat manager can do is be on the alert for signs a last straw has fallen. At the same time, the threat manager should do everything possible to prevent last straws within his or her control. Doing so usually requires the threat manager to adopt a social worker approach to the subject. Is there a problem confronting the subject that the threat manager can help fix? These situations require using the assist strategy. For example, when an employee is terminated from a job, the threat manager should make sure that the out-processing, especially the delivery of any monies owed the employee, is processed expeditiously. From the subject's point of view, getting fired is one thing, not getting compensated for unused annual leave or any delays in receiving the last paycheck might turn into a last straw. Identifying potential last straws requires the threat manager to see the situation from the subject's point of view.

5. *Always approach the problem flexibly and innovatively.*

   The dynamics of threat management require flexibility and innovation on the part of the threat manager. Frequently, this can be generated through a multidiscipline team approach, with each member of the team encouraged to bring his or her expertise and creativity to each case. Not only is there chemistry at play between the management strategies and the subject, but also team approaches generate interactions, leading to better alternatives and better ideas. These should be encouraged and commended.

6. *Always remember that hunters engage in attack-related behaviors and howlers engage in inappropriate communications.*

The threat management process is all about observable behaviors. Potential targets, their staffs, and their families should be thoroughly briefed on the threat manager's definition of inappropriate communication or contact and trained where to report such inappropriate communications or contacts. Once reported, the threat manager should assess the subject's known behaviors, whether writing letters, stalking, telephoning, obtaining a weapon, or anything else. Because, by definition, hunters behave differently from howlers, the threat manager should move quickly to determine the category into which the current subject falls. That determination will help with the selection of the most appropriate threat management strategy. For example, a sinister howler upset at some adverse decision against him or her may make an angry, threatening contact using some distance communication. After assessing the subject as a howler, the threat manager may use a watch-and-wait strategy for a few days, then switch to a take-no-further-action-at-this-time strategy once it becomes clear the subject intends no further contacts. In the end, everything depends on how the subject behaves.

7. *Always keep your word and be prepared to do what you told the subject you would do.*

Threat management holds no place for bluffing, exaggerating, or distorting, to oneself, to others, and especially not to the subject or target. In any dealing with the subject, the threat manager should again stick with the facts, keep the subject focused on the facts, and always ensure that if the subject is warned or told something will happen, the warning or the something will come to pass. Warning the subject and then not following up is worse than unenforced civil orders because the lack of action reflects directly on the threat manager.

8. *Always treat the subject with respect and ensure the "dignity domino" remains upright.*

In threat management, a subject's inhibitors* act like falling dominoes. When one falls, it risks toppling over the next in line. At the end of the row stands the "dignity domino," the last and most dangerous to fall. Last straws frequently topple the dignity domino; threat managers should never do so. Subjects often lash out over the feeling that they have been dissed, that no one treats them as they expect, and that they need to be respected. Simply by treating the subject politely, albeit firmly if necessary, the threat manager can help prop up that last domino.

9. *Always stick to the facts as you know them and avoid playing the "What if?" game.*

The "What if?" game is always enticing because it allows the imagination full freedom to stretch as far and as frighteningly as a Stephen King horror story. Targets especially like to play the game. Threat managers should not. The best antidote is to stick with the known and avoid speculating about the unknown.

10. *Always manage the case for as long as it needs managing.*

Threat management cases tend to have long durations. Howlers may howl for years. Hunters, too, may take a long time before they try to consummate the hunt. Frequently, neither hunters nor howlers break any laws or give sufficient evidence

---

* Inhibitors are pieces of his or her life that have some value to the subject, such as a job, finances, family, reputation, religion, self-esteem, and, most important of all, dignity.

for mental health commitments or give the threat manager any reason to institutionalize them. Thus, this type of subject must be managed on an ongoing, long-term basis. That means managing the target's expectations as well, for too often, threat management offers no easy solution to handling the hunter or the howler.

Summary

In this chapter, we discussed the fact that the various categories describing howlers also apply to hunters, although not always as quickly and readily identifiable as they are with howlers. That is because howlers rarely hide their motives; hunters frequently do. Next, we discussed the last-straw syndrome. We defined that syndrome as a triggering event that can transform a howler into a hunter. We strongly recommended that threat managers be on the lookout for its possibly falling and taking care not to toss out the last straw themselves. We next discussed other concepts that affect the threat management process, such as case dynamics, intervention synergy, and silos and bunkers. We concluded the chapter with a set of guiding principles threat managers should use in managing hunters and managing howlers.

As a final word, threat managers can best understand both hunters and howlers by their respective behaviors. By focusing on those distinctive behaviors, the threat manager can identify, assess, and manage howlers and hunters effectively. Seen against the backdrop of intended violence, the behaviors of those who pose threats and those who make threats can be spotlighted with great precision. Concepts such as *attack-related behaviors*, *intimacy effect*, *last-straw syndrome*, *sinister howlers*, and *binder howlers* offer powerful tools for enhancing the threat management process. By the nature of their task, threat managers need all the tools they can get.

Situation Analysis: The Relentless Pursuer

The Facts

A state official contacted the state threat management office concerning a problem at his residence. He told the threat manager that he lives with his wife, their son, and her father. The official was known nationally owing to political radicalism during the 1960s and a previous marriage to a famous activist movie star. The official expressed concern about a man who, over the past year, had been leaving messages in the official's mailbox. Recently, the man confronted the father-in-law on the front lawn of the residence. The man demanded a meeting with the official, stating he "didn't care how he did it."

The threat manager immediately arranged to interview the state official, his wife, and the father-in-law. They told him that Daniel B. has been communicating with them by letter and personal visits to the home for well over a year. Daniel regularly left messages in their mailbox. The messages contained poems, rambling discourses, and small, hand-drawn pictures. Daniel had even managed to talk with the wife and father-in-law in front of the house on several occasions. His conversations rambled across various political topics. Two weeks earlier, Daniel showed up at a well-publicized town meeting where the official was scheduled to speak. One of the official's assistants diverted Daniel from approaching the official.

The official decided not to report any of these encounters and communications because he considered Daniel a harmless "nut case." That opinion changed, however, after the last contact with the father-in-law and Daniel's ominous statement about doing anything to get a meeting with the official. The official now felt concerned for his family's safety, although he declined any kind of protective detail at his residence.

Threat Assessment

On the basis of the facts available at the time of this assessment, Daniel was assessed as acting like a hunter through his persistent approach behavior. Although his grievance was unknown at this time, Daniel researched the location of the official's residence. He also appeared at a publicized meeting that he knew the official was scheduled to attend. Daniel was persistent in his desire to contact the official. More disturbingly, his method of contacting the official changed from leaving messages in the mailbox to direct confrontations with family members and staff employees, during which he exhibited aggressive behavior. Daniel is assessed as presenting a high risk of violence against the official, his wife, and his father-in-law.

Recommended Protective Response

Because the official declined posting a patrol car outside his residence, the threat manager arranged for frequent patrols of the house and surrounding neighborhood by local law enforcement. The threat manager also briefed the family on security precautions and measures they could take if confronted again by Daniel.

Recommended Threat Management Strategy

Because Daniel had never made clear just what he wanted or expected from meeting with the official, the first threat management strategy should be to interview Daniel for information. During the interview, it might be possible to refocus Daniel onto the threat manager. Depending on the information gleaned from the interview, such other strategies as confronting and warning him to stop, obtaining a restraining order, attempting a mental health commitment, or even gaining cause for arrest might develop. Daniel's aggressive approaches rule out any of the nonconfrontational strategies. The key to this case will be to remain as flexible as possible and take advantage of new opportunities to deploy the full range of confrontational strategies.

The Outcome

The threat manager determined that Daniel lived less than a mile from the state official. The threat manager and her partner went to the front door. Daniel answered the doorbell naked. He refused to let the threat manager inside his house, forcing the threat manager to interview him through the screen door. He remained very confrontational and uncooperative throughout the interview and refused to answer most of the threat manager's questions. Daniel stated that he could talk to the official if he wanted to. Further, he denied any violent intent. He admitted to seeing doctors in the past but claimed he no longer needed to take the medications they had prescribed for him. The threat manager finally wrested an agreement from Daniel not to attempt to contact the official again but, rather, to call the threat manager if he had a problem.

The threat manager then canvassed the neighborhood interviewing Daniel's neighbors. All of them claimed they feared Daniel because of his confrontational demeanor. He frequently prowled the neighborhood at night. On a number of occasions, he had become agitated and begun knocking on doors looking for people who did not live there. The local police knew Daniel as a local problem involved in numerous disturbances in the neighborhood. They also had a report that Daniel had harassed a local restaurant owned by a movie star. On occasion, Daniel had gone to the restaurant demanding to meet the owner.

A week later, Daniel left another letter in the official's mailbox. Later that day, he confronted the father-in-law in front of the house. Daniel again demanded to see the official. The father-in-law, based on the security briefing he had received, quickly disengaged himself from the confrontation. Daniel left and the father-in-law immediately reported the incident to the threat manager.

On the basis of the information gleaned from the interviews with Daniel and his neighbors, the police report, and the latest incident, the threat manager decided to get more confrontational with Daniel. She also wanted to gather more information to justify a mental health commitment based on erratic behavior and Daniel's posing a threat to the official and his family. Over the years, she had developed a professional relationship with the staff at many of the mental health facilities in the area, so she had a clear idea of what information they would need. She also knew how to put the information in the right format.

The second interview took place in front of Daniel's house. He again claimed the right to contact the official and maintained he had done nothing wrong. He did not exhibit sufficient signs of mental illness to justify a commitment at that time. Instead, the threat manager adopted a much sterner attitude toward Daniel. She bluntly told him to stop the behavior. Daniel seemed more cooperative at the end of the interview.

Daniel stayed away from the state official for over a month. Then he again went to the residence. As the official returned home with his son, he saw Daniel pacing in front of his house acting very upset and agitated. When Daniel saw the official, he immediately threatened to "kick his ass." The official, per the security briefing, refused to be drawn into a discussion. He went into the house and called the police. Daniel left the area before the police arrived. The police checked his residence but did not find him.

At this point, the official agreed to allow a curb watch at his home until the police could locate Daniel. An hour later, Daniel returned to the house. The officers in the patrol car took him into custody and dropped him off at a mental health facility for evaluation.

The threat manager took advantage of this opportunity to get a commitment. She gathered all the information she had collected on the case and spelled it out in chronological order in an affidavit format. The threat manager also met with the director of the clinic to express her concerns and deliver the affidavit. The doctor's evaluation of Daniel, informed as it was by the facts in the case, led to a determination to effect a mental health conservatorship. The facility arranged to send Daniel to a locked facility for long-term treatment.

Issues of Interest

The case of this hunter offers some fascinating insights:

1. Targets will not always report incidents until they actually feel threatened. The training of protectees, their staffs, and families helps alleviate this hesitation. However, because lack of reporting is not unusual, the threat manager should always ask about past incidents to get a complete picture.
2. Targets will not always accept protection, even if it is recommended. This requires threat managers to make other arrangements that are usually less effective. The security briefing and emergency plan provide a starting point for more security later.
3. Daniel's mental illness made his grievance and motive impossible to determine. However, his behavior clearly showed he was acting like a hunter. Whatever his motive, he was determined to make repeated approaches.
4. Interviews and interventions do not always work as intended. The threat manager must be prepared to employ different strategies as circumstances change. For example, the mental health strategy could not be employed at the second interview because Daniel did not meet the necessary criteria. When he again approached the official in an agitated state and made a threat, he did meet the criteria for mental health evaluation.
5. Previous liaison with the director of the mental health facility along with providing him specific information on Daniel's behaviors made the strategy work.
6. Most government officials live within the community they serve without security other than what they provide themselves. Indeed, for many government officials, the idea of seeking protection makes them uncomfortable. It may also become a political issue during election campaigns because of the high cost.
7. Public officials living in the community are accessible to people who are angry or obsessed regarding an issue. When approached, many officials feel obliged to resolve, or try to resolve, the issue themselves until they get in over their heads.
8. Hunters frequently hide their grievances or motives, because revealing them might make them more susceptible to being managed. Consequently, threat managers need to manage the hunter's behavior without regard to what is prompting that behavior.

Appendix:
When Should Threats
Be Seen as Indicative
of Future Violence?
Threats, Intended Violence,
and the Intimacy Effect

DEBRA M. JENKINS

Introduction

In the emerging field of threat management, law enforcement personnel and other criminal-justice professionals must assess the potential for planned or intended violence. Cases of intended violence cross various venues, that is, intimate partners, students at school, persons in the workplace, and against public figures, government officials, and members of the judiciary. In state and federal jurisdictions, the law has established punishments for those who make explicit threats of violence. This has the effect of focusing law enforcement attention only on actual threateners, as many assumed that those who make threats to public figures also pose threats (Fein & Vossekuil, 1999). For years, conventional law enforcement thinking held that threats were strong pre-incident indicators of future violence (Calhoun & Weston, 2003; Fein & Vossekuil, 1999).

Research has thrown that thinking into doubt—at least in certain venues (Calhoun, 1998; Dietz, Matthews, Martell et al., 1991; Dietz, Matthews, van Duyne et al., 1991; Fein & Vossekuil, 1999). Research on acts of intended violence has raised significant issues concerning the relationship between threats of physical harm and actual acts of physical injury. Secret Service researchers stated flatly that threats to public figures have no bearing on predicting assassination (Fein & Vossekuil, 1999). A study of threatening and otherwise inappropriate letters sent to members of Congress indicated that threateners were significantly less likely to pursue an encounter when compared with those who did not threaten (Dietz, Matthews, Martell et al., 1991). A U.S. Marshals Service researcher came to a similar conclusion in a study of threats and violence against federal judicial officials (Calhoun, 1998). These researchers all recommended discounting the value of threats as indicators of future violence toward public figures.

While these findings are important for understanding and managing the potential for violence in the venues of public figures, they may not be applicable to other venues where parties are more familiar or intimate with each other. Yet, these findings have been applied to intended violence generally—risk-related decisions about pretrial release and parole (Borum, Fein, Vossekuil, & Berglund, 1999), the workplace, (Turner & Gelles, 2003), and school violence (Fein, Vossekuil, Pollack, & Borum, 2002; Reddy et al., 2001). Dr. Reid

Meloy, the noted California forensic psychologist, could not reconcile the discrepancy in the findings about the threat/violence outcome in the public figure venue compared with the venue for domestic violence. Consequently, he discounted threats altogether. He wrote:

> Those that pose a threat toward public figures usually do not threaten the person beforehand. On the other hand, in the stalking of private figures (usually prior sexual intimates), false negative rates (where subjects who were violent toward a target but did not directly threaten beforehand) are usually quite low. Articulated threats appear to have a positive and significant relationship to violence risk. (Meloy, 2001)

Therefore, Meloy suggested that "threats are much less useful in assessing actual violence risk than we have assumed in the past" (Meloy, 2001).

However, research studies on intended violence in different venues have reached opposite conclusions. Threats of violence in domestic venues may be ubiquitous, but they should not be ignored. A tragic consequence of dismissing threats in intimate settings can be seen in the 1999 case of the Castle Rock, Colorado, police department's decision to take no action after Jessica Gonzales pleaded with them to enforce a restraining order against her husband who had abducted their three daughters. Mr. Gonzales had a history of threats (*Gonzales* v. *Town of Castle Rock*, 307 F.3d 1258, 1261 [10th Cir., 2002]). He eventually emerged on the doorstep of the Castle Rock Police Department firing his weapon, resulting in his death by law enforcement. He had already killed his three children. The National Sheriff's Association opined that "the police could not have predicted the terrible outcome" (Meier, 2005). Of course, prophesy is not a talent we expect our criminal justice professionals to possess, but we might ask for greater understanding of the relationship of threats of violence to actual violent outcomes in various scenarios.

A study published in 2003 in the *American Journal of Public Health* suggested that there were "identifiable risk factors for intimate partner femicides," one of which was threats (Campbell et al., 2003). In addition, analysis of data from the National Violence Against Women Survey found links between individuals receiving threats and future victimization in the venue of domestic violence (Tjaden & Thoennes, 2000b). Research on school violence and workplace violence also suggests that threats, threatening statements, or talk of acting violently are linked to future violent acts in that setting (McGee & DeBernardo, 1999; Northwestern, 1993; O'Toole, 2001; Scalora, Washington, Casady, & Newell, 2003).

In their book *Contemporary Threat Management*, Dr. Frederick S. Calhoun and California Highway Patrol lieutenant Stephen W. Weston (2003) developed an untested hypothesis they call the *intimacy effect*. They suggested that the more intimate the relationship between threatener and target, the more likely the threatening statement can serve as a pre-incident indicator of intended violence. As they pointed out, however, researchers have not yet fully explored this aspect of threats and their relationship to intended violence (Calhoun & Weston, 2003).

This Appendix explores the validity of the intimacy effect by examining available research on threats of violence across several venues of intended violence. The paper will address the concept's validity from the perspective of the criminal justice system and its potential response to threats of violence. If the intimacy effect holds up, it offers criminal justice officials insight into the practical aspects of their responses to threats of violence by understanding their context within the social setting in which they occur.

A Framework for the Discussion of Threats and Intended Violence

No shortage of studies about violence exists. As a result, a variety of theories and categories have been developed. Individual, life-cycle, socioeconomic, and situational theories (Tittle, 2000) provide insight into violence and crime which, when studied together, often offer theories and explanations that overlap. Traditionally, certain criminologists have categorized violence into interpersonal and political categories (Siegel, 2001). An act of murder may fit both categories. In 1993, the National Research Council published four volumes titled *Understanding and Preventing Violence*. As a result of the consensus by the Panel on the Understanding and Control of Violent Behavior, the council adopted a definition of violence as "behaviors by individuals that intentionally threaten, attempt, or inflict physical harm on others" (Reiss & Roth, 1993). The panel's definition included intent, which is in line with the legal treatment of violence. Intent is the essential ingredient in establishing criminal violence in law. The panel also considered reactive violence as intentional (Reiss & Roth, 1993). However, by separating reactive or impromptu violence from more deliberate (intended) acts, new hypotheses may be suggested to help threat assessors detect, intervene, and prevent intended violence.

Violence and Its Intent

The bulk of the research on violence has focused on social causes, both microsocial and macrosocial, and on individual causes, both psychological and biological. The results of such research continue to provide various useful perspectives and indicators of risk. In 1993, the National Academy of Sciences (NAS) reported that "it was still not possible to link [existing research] together in a manner that would provide a strong theoretical base on which to build prevention and intervention programs" (Reiss & Roth, 1993). The NAS panel, in the interest of understanding and preventing violence, referred to social phenomena and processes of criminal justice treatment or social changes. Citing the problem of school violence, Marisa Reddy et al. wrote that "while eliminating all forms of antisocial aggression and violence is a laudable goal, different types of violence have different antecedents and thus require different approaches for assessment and intervention" (Reddy et al., 2001).

Methods of violence prevention concern the understanding of processes that lead to violent events and establishing measures to prevent them. A promising field of criminological review is *symbolic interactionism*. It focuses on "sequential, reciprocal response patterns in which interactants adjust to each other's behavior, note responses to their actions, interpret the meanings of those responses, and then adapt their next moves in accordance with those interpretations" (Tittle, 2000).

Preventive measures are often seen in hindsight. For example, on October 29, 2004, Sarah Crawford moved away from the apartment she and her abusive husband shared near Charlottesville, Virginia, while police stood nearby. The following day, her husband called her to say that "he understands why husbands kill their wives" (Shapira, 2004). On November 1, 2004, a county judge refused her request to extend a temporary restraining order against her estranged husband. Six days later, she was found dead in a Charlottesville hotel room. Dale Crawford, her husband, was arrested and charged with abduction and first-degree murder after he was located driving his wife's car near Jacksonville, Florida.

(Shapira, 2004). The lethality (murder) and deliberateness (abduction) of this event suggest Crawford's violent intent. Was Dale Crawford's veiled threat in this case a signal to the victim and to law enforcement to take steps to prevent this murder?

Practitioners of violence prevention need a greater understanding of the steps taken toward consummating an act of intended violence. Through this understanding, they may develop intervention strategies. The legal classifications of homicide may help point us in the right direction. The American model penal code suggests that homicide committed as part of another felony or in a premeditated fashion—first-degree or capital murder—is more heinous than that committed in the heat of passion—second-degree murder (Kerper, 1972). Thus, intent is an important factor in determining legal penalties. The ingredient of intent is the common denominator, whether the victims are presidents, domestic partners, coworkers, or classmates (Calhoun & Weston, 2003).

Researchers and theorists have posited a variety of classifications of violence. For example, some distinguish between interpersonal and political violence (Siegel, 2001). Interpersonal violence is either instrumental or expressive. Instrumental violence is designed to improve the financial or social position of the criminal. Expressive violence vents rage, anger, or frustration (Siegel, 2001). Within this traditional breakdown, politically motivated violence by a lone individual against the U.S. president would not be interpersonal but political. Such categorizations look at motivation or reason for committing a violent act. Doing so may create useful concepts to support various criminal theories. However, professionals and organizations responsible for security and protection are better served with studies of detectable actions and behaviors that might be helpful in interventions. Whereas actuarial and clinical approaches have dominated the pursuit of identifying the dangerous person who is likely to commit violent acts, James Clark proposed ground breaking "situational variables" to provide "useful clues in short-term assessment of dangerousness" (Clark, 1989). Clark's work has served as a springboard to other more recent research studying violent acts and their preceding processes.

In their important research report, *Protective Intelligence and Threat Assessment Investigation* (Fein & Vossekuil, 2000), Secret Service researchers offered a new type of violence. More fitting to their research approach, they focused on targeted and non-targeted violence. "Targeted violence is the end result of an understandable, and often discernible, process of thinking and behavior" (Fein & Vossekuil, 2000). The study offered proof that assassinations and attempted assassinations were not spur-of-the-moment acts. Attempts on the life of a public figure may initially appear as impetuous or spontaneous, but that appearance does not hold up under scrutiny. The Secret Service offered a "new way of thinking and a new set of skills for criminal justice professionals. These investigations involve analysis of a subject's behavior and examination of patterns of conduct that may result in an attack on a particular target(s)" (Borum et al., 1999). Targeted violence includes traditional criminology's elements of not only interpersonal (both instrumental and expressive), but political violence as well. The Secret Service's definition enabled threat assessors to better understand attack behaviors in preventing violence.

The Secret Service's concept of targeted violence does not account for acts of violence that appear to be deliberate, even though the targets are not clearly defined or identified. Curiously, however, this was the case in several of their study subjects. For example, John Hinckley focused his attention on the presidency and attended campaign appearances for President Carter. After the presidential election of 1980, Hinckley shifted his attention to President Reagan. On the day he shot Reagan, he had debated whether to shoot

Ted Kennedy, Reagan, or himself. Reagan, Hinckley decided, was closer (Clark, 1989). In other cases, however, the opportunity to attack was the reason for the target selection. For example, a subject called "P.V." traveled to a movie studio in Los Angeles (after killing three persons in a bagel store in another state) in order to kill a famous actor. When he failed to find the actor, he shot two security guards at a film studio gate instead (Fein & Vossekuil, 1999). In these cases, the target appeared less important than the violence intended.

In their article published in the *Annals of the American Academy of Political and Social Sciences* entitled "Understanding and Controlling Violence," authors Neil Weiner and Don Hardenbergh (2001b) proposed a narrower definition for targeted and non-targeted violence. Derived from the NAS definition, Weiner and Hardenbergh defined judicial violence as behavior by individuals that intentionally threatens, attempts, or inflicts physical harm on persons at work or on duty in the judiciary (Weiner & Hardenbergh, 2001b). For the purpose of discussing the control of judicial violence, the authors further offered a breakdown of targeted violence as involving an "ideational and behavioral sequence—a pathway—directed at or focused on a specific person or group," judicial officials, in their example. Non-targeted violence involved "less deliberation and focus and shorter duration" (Weiner & Hardenbergh, 2001b). Again, this definition of targeted violence fails to take into consideration persons who intend to commit a violent act, but who also may not have set their sights on a particular individual or who may substitute targets of opportunity.

Borrowing from the animal kingdom, Dr. Reid Meloy has adopted types of violence he calls *predatory* and *affective*. With a decidedly psychological perspective, Meloy likens human violence to feline violence. A cat can behave in a predatory manner when stalking prey in the backyard. Yet, when confronted with an unexpected threat, the cat arches, hisses, and displays teeth and claws. Meloy's predatory violence includes characteristics such as planned or purposeful violence, variable goals—primarily cognitive, a heightened and focused awareness, and no displacement of target (Meloy, 2000). Affective violence is autonomic and usually directed toward a prior intimate or acquaintance. According to Meloy (2001), "public figures appear to be victimized by predatory violence," planned and purposeful. However, Dale Crawford's abduction and murder of his wife demonstrated the same deliberation and planning shown by John Hinckley toward President Reagan. P.V., who traveled with violent intent to meet a public figure, also showed the same deliberate behaviors.

Meloy's focus on a "target" is similar to the focus of the Secret Service's, as well as to the focus of Weiner and Hardenbergh. What about the cat that stalks a mouse, but whose attention is redirected toward a moth crossing its line of vision? The cat's predatory actions and its will to hunt remain intact while its target may change. Perhaps Meloy's definition of predatory violence—especially the needed ingredient of "no displacement of target" (Meloy, 2000)—narrows his definition to one that is not entirely useful for understanding the process of preventing violence.

Calhoun and Weston (2003) propose another way of looking at violence that might be the most practical yet in preventing certain acts of violence. Rather than trying to forge a conceptual link through the victims, which is the problem with inserting the target into the previous definition, a concept of intended violence can be drawn from the perpetrators. Eliminating crimes motivated by passion or profit, their concept of violence links certain modes of "domestic violence, workplace violence, school violence, public-figure assaults and hate crimes" under the umbrella concept of intended violence (Calhoun & Weston, 2003). Someone intent on violence has already made the decision to commit a violent act.

Table A.1   Types of Violence

Author	Some Violence Typologies
Siegel (2001)	*Interpersonal versus political.* Interpersonal violence is either (1) instrumental—designed to improve the financial or social position of the criminal or (2) expressive—to vent rage, anger, or frustration; political violence is motivated by ideology
Reiss & Roth (1993) (NRC)	*Intentional versus collective.* Intentional is inflicting physical harm (or attempt); collective is riots, state violence, some actions by organized crime
Fein & Vossekuil (2001)	*Targeted violence.* Target is chosen by virtue of association with a certain venue, for example, national political figures, judges
Weiner & Hardenbergh (2001a, 2001b)	*Targeted versus nontargeted (specific to courthouse venues).* Targeted involves an individual expressly intending to engage in violence, deliberate, includes planning; nontargeted involves individuals with no preexisting intention of engaging in violence but unexpectedly acts out in courtroom or courthouse
Meloy (2001)	*Predatory versus affective.* Predatory is planned or purposeful, cognitive, and with variable goals; affective is with intense autonomic arousal, reactive and immediate violence, and the goal is defense
Calhoun & Weston (2003)	*Intended versus impromptu.* Intended is when the perpetrator is inspired to engage in violence for whatever reason; it includes (1) targeted—specific choice of victim and (2) opportunistic—general in selection of victims; impromptu is a spontaneous outburst sparked by circumstances of the moment

The secondary consideration then becomes target and/or opportunity (Calhoun & Weston, 2003). In a previous example given by the Secret Service, P.V. clearly intended to commit a violent act. He even had a target in mind. However, the opportunity to meet his target did not occur, so he turned a chance encounter into an act of violence toward two unfortunate security guards. Certainly, these various venues can also host violent acts that are impromptu or reactive. However, by separating intended or deliberate from impromptu or reactive, threat assessors may have a window of opportunity to detect and intervene along the path to intended violence.

In March 2000, Michael McDermott began working at a computer consulting company just outside Boston. He brought with him IRS troubles. By December, the IRS was deducting from his wages. The forced withdrawals outraged McDermott, so he directed his wrath at the company accounting department. Shortly before Christmas, he began yelling at the accountants for garnishing his wages. The day after Christmas, McDermott went to work heavily armed, the weapons hidden in a duffle bag. For his midmorning coffee break, McDermott took an AK-47, a shotgun, and a pistol from his cubicle and walked toward the accounting department. He began killing people in the reception area, then in accounting—a total of seven died (Calhoun & Weston, 2003). McDermott clearly intended to kill that day. His targets varied among people whom he perceived had wronged him as well as people who presented him with additional opportunities to exercise his intent to kill.

Table A.1 presents the various types of violence discussed in this section.

Venues

Thanks to the work of various threat-assessment professionals and researchers, threat assessment venues have emerged to help provide better context in which to understand indicators for intended violence. These venues include (1) situations involving public

Table A.2   Intended Violence across Venues

Public Figure	Workplace	School	Domestic
Violence inflicted or attempted by person(s) intent on harm that may be directed at a public figure (Fein & Vossekuil, 2000; Meloy, 2001)	Violence inflicted or attempted by persons(s) intent on harm "against coworkers, supervisors or managers by a present or former employee" (Rugala, 2003)	Violence inflicted or attempted by person(s) intent on harm, that are "service recipients or customers of the school, parents or guardians of students or those who are currently or formerly in relationships with students" (Mohandie, 2000)	Violence inflicted or attempted by person(s) intent on harm, that are current or former sexual intimates
Relationship: noninterpersonal	Relationship: mixed noninterpersonal and interpersonal	Relationship: mixed noninterpersonal and interpersonal	Relationship: interpersonal
Nonintimate	Semi-intimate	Semi-intimate	Intimate

figures, (2) the workplace, (3) schools, and (4) domestic or intimate partner situations. For example, Dr. Chris Mohandie described intended violence in the school venue. His definition from a threat-assessment point of view is that preventable school violence is perpetrated by someone who is a service recipient or customer of the school, a category which, in addition to students, may also include parents or guardians of students and those who are currently or formerly in relationships with students (Mohandie, 2002). The FBI, in concert with other researchers, has a parallel classification for the workplace-violence venue: "Violence against coworkers, supervisors or managers by a present or former employee" (Rugala, 2004). Intended violence is present in each of these venues. We are able to see intended violence along the spectrum of venues as well as the degree of intimacy for each venue (Table A.2).

The Nature of Threats

Within the past decade, the discourse on threats and their relationship to violence has increased (Calhoun, 1998; Calhoun & Weston, 2003; de Becker, 1997; Dietz, Matthews, Martell et al., 1991; Dietz, Matthews, van Duyne et al., 1991; Fein & Vossekuil, 1999; Meloy, 2001; Scalora et al., 2003). "In the spirit of symbolic interactionism… theorizing about crime-provoking situational characteristics has most often focused on events and action interpreted by participants as threatening their status or positions or their ideas about self" (Tittle, 2000). Long considered a protection of free speech, laws against threats were slow to appear. In 2015, the U.S. Supreme Court overturned the conviction of Anthony Elonis, who repeatedly threatened his ex-wife using Facebook. While the trial jury in this case was convinced that Elonis's threats were indeed a crime, Justice Roberts opined for the majority that no crime was apparent as the jury was not required to consider his "mental state" at the time he put the threatening postings on Facebook.

In 1993, the NAS Panel on Understanding and Preventing Violence called for additional research for preventive interventions with specific emphasis on the relationships between aggressive and violent behavior, as well as analyses of protective and aggravating conditions and factors in families, peer groups, schools, and communities (Reiss & Roth, 1993). Violence prevention can exist in several forms such as responses and actions by enlightened people or institutions charged with dealing with potential violent offenders such as medical professionals, social workers, and criminal justice officials.

According to *Webster's Encyclopedic Unabridged Dictionary of the English Language* (1989), a "threat" is a declaration of an intention or determination to inflict punishment, injury, death, or loss to someone in retaliation for, or conditionally upon, some action or course. For the purposes of this discussion, these declarations of violent intention are communicated and differentiated from structural threats or threats from weather or disease. Communicated threats occur in many forms. A mother may make a threat to her children that a promised visit to the ice cream parlor will not occur if their behavior does not improve. A candidate for state political office may threaten his opponent with "revealing evidence of prior sexual harassment." A gunman may say to his robbery victim, "Give me your wallet or I will shoot you." Most have at least heard about such scenarios where threats are used. But, when should threats be taken seriously and seen as predictive of intended violence?

A letter writer may mail a letter to the White House containing the words, "I have the President in my sights and I will shoot him on his next trip to New York City for his policy on school prayer." This may seem similar to a husband who threatens his wife with: "I will take my hunting rifle out of the truck and kill you if you don't listen to me next time." But, how much do spoken or written threats mean from situation to situation—from venue to venue? Does the Secret Service need to respond to the presidential threat differently than how the local county police respond to the husband's threat to his wife?

Communicated threats are made to convince us of an intention but, according to personal security expert Gavin de Becker, "threats actually convince us of an emotion: frustration" (de Becker, 1997). Furthermore, the threat boosts the power of the threatener from the fear instilled in the victim. As de Becker points out, threats are promises, many of which are broken—but some of which are kept.

Milburn and Watman (1981) wrote that threats are ubiquitous and that they can be explicit, implicit, and structural. Explicit threats—the focus of this study—offer the source considerable control over his or her own phrasing, clarity, and tone. However, according to Milburn and Watman, such threats have a high failure rate, usually owing to the reaction of the target. In fact, threats are effective in inverse relation to the degree of personal involvement of the threatener. Whereas the source of the threat intends to threaten and the target sees the threat, the communication is accurate. However, the farther away the target is from the source of the threat and the less the target sees the threat, the less effective the threat (Milburn & Watman, 1981).

For workplace violence venues, Drs. Turner and Gelles (2003) recommend examining aspects of the threat, looking for organized, fixed, focused, and action- and time-imperative communications as potential precursors of violence. The degree to which threatening communications deviate from these characteristics in workplace scenarios helps to determine the immediacy of the intervention or action to be taken (Turner & Gelles, 2003).

The Relationship of Threats to Intended Violence

In James Tedeschi's work within social interactionist theory, threats and resulting physical harm are put into the context of coercive actions. Coercive actions can be motivated by a need to ensure another party's compliance, to restore justice, and/or to project a particular social identity. Tedeschi suggests that where compliance is a motive, people who possess greater relative power than others may be encouraged to use coercion because they expect to be successful at little cost (Tedeschi & Feldson, 1994).

An application of coercion theory (part of social interactionist theory) to situations where people make threats might help to explain why threats made by people in various situations are associated with different outcomes. For example, in a domestic conflict situation, control and compliance are common motives. Over time, the male spouse, who usually has greater physical strength and aggressive tendencies, uses these as tools to maintain control (Tedeschi & Feldson, 1994).

Making threats to gain compliance, as seen in domestic violence situations, are often about a perpetual conflict between the parties. However, in matters of school and workplace violence, threats may be motivated by a desired outcome spawned by justice seeking. For example, in 1998, Robert Scott Helfer sought revenge at his workplace in Greeley, Colorado. He exhibited many of the characteristics of a troubled employee, but he particularly focused on a coworker, Donna Archuleta, who had altered an office furniture order he had placed. He threatened her with violence. On the morning of a disciplinary hearing over his transgressions on the job, he pulled out a handgun and began shooting, killing one person and wounding another. He left the room and began seeking out Donna. Along the way, he encountered other coworkers telling them "Don't worry. I'm not here for you." As Donna heard Helfer getting closer, she instinctively realized that he was after her. Her instincts saved her life as she hid herself from the gunman (Moffatt, 2000).

In contrast, however, actors with an interest in public figures may see the act of making threats less useful than striking the victim without them. After all, if one intends to assault or kill a public official, what is the point of warning by issuing threats? The motive is more likely punitive or justice seeking. Secret Service researchers have reported that in a study of 83 public figure attackers, "fewer than one tenth of all 83 attackers and near-lethal approachers communicated a direct threat to the target or to a law enforcement agency" (Fein & Vossekuil, 2000). However, public figure attackers and near-lethal approachers were not completely secretive about their aims and intentions. John Hinckley wanted maximum attention for his actions. Although he visited the offices of a number of major Washington figures during the fall and winter of 1980, Hinckley focused his attention on the presidency. In the fall of 1980, Hinckley, traveling with a gun, attended campaign appearances by President Carter (Fein & Vossekuil, 1999).

Alarming words contained in threats cause people to react by going into a defensive posture (de Becker, 1997). In evaluating threats, experts stress context. Rather than evaluating the words used to make the threat, an investigation into the whole situation is required. To illustrate the difference from one case to the next, de Becker (1997) wrote that in interpersonal situations a "threat tends to actually increase the likelihood of violence by eroding the quality of communication and increasing frustration, but the very same threat conveyed to a public figure does not portend violence at all" (de Becker, 1997).

In fact, as two security experts have noted (Batza & Taylor, 1999), one of the most common misconceptions in the assessment of public figure stalking is the alarm caused by death threats. These particular security experts categorize stalkers as attachment-seeking, identity-seeking, rejection-based, or delusional. They claim, "No known modern-age, public-figure attacker threatened to kill his or her victim prior to doing so" (Batza & Taylor, 1999). This does not, however, hold true in other types of stalking situations in which threats are important predictors of future violence. Consequently, while each type may be seen in stalking directed toward public figures or in interpersonal cases, threats made are not as important when factored into assessments of public figure cases (Batza & Taylor, 1999). However, assessing direct threats is important in interpersonal cases.

The importance of the research on threats and violence toward public officials has significantly helped threat assessors realize that it is a myth that most attacks on public officials are preceded by direct threats. The findings by the U.S. Marshals Service on threats to federal judicial officials helped change the attention of threat assessors from merely direct threats to other detectable behaviors. In 1996, the U.S. Marshals Service revised its reportable behaviors from merely threats to "other less obvious language or behavior" (Jenkins, 2001).

While research has helped to advance threat management for the protection of public officials, the same findings may have had some deleterious effect on other venues where threats and violent outcomes exist. For example, in a Department of Justice publication reviewing batterer intervention programs, lethality assessments were encouraged and the process that was promoted by the Secret Service, based on its study of public figure attackers or near-lethal approachers, was referenced (Healey, Smith, & O'Sullivan, 1998). The Secret Service process may not, however, be applicable and even might be harmful if taken into account for domestic situations when evaluating direct threats to harm. Threats may indeed be important to risk assessment in venues where the threateners and their targets are more familiar with each other.

Very revealing research conducted in 1999 has provided indicators toward the effect intimacy has on dangerousness. The study compared 233 intimate and non-intimate stalking cases managed by the Los Angeles Police Department. The researchers defined intimates as married, cohabitating, dating, or having a prior sexual relationship. Non-intimates were defined as coworkers, schoolmates, roommates, neighbors, or those in professional business relationships. No stranger relationships were noted in the definition. The results of the analysis revealed that in this data set, "intimate stalkers threatened persons and property more often, committed more violence against persons and property (including physical violence toward the victim), were more likely to 'make good' on their threats... and used more physical approach behaviors" (Palarea, Zona, Lane, & Langhinrichsen-Rohling, 1999). As noted in the report's discussion: "The results illustrate the importance of accounting for the presence of an intimate relationship when assessing for violence" (Palarea et al., 1999).

In his discussion of stalking, threats, and violence, Dr. Reid Meloy asserts that "threats are very common, and therefore provide us with little guidance in determining how dangerous someone is" (Meloy, 2000). Meloy observed from his studies concerning prior sexual intimates that when threats were made, there was no follow-up violence 75% of the time. Meloy wrote that false negative rates among violent stalkers were typically less than 15% when the victim was a prior sexual intimate, "[but] if the victim is a public figure, false negative rates jump to at least 90% " (Meloy, 2000). He explained this discrepancy as the difference between private stalking, which he considered affective (autonomic or impulsive) behavior, and public stalking, which he considered predatory (planned or instrumental) behavior. In another publication, Meloy reported on a review of studies of stalking, threats, and violence. The review yielded 736 subjects who stalked or attacked across various venues. Among the studies, Meloy found a positive and significant relationship between communicated threats and violence risk, with one striking exception. In the study involving public figures attacked or assassinated, Meloy cited that only one out of ten subjects "communicated a direct threat to the target or to law enforcement before they were violent" (Meloy, 2001). In his discussion, Meloy offered an explanation citing the nature of the violence:

> Private targets are typically shoved, pushed, punched, slapped, choked, fondled or hair pulled by the perpetrator, and he usually does not use a weapon… This is a mode of violence which is *affective*: highly autonomically arousing, accompanied by anger or fear, unplanned, and an immediate reaction to a perceived threat, usually rejection by the person who is the target of the pursuit, usually a prior acquaintance or intimate. On the other hand, public targets appear to be victimized by a *predatory* mode of violence: it is planned for days, weeks or months, is purposeful (instrumental), has variable goals, and is primarily cognitively motivated. (Meloy, 2001)

Apparently, Meloy does not associate predatory behavior with violence among intimates. Unwittingly, Meloy might be helping to explain the discrepancy in the likelihood of intended violence after a threat is made between intimates and non-intimates.

To explore the intimacy effect on threats, we will look at the spectrum of intended violence from non-intimates to intimates. The exploration of intended violence and threats in school and workplace venues focuses on the familiarity of the offenders and the victims. The purpose will be to try to understand why the research on threats appears to contradict itself. The goal is to develop some practical standards that law enforcement and other threat assessment professionals can use in evaluating threats. Essentially, the paper asks: When should threats be seen as indicative of future violence?

Findings on Public Figure Violence

While the American public was still reeling from the terrorist attacks of September 11, 2001, deadly anthrax arrived through the mail in then Senate Majority Leader Tom Daschle's office at the Hart Senate Office Building in Washington, DC. Three years later, the deadly poison ricin was discovered in the mailroom for the offices of Senate Majority Leader Bill Frist. These incidents are reminders that public figures are not immune to potentially deadly attacks from persons intent on violence toward them. Each year, federal, state, and local law enforcement officials and private security officers intercede with thousands of individuals who demonstrate inappropriate or unusual interest in a public official or figure. Some of these individuals were intercepted within lethal range of a target just before they attempted to mount an attack (Fein & Vossekuil, 2000).

Public officials taking positions in political debates on issues such as abortion, capital punishment, and military spending naturally garner resentment and publicity over their positions. Under these circumstances, even the most politically adroit cannot fail to alienate large numbers of individuals. The publicity that public officials receive also brings them to the attention of mentally disturbed or jealous individuals. Not surprisingly, public officials receive a steady stream of hostile and inappropriate communications in the form of mail, telephone calls, and unwanted visits (Dietz, Matthews, Martell et al., 1991). In many cases, the incumbent's title alone is enough to attract those who wish to harm a public official. John Hinckley stalked President Jimmy Carter, then switched to Ronald Reagan after Reagan's election to office (Clark, 1989). Another subject from the Secret Service sample was "FT," a lonely, angry young man who spent 18 months preoccupied with selecting and shooting a national leader (Fein & Vossekuil, 1999). Such unwanted attention poses a significant challenge to law enforcement.

Several attempts have been made to study the behavior leading up to violent approaches toward public figures. James Clark published groundbreaking research in 1981, *American Assassins* (Clark, 1982), which carefully portrayed the characteristics and actions of 16 assassins and would-be assassins of American presidents or presidential candidates as well as Martin Luther King. Clark identified a number of significant exceptions to the then conventional wisdom concerning the motives and tactics (or actions) of assassins. Rather than accept a preexisting myth that assassins and would-be assassins commit political violence brought on by some psychosis, he discovered nuances among his study subjects that serve to enlighten us about the thinking that led to violence. For example, Samuel Byck, who attempted to assassinate Richard Nixon, and Lee Harvey Oswald both translated their very real domestic difficulties into political extremism. Employment problems and marital difficulties were the real reasons for their frustration and anger (Clark, 1989). Only the target selection makes Oswald any differently motivated than Charles Whitman, who in 1966 climbed a tower at the University of Texas, heavily armed, and methodically took aim at people below. He killed 12 and wounded 31 (Calhoun & Weston, 2003). Both Oswald and Whitman planned and prepared for their violent acts, leaving clues along the way. This similarity was profound. These and similar cases opened the door to the study of violence as an intended act.

In an update to his *American Assassins*, James Clark later wrote about his psychological profiles of known assassins, remarking that the characteristics of his small sample of known assassins were not dissimilar from those of millions of others who do not attempt such actions. "Most assassins are drawn to identifiable behavior patterns before they strike" (Clark, 1989). In a small portion of these cases, threats were known to have been made. However, not all threats were considered direct. Only 4 of the 17 subjects actually made threats prior to their attacks. Although from this, as Clark warned, "threats cannot be ignored," the behaviors of the assassins prior to their acts were more telling. For example, Lynette Fromme drew considerable attention to herself through her well-known attempts to publicize the alleged injustice of Charles Manson's trial. She combined these acts by wearing bizarre red robes as she waited for President Ford to pass by. In another incident, John Hinckley arrived at the Nashville airport with three handguns in his suitcase on the day President Carter was scheduled to speak there (Clark, 1989). Clark made a practical contribution by shifting the research focus to behaviors and away from merely the mental condition of the perpetrator.

In 1991, a team of researchers led by Park Dietz published two articles reporting on their study of inappropriate communications sent to Hollywood celebrities and similar types of letters mailed to members of Congress. Both studies led Dietz and his colleagues to a startling conclusion. They found that explicit threats of physical harm had little bearing—even an opposite bearing—on the actual behavior of the person uttering the threat. For Hollywood celebrities, Dietz et al. found "no association between threatening and approaching." It followed, then, that "the presence or absence of a threat in the communication is no indication whatsoever of whether a subject is going to pursue an encounter" (Dietz, Matthews, van Duyne et al., 1991). Their initial conclusion ran against common sense and traditional practice, both of which held that threateners were dangerous individuals.

The finding that emerged from the team's study of communications to members of Congress was even more pronounced. "Subjects," the research team wrote, "who sent threats to a member of Congress were significantly less likely to pursue a face-to-face encounter with him or her." The team elaborated:

> The finding regarding threats was particularly robust. Each of the following aspects of threats, taken alone, was significantly associated with not approaching: threatening any kind of harm toward any public figure; threatening to kill any public figure or those around a public figure; indicating that a threat would be executed by the subject or his agent; making any conditional threat; and making any implausible threat. (Dietz, Matthews, Martell et al., 1991)

The researchers selected 100 cases from the Capitol Police case files. All contained some form of written communications; 50 cases indicated positive approach behavior and 50 cases indicated negative approach behavior. From this collection, a stratified random sample of 86 cases was analyzed for content of the correspondence.

Defining a threat as any offer to do harm, however implausible, the study found that in 58% of the cases, a threat was communicated (Table A.3). However, the subjects who threatened were significantly less likely to approach. "Nearly every feature of threats studied bore a significant relationship to approach behavior, always in the direction of threateners approaching less often" (Dietz, Matthews, Martell et al., 1991).

From this finding, Dietz concluded that waiting for a threat before contacting law enforcement, or law enforcement waiting for an explicit threat before opening an investigation or taking measures to thwart "dangerous encounters," would be a serious mistake.

Subsequent research on public figure attacks has confirmed Dietz's finding. Secret Service researchers analyzed 83 attackers and near attackers of presidents, celebrities, jurists, and other public figures. Like Dietz, the Secret Service researchers concluded that "persons who pose threats most often do not make threats, especially explicit threats." Less than a tenth of the 83 attackers and near-attackers communicated threats. More tellingly, none of the 43 individuals in the study who actually attacked a public figure ever made an explicit threat to the target (Fein & Vossekuil, 2000). When asked why he did not send a threat letter before he approached, one study subject responded that if he "had sent a letter, the police would have come and arrested me. I did not want to be stopped then" (Fein & Vossekuil, 1999).

From this study, the Secret Service has moved away from relying on descriptive, demographic, or psychological profiles. Furthermore, "the threat assessment approach does not rely on direct communication of a threat as a threshold for an appraisal of risk or protective action. Investigators make a distinction between people who *make* threats and those who *pose* a threat. Persons who appear to pose a threat provoke the greatest level of concern. Although some people who make threats ultimately pose threats, many do not" (Borum et al., 1999). As with Clark and Dietz, the Secret Service research discounted the value of threats while it inflated the value of behaviors.

Table A.3   Threat Made and Approach Behaviors—Letters to Congress

Approach Behavior	Threat Yes	Threat No
Approach negative	84%	16%
Approach positive	33%	67%

Source: Dietz, P. E., Matthews, D. B., Martell, D. A., Stewart, T. M., Hrouda, D. R., & Warren, J., *Journal of Forensic Sciences*, 36(5), 1445–1468, 1991.

A study of threats and assaults against federal judicial officials by Dr. Frederick S. Calhoun drew a distinction between attackers, whom he called "hunters," and threateners, whom he called "howlers." Between the two, Calhoun concluded,

lies a world of difference. They are extremes: one an actor, one a talker: one a doer, one a writer. Between them is a huge chasm, a clear distinction. The hunters hunt and rarely howl; the howlers howl and only rarely hunt. (Calhoun, 1998)

Based on this fundamental difference between hunters and howlers, the study identified distinctive characteristics of each. Howlers communicated their threats to their targets in writing or over the telephone. Hunters did not communicate, but engaged in face-to-face confrontations or suspicious activities, including physical assaults (Calhoun, 1998).

According to Dr. Calhoun, "the courts are now imperiled in a way that no one imagined even [two] decades ago. In the last 20 years, more federal judges have been brutally assassinated than in the 175 years before" (Calhoun, 1998). This new reality exposes potential unprotected victims to violence. In 1988, Charles Koster carried his daughter's discrimination suit to federal court in New York. He expected Judge Richard Duronco to sustain her. When the verdict affronted him, Koster tracked down the judge at his home and, without warning, shot him to death in his backyard (Calhoun, 1998). Similarly, Bart Ross, dejected by Judge Joan Lefkow's dismissal of his lawsuit against Northwestern Hospital, broke into her house in February 2005 to wait for her to come home. Once discovered by the judge's husband, Ross killed the husband and the judge's mother, then fled (Calhoun and Weston, 2009).

Even though 3,096 inappropriate communications to federal judicial officials were recorded between 1980 and 1993, the vast majority of federal judicial officials end their service without intimidation, harassment, or violence. "Even among those officials who were pestered, the proportion who were physically imperiled was even smaller. Of the 2,996 reported inappropriate communications and assaults that could be rated by outcome, 242 of them posed some enhanced risk to the victim. In other words, some 91.9% of the rated cases were specious, the communications empty and ultimately harmless" (Calhoun, 1998).

Based on a career providing security services to public figures in the United States, Gavin de Becker fully embraced what the research told him. As he explained in *The Gift of Fear*:

It is a tenacious myth that those who threaten public figures are the ones most likely to harm them. In fact, those who make direct threats to public figures are far less likely to harm them than those who communicate in other inappropriate ways (lovesickness, exaggerated adoration, theses of rejection, the belief that a relationship "is meant to be," plans to travel or meet, [or] the belief that the media figure owes them something). Direct threats are not a reliable pre-incident indicator for assassination in America, as demonstrated by the fact that not one successful public-figure attacker in the history of the media age directly threatened his victim first. (de Becker, 1997)

The "demythologization" of threats to public figures as indicators of future action led several law enforcement agencies charged with public-figure protection responsibilities to shift away from waiting for a threat (Calhoun & Weston, 2003). Instead, they have broadened their investigations to include inappropriate communications or contacts between the protectees and those who might cause them harm (Calhoun & Weston, 2003; Fein & Vossekuil, 2000; Jenkins, 2001). These agencies taught their targets to report inappropriate communications or contacts even if they lacked explicit expressions of an intent to cause harm. In effect, the focus shifted from what individuals said to what they did. "Actions spoke louder than words," Calhoun and Weston (2003) concluded.

Observations

- Public figures receive threatening and inappropriate communications.
- Public figures are attacked without first being threatened in most cases studied.
- There is little motivation to threaten a public figure if violence is the desired outcome.
- Many attackers of public figures intend to act out violently, rather than resort to violence spontaneously.
- Consequently, the research shows that threats are not good pre-incident indicators for violence against public figures.

Findings on Workplace Violence

Since 1986, when Patrick Henry Sherrill, a postal worker in Edmond, Oklahoma, shot and killed six coworkers and then committed suicide, workplace violence has been the focus of intense research (Layden, 1996). According to the U.S. Department of Labor, violence in the workplace decreased from 891 incidents in 2012 to 751 incidents in 2013 (Department of Labor, 2014). Workplace homicide rates have fallen along with rates of overall violent crime since the mid-1990s, but we do not know the extent to which we can attribute these decreases to industry-based prevention programs (Peek-Asa, Runyan, & Zwerling, 2001). A 2001 report on workplace violence intervention opined that homicide remained (at the time of the report) the second leading cause of fatal occupational injuries for all workers and the leading cause of fatal occupational injuries for women. Although worker-on-worker violence accounted for about 7% of workplace homicides (Merchant & Lundell, 2001), such events leave us horrified and asking if predictive signs might have been detected to prevent such violence.

In cases of workplace violence, the U.S. Office of Personnel Management listed "direct or veiled threats of harm" among the warning signs of potential coworker violence (Office of Personnel Management, 1998). The Workplace Violence Research Institute advised employers in 1998 that "one of the most important elements in any prevention program is a zero tolerance policy for threats, harassment, intimidation and weapons possession" (Mattman, 1998). The institute analyzed more than 200 incidents of workplace violence and found that coworker violence was associated with a number of changed behaviors. One such "pre-incident indicator" included individuals who threaten or verbally abuse coworkers and supervisors (Mattman, 1998).

In an early work, James Alan Fox and Jack Levin (1994) steered away from the purely mental state of the workplace violence perpetrator. While recognizing mental anguish and possible mental and personality disorders, Fox and Levin saw episodes of workplace violence as a process. They found that most vengeful, violent workers do not act spontaneously and "just explode," but deliberate and engage in well-planned ambushes to gain revenge. "Workplace killers may be despondent, disillusioned, disappointed and even clinically depressed—but generally [are] not deranged" (Layden, 1996). Other researchers have also developed a baseline profile but found a "secondary but crucial set of risk factors [including]... threats of physical assault" (Layden, 1996).

Workplace violence is now recognized as a specific category of violent crime. In a recent publication, the FBI announced that specialists have come to a consensus that workplace violence falls into four broad categories. These are:

- Type 1—violent acts by criminals who have no other connection to the workplace, such as robbery.
- Type 2—violence directed at employees by persons for whom an organization provides services, such as customers or students.
- Type 3—violence against coworkers, supervisors, or managers by a present or former employee.
- Type 4—violence in the workplace by someone with a personal relationship with an employee, such as a domestic partner (Rugala, 2004).

According to data collected by the Bureau of Labor Statistics, coworker-on-coworker violence has been notably more deadly than violence directed at employees by customers or clients (Duhart, 2001). The data suggests that these events, motivated by revenge—not profit—are planned, purposeful, and intended (Table A.4).

This report focuses on the FBI's Type 3 workplace (coworker-on-coworker) violence to remain consistent with the concept of intended violence. Although domestic violence is a certain problem at the workplace, it is addressed in this report in the section reviewing the research on domestic violence.

In 1994, James Alan Fox and Jack Levin wrote that workplace violence—referring to the Type 3 category above—typically originated from the "vengeful employee." They elaborated by suggesting a profile of a middle-aged, white male facing termination or perceived injustices on the job. While aggregated characteristics resulting in profiles are interesting and may even describe the typical workplace attacker today, such profiles may not be practical for prevention efforts. "Given the relative infrequency of events such as workplace violence... the vast majority of people who 'fit' any given profile will not engage in that behavior" (Borum et al., 1999).

Where the potential for preventing intended violence exists is in the detection of behaviors indicating that an individual is on a "pathway to violent action" (Borum et al., 1999). A subject's appearance or profile is less important than his observable behaviors. In the workplace, threats appear to be part of a continuum of escalating behaviors that may help to predict the potential for violence.

A review of the literature on workplace violence reveals a growing interest in learning causes and prevention. The making of threats and its relationship to violent outcomes is not obvious. Some of the research treats threats as separate victimizations. Regardless, a pattern does emerge indicating that the making of threats among coworkers is prevalent and, as some data show, associated with physical violence (Northwestern, 1993; Scalora et al., 2003; Tjaden & Thoennes, 2001).

Table A.4   Distribution of Workplace Homicides by Relationship ($n = 130$)

Homicides—coworkers (more familiar)	67	65%
Homicides—clients (less familiar)	36	35%

Source: Duhart, D., *Violence in the workplace, 1993–99*. Washington, DC: Bureau of Justice Statistics, Department of Justice, 2001.

For the purpose of helping employers solve workplace violence problems and identify future trends, the Northwestern National Life Insurance Company, Minneapolis, Minnesota, conducted its own research and published its findings in 1993. Northwestern surveyed a representative sample of 600 full-time American workers conducted during 15-minute telephone interviews. The workers polled were from a national random sample excluding military personnel and the self-employed. The sample was drawn to accurately reflect the male–female ratio as well as the distribution of the workforce among the four census regions in the United States (Northwestern, 1993).

The survey made distinctions among threats, harassment, and physical attack at the workplace. Harassment was defined as the act of someone's creating a hostile work environment through unwelcome words, actions, or physical contact not resulting in physical harm. Threats were defined as expressions of the intent to cause physical harm. Physical attack was aggression resulting in a physical assault with or without the use of a weapon (Northwestern, 1993).

The study addressed the broader scope of workplace violence, including violence from strangers, clients, and coworkers. Key findings, however, give a glimpse of the intimacy effect on violence in the workplace. For example, one key finding of the study indicated a strong relationship between job stress and workplace harassment and violence. Highly stressed workers experienced twice the rate of violence as less stressed employees. Threats of violence were linked with higher burnout rates. The intimacy effect may also be seen as another key finding of the study that claimed that harassers are usually coworkers or bosses, while attackers are more likely to be customers. Victims identified interpersonal conflicts with coworkers as the most likely reason they were harassed or threatened as compared with attacks by clients or patients precipitated by irrational behavior. Coworkers and bosses accounted for 86% of all harassment at work, one third of threats, and one fourth of workplace attacks. Forty-six percent of workplace harassment victims and 27% of workers who had been threatened identified job-related interpersonal conflict as the likely cause (Table A.5).

Threats among current and former workers in this study exceeded rates among less intimate or less familiar types.

Forty-seven-year-old pressman Joseph Wesbecker of Louisville, Kentucky, was furious about his perceived mistreatment by management at the Standard Gravure Printing Plant. He was so angry that he told a coworker that he planned to get even with the company and even showed him the gun with which he intended to carry out his plan of attack. Months later, Wesbecker roamed the corridors with his AK-47, systematically seeking out his intended targets. He killed eight and wounded a dozen others (Fox & Levin, 1994). Wesbecker preceded his attack with a threat of his intent, leading to the devastating lethality of this event.

Table A.5 Results of the Northwestern Survey

Perpetrator	Workplace Attack Victims (%)	Workplace Threat Victims (%)	Workplace Harassment Victims (%)
Coworker other than boss or former employees	30	43	88
Customers/clients	44	36	15
Stranger	24	16	2
Other	3	7	2
Total	101	102	107

Source: Northwestern National Life Insurance Company, *Fear and violence in the workplace.* Minneapolis, MN: Northwestern National Life Insurance Company, 1993.

Research published as *Nonfatal Workplace Violence Risk Factors* (Scalora et al., 2003), involved incidents of workplace violence from January 1, 1997, through June 30, 1998, investigated by the Lincoln, Nebraska, Police Department. Using a workplace violence definition that required workplace location, offense type (threats and attacks), and only employees as victims, yielded the researchers 281 reported incidents. The sample was bifurcated according to who posed the danger—sources either external or internal to the workplace. Internal threat cases involved conflicts between coworkers, but also included domestic partners. External threat cases were classified as originating from strangers or clients (Scalora et al., 2003).

Across the total sample, nearly one third of the perpetrators threatened their victims before the violent incident. The researchers claimed that prior threat was inversely related to the presence of subsequent assaultive behavior. For both external and internal situations, perpetrators of threats were significantly less likely to have engaged in assaultive behavior. However, when the data were analyzed separately for external and internal circumstances, the results appeared to support the intimacy effect. For the internal circumstances group, discriminant analysis revealed that coworkers were more likely to engage in threats and violent behavior than the other victim-offender types (Table A.6).

Although the authors described their analysis as revealing that prior threatening behavior was inversely related to violent behavior in a workplace, comparing these results to the results for the external circumstances group reveals that the association of threats preceding violence was greater in closer relationships compared with stranger relationships.

In a review of survey results published in *Coworker Violence and Gender* (Tjaden & Thoennes, 2001), analysts using data collected as part of the National Violence Against Women (NVAW) Survey reviewed coworker violence. The review was undertaken to further the understanding of coworker violence compared with violence in other venues and by other perpetrators. While the analysis of the NVAW data indicated that 193,455 people 18 years old or older suffer annually from coworker violence, the phenomenon is relatively rare compared with other violence, such as that committed at home or by strangers (Tjaden & Thoennes, 2001).

Workplace victimizations were classified into rapes, physical assaults, stalking, and threats. The type of violence experienced by males and females differed significantly. For women, stalking and rape were reported in greater numbers than by men. Men reported significantly greater numbers of physical assaults. While both genders reported that they were threatened with violence by coworkers, men reported that they were threatened with violence the most (Tjaden & Thoennes, 2001) (Table A.7).

Although this study did not specifically address threatening statements and their relationship to violent outcomes, the analytical results indicate that threatening statements and violent behavior are certainly present among coworkers (Tjaden & Thoennes, 2001).

According to *Violence in the Workplace, 1993–99*, about 900 work-related homicides occurred annually between 1993 and 1999 and an average of 1.7 million violent victimizations per year were committed against people aged 12 or older who were at work (Duhart, 2001). Workplace violence accounted for 18% of all violent crime over the 7-year period.

Table A.6 Percentage of Cases Where Prior Threat Was Made

External Threat w/ Assault	External Threat w/ No Assault	Internal Threat w/ Assault	Internal Threat w/ No Assault
10%	40%	21.6%	55.6%

Source: Scalora, M., Washington, D., Casady, T., & Newell, S., *Journal of Interpersonal Violence*, 18(3), 310–327, 2003.

Table A.7   Distribution of Female and Male Coworker Violence Victims by Type of Victimization as Measured by the NVAW Survey

Type of Victimization	Female Victims ($n = 86$)	Male Victims ($n = 184$)
Rape	26.7	3.8
Physical Assault	33.7	79.3
Stalking	39.5	6.5
Threat	8.1	15.8

Source: Tjaden, P., & Thoennes, N., *American Journal of Preventive Medicine*, 20(2), 85–89, 2001.

While most of the nonfatal violence was perpetrated by strangers against workers in high-risk occupations, that is, police officers, mental health workers, and taxi drivers, some of this violence was committed by coworkers against other coworkers involved in interpersonal circumstances (Duhart, 2001). In fact, according to data from the U.S. Department of Labor presented in Duhart's publication, an annual average of workplace homicides involving coworkers was 67, or 7% of the total of all workplace homicides. "Coworkers or former coworkers committed a higher percentage of homicides in the workplace when compared to customers or clients" (Duhart, 2001). The assumed familiarity among coworkers compared with client–worker relationships coupled with the greater lethality in the coworker-on-coworker group may suggest a certain intent. For example, a client may lash out at a worker who denies a certain expected service by slapping or kicking. However, the murders using firearms and other weapons require some preparation and planning.

Data available from the 2003 National Crime Victimization Survey (NCVS) revealed that threats to harm frequently preceded violent action among coworkers. In an estimated 53,540 nonfatal victimizations among coworkers and employees, both current and former, 4,661 current and former employees threatened harm before they attacked compared with 3,628 who attacked without threatening. Although threats from current and former coworkers were present in this survey, the percentage of threats prior to attack was somewhat less (Bureau of Justice Statistics, 2003). The NCVS data does not differentiate between intended and impromptu violence (Table A.8).

On February 9, 1996, Clifton McCree arrived at the trailer where Fort Lauderdale, Florida, beach maintenance workers gathered at the beginning of the workday. McCree entered the trailer and began shooting. One employee, Nancy Ann Ellers, escaped through a rear door as McCree fired in her direction. A total of six employees were killed. However, one employee, Ivan McDonald, survived because he remembered McCree's threats. Practicing his own personal security routine, he rarely went into the trailer. Rather, he would greet fellow employees, clock in, and wait in his vehicle to join the crews as they left for their maintenance tasks. On the day of the shooting, McDonald was waiting in his vehicle as he observed Ellers running from the trailer (Moffatt, 2000). Believing McCree's threats probably saved his life.

Table A.8   Comparison of Means in Attack Incidents Where Threats Were Made or Not

Type	Threats Before Attack	No Threat Before Attack
Employee (current or former)	56.2	43.8
Coworker (current or former)	27.7	72.3

Source: National Crime Victimization Survey, 2003.

In 2002, the FBI's National Center for the Analysis of Violent Crime (NCAV) conducted a symposium on workplace violence resulting in the monograph *Workplace Violence: Issues in Response* (Rugala, 2004). For this project, the FBI focused on non-stranger workplace violence, that is, coworkers, clients, and intimates.

> When violence comes from an employee or someone close to an employee, there is a much greater chance that some warning sign will have reached the employer in the form of observable behavior. That knowledge, along with the appropriate prevention programs, can at the very least mitigate the potential for violence or prevent it altogether. (Rugala, 2004)

Threats may be an important starting point in the prevention efforts. As part of an overall program that reinforces employee trust and ensures responsible employer response, the FBI has identified homicidal and suicidal comments and threats at the workplace as a significant risk factor. "Many times, a violent act is preceded by a threat" (Rugala, 2004). Threats can be explicit or veiled, verbal or written, even vague. For example, the FBI monograph cited the case of a 46-year-old subject who exhibited inappropriate behavior while engaged in a worker-training program. After several months of this behavior and several management-approved leaves of absence, the worker's focus began to crystallize on five specific coworkers, then on one in particular.

> While the police investigation was under way, the subject made threats against five former female coworkers. A threat assessment was conducted analyzing letters, voice mail, reports from EAP, and interviews with various individuals. The subject's communications were organized and contained specific threats. For example, he wrote… "I will in my own time strike again, and it will be unmerciful." The material suggested that he was becoming increasingly fixated on the targets and his communications articulated an action imperative which suggested that the risk was increasing. (Rugala, 2004)

The threat assessment and legal review resulted in the arrest of the subject, who was eventually found not guilty by reason of insanity. The arrest may have prevented a violent attack on his coworkers. The monograph suggested that further research was needed to study threats, different patterns of threatening behavior, different forms of threats, and threat evaluation procedures to better help determine validity.

Drs. James Turner and Michael Gelles (2003) examined threats in their published risk management approach to threat assessment. In the workplace, threatening statements are often the triggering events that set into motion evaluations, assessments, and interventions, if necessary. In fact, in cases studied by the authors, 99% included threats or verbal abuse preceding a violent act. Although vast numbers of threats occur without leading to physical violence, the level of risk associated with threatening behavior and verbal abuse must still be determined. "Almost every published paper or report on incidents of workplace violence involving known perpetrators shows the same information—a pattern of threatening behavior and verbal abuse prior to physical acts of violence" (Turner & Gelles, 2003). Turner and Gelles have developed a five-tiered approach to threat assessment. The first tier is high risk calling for immediate intervention in the form of arrest, hospitalization, or major organizational response (e.g., bomb threats requiring emergency resources and evacuation of employees). In this category, threats are characterized as repeated threats of intent to do harm, threats accompanied by actions that will likely bring harm, and bomb or biological threats or written or e-mail threats (Turner & Gelles, 2003).

Turner and Gelles also qualify conditional threats. If the threats contain qualifications or conditions in a workplace setting, that is, if some event does or does not occur in the future, then the threat would be carried out; immediate intervention may not be necessary. Such scenarios call for prompt evaluation, but may be mitigated through organizational channels. Likewise, threatening statements that provoke fear in targeted individuals, but which are not accompanied by approach behavior, deserve prompt attention, but can often be resolved through human resource processes such as removals or transfers of the employees. Threats made by individuals in the workplace that are isolated and not clearly distressful to the receiver fall into Turner and Gelles' tier calling for evaluation with a view toward communication training or employee assistance. Their lowest tier involves the false reports of threats in the workplace. Clearly, this research points to the importance of threatening statements in the predictability of workplace violence (Turner & Gelles, 2003).

A review of research on workplace violence in *Violence, the Emotionally Enraged Employee, and the Workplace* (Layden, 1996) concluded that employers must have "policies and procedures for handling threats." Several warning signs of violence were identified. A common risk factor found by most researchers was the occurrence of threats toward the potential victim(s). From his research, S. Anthony Baron concluded that most workplace violence perpetrators exhibited severe psychoses. He outlined three levels in the forms that violence may take. Level 1 is mostly a mildly belligerent state whereas Level 3 is actual violence. Level 2 was described as increased belligerence including "verbalizing wishes to hurt co-workers and/or management" (Layden, 1996).

A series of writers claiming expertise or stakes in workplace violence have asserted that violence was not a spur-of-the-moment occurrence, that observable behaviors, including threats, were often present (Batza & Taylor, 1999; Carll, 1999; Duncan, n.d.; Merchant & Lundell, 2001). Stanley Duncan's article "Death in the Office: Workplace Homicides" (undated) reported that current or former employees accounted for the majority of workplace homicides compared with perpetrators who were strangers, customers, or clients. The fact that most homicides of this type involved the use of firearms indicated that "these crimes reflect extensive planning by the offender… [who] usually have plenty of time to prepare" (Duncan, undated). Duncan advised that management must take any threat of violence seriously.

In workplace venues, particular attention should also be paid to inappropriate communications to coworkers and supervisors and repeated accusations of other people's causing one's problems (Batza & Taylor, 1999). "One of the most common misconceptions in the assessment of public-figure stalking is the alarm caused by death threats," wrote David Batza and Michelle Taylor (1999) in their article "Stalking in the Community and Workplace." They added that it does not hold true for interpersonal stalking situations. As security and threat assessment professionals, Batza and Taylor held that factors to be considered in interpersonal stalking cases include "use of threats, intimidation, or manipulations" (Batza & Taylor, 1999).

The U.S. Office of Personnel Management published *A Guide for Agency Planners* (1998) in which it stated that a major component of any workplace violence program is prevention. While no one can predict human behavior and no specific profile of a potentially dangerous individual exists, there are indicators of increased risk which include "direct or veiled threats of harm" (Office of Personnel Management, 1998).

In a review of workplace violence intervention research, James Merchant and John Lundell (2001) declared that "despite existing research, significant gaps remain in our knowledge of the causes and potential solutions" to violence in the workplace. For worker-on-worker violence, part of the research agenda called for includes

- Determining the importance of corporate culture, organization, and security in workplace violence
- Discovering how surveillance data on threats and violence can be improved
- Assessing effectiveness of zero-tolerance policies and profiling (Merchant & Lundell, 2001)

Dr. Elizabeth Carll (1999) wrote that workplace violence prevention plans and policies are in the same position as sexual harassment policies were several years ago. Comprehensive prevention strategies included training for employees and managers to recognize impending and escalating problems. Cautioning against identifying people as dangerous simply because they match a list of characteristics, Dr. Carll encouraged a review of signs that could alert employers to possible trouble. Among the myriad factors that help identify a potentially violent personality, Dr. Carll included intimidation of others and "threats toward company or another employee" as important (Carll, 1999).

The reactions of people to threatening statements made in the workplace differ. However, threatening statements made at work have been touted as one of several warning signs that should be reported and evaluated, especially considering their association with violent outcomes in this venue (Batza & Taylor, 1999; Carll, 1999; Rugala, 2003; Turner & Gelles, 2003). In contrast to threats directed at public figures, threats in the workplace appear to have considerable relationship to violent outcomes.

Observations

- Coworker or ex-coworker violence can take the form of intended violence.
- Threats are more prevalent among coworkers than from other sources in the workplace.
- Researchers should investigate the familiarity among study subjects before coming to conclusions about the relationship of threats and violence outcomes.
- Although threats are indeed separate victimizations, they are also part of a violence continuum.
- Workers suffer attacks of greater lethality from coworkers than from clients.
- Most threat assessment professionals believe that threats among coworkers are important in determining level of dangerousness.
- Consequently, the research suggests that the intimacy effect may be present in coworker workplace violence.

Findings on School Violence

In the wake of infrequent but highly publicized and deadly events, school administrators, mental health professionals, law enforcement professionals, and policymakers have come under increasing pressure to take steps to prevent school violence in their communities (Reddy et al., 2001). The number of deaths in school settings may have declined over the past decade, but the number of violent incidents involving multiple victims has increased.

These highly publicized lethal incidents may be attributable to increased concerns about school safety (McCann, 2002; Mohandie, 2000). In addition, FBI researchers have acknowledged that adolescent violence in general, and homicides in particular, have "decreased since 1993 but that... trend has been... obscured in the nationwide wave of concern over school shootings of the type examined in the NCAVC's study" (O'Toole, 2000).

Violence occurs in and around schools in various forms. While eliminating all forms of antisocial aggression and violence is a laudable goal, different types of violence have different antecedents and thus require different approaches for assessment and intervention (Reddy et al., 2001). School violence ranges from such events as the 1996 Dunblane, Scotland, shooting, in which an adult with no apparent ties to a primary school opened fire on a crowd of school children to the mass murder at a school in Bath, Michigan, where the perpetrator rigged and detonated explosives in the basement of the school in retaliation for a tax levy (Mohandie, 2000). While these acts were clearly intended, the perpetrators were not associated with the school and could not have been observed in the school setting.

However, Dr. Mohandie provides us with another type of school violence. It is a "lethal and non-lethal event that occurs at school, and since it most often involves students, offers significant opportunity to observe early warning signs and the developing problem" (Mohandie, 2000). According to Dr. Mohandie, these events are perpetrated by someone who is a service recipient or customer of the school, a category which, in addition to students, may also include parents or guardians of students and those who are currently or formerly in relationships with students (Mohandie, 2000). McGee and DeBernardo (1999) have described the same category of school violence as unlike the more conventional adolescent shooting incidents. He labeled the actors "classroom avengers" whose motives are "personal vengeance and achievement of notoriety rather than being drug, inner city, or juvenile-gang related." Examples of this type of school violence include the March 2005 shooting by a 16-year-old in Red Lake, Minnesota, that killed ten people; the April 1999 shootings by two 17-year-olds in Littleton, Colorado, that killed 13 people; the October 1997 shooting by a 16-year-old in Pearl, Mississippi, that killed two students and wounded seven; and the March 1998 shootings by a 13-year-old and an 11-year-old that killed four students and one teacher in Jonesboro, Arkansas.

The FBI studied non-inner-city school shootings—although such incidents are quite rare—to help prevent similar incidents in the future. Their research began with an analysis of 18 school shooting cases around the country. They also drew from a small number of cases on which they had been asked to conduct a threat assessment. The findings of the analysis were used to formulate questions and topics for discussion at a symposium in 1999. Their report, published in 2000, drew from their own analysis as well as from expert opinions provided by symposium participants. The FBI concluded that, among other things, "easy access to weapons is not the most significant risk factor and that school shootings are exclusively revenge motivated" (O'Toole, 2000). Violence motivated by revenge is intended violence. From such examples of intended violence in schools, assessment of threatening and potentially violent behavior in school settings might best be based on a process-oriented approached. The focus is on behavior, patterns of behavior, and situational factors (Reddy et al., 2001). Threats of violence in school settings may be an important part of this process toward violence. For example, Columbine shooter Eric Harris "posted death threats against fellow students on his web site" (Pisciotta, 2000). In a more recent incident, talk and warning signs preceded the Red Lake Indian Reservation school shootings. More than ten other adolescents knew about the plot (Hedgpeth, 2005). An example of this type of event occurred in 1992 in Yuba, California, at a high school where a 21-year-old former student shot and killed three students and one of his former teachers and wounded ten others. He eventually surrendered to the police, but one of his friends had called police during the standoff identifying the gunman because the gunman had talked about his plans and fantasies beforehand (Houston Chronicle News Services, 1992).

The limited research on school shootings suggests that threats and talk of violence frequently precede the violence (McGee & DeBernardo, 1999; Mohandie, 2002; O'Toole, 2000). An FBI report on non-inner-city school shootings highly recommended that schools establish a threat assessment procedure "managed by properly trained staff" (O'Toole, 2000). In a study of selected school shootings, Secret Service researchers found many instances in which the eventual school shooter had discussed his plans with friends (Reddy et al., 2001). Similarly, the U.S. Department of Education compiled a list of "early warning signs" for school violence. The list included "expression of violence in writings and drawings" and "serious threats of violence" as behaviors school officials should be on the lookout for (O'Toole, 2000).

Eric Harris, one of the Littleton, Colorado, shooters, posted his threats on a Web site:

> Dead people can't do many things, like argue, whine bitch, complain, narc, rat out, criticize or even fucking talk. So that's the only way to solve arguments with all you fuckers out there, I just kill! (Mohandie, 2000)

The swift response to threats of violence in schools suggest a greater concern or even awareness that threats are closely associated with violent and lethal acts. In January 2005, two boys were arrested in Ocala, Florida.

> The 9- and 10-year-old boys were arrested … and charged with making a written threat to kill or harm another person. They were also suspended from school.
> One drawing showed the two boys standing on either side of the other boy and "holding knives pointed through" his body, according to a police report. The figures were identified by written names or initials.
> Another drawing showed a stick figure hanging, tears falling from his eyes, with two other stick figures standing below him. Other pieces of scrap paper listed misspelled profanities and the initials of the boy who was allegedly threatened. (AP, 2005)

The boys, ages nine and ten, were also suspended from school. They were charged with making a written threat to kill or harm another person. The boys' parents said they thought the children should be punished by the school and families, not the legal system (AP, 2005).

The criminal justice system responded in much the same way when, in 2001, New Bedford (Massachusetts) High School students revealed discussions among them to "smuggle guns under black trench coats, detonate explosives and kill as many students and faculty as possible" at the school. Police learned of the plan from one of the conspirators who tipped off her favorite teacher, as well as from a note discovered by a school janitor (AP, 2001). All the student conspirators were arrested. Clearly, law enforcement perceived a connection between threats at schools and violence at schools, but what does the research say?

Based on their research on assassinations and attacks on public officials, Secret Service researchers developed a "threat assessment approach." They reported that the approach holds some promise for assessing the risk of targeted violence in schools (Reddy et al., 2001). While this may be true for certain aspects of assessing approach behavior, a conflict may arise in the context of threats in the different venues. The defining element of targeted violence "is that the perpetrator selects a target prior to the violence incident" (Reddy et al., 2001). The Secret Service took its finding from public-figure research into the school violence arena and asserted that threats (direct, indirect, conditional, and otherwise) should be taken seriously but they are not the most "reliable indicators of risk" (Reddy et al., 2001).

> Indeed, a youth who is committed to mounting an attack may be less inclined to threaten a potential target directly, particularly if he or she does not want to be stopped. The youth may, however, discuss ideas of harm among friends and peers. (Reddy et al., 2001)

In the same report, the Secret Service researchers admit, however, that they "recognize that although the threat assessment approach is based upon empirical research on targeted violence [public-figure research], it too lacks the benefit of comprehensive empirical knowledge on targeted violence in schools" (Reddy et al., 2001).

Kipland P. Kinkle shot and killed his parents and went on a shooting rampage the next day at his high school. Kinkle left a note expressing sorrow for having to kill his parents (Bernstein, 1999). Kinkle's diary indicated his prior expression of desire to commit violent acts.

> I feel like everyone is against me, but no one ever makes fun of me, mainly because they think I am a psycho. There is one kid above all others that I want to kill. I want nothing more than to put a hole in his head. The one reason I don't: Hope. That tomorrow will be better. As soon as my hope is gone, people die. (Kinkle, 1999)

According to the FBI's 2000 report, threat assessments should be initiated once a threat is made. A threat was defined as an expression (written, spoken, or symbolized) of intent to do harm or act out violently against someone or something. While all threats are not the same, all "must be taken seriously and evaluated" (O'Toole, 2000). The motivation for making threats in the school environment can be for a variety of reasons ranging from warning signals to reaction to fear of punishment to a demand for attention to a strikeback for a perceived injustice. As a possible signpost preceding school violence, "a threat is one observable behavior among others that may be less obvious, that is, brooding, conversations or writings about violent revenge" (O'Toole, 2000).

The FBI has described threats as direct, indirect, veiled, and conditional. In order to assess threats made in the school environment, the FBI ranked the risk as high, medium, and low. With such classifications, "schools [would] be able to recognize and act on the most serious threats, and to address all other threats appropriately and in a standardized and timely fashion" (O'Toole, 2000). For example, a note stating:

> At eight o'clock tomorrow morning, I intend to shoot the principal. That's when he is in the office by himself. I have a 9 mm. Believe me, I know what I am doing. I am sick and tired of the way he runs this school. (O'Toole, 2000)

Per the FBI's report, this is a "high level of threat" since it is direct, specific, and plausible, and it indicates concrete steps that may have been taken toward carrying out the threatened act. Medium-level threats may be as "direct" as those seen in high-level threats; however, other evidence indicates that the threatener has not taken preparatory steps toward a violent act and there may be less specificity of intent. Low-level threats were described by the FBI as vague and indirect and that information contained within the threat is inconsistent or implausible, or it lacks detail (O'Toole, 2000).

Once a threat of violence has been made in the school environment, according to the FBI report, a four-pronged examination of the student should be made. The four prongs include: (1) personality traits and behavior, (2) family dynamics, (3) school dynamics, and (4) social dynamics. Perhaps the FBI has made an important breakthrough in the collective thinking about threats of violence in schools. Within the personality traits and behavior category, the FBI addressed a phenomenon it termed "leakage." This occurs when a student intentionally or unintentionally reveals clues to feelings, thoughts, fantasies, attitudes, or intentions that may signal an impending violent act. At the FBI's NCAVC Symposium held in 1999 to support its research, experts developed recommendations that leakage should be further studied for its relevance in predicting future violence. The FBI's report stated that "leakage is considered to be one of the most important clues that may precede an adolescent's violent act" (O'Toole, 2000). The fact that ten or more adolescents associated with the Red Lake High School knew about the attack in advance may be an example of leakage.

The Secret Service, in conjunction with the U.S. Department of Education, has conducted its own research. From its analysis of a sample of 37 school shootings, the service concluded that "most attackers did not threaten their targets directly, but did engage in pre-attack behaviors that would have indicated an inclination toward the potential for targeted violence had they been identified" (Vossekuil, Fein, Reddy, & Borum, 2002).

According to the Secret Service, most perpetrators of the school shootings it studied did not make a threat prior to a violent act. However, in most cases, other people knew about the attack before it took place. In over three quarters of the incidents, at least one person had information that the attacker was thinking about or planning the school attack. In nearly two thirds of the incidents, more than one person had information about the attack before it occurred. In nearly all of these cases, the person who knew was a peer—a friend, schoolmate, or sibling. Some peers knew exactly what the attacker planned to do; others knew something "big" or "bad" was going to happen, and in several cases knew the time and date it was to occur. An adult had information about the idea or plan in only two cases. Almost all the attackers engaged in some behavior prior to the attack that caused others—school officials, parents, teachers, police, fellow students—to become aware of the plot. In one example cited by the Secret Service report, a school shooter submitted a series of poems to his English teacher prior to his attack. They read, in part:

> Am I insane
> Wanting to spill blood like rain
> Sending them all to Hell
> From humanity I've fell.

In most of the cases, at least one adult was concerned by the attacker's behavior. In three quarters of the cases, at least three people—adults and other children—were concerned by the attacker's behavior. In one case, for example, the attacker made comments to at least 24 friends and classmates about his interest in killing other kids, building bombs, or carrying out an attack at the school. A school counselor was so concerned about this student's behavior that the counselor asked to contact the attacker's parents. The attacker's parents also knew of his interest in guns (Vossekuil et al., 2002). The Secret Service recognized this phenomenon and termed it "signaling the attack," which is a summation of any threatening communications or warnings made by most school shooters studied, described previously (Vossekuil et al., 2002).

While the Secret Service report encouraged a school threat-assessment process based primarily on an "appraisal of behaviors, rather than on stated threats," threats may have more importance than realized when looking at intended violence rather than targeted violence in the school venue.

The Secret Service focus on targeted violence, that is, an act carried out targeting a specific pre-identified individual or thing and targeted threats of violence, distracts the Secret Service researchers from the importance of recognizing the threat-assessment potential using threats in the form of signaling the attack or leakage as pre-incident indicators. Although the majority of their sample of school shooters did not directly threaten the victims they targeted, by defining the violence as intended, a broader view of persons who have a violent intent signaled by threatening communications with or without a particular target emerges. In fact, the Secret Service reported that 75% of their sample-subject school shooters had a history of suicidal thoughts, threats, gestures, or attempts and in almost all incidents a peer or sibling was informed of the planned attack (Vossekuil, Reddy, & Fein, 2000).

While many threats of violence are made among school students that are never carried out, to dismiss a threat as not a pre-incident indicator of intended violence in the school environment may risk leaving out an important ingredient in assessing risk. "Verbal behavior" by adolescents in the school environment is communication that has an expressive or instrumental function. Dr. Kris Mohandie (2002) wrote that "violence in many school-associated circumstances represents a desire to express a feeling, or to influence some course of events. The talk of violence represents the individual's attempts to 'get their point across'" (Mohandie, 2002). Another way of looking at this is to identify this behavior as "breakthrough behavior" or leakage. Threats and leakage are breakthrough behaviors that can be observed by others and used as a signal to be reported, evaluated, and addressed (Mohandie, 2002). A retrospective view rather than a prospective view of threats and their outcomes is needed. Although the Secret Service reported in both its public figure and safe school research that most individuals who threatened violence do not attempt it, the data in most studies indicate that those who did carry out an attack in the school venue did, in fact, make threats. In school settings, this often took the form of leakage (Mohandie, 2002).

In a review of 18 school shootings resulting in homicide(s), explicit threats were made by the perpetrator(s) prior to the incident 100% of the time (McGee & DeBernardo, 1999). Verbal or written expressions of intent to kill or commit suicide or do something highly dramatic within the very near future, when made in this context and in the presence of the other primary variables of this profile, were highly predictive of an imminent attack. The authors presented a hypothetical behavioral composite of the "Classroom Avenger." This was a depressed and suicidal, usually Caucasian, adolescent male from a rural, suburban, or small community who perpetrates a nontraditional, multivictim homicide in a school or classroom setting. Classroom Avenger shootings are evolving over time in the direction of greater complexity and sophistication, and a media-based copycat or contagion effect is almost certainly present. Seasonality was also a factor, with most of the incidents studied occurring between December and May.

According to a report published by the U.S. Department of Education (Dwyer, Osher, & Warger, 1998), idle threats are common in response to frustration. Alternatively, one of the most reliable indicators that a youth is likely to commit a dangerous act toward himself or others is a detailed and specific threat to the use of violence. Recent incidents across the country clearly indicate that threats to commit violence against oneself or others should be taken very seriously. Steps must be taken to understand the nature of these threats and to prevent them from being carried out (Dwyer et al., 1998).

Interestingly, the concept of leakage gives further credence to the intimacy effect. The concept depends on the fact that students who notice the leakage all know the student or students doing the leaking. The recipient students go to school with the plotters, hear them talking, read their writing, or observe their actions. From this interpersonal relationship, the leakage occurs. The intimacy effect explains why leakage takes place in school settings, but not in public figure settings.

Observations

- Researchers are conflicted about how important threats are in the assessment of potential violence in the school venue.
- Schools and criminal justice officials must choose between punishment for threats presenting liability risks or risk violent actions.
- Threats of violence in the school venue may more likely be in the form of leakage.
- Leakage supports the intimacy effect hypothesis since it occurs within interpersonal settings.

Findings on Domestic Violence (Intimate Partners)

According to *Crime in the United States* (Federal Bureau of Investigation, 2003), murders among intimates in 2002 numbered 1,320. This included victims who were related to the offenders as husbands, wives, boyfriends, and girlfriends. Seventy-eight percent of the victims were women. Although the rate of intimate partner murder from 1976 to 1996 dropped by 36%, the decline was due primarily to the drop in the number of male victims. The murder rate for female victims of intimate murder remained relatively steady over the same period of time (Bureau of Justice Statistics, 1998). While most intimate lethal violence occurred in or near the victim's home, reports of nonlethal violence locations included another's home, commercial places, schools, and parking lots (Bureau of Justice Statistics, 1998). The distance from the home may indicate a determined purpose or some planning to the attack, which are parts of our definition for intended violence.

For years, local law enforcement well understood the importance of threats as pre-incident indicators of domestic violence. The Danvers, Massachusetts, police department has put threats of homicide or suicide at the top of its list of various warning signs of potential domestic homicide. Similarly, the Nashville police department has emphasized the importance of taking intimidation and threats against a domestic partner seriously (Calhoun & Weston, 2003). In a study of criminal justice strategies toward intimate-partner violence, Kerry Healey and Christine Smith reported that "prior threats to kill" and suicide threats were among the most important warning signs of potential domestic abuse (Healey et al., 1998).

Unfortunately, not all jurisdictions take threats of violence in domestic or intimate venues seriously. In 1996, in Brooklyn, New York, after a 2-year history of stalking, beating, and threatening his estranged girlfriend, Galina Komar, a judge allowed the release of Benito Oliver, jailed for violating his restraining order. After Oliver's release, he walked into the Koeppel Volkswagen dealership where Ms. Komar worked and shot her once in the head with a .44-caliber revolver. Mr. Oliver then shot himself in the head. Three weeks earlier, Oliver had been arrested for placing three threatening phone calls from his jail cell (Van Natta, 1996).

Studies of domestic violence bring forth various theories and classifications, none of which are specifically designed to make a distinction between intended and impromptu violence. Domestic violence is often seen as a quagmire of abusive and assaultive behavior rather than a clear sequence of events. However, "findings from a variety of sources indicate that woman abuse among separated women is a more serious problem than abuse experienced by married women living with their husbands" (Ellis, 1992). For violence to occur between former intimates, planning and travel are required to successfully accomplish it. Such planning and travel indicate that this category of domestic violence is intended violence. Intended, and therefore more lethal, violence in domestic situations can be brought about by stress, revenge, anger induced by loss of attachment, or perceptions of betrayal, jealousy, or challenges to male hegemony (Ellis, 1992). Whatever the motive, the key to intended violence is that it is planned beforehand.

Author Gregory Moffatt has developed the "principle of least interest," which he contends operates in every relationship. A woman in an abusive relationship may decide "she has had enough and choose to leave. When she leaves, the husband discovers that he has lost power or control, and even though she may not realize it, the wife has gained immense power in the relationship. In an attempt to regain power or control, the husband will make promises, beg forgiveness, or threaten. The more he sees that he cannot regain the power in the relationship, the more desperate he becomes" (Moffatt, 2000). An early study of families involved in divorce proceedings also revealed that males who behaved violently suffered from feelings of underachievement and felt deficient in certain status characteristics relative to their wives. These findings provided further evidence that violent behavior most often involved the use of coercive force by a person of superordinate status at times when he found his stature threatened (O'Brien, 1971).

In November 2013, William Gardner killed his on-again, off-again girlfriend, Leslie Pinkston, the day after she texted him that she was now romantically involved with someone else—the ultimate departure from an intimate relationship. In response to her text, Gardner responded with a threat, telling her she was going to die (see Chapter 2 above). Gardner no doubt realized that taking up with a new boyfriend stripped him of any power, save violence, over Pinkston.

For 16 years, Steven and Janice Lancaster maintained a happy marriage, living in southern Maryland with their two children. Things changed, however, when Steve took a mistress, yet refused to give Janice a divorce. He began to beat her, and Janice had him arrested. She dropped the charges the first time, but had him arrested again. In February 1999, Steven told Janice that he would kill her and himself. After months of more threats, abuse, and battering, a Maryland court issued a protection order compelling Steve to move out of their house and to keep away from his wife. On January 3, 2000, Steve parked a mile from his wife's house just before dawn. Dressed in dark clothes and a stocking cap, he walked to the house carrying a shotgun. He killed Janice and himself. Their son heard the shotgun blasts while waiting at his school bus stop and said, "I think that came from my house" (St. George, 2000).

As part of the NAS study of violence, Jeffrey Fagan and Angela Browne (1994) reviewed the research on physical aggression between men and women in intimate relationships. Harmful behaviors in intimate relationships include "psychological abuse, economic deprivation, threats to others in the family, and threats as a method of coercion... which are part of the 'ecology of aggression' that characterizes marital violence" (Fagan & Browne, 1994). The closeness of intimates makes it particularly challenging to discern the difference between intended, or planned, violence and the more emotive, spontaneous, impromptu violence often seen in the dynamics of the domestic venue. The ongoing forms of victimization seen in domestic violence may prove challenging in discerning temporal order or defining "discrete and definitionally tidy events" (Mirrlees-Black, 1999).

An 11 U.S.–city study sought to identify risk factors for femicide in abusive relationships. Proxies of 220 intimate partner femicide victims identified from police or medical examiner records were interviewed, along with 343 abused women who served as controls. Pre-incident risk factors associated in multivariate analyses with increased risk of intimate partner femicide included perpetrator's access to a gun and previous threats to kill, perpetrator's stepchild in the home, and estrangement, especially from a controlling partner. Table A.9 is an excerpt from the Risk Factors for Femicide in Abusive Relationships study.

The difference is striking when threats of violence are compared with nonlethal violence. These findings were incorporated into recommendations for medical professionals who assess the potential for lethal violence among battered women. "It is important to assess perpetrators' access to guns and to warn women of the risk guns present. This is especially true in the case of women who have been threatened with a gun or another weapon under conditions of estrangement" (Campbell et al., 2003).

An analysis of NCVS data (Felson & Messner, 2000) indicated that men who assault their female partners were more likely to issue threats beforehand than offenders in assaults involving other relationships or other gender combinations. The study used a multivariate statistical model to examine whether violence by men against their female partners was more likely than other violence to involve a control motive. The approach of the study was based on the assumption that assailants who issued threats before attack were more likely to have control motives than those who did not issue threats. In a subset of incidents from the NCVS, 2,597 cases of physical attacks without the ambiguities of weapons involvement, other crimes, or multiple victims or offenders were selected. Within the set of variables for gender and relationship, the variable of whether or not a threat was made before the attack was applied. The results of logistic regression analysis supported the hypothesis about control motive in partner violence. In fact, the analysis indicated for this data set that the odds of a threat before the assault were three and one-half times greater for men who assault their female partners. The analysis revealed that for this sample set, females were less likely to threaten before an assault (Felson & Messner, 2000).

In a study designed to look at psychological aggression and its relationship to physical assault and gender, researchers found evidence that certain behaviors—including threats of

Table A.9   Partial Results: Risk Factors for Femicide in Abusive Relationships

	Abused Control Women (n = 343)	Homicide Victims (n = 220)
Partner threatened to kill women	50 (14.6%)	142 (73.6%)

Source: Campbell, J. C., Webster, D., Koziol-McLain, J., Block, C., Campbell, D., Curry, M. A., Gary, F. et al., *American Journal of Public Health*, 93(7), 1089–1097, 2003.

violence—associated with conflict among couples can help to discriminate between "common couple violence" and "patriarchal terrorism" (Hamby & Sugarman, 1999). In this study, a sample of male and female undergraduates (*n* = 374) completed the Revised Conflict Tactics Scales about a courtship relationship. Behaviors were categorized as minor or severe forms of psychological aggression. The hypothesis proposed was that individuals who engage in instrumental, malicious, and explicit acts of violence are more likely to be physically aggressive, especially severely physically aggressive, toward their partners than those who do not engage in such acts. The findings of the analysis indicated that destroying the property of a partner, malicious name calling, and threatening physical violence all occurred more often with severe physical assault than other forms of psychological aggression (Hamby & Sugarman, 1999). The significance of the data was shown in the finding that threats to harm were rarely associated with minor physical assault and even less with no physical assault (Table A.10).

Findings from a British Crime Survey (BCS) self-completion questionnaire administered in 1995 indicated that "frightening threats" were prevalent in domestic violence situations. In fact, "women were far more likely than men to have experienced both assault and threats" (Mirrlees-Black, 1999) than merely assaults or threats alone. These findings suggest that the experiences of female victims are qualitatively different from those of most male victims. The survey revealed that for women and men the lifetime prevalence of domestic violence where threats, assaults, and threats combined with assaults were delineated, threats combined with assaults occurred a greater percentage of the time—26% of women and 17% of men (Table A.11).

The findings suggest that threats were closely associated with violence among the study subjects.

Threatening statements and intended violence are not exclusive to male perpetrators. In a study of female stalkers, Meloy and Boyd (2003) list anecdotally two cases where two women intentionally killed three victims in San Diego County, California. Both women were prior sexual intimates of their victims and "committed acts of predatory violence that were planned, purposeful, and emotionless." They reported:

A 26-year-old woman threatened and intruded on her former boyfriend for more than a year, rented an apartment near him, and shot him to death with a .357 magnum revolver in front of his apartment.

Table A.10   Partial Results of Analysis. Means or Averages for Perpetrating Specific Forms of Psychological Aggression as a Function of Severity of Physical Assault

	No Physical Assault	Minor Physical Assault	Severe Physical Assault
Threatened to hit partner	0.02	0.12	0.52

Source: Hamby, S., & Sugarman, D., *Journal of Marriage and the Family*, 61(4), 959–970, 1999.

Table A.11   Lifetime Prevalence of Domestic Violence: BCS Self-Completion Questionnaire

	Women Aged 16–59	Men Aged 16–59
Threats only	16	5
Assault only	23	15
Threats and assaults	26	17

Source: Mirrlees-Black, C., *Home Office Research Study*, 191, 1999.

In the second case,

> A 41-year-old woman engaged her former husband in five years of vandalism, threats, telephone calls, trespassing, property damage, and financial and child custody disputes. She then shot and killed him and his new wife with a .38 caliber revolver in the early morning hours as they lay sleeping in their bed.

Meloy and Boyd (2003) studied an assembly of sample cases of stalking by females from the archival records of mental health and law enforcement professionals. Threats by the subjects were defined as written or oral communication that implicitly or explicitly stated a wish or intent to damage, injure, or kill the target. Although the study confirmed that most female stalkers were not former intimates, the authors assert that the female stalkers threatened their victims at about the same rate as the males and that there was a greater likelihood of violence if a threat was communicated by the female stalker to her victim. The strength of the relationship was mild, underscoring Meloy's belief that in private stalking cases, threats are so common that they do not predict violence (Meloy & Boyd, 2003). That may well be true if one looks only at domestic violence cases. However, compared with public figure cases, the ratio of threats to assaults in domestic violence cases is striking.

An analysis of survey data reported in *Extent, Nature, and Consequences of Intimate Partner Violence* (Tjaden & Thoennes, 2000a) found evidence that violence committed against women by intimates tends to be more threatening and severe than violence committed against men by intimates. In addition, women were significantly more likely to employ the use of restraining orders, even though at least half of them were violated. Injuries suffered by victims ranged from scratches to being knocked unconscious. Women who were physically assaulted by an intimate partner were significantly more likely to be injured if their perpetrator threatened to harm or kill them or someone close to them and if the perpetrator was using drugs or alcohol at the time. Male victims of physical assault were also significantly more likely to be injured if their perpetrator threatened to harm or kill them (Tjaden & Thoennes, 2000a). These findings imply that threats of violence should be taken seriously. Violence prevention strategies, including law enforcement's response, should emphasize this fact.

Dr. Elizabeth Carll provided warning signs of impending violence in intimate relationships. She wrote that among other predispositions in personality and thinking, four behavior traits actually indicate the beginning of battering in a relationship and may signal the onset of more extreme violence to come. These include throwing, breaking, or striking objects; abusing or killing pets; using force during an argument, such as shoving or holding up against a wall; and making threats of violence (Carll, 1999).

While much domestic violence is heated and impromptu, some is clearly planned and clearly intentional. Researchers need to think about future studies to determine how to recognize indicators of preventable violence.

Observations

- Threats of violence are common among intimate partners.
- It is possible to discern intended (planned) violence from impromptu (impulsive) violence in the domestic venue.
- Separation of an intimate couple may trigger more lethal intended violence.
- Female intimate partners are less likely to threaten prior to violent attack.

- Control motive is prevalent in male intimate-partner threats.
- Loss of control may prompt male intimate-partner attacks.
- Intimate partners who are severely or lethally violent are likely to have made prior threats of violence.
- The research on threats and violence in the domestic violence venue supports the intimacy effect.

General Observations

Threat assessors may be able to evaluate direct threats differently depending on familiarity of victim and target.

- There is a stronger relationship between threats and intended violence in the domestic violence venue than in the public figure violence venue.
- The enforcement of laws against threats of violence is less likely in the domestic venue than when directed toward public figures.
- If threat assessors wait for direct threats to occur against public figures, they may be misdirecting their attention away from real dangers.
- Within the domestic violence venue, the separation of intimates may be the most lethal stage of the relationship.
- Workplaces and schools provide social environments of familiarity where threats and talk of violence before an attack are common.
- In workplaces and schools, others are likely to know or suspect an attack is likely or imminent.
- Research drawn from the various venues for intended violence supports the intimacy effect hypothesis that the value of a threat as a pre-incident indicator increases in proportion to the degree of familiarity between subjects and targets.

Conclusions

The intimacy effect postulates that the more intimate the relationship between someone making a threat of violence and the target of that threat, the more likely the threatening statement portends future violence against the person threatened. No one has tested the validity of the intimacy effect through original or primary research. However, this review of the major recent research on the various venues of intended violence found considerable support for the hypothesis, especially at the extreme ends. That is to say, the hypothesis holds up at the most interpersonal of all relationships, domestic violence. It also can be validated at the opposite end—public-figure violence.

Findings from the research in the workplace and school venues are not quite as striking in support of the hypothesis. However, that may be due to the fact that the various research studies reviewed did not specifically address the role of threats as pre-violence indicators. Still, many of the studies give credence to the view that threats in interpersonal settings did frequently portend future violence. That strongly suggests that research specifically designed to test the intimacy effect hypothesis would provide further support for the hypothesis.

These findings have important implications for threat assessors who must evaluate various behaviors and whether they associate or not with severe forms of physical violence. As many as 20 teenagers may have known ahead of time about plans for the shooting spree that resulted in the deaths of ten people at the hands of a former student on the Red Lake, Minnesota, Indian reservation (Hedgpeth, 2005). Had law enforcement known what those 20 knew and accepted that knowledge as credible, lives may well have been saved. If the Castle Rock, Colorado, police department had acted on Jessica Gonzales' request for help, three murders and one suicide might have been prevented (Table A.12).

Today, criminal justice officials are presented with information and concerns about a possible future violent crime, yet the law and the research on threats are out of sync. Currently, law enforcement officials react quickly and decisively to threats to public officials. They do not react nearly as quickly nor as decisively to threats against domestic partners. The findings drawn from this research review suggest that threats need to be assessed within the social setting in which they are uttered. By taking into account the relationship between the threatener and the target of the threat, the assessor can determine the seriousness of the threat. The rule is simple: the more intimate the relationship, the more serious the threat.

This is not to say that threats of violence toward intimates always portend violence. The field of threat assessment knows no such absolutes. Rather, the research suggests that threats precede violence at a much higher rate in interpersonal settings than threats toward public officials. Conversely, the research also indicates that violent outcomes and threats are not probable when made by strangers toward public figures. Those probabilities have a profound impact on how law enforcement should respond to a threat.

Threats made in social settings are ubiquitous, and laws have arisen over the years to deal with this behavior. Enforcement efforts vary among jurisdictions. For example, threats to the president receive intense scrutiny from the Secret Service and federal prosecutors. Local officials exercise considerable discretion when complaints of being threatened are reported in domestic violence settings.

According to Capitol police authorities, in the summer of 2004, 70-year-old Gerry Dunphy shouted at them while pointing at the U.S. Supreme Court building that his son

Table A.12 Threats of Intended Violence and Outcomes across Venues

Public Figure	Workplace	School	Domestic
Violence inflicted or attempted by person(s) intent on harm that may be directed at a public figure (Fein & Vossekuil, 2000; Meloy, 2001)	Violence inflicted or attempted by person(s) intent on harm "against coworkers, supervisors or managers by a present or former employee" (Rugala, 2003)	Violence inflicted or attempted by person(s) intent on harm that are "service recipients or customers of the school, parents or guardians of students and those who are currently or formerly in relationships with students" (Mohandie, 2000)	Violence inflicted or attempted by person(s) intent on harm that are current or former sexual intimates
Relationship: noninterpersonal	Relationship: mixed noninterpersonal and interpersonal	Relationship: mixed noninterpersonal and interpersonal	Relationship: interpersonal
Threats of violence not associated with violent outcomes	Threats of violence associated with violent outcomes	Threats of violence associated with violent outcomes	Threats of violence associated with violent outcomes

was "going to use the [Amtrak] train and tunnel to blow up that building" (Leonnig, 2005). Dunphy, frustrated by the increasing security on Capitol Hill that hampered his travel, railed against public figures and their structure. He was charged and subsequently convicted of making a false threat and ordered to pay $15,328. The largest portion of Mr. Dunphy's fine went toward restitution for Amtrak. In response to Mr. Dunphy's threat, Amtrak had evacuated Union Station, thus causing considerable train delays. Friends and defenders of Mr. Dunphy claimed that the government overreacted (Leonnig, 2005). Compare the reaction of the criminal justice system in Mr. Dunphy's case with the reaction in the cases of Sarah Crawford (Shapira, 2004), Janice Lancaster (St. George, 2000), and Galina Komar (Van Natta, 1996), all three of whom were slain by intimate or former intimate partners after threats of violence were made known to law enforcement and the courts. Neither law enforcement nor the courts did anything in response to the threats directed at these women. Armed with a better understanding about how threats can be assessed in context with the social setting, law enforcement may avoid delaying travelers unnecessarily in some venues while saving lives in others. The intimacy effect provides an excellent barometer for law enforcement to use when assessing threats of intended violence.

Researchers should continue to evaluate and refine violence prevention programs to determine which strategies appear most effective in decreasing rates of violence. This includes "a study of threats, including the analysis of different patterns of threatening behavior, different forms of threat, and methods of evaluating when a threat is likely to be carried out" (Rugala, 2003). With more comprehensive, reliable, and detailed data directly related to threats, intended violence, and the intimacy effect, researchers may develop more sophisticated tools to help create or improve prevention techniques and programs.

Bibliography

Associated Press (AP). Boy Arrested for Stick Figure Drawing. January 26, 2005.

Batza, D., & Taylor, M. (1999). Stalking in the community and the workplace. In E. Carll (Ed.), *Violence in our lives* (pp. 66–96). Needham Heights, MA: Allyn & Bacon.

Bernstein, M. (1999, November). Defense describes voices. *The Oregonian*.

Borum, R., Fein, R., Vossekuil, B., & Berglund, J. (1999). Threat assessment: Defining an approach for evaluating risk of targeted violence. *Behavioral Sciences and the Law, 17,* 327–337.

Bureau of Justice Statistics. (1998). *Violence by intimates.* Washington, DC: Department of Justice.

Bureau of Justice Statistics. (2003). *National crime victimization survey, 1992–2001 computer file.* Ann Arbor, MI: Inter-University Consortium for Political and Social Research.

Calhoun, F. S. (1998). *Hunters and howlers: Threats against federal judicial officials in the United States, 1989–1993.* Arlington, VA: Department of Justice, U.S. Marshals Service.

Calhoun, F. S., & Weston, S. W. (2003). *Contemporary threat management: A practical guide for identifying, assessing, and managing individuals of violent intent.* San Diego, CA: Specialized Training Services.

Calhoun, F. S., & Weston, S. W. (2009). *Threat assessment and management strategies: Identifying the howlers and hunters* (1st ed.). Boca Raton, FL: CRC Press.

Campbell, J. C., Webster, D., Koziol-McLain, J., Block, C., Campbell, D., Curry, M. A., Gary, F., Glass, N., McFarlane, J., Sachs, C., Sharps, P., Ulrich, Y., Wilt, S.A., Manganello, J., Xu, X., Schollenberger, J., Frye, V., & Laughon, K. (2003). Risk factors for femicide in abusive relationships: Results from a multisite case control study. *American Journal of Public Health, 93*(7), 1089–1097.

Carll, E. (1999). *Violence in our lives: Impact on workplace, home, and community.* Needham Heights, MA: Allyn & Bacon.

Clark, J. W. (1982). *American assassins*. Princeton, NJ: Princeton University Press.

Clark, J. W. (1989). Identifying potential assassins: Some situational correlates of dangerousness. In T. R. Gurr (Ed.), *Violence in America* (Vol. 1, pp. 178–196). Newbury Park, CA: Sage Publications.

de Becker, G. (1997). *The gift of fear*. New York: Random House.

Department of Labor, U.S., Bureau of Labor Statistics. (2014, September). *National census of fatal occupational injuries in 2013 (preliminary results)*. Retrieved from http://www.bis.gov/new .release/pdf/cfoi.pdf.

Dietz, P. E., Matthews, D. B., van Duyne, C., Martell, D. A., Parry, D. H., Stewart, T., Warren, J., & Crowder, J. D. (1991). Threatening and otherwise inappropriate letters to Hollywood celebrities. *Journal of Forensic Sciences, 36*(1), 185–209.

Dietz, P. E., Matthews, D. B., Martell, D. A., Stewart, T. M., Hrouda, D. R., & Warren, J. (1991). Threatening and otherwise inappropriate letters to members of the United States Congress. *Journal of Forensic Sciences, 36*(5), 1445–1468.

Duhart, D. (2001). *Violence in the workplace, 1993–99*. Washington, DC: Bureau of Justice Statistics, Department of Justice.

Duncan, S. (n.d.). Death in the office: Workplace homicides. *FBI Law Enforcement Bulletin*.

Dwyer, K., Osher, D., & Warger, C. (1998). *Early warning, timely response: A guide to safe schools*. Washington, DC: U.S. Department of Education.

Ellis, D. (1992). Woman abuse among separated and divorced women: The relevance of social support. In E. Viano (Ed.), *Intimate violence: Interdisciplinary perspectives* (pp. 177–189). Washington, DC: Hemisphere Publishing Company.

Fagan, J., & Browne, A. (1994). Violence between spouses and intimates: Physical aggression between women and men in intimate relationships. In A. Reiss, & J. Roth (Eds.), *Understanding and preventing violence: Social influences* (Vol. 3, pp. 115–292). Washington, DC: National Academy Press.

Federal Bureau of Investigation. (2003). *Crime in the United States, 2002: Uniform crime reports*. Washington, DC: Department of Justice.

Fein, R., & Vossekuil, B. (1995). *Threat assessment: An approach to prevent targeted violence*. Washington, DC: National Institute of Justice, Department of Justice.

Fein, R., & Vossekuil, B. (1999). Assassination in the United States: An operational study of recent assassins, attackers, and near-lethal approachers. *Journal of Forensic Sciences, 44*, 321–333.

Fein, R., & Vossekuil, B. (2000). *Protective intelligence and threat assessment investigations: A guide for state and local law enforcement officials*. Washington, DC: U.S. Department of Justice, Office of Justice Programs.

Fein, R., Vossekuil, B., Pollack, W., & Borum, R. (2002). *Threat assessment in schools: A guide to managing threatening situations and to creating safe school climates*. Washington, DC: U.S. Secret Service & U.S. Department of Education.

Felson, R., & Messner, S. (2000). The control motive in intimate partner violence. *Social Psychology Quarterly, 63*(1), 86–94.

Fox, J., & Levin, J. (1994). Firing back: The growing threat of workplace homicide. *The Annals of the American Academy of Political and Social Science, 536*, 16–30.

Gelles, R., & Straus, M. (1988). *Intimate violence*. New York: Simon & Schuster.

Gilligan, J. (1997). *Violence: Reflections on a national epidemic*. New York: Vintage Books.

Gondolf, E. (1996). *Characteristics of batterers in a multi-site evaluation of batterer intervention systems*. Indiana, PA: Minnesota Center against Violence and Abuse.

Greenhouse, L. (2005, March). Justices hear debate on whether police must intervene. *New York Times*, p. 20.

Hamby, S., & Sugarman, D. (1999). Acts of psychological aggression against a partner and their relation to physical assault and gender. *Journal of Marriage and the Family, 61*(4), 959–970.

Healey, K., Smith, C., & O'Sullivan, C. (1998). *Batterer intervention: Program approaches and criminal justice strategies*. Washington, DC: National Institute of Justice.

Hedgpeth, D. (2005, April). Others aware of Red Lake plans, officials say. *Washington Post*, p. 3.

Hornung, C., McCullough, C., & Sugimoto, T. (1981). Status relationships in marriage: Risk factors in spouse abuse. *Journal of Marriage and the Family, 43*(3), 675–692.

Houston Chronicle News Services. (1992, May). Dropout kills four at school in California. *Houston Chronicle*, p. 1.

Jenkins, D. (2001). The U.S. Marshals Service's threat analysis program for the protection of the federal judiciary. *The Annals of the American Academy of Political and Social Science, 576,* 69–77.

Kerper, H. (1972). *Introduction to the criminal justice system.* St. Paul, MN: West Publishing Company.

Kinkle, K. (Fein, R.). (1999, November 4). *Kinkel's Journal.* E-mail to F. Calhoun.

Kinney, J., & Johnson, D. (1993). *Breaking point: The workplace violence epidemic and what to do about it.* Chicago: National Safe Workplace Institute.

Kivimaki, M., & Elovainio, M. V. J. (2000). Workplace bullying and sickness absence in hospital staff. *Occupational Environmental Medicine, 57,* 656–660.

Kostinsky, S., Bixler, E., & Kettl, P. (2001). *Copy cats that kill.* Retrieved from http://www.center4 research.org/violencen.html.

Layden, D. (1996). The emotionally enraged employee. In R. Curry, & T. Allison (Eds.), *States of rage: Emotional eruption, violence, and social change* (pp. 35–61). New York: New York University Press.

Leonnig, C. (2005, March). Cost of roadblock rage on hill: $15,328. *Washington Post*, p. 1.

Macmillian, R., & Gartner, R. (1999). When she brings home the bacon: Labor-force participation and the risk of spousal violence against women. *Journal of Marriage and the Family, 61*(4), 947–958.

Mattman, J. W. (1998). *Preventing violence in the workplace.* Retrieved from http://www.workviolence .com/articles/preventing_violence.htm.

McCann, J. (2002). *Threats in schools: A practical guide for managing violence.* Binghamton, NY: Haworth Press.

McGee, J., & DeBernardo, C. (1999). The classroom avenger. *The Forensic Examiner, 8,* 5–6.

Meier, J. (2005, March). Battered justice for battered women. *Washington Post*, p. 25.

Meloy, J. (2000). *Violence risk and threat assessment: A practical guide for mental health and criminal justice professionals.* San Diego, CA: Specialized Training Services.

Meloy, J. (2001). Communicated threats and violence toward public and private targets: Discerning differences among those who stalk and attack. *Journal of Forensic Sciences, 46*(5), 1211–1213.

Meloy, J., & Boyd, C. (2003). Female stalkers and their victims. *Journal of American Academy of Psychiatric Law, 31,* 211–219.

Merchant, J., & Lundell, J. (2001). Workplace violence intervention research workshop, April 5–7, 2000, Washington, DC. *American Journal of Preventive Medicine, 20*(2), 135–140.

Milburn, T., & Watman, K. (1981). *On the nature of threat: A social psychological analysis.* New York: Praeger.

Mirrlees-Black, C. (1999). Domestic violence: Findings from a New British Crime Survey self-completion questionnaire. *Home Office Research Study, 191.*

Moffatt, G. (2000). *Blind-sided: Homicide where it is least expected.* Westport, CT: Praeger.

Mohandie, K. (2002). *School violence threat management.* San Diego, CA: Specialized Training Services.

Murty, K., & Roebuck, J. (1992). An analysis of crisis calls by battered women in the city of Atlanta. In E. Viano (Ed.), *Intimate violence: Interdisciplinary perspectives* (pp. 61–70). Washington, DC: Hemisphere Publishing Company.

National Victim Assistance Academy. (2002). *National victim assistance academy textbook.* URL http://www.ojp.usdoj.gov/ovc/assist/nvaa2002/welcome.html.

Nigro, L. G., & Waugh, W. L. Jr. (1996). Violence in the American workplace: Challenges to the public employer. *Public Administration Review,* 326–333.

Northwestern National Life Insurance Company. (1993). *Fear and violence in the workplace.* Minneapolis, MN: Northwestern National Life Insurance Company.

O'Brien, J. (1971). Violence in divorce prone families. *Journal of Marriage and the Family, 33*(4), 692–698.

Office of Personnel Management. (1998). *Dealing with workplace violence: A guide for agency planners.* Washington, DC: Government Printing Office.

O'Toole, M. E. (2000). *The school shooter: A threat assessment perspective*. Critical Incident Response Group, National Center for the Analysis of Violent Crime, FBI Academy.

Palarea, R., Zona, M., Lane, J., & Langhinrichsen-Rohling, J. (1999). The dangerous nature of intimate relationship stalking: Threats, violence, and associated risk factors. *Behavioral Sciences and the Law, 17,* 269–283.

Peek-Asa, C., Runyan, C., & Zwerling, C. (2001). The role of surveillance and evaluation research in the reduction of violence against workers. *American Journal of Preventive Medicine, 20*(2), 141–148.

Pennsylvania Department of Education, Pennsylvania Emergency Management Agency, and Center for Safe Schools. (2001). *Assessing threats of violence*. Lemoyne, PA: Pennsylvania Department of Education, Pennsylvania Emergency Management Agency and Center for Safe Schools.

Pisciotta, L. M. (2000). Beyond sticks and stones: A first amendment framework for educators who seek to punish student threats. *Seton Hall Law Review, 634.*

Pynchon, M., & Borum, R. (1999). Assessing threats of targeted group violence: Contributions from social psychology. *Behavioral Sciences and the Law, 17,* 339–355.

Reddy, M., Borum, R., Berglund, J., Vossekuil, B., Fein, R., & Modzeleski, W. (2001). Evaluating risk for targeted violence in schools: Comparing risk assessment, threat assessment, and other approaches. *Psychology in the Schools, 38*(2), 157–172.

Redfield, S. E. (2003). Threats made, threats posed school and judicial analysis in need of redirection. *BYU Education and Law Journal, 663.* Retrieved from http://digitalcommons.law.byu.edu/elj/vol2003/iss2/9.

Reiss, A., & Roth, J. E. (1993). *Understanding and preventing violence* (Vol. 1). Washington, DC: National Academy Press.

Rhodes, N. R. (1992). The assessment of spousal abuse: An alternative to the conflict tactics scale. In E. Viano (Ed.), *Intimate violence: Interdisciplinary perspectives* (pp. 27–35). Hemisphere Publishing Company.

Rugala, E. A. (2004). *Workplace violence: Issues in response*. Quantico, VA: Department of Justice, Federal Bureau of Investigation.

Scalora, M. et al. (2002). Risk factors for approach behavior toward the U.S. Congress. *Journal of Threat Assessment, 2*(2), 35–55.

Scalora, M., Washington, D., Casady, T., & Newell, S. (2003). Nonfatal workplace violence risk factors. *Journal of Interpersonal Violence, 18*(3), 310–327.

Shapira, I. (2004, November). Virginia wife slain after court denies protection. *Washington Post*, p. 1.

Siegel, L. J. (2001). *Criminology: Theories, patterns, and typologies*. Belmont, CA: Wadsworth.

St. George, D. (2000, January). Warrant unserved, Md. man kills wife. *Washington Post*, p. A01.

Straus, M. A. (1979). Measuring intrafamily conflict and violence: The conflict tactics (CT) scales. *Journal of Marriage and the Family, 41*(1), 75–88.

Tedeschi, J., & Feldson, R. (1994). *Violence, aggression and coercive actions*. Washington, DC: American Psychological Association.

Tittle, C. R. (2000). Theoretical developments in criminology. In *Criminal justice 2000. The nature of crime: Continuity and change* (Vol. 1, pp. 51–101). Washington, DC: Department of Justice, National Institute of Justice.

Tjaden, P., & Thoennes, N. (1998). *Stalking in America: Findings from the National Violence against Women Survey*. Washington, DC: National Institute of Justice, Department of Justice.

Tjaden, P., & Thoennes, N. (2000a). *Extent, nature, and consequences of intimate partner violence*. Washington, DC: National Institute of Justice; Center for Disease Control.

Tjaden, P., & Thoennes, N. (2000b). *Full report of the prevalence, incidence, and consequences of violence against women: Findings from the National Violence against Women Survey*. Washington, DC: National Institute of Justice; Center for Disease Control.

Tjaden, P., & Thoennes, N. (2001). Coworker violence and gender. *American Journal of Preventive Medicine, 20*(2), 85–89.

Turner, J., & Gelles, M. (2003). *Threat assessment: A risk management approach.* New York: Hayworth Press.

Van Natta, D. (1996, February). Judge rebuked after a woman is slain. *New York Times,* p. 3.

Viano, E. (1992). *Intimate violence: Interdisciplinary perspectives.* Washington, DC: Hemisphere Publishing Corporation.

Vossekuil, B., Borum, R., Fein, R., & Reddy, M. (2001). Preventing targeted violence against judicial officials and courts. *The Annals of the American Academy of Political and Social Science, 576,* 78–90.

Vossekuil, B., Fein, R., Reddy, M., & Borum, R. (2002). *The final report and the findings of the safe school initiative: Implications for the prevention of school attacks in the United States.* Washington, DC: United States Secret Service; United States Department of Education.

Vossekuil, B., Reddy, M., & Fein, R. (2000). *Safe school initiative: An interim report on the prevention of targeted violence in schools.* Washington, DC: U.S. Secret Service; U.S. Department of Education; National Institute of Justice.

Webster's encyclopedic unabridged dictionary of the English language. (1989). New York: Gramercy Books.

Weiner, N., & Hardenbergh, D. (2001). Understanding and controlling violence. *The Annals of the American Academy of Political and Social Science, 576,* 23–37.

Wilson, M. (1996, September). Why did he do it? Nobody knows. *The Mobile Press,* p. 1.

Index

Page numbers followed by f and t indicate figures and tables, respectively.

Printed in the United States
by Baker & Taylor Publisher Services